DEVELOPING INDEPENDENT READERS

Strategy-Oriented Reading Activities for Learners with Special Needs

CYNTHIA CONWAY WARING

**THE CENTER FOR APPLIED
RESEARCH IN EDUCATION**
West Nyack, New York 10994

Library of Congress Cataloging-in-Publication Data

Waring, Cynthia Conway.
  Developing independent readers : strategy-oriented reading
activities for learners with special needs / Cynthia Conway Waring.
    p.   cm.
  Includes bibliographical references.
  ISBN 0-87628-266-4
    1. Reading disability—Handbooks, manuals, etc.   2. Reading—
Remedial teaching—Handbooks, manuals, etc.   3. Learning disabled
children—Education—Reading—Handbooks, manuals, etc.   I. Title.
LB1050.5.W37   1995   94-32336
                                                                  CIP

© 1995 *by* Cynthia Conway Waring

Printed in the United States of America

10   9   8   7   6   5

ISBN 0-87628-266-4

ATTENTION: CORPORATIONS AND SCHOOLS

The Center for Applied Research in Education books are available at quantity
discounts with bulk purchase for educational, business, or sales promotional use.
For information, please write to: Prentice Hall Special Sales, 240 Frisch Court,
Paramus, New Jersey 07652. Please supply: title of book, ISBN number,
quantity, how the book will be used, date needed.

**THE CENTER FOR APPLIED RESEARCH
IN EDUCATION**
West Nyack, NY 10994
A Simon & Schuster Company

On the World Wide Web at http://www.phdirect.com

Prentice-Hall International (UK) Limited, *London*
Prentice-Hall of Australia Pty. Limited, *Sydney*
Prentice-Hall Canada Inc., *Toronto*
Prentice-Hall Hispanoamericana, S.A., *Mexico*
Prentice-Hall of India Private Limited, *New Delhi*
Prentice-Hall of Japan, Inc., *Tokyo*
Simon & Schuster Asia Pte. Ltd., *Singapore*
Editora Prentice-Hall do Brasil, Ltda., *Rio de Janeiro*

for

Nat, Nathaniel, and Molly Waring

with thanks to

Susan Kolwicz
J. Porter Smith
and
Cynthia and Robert Stowe

and to

Les Edinson
Joanne Clapp Fullagar
Cynthia Haskell
Genie Hersh
Susan Hurley
Dale Halsey Lea
Susan Riley
and
Marie and Topher Waring

About the Author

Cynthia has an M.Ed. from the Reading Specialist Program at Lesley College, an M.A. in Special Education/Learning Disabilities from the University of Connecticut, and a B.A. in English–Honors and Psychology from the University of Massachusetts. She is certified as an elementary teacher (K–8), teacher of children with moderate special needs (N–12), reading specialist/consulting teacher of reading (K–12), and Orton-Gillingham Therapist. She is a registered educational therapist and member of The Learning Disabilities Network (based in New England) and her local TAWL (Teachers Applying Whole Language).

During her more than twenty years of teaching in the areas of reading, language, and learning disabilities, Cynthia has developed and used *Developing Independent Readers*. She has taught students with diverse special needs from kindergarten age to adult in full inclusion, classroom, clinic, adult literacy program, and resource room settings and in private tutoring practice. Cynthia has made presentations at professional conferences, lectured in graduate-level courses, and conducted in-service workshops and teacher training. Her article "Keys and a Clue" was published in *Teaching Exceptional Children*.

Currently, Cynthia is a full-time teacher of children with special needs at Shutesbury Elementary School in Massachusetts, where teachers support all children in their classrooms in a full inclusion special education model. In addition, Cynthia tutors children and adults in private practice using *Developing Independent Readers*, conducts in-service workshops and teacher training, and consults with teachers in elementary schools and adult literacy programs.

ABOUT
THIS
BOOK

Developing Independent Readers is designed to support the growth of readers who will read throughout their lives for both enjoyment and the fulfillment of their own personal goals. It is a resource for teachers of children and adults with special needs including special education teachers, reading specialists, and classroom teachers. The activities support readers (starting with the beginning of second grade and continuing onward) who may have diverse learning styles and a variety of special needs: learning or reading disabilities; weaknesses in attention, memory, and/or language and speech areas, including hearing loss; or the challenges of learning English as a second language. Activities can be presented successfully in a variety of educational settings. They are effective for individual and group lessons and as part of classroom reading and writing programs.

Developing Independent Readers suggests ways in which teachers can present productive strategies and important elements for reading consistent with the whole language philosophy of literacy development. It integrates understandings about the interactive nature of the reading process with a sequential, multisensory presentation of the phonetic structure of the English language for reading and spelling.

Conceived and written as an early intervention program, this program enables students to read independently before they experience confusion or failure, develop counterproductive strategies or habits, or become dependent on one cueing system or on other people for support. It is also a highly effective remedial program for learners of elementary school age through adult.

STRATEGY-ORIENTED READING ACTIVITIES

Developing Independent Readers is based on the understanding that the most effective program for supporting beginning readers with special needs emerges from observations of successful readers. Thus, its purpose is to enable readers to develop and use independently the productive strategies of skilled readers, such as predicting, reading on, rereading, cross-checking, and confirming or self-correcting as they seek meaning. These strategies enable readers to use information simultaneously from combinations of cueing systems: semantic (meaning), syntactic (language structure and order or grammar), and grapho-phonic (letter-sound correspondences). Readers who independently apply strategies to seek meaning continue to improve.

FOR LEARNERS WITH SPECIAL NEEDS

Many young children learn to read easily and naturally—a few before entering school and many as the result of classroom instruction. Others need extra support with the process. They continue to be emerging readers at the beginning of second grade (or later, if they have not received appropriate support). They form a heterogeneous group in terms of learning styles and special needs.

Some of these learners have not mastered a sufficient sight vocabulary and/or are not proficient enough in using grapho-phonic information to gain easy access to the text. Some have relative strengths in their ability to utilize information from semantic and syntactic cueing systems; some do not. Some students who predict well have weaknesses in visual and/or auditory areas or memory. Others have strengths in word identification strategies but have weaknesses in language and vocabulary areas and/or in attention. And some are learning English as a second language or with a hearing loss.

These learners all have a need for explicit teaching and modeling of productive strategies to construct and maintain meaning. They need many opportunities to practice and apply strategies in natural, meaningful contexts. The activities in *Developing Independent Readers* provide students with success that enables growth. From the beginning, students develop confidence as they learn how to use their relative strengths to support their weaknesses. Teachers and peers provide support only as needed as readers master strategies and elements that they can use independently.

A LITERATURE-BASED PROGRAM

Reading for Meaning

The focus of each reading session in *Developing Independent Readers* is sustained reading of, engagement in, and response to meaningful text. The goal of all activities is reading for understanding and enjoyment. Activities include **Sustained Reading in Context**, **Motivation and Extension Activities**, and **Strategy-Oriented Mini-Lesson Activities**. These are described more fully in the next section.

Group and Individual Presentation

Suggested activities can be completed successfully by groups of learners as well as by individual students. Units can be presented effectively in a classroom context as well as in individual tutorial settings. Themes can be the focus of classroom units of study, with the suggested books and activities as the basis of the picture book component. Supported reading can occur during individual reading conferences and shared reading (paired or group). Students can keep books in their individual book boxes, folders, or bags in the classroom. They can read and reread them during independent reading time, partner or group reading, or reading conferences with adults. Together, the Mini-Lesson Activities comprise a spelling program that can be used with individual students and with groups. Students can complete reinforcement activities independently or with support in school and at home.

The Lesson Plan Student Record

The Lesson Plan Student Record suggests a format and sequence for teachers to use in presenting lessons for each element in *Developing Independent Readers*. Teachers use it to record activities completed by students. A reproducible master for photocopying is included in Appendix B. Teachers fill in student names and the element for each unit.

HOW TO USE THIS PROGRAM

The following suggested procedures are for teachers to use to present activities that support growth and independence in reading. Included are the following components:

- Book Lists for Sustained Reading in Context
- Motivation and Extension Activities
- Strategy-Oriented Mini-Lesson Activities

BOOK LISTS FOR SUSTAINED READING IN CONTEXT

The Books

Books of Progressive Difficulty by Thematic Units

Annotated book lists that accompany each chapter organize books by thematic units that correspond to phonetic elements chosen for their high utility and frequency in reading. Books are listed by progressive difficulty within each unit and throughout the program. Each unit includes books at a range of reading levels that students read with different kinds of support. The teacher selects books from the book list to meet the needs of students and provides the appropriate support to make the books accessible. Learners practice and apply presented elements in context and make additional connections that aid memory as they respond to the literature and engage in related activities.

Supportive Literature

Meaningful, highly motivating, and enjoyable picture books that are, by nature, supportive of the beginning reader with their rich meanings, natural language, and predictable patterns are used in this program. Reading these books allows readers to draw on their areas of relative strength and encourages their drive to seek meaning which propels the reading process.

Multicultural Literature

These books depict the lives, challenges, and victories of people of diverse cultures, ages, and times in history. Universal themes of human experience emerge for discussion. Students expand their own and their peers' understandings and vocabularies as they relate and share their experiences. Learners have opportunities to broaden their understandings and concepts about the world through globe, map, and time-line activities.

Traditional Literature

A large number of the suggested books are traditional literature with predictable plots, themes, characters, patterns, and motifs. Many are familiar to students from previous oral experiences—folk tales, legends, songs, fables, proverbs, myths, and other folk literature. The language of these books is natural, often conversational. Beginning readers experience fluency and competence as they engage themselves in the reading process and in the study of literature.

Sustained Reading in Context

The goal of all activities in *Developing Independent Readers* is reading for understanding and enjoyment. For this reason, every lesson focuses on sustained reading in context. Each activity is designed to help readers become more active learners who independently use a balance of productive strategies to reach this goal.

Teachers support students' growth in reading as they share books and other reading material with them. In the midst of the reading process, teachers engage students in activities and discussions, model and teach strategies, make and enlist responses, and ask and encourage questions. These teacher behaviors have a powerful influence on students' reading and are a critical part of the art of teaching. Suggested teaching strategies are presented in Appendix A, and the following five books present this important understanding:

> ***The Early Detection of Reading Difficulties*** by Marie Clay (Auckland: Heinemann Education, 1979)
>
> ***The Foundations of Literacy*** by Don Holdaway (Sydney: Ashton Scholastic, 1979)
>
> ***Independence in Reading*** by Don Holdaway (Sydney: Ashton Scholastic, 1980)
>
> ***Reading with the Troubled Reader*** by Margaret Phinney (Portsmouth, New Hampshire: Heinemann, 1988)
>
> ***Transitions: From Literature to Literacy*** by Regie Routman (Portsmouth, New Hampshire: Heinemann, 1988).

Periods of at least ten or fifteen minutes of sustained reading give learners opportunities to engage fully in the reading process. Students learn new elements and review elements as they read them frequently in the suggested books, and they experience fluency as they are provided with appropriate books and the support they need to master productive strategies and important elements. Fluency is vital to continued interest and enjoyment in reading.

Students and/or the teacher hold a book upright, rather than flat on a table or desk, as they read. This diminishes the foreshortening effect on the print, which occurs when the book is held at an angle. Students also experience less tension and fatigue in neck and shoulder muscles.

MOTIVATION AND EXTENSION ACTIVITIES

Each unit contains a variety of suggested Motivation and Extension Activities that correspond to the books presented in the annotated book lists and encourage student enjoyment, response, and involvement with books. Students make connections for learning and remembering strategies and elements through discussion, writing, art, drama and puppetry, science, cooking, and music. Activities provide background information, vocabulary enrichment, and a motivation to read through opportunities to relate, interpret, and apply. Students respond creatively and critically to that which has been read and discussed. Often activities call on students' strengths; frequently they promote growth in areas of relative weakness.

The teacher selects activities according to student learning styles, strengths, needs, experiences, and interests. Field trips to provide experiences and background information and to collect data (to compare and contrast goats and sheep, for example) are valuable additions to units.

Activities are not suggested for every book listed. Frequently, the most authentic and meaningful responses and activities follow naturally and spontaneously from the shared book experience. Many books are best read and savored for their own sakes.

STRATEGY-ORIENTED MINI-LESSON ACTIVITIES

Strategy-Oriented Mini-Lesson Activities provide students with brief opportunities (of approximately fifteen minutes) to focus on productive strategies for reading and writing. Activities are designed to be presented occasionally during a thematic unit. Typically, Mini-Lesson Activities are presented after students read a book or complete a related Motivation and Extension Activity. Activities are interactive and integrate the reading and writing processes. They are multisensory—using a variety of input and output modalities—and designed to engage learners with short attention spans. Writing and spelling reinforce learning by providing multisensory feedback (visual, auditory, and kinesthetic/motor/tactile). Activities present grapho-phonic elements important to successful beginning reading and writing. These elements were chosen for their high utility and frequency in books: letter-sound correspondences, syllable types, structural analysis and syllable division strategies, and capitalization and punctuation usage.

Strategy-Oriented Mini-Lesson Activities are as follows:

- Auditory Pattern Discovery
- Visual Pattern Discovery
- Word List Reading with Oral Sentences
- Theme and Key Word Clue Game and Introduction of New Card(s)
- Word List Clue Game
- Letter-Sound-Key Word Practice
- Sound-Letter Practice
- Spelling and Reading List Words for Cloze Sentences
- Cloze Sentences
- Dictation and Editing

Each section that follows includes Materials and Procedures for each activity.

Auditory Pattern Discovery

Materials

Word List 1 (color coded) for teacher reference

Word lists present element words in alphabetical order as follows:

Column 1: One-syllable words with no or single consonants in initial and final positions and/or consonant blends and/or digraphs in initial and/or final positions

Column 2: Compound and other multisyllabic words (beginning with Chapter 6)

NOTE: Appendix A: Teaching Strategies contains "Syllable Division and Structural Analysis Strategies for Reading and Writing."

The Word List 1 master is designed to reproduce the black letters when photocopied. The teacher then adds red letters with a thin marker. The teacher photocopies the master as presented, with two columns of words (single and multisyllable), or covers one or the other list as he or she copies to select one list appropriate for students. The teacher prepares Word List 1 by placing a double layer of removable label tape over the letters (on the left), sound representation (in the middle), and key word/picture (on the right). Students have been known to see through a single layer of tape!

Word lists may also be presented to groups of students using poster-sized chart paper on an easel or chart stand. Wide colored markers work well for writing words. Oaktag masks cut to size cover information at the top of the chart paper.

Procedures

1. Without showing students Word List 1, the teacher slowly reads words aloud from the list, one word at a time. The teacher asks after each word, "What do you notice when you *listen* to these words?", "What do you *hear* that is the same about these words?", or "What do your *ears* tell you about these words?" Once familiar with these procedures, the teacher only reminds students of the procedure at the beginning of the activity.

2. The teacher allows an interval of time after each word for students to make hypotheses about the pattern. The teacher encourages students to confirm or correct predictions as each new word is added. After hearing the words *boo, coo, moo, shoo, too,* and *zoo,* for example, students might respond that they rhyme. When *boot* (and next, *cool*) is added, the teacher might say, "You said that they all rhyme. Do you still think so? What else could be the same?" At this point, if necessary, the teacher repeats the words, exaggerating the pronunciation of the (o͞o).

3. When they have determined the pattern, students confirm it by checking the rule with a few subsequent words that the teacher reads aloud. Students then remove the tape from the middle position to uncover the sound representation. The teacher encourages students to "Take a look to see if you're right. Are you?"

NOTE: The representation for sounds used in *Developing Independent Readers* is simple and makes sense to students. At the beginning of the program the teacher explains that the sounds that letters represent are written between marks called parentheses. Rather than parentheses, most dictionaries use diagonal lines to represent respellings. Together, the teacher and students look at different dictionary phonetic respellings. They compare and contrast them with the way respellings are represented in this program.

Visual Pattern Discovery

Word List 1 (color coded) is used. The color coding aids students in focusing on the pattern. It is removed as a cue in activities using Word List 2. The Word List is prepared with tape masks in two positions—letters (on the left) and key word/picture (on the right).

Procedures

1. Immediately after completing Auditory Pattern Discovery, the teacher shows students Word List 1. The teacher asks, "What do you notice when you *look* at these words?", "What do you *see* that is the same about these words?", or "What do your *eyes* tell you is the same about these words?" The teacher encourages students to verbalize their observations. For example, "I see oo in all the words" or "There's oo in all of them."

2. After students describe the pattern, they remove the tape from the left position. This uncovers and reveals the letters. The teacher encourages students to confirm: "Take a look. See if you're right. Are you right?"

3. The teacher then models the connection between the letter(s) and sound by saying, "Yes, oo spells ($\overline{oo}$) in these words." Students practice this important letter-sound correspondence in Letter-Sound Key Word Practice (described later).

Word List Reading with Oral Sentences

Materials

Word List 1 (color coded) is prepared with tape mask on one position—key word/ picture (on the right).

Procedures

1. Students (or students and the teacher) read words down lists from the top of the page to the bottom. They read the list on the left first and progress to the lists that follow to the right. They read words from the list one at a time, or student(s) and the teacher take turns reading the words. After each word, students or the teacher create and say a sentence that uses the word and shows its meaning.

2. The teacher encourages students to make more than one sentence to show the meanings of words with multiple meanings and of homographs (words with the same spelling but different meanings and origins, such as *fly* used as a noun or as a verb). The teacher also highlights homophones (words that sound the same but have different meanings and are usually spelled differently, such as *meat* and *meet*).

3. To provide a more challenging task, some students and the teacher create a serial story with the words. Each sentence relates to a common topic.

NOTE: Some students need a great deal of support and practice to blend or fuse sounds to come up with a meaningful word. Anticipating and using meaning and language structure and order is often a factor critical to success. To support these students (and only as long as it benefits them), the teacher precedes each word with an oral sentence, and students read the word immediately following. In addition to providing semantic and syntactic cues, the teacher's sentences provide a model for students to use when they generate their own sentences. The teacher models using grapho-phonic and semantic and syntactic clues together. "Let's sound together (or sample those sounds) and think about what would make sense in the definition or sentence." The teacher pronounces the sounds in order in the word with the student, slowly drawing and fusing the sounds. Together, the teacher and students cross-check using the other cueing systems—for example, "(r)-(ing). Is a ring a piece of jewelry?" or "(r)-(ing). I got a diamond ring for my birthday. Does that make sense? Does that sound right?" When students encounter challenging words while reading, the teacher often says, "Let's sample those sounds and read on" and then encourages students to reread to confirm. When students appear to be stuck as they try unproductively to sound a word, the teacher often says, "Keep going" or "Blank and keep reading." Students are often surprised at first and delighted to discover that the challenging word pops into their heads when meaning and structure cues are added to the sampling of sounds. The teacher often restates or encourages students to verbalize what has happened when they have followed this procedure. This reinforces and brings this powerful strategy to students' conscious awareness.

Some students need even more support with blending and fusing sounds into words. They benefit from moving cards with letters that represent phonemes printed on them as they blend:

Other students benefit from having the process modeled using a tachistoscope. The teacher uses these types of supports or scaffolds only as long as needed by individual students. The goal is independent reading in context.

Theme and Key Word Clue Game

Materials

Word List 1 (color coded) prepared with a tape mask in one position—key word/picture (on the right).

Letter-Sound Key Word/Picture Card(s)

Procedures

1. The teacher introduces each unit by reading aloud one of the books from the suggested **Book List** or by presenting a **Motivation and Extension Activity**. The books and activities provide important background information and opportunities to discuss concepts and vocabulary related to the theme so students can connect the key word for the element with the thematic unit.

2. Students look at Word List 1 while the teacher gives clues about the key word, which is one of the words in the list. The clues are directly related to the book they have heard read aloud or to the **Motivation and Extension Activity** students have completed.

3. The teacher gives clues one at a time that are more general in the beginning and then become more specific. After each clue, students make hypotheses. They then confirm or correct their predictions as each new clue is added.

4. The teacher proceeds with at least one clue after students have guessed the word. This encourages students to continue on (as in reading on when reading in context) to cross-check and confirm or correct as each new bit of information is added.

5. When students have identified the theme and key word for the unit and have confirmed it by using subsequent clues, they remove the tape from the right position. This uncovers and reveals the key word and picture. The teacher encourages students to "Take a look and see if you are right. Did you guess the word?"

Introduction of New Card(s)

6. The teacher then introduces the Letter-Sound Key Word/Picture card(s) (located in Appendix C) for the unit. The teacher shows students the card and models the response: "*ee* is ($\bar{e}$) in *seeds*" or "*ee* ($\bar{e}$) *seeds*." The teacher adds and shuffles the new card(s) into the students' pack for later and subsequent practice.

Word List Clue Game

Materials

Word List 2 (as presented, with no color coding or tape masks) is used. The game involves two or more players and works well with pairs and groups of students. In individual tutorial settings, the teacher and the student play.

Procedures

1. The teacher places the word list in view of all players. Players take turns choosing a word from the list for the other player(s) to guess.

2. Without indicating which word they have chosen, players give clues in riddle form, definitions, or a cloze sentence containing the word and showing its meaning. They say "blank" where the word fits.

3. After the first clue is given, one of the players makes a guess and places a check mark next to the predicted word in the list. The clue giver does not tell if the guess is correct; he or she gives another clue. Other players use the additional information to confirm or correct the first prediction. If the word is confirmed by the second clue, a player circles it on the word list. If the word is not confirmed, the clue giver continues to give clues, one at a time, and players check off predicted words until the word is correctly identified and circled.

4. Another player chooses a word, and play continues until all words on the list have been guessed.

NOTE: Occasionally, students act out clues for an entire list (as in charades). At other times, students draw clues for a list of words. Most often, though, students play the game as it was presented in the preceding list, which provides practice using oral language.

Letter-Sound Key Word Practice

Materials

Letter-sound key word/picture cards are approximately 3″ × 5″ in size. They are made by photocopying the reproducible masters in Appendix C onto white card stock.

Each card is divided vertically by lines into three segments or frames, with the following information represented:

1. On the left is the letter or letters that represent a phoneme/sound.
2. In the middle is the sound represented by the letters enclosed in parentheses.
3. On the right is a key word and picture. For most sounds, the letters are embedded in the picture. (The teacher may add hand motions corresponding to the pictures to help some students remember and retrieve consonant digraphs. For *ch* the teacher pretends to sneeze, with his or her index finger forming a *c* under the nose; for *sh* the teacher forms an *s* in the air as if tracing the fin of the shark to signal the *s* of the *sh* combination; for *th* the teacher puts up his or her thumb as it is represented in the *t* in the *th* combination in the picture; and so on.)

Each student (or group of students) has a pack of Letter-Sound Key Word/Picture Cards. The pack contains a card for the new element presented and a card for every review element (included for practice, as needed). For this activity, the teacher includes in the pack new and review cards which represent more than one sound for each letter or combination of letters. These include *a, e, i, o, u, y, oo, ow, ou, g,* and *c*.

A card is used as a mask to cover the last two frames (middle and right) of each letter-sound key word/picture card durinig the One Frame Exposed activity. A template for making masks from colored card stock or oaktag is also included in Appendix C.

Procedures

1. Each student (or group of students) has a pack of Letter-Sound Key Word/Picture Cards. The pack contains a card for the new element presented and a card for every review element (included for practice, as needed).

2. In tutorial, the student and teacher sit next to and turn to face each other at a table. In group presentation, the teacher sits in front of students. The teacher presents the cards, one at a time, with the symbols toward the students. The teacher holds the pack with the left hand (which is to students' right) and turns cards with the right hand (which is to students' left). This provides a movement that cues readers to return their eyes to the left of each card, as in the return sweep of the eyes from the right in reading text.

3. *Three Frames Exposed.* The student reads each section of the card in order from left to right: (1) the *name* of the letter(s), (2) the *sound* the letter(s) represent, and (3) the *key word/picture.* The teacher places each card successfully read in front of students and states, at first, and then implies the question, "Are you right? Take a look and check to be sure." Cards that students are unsure of or are read unsuccessfully are returned immediately to the pack for additional tries and practice (as needed) during this activity. Students enjoy having their pile of cards to compare with the teacher's pile, which is usually nonexistent because students are provided with several opportunities for success with challenging cards.

4. *One Frame Exposed.* The procedure is the same as for the Three Frames Exposed activity, except that the second and third frames for each card are covered with the mask. The teacher removes each card students read from the pack with the right hand and holds the mask in place with the left hand. In this more difficult task, students name the exposed letter(s) and give the sound and key word from memory.

When useful, the teacher points to or guides students to point to the section under the mask that represents each response. Memory and retrieval appear to be aided by this additional spatial and motor cue.

NOTE: Some students need practice with the Three Frames Exposed activity before they complete the One Frame Exposed activity. Other students need less practice. They need only to see each new card with the three frames exposed once when it is introduced after the Theme and Key Word Clue Game. All students have practice reading the three frames when the teacher places cards in front of students to check after they respond to each card in the One Frame Exposed practice.

Sound-Letter Practice

Materials

Students' pack of letter-sound key word/picture cards for teacher reference

Lined paper and pencil (for Oral and Writing activity)

For this activity, the teacher substitutes cards. He or she removes new and review cards from the pack which represent more than one sound for each letter or combination of letters and replaces them with cards that represent one sound for each letter or combination of letters, including *a, e, i, o, u, y, oo, ow, ou, g,* and *c.* The teacher replaces the multiple-sound cards after this activity is completed. This prepares the pack for the next Letter-Sound Key Word Practice.

The teacher arranges cards from individual students' packs by putting together cards that represent the same sound. Card packs differ according to where individual students and groups of students are in the program's sequence. For example, one student (or group of students) might have for (ō): o (open syllable) and (vowel-consonant-e syllable), and ow (grow). For the same sound, (ō), another student (or group) might have: o (open syllable) and (vowel-consonant-e), ow (grow), and oa (goat). If students complete the Oral and Sorting activity of Letter-Sound Key Word Practice, they do the arranging of the pack for this activity themselves.

A chart of **Sound-Letter Correspondences Presented in *Developing Independent Readers*** is presented on page xviii:

Procedures

1. The teacher refers to the cards in the pack and says the sound represented on each card (or group of cards that represent the same sound). Students see only the backs of cards until after they make their response.

2. After students respond, the teacher shows students the face of the card and asks (at first explicitly and later by implication), "Are you right? Check and see."

3. Students respond in three ways: oral, oral and sorting, and/or oral and writing. In each case, the first response is *always* oral. The teacher is able to help students correct any errors at this point so that they do not practice errors in writing. Students who hear and feel themselves say the letters that represent sounds also receive important feedback and reinforcement for learning and remembering.

4. *Oral.* The teacher refers to the cards and says the sound, one sound at a time, represented on each card (or group of cards that represent the same sound). Students say the names of the letters that spell the sound. When there are multiple ways to

	Consonant Sounds			Vowel Sounds
(b)	b	(r)	r	(ă)	a
(k)	c, k	(s)	s, c (e, i, y)	(ĕ)	e
(d)	d	(t)	t	(ĭ)	i
(f)	f	(v)	v	(ŏ)	o
(g)	g	(w)	w	(ŭ)	u
(h)	h	(ks)	x	(ā)	a, a-e, ay, ai
(j)	j, g (e, i, y)	(y)	y	(ē)	e, e-e, ee, ea, y
(l)	l	(z)	z	(ī)	i, y, i-e, igh
(m)	m	(ch)	ch	(ō)	o, o-e, ow, oa
(n)	n	(sh)	sh	(ū)	u, u-e
(p)	p	(th)	th	(ar)	ar
(kw)	qu	(t̲h̲)	th	(or)	or
				(er)	er, ir, ur
				(o͞o)	oo, ou
				(oo)	oo
				(ow)	ow, ou
				(oy)	oy, oi
				(aw)	aw, au
				(ing)	ing

represent a sound, the teacher asks for all of the ways that have been presented up to that point in the program. The teacher gives students that information by saying, "Tell me four ways to spell (ō)" or "Tell me two ways to spell (k)."

5. *Oral and Sorting.* The teacher places all of the cards from the prepared pack in random order face up on a table in front of students. The teacher says one sound at a time. Students (1) say the names of the letters that spell the sound, (2) point to or pick up the card or cards that correspond to their oral responses, and (3) check their responses. This includes all possible cards in cases of multiple spellings.

6. *Oral and Writing.* The teacher refers to the cards and says the sound, one sound at a time, represented on each card (or group of cards that represent the same sound). Students (1) say the names of the letters that spell the sound, (2) write the letters while looking at and naming them ("Tell your hand what to write"), (3) check to see that what they have written is what they intended (first without the card as a reference and then with the card after the teacher places it in front of them), and (4) correct the response, if needed.

Spelling and Reading List Words for Cloze Sentences

Materials

Word List 1 or 2 for teacher reference
Lined paper and pencil

1. The teacher asks students to say the names of the letters that spell the sound represented by the element being presented. Students say the names of the letters and then write them at the top of the paper. For example, the teacher says, "How do you spell (ō) in goat?" Students respond by saying and then writing *oa*.

2. The teacher then dictates words, one word at a time, from Word List 1 or 2 for students to write. Some students benefit from reading a word list before they spell the words. Others do not need this practice.

3. Rather than dictate the words, the teacher may give clues for each word—for example, "It is another name for a street" instead of dictating "road."

4. After the teacher dictates or gives clues for a word, students repeat the word and spell it (orally first for some students). Students write words in a list on the paper. The teacher reminds students, as appropriate, to say the names of the letters as they write the words: "Tell your hand what letters to write." Students read each word after they write it to check the spelling. They read the entire list when all words have been written in preparation for the Cloze Sentences activity, which follows immediately.

Cloze Sentences

Materials

Student word list from Spelling and Reading List Words for Cloze Sentences activity

Cloze sentences activity sheets, cut by the teacher into strips by sentence, folded in half, and placed in an envelope

Business-size envelope

The teacher prepares the cloze sentences that correspond to the column(s) of the word lists he or she has selected for students. Word lists include single- and multisyllable words beginning with Chapter 6. Within each of the sections headed "Single Syllable" and "Multisyllable," sentences are in an order that differs from the alphabetical order of the words in the word lists.

The teacher copies the cloze sentences using the reproducible masters provided for each unit. The teacher presents the sentences as activity sheets or cuts the pages into strips by sentences, folds the strips in half, and puts them in an envelope for a game format. Students can use the strips cut from the tops of the pages (which contain the Letter-Sound Key Word/Picture) as bookmarks when they read books for the units. The bookmarks provide students with additional exposure to this important information.

Procedures

1. The teacher places the student's word list under a book or folder for students to refer to only as needed. The student has written this list in the Spelling and Reading List Words for Cloze Sentences activity, which immediately precedes the Cloze Sentences activity.

2. If they play the game using the sentence strips, students take turns with other students or with the teacher. Players select one sentence strip at a time from the

envelope. Often, students like to search the envelope for long or short sentences (wide or narrow folded strips) according to their preferences.

3. Players, in turn, read an entire sentence (with support as needed) and say "blank" or pause to indicate the omitted word. They then write the appropriate word in the blank that completes the sentence from the word list. Students write the word from memory, if possible. They use the list to check spelling or to copy, if necessary. Students reread each sentence after completing it to check that it makes sense and sounds right and to check for spelling.

NOTE: Students who need a system for motivation can earn the following points. The teacher places the rules where all players can read them. The goal is to earn the greatest number of points.

3 points: If you do not look at the list and you spell the word right

2 points: If you do not look at the list and you do not spell the word right

1 point: If you look at the list and you copy the word right

0 points: If you look at the list and you do not copy the word right

Some students enjoy the opportunity to steal sentences from the teacher (*not* from other students). If a student is able to read the sentence and say the omitted word before the teacher finishes reading his or her sentence silently (and *slowly*), that student steals the sentence, writes in the appropriate word, and adds it to his or her pile of completed sentences.

Dictation and Editing

Materials

Paragraphs for dictation and editing for each unit for teacher reference

Reproducible masters of paragraphs for dictation and editing in cloze sentence format for student response are included in Chapters 1 through 4. Teachers may cut reproduced sheets into separate dictations before they give them to students to complete. Students write element words in the blanks as they follow the procedures.

Lined paper and pencil

Procedures

Dictation

1. To begin, students head the paper with the element from the unit which will recur in the dictated paragraph(s). The teacher says, "How do you spell (ō) in goat?", for example. Students say and then write *oa* at the top of the paper.

2. The teacher reads aloud the entire paragraph. The teacher and students discuss the content of the paragraph (meaning and vocabulary). Some students benefit from visualizing the passage to aid memory. Some students enjoy drawing pictures that illustrate the dictated passages.

3. The teacher writes (for students' reference) any words that require visual memory. The teacher places these given words in view, where students can copy them.

4. The teacher then dictates the paragraph by meaningful phrases. As students pro-

gress through the program or as they demonstrate increased auditory memory, the teacher dictates increasingly longer phrases and sentences. Students repeat each phrase or sentence and write it. Students skip a line between each line of writing in anticipation of editing. The teacher says "end of sentence" and "beginning of sentence" to signal punctuation and capitalization as appropriate for individual students.

Editing

1. Students edit for the following: content, form, capitalization and punctuation, and spelling.
2. Students read and reread the paragraphs several times for different purposes during the writing and editing processes. This gives students opportunities to read element words in meaningful contexts and to read their own handwriting. Some students benefit from rereading the paragraphs during the next session.

   Content: Students read the paragraph they have written to check that it makes sense, sounds right, and has no omitted or inserted words. In the beginning, the teacher reads the passage as students follow along. As soon as possible, students read aloud or silently, as appropriate.

   Form: Students check organization of the paragraphs, such as spacing (between words, sentences, paragraphs, and lines), left and right margins, and indentation (to signal paragraphs). They also check letter formation and legibility.

   Capitalization and Punctuation: Students check the beginnings of sentences for uppercase letters and the ends of sentences for appropriate punctuation.

   Spelling: Students underline and check the spelling of all new element words. Students and teacher each count the new element words in their respective copies of the paragraph and check that they have the same number. Students check the spelling of all review element words. Students and teacher discuss given words, as appropriate.

CONTENTS

1 ing king ✦ 1

2 oo moon ✦ 13

3 Open Syllable go ✦ 25

34 x fox • 390

A Note to Teachers Before Beginning Lessons

The *Developing Independent Readers* program begins with students' knowledge (but not necessarily mastery) of most single consonant sounds. Knowledge includes letter recognition and sound correspondence. It includes the ability to (1) name each consonant letter (upper- and lowercase forms), (2) associate a sound with each letter, (3) write the letter when given the letter name (upper- and lowercase forms), and (4) name and write the letter when the sound it represents is presented orally.

The teacher determines each student's alphabetic knowledge before beginning the lessons in *Developing Independent Readers*. Appendix D contains an "Alphabet Knowledge" assessment of consonants; consonant digraphs *ch*, *sh*, and *th*; and single vowels.

To begin lessons, the teacher prepares a pack of Letter-Sound Key Word/Picture Cards for each student or group of students. Masters for these cards are in Appendix C. The pack contains a card for each element as it is introduced. The first cards placed in the pack are single consonants and consonant digraphs not mastered as determined on the "Alphabet Knowledge" assessment. (Procedures for using the Letter-Sound Key Word/ Picture Cards are described in detail in the section "Letter-Sound Key Word Practice" beginning on page xv.)

Beginning with Chapter 1, *ing (ing) king*, students complete activities for each unit in the sequence presented in the Table of Contents and in the following Scope and Sequence Chart.

The elements *ing (ing) king* and *oo (oo) moon* are beginning elements because of their high frequency and utility in reading. They are frequently among the elements that students know from their previous reading and writing experiences. They are easy patterns for students to discover auditorally and visually. In addition, they are concrete elements effective for introducing the procedures of the lesson.

SCOPE AND SEQUENCE

The Scope and Sequence Chart for *Developing Independent Readers* follows on page xxx. It is included for teacher reference only. Students need to know letter-sound relationships for reading and sound-letter relationships for writing.

SYLLABLE TYPES

Developing Independent Readers presents the following seven syllable types, which comprise the words in the English language:

* *Open syllable:* One vowel ends the syllable and represents a long sound—for example, go, raven.
* *Closed syllable:* One or more consonants follow a single vowel which represents a short sound—for example, cat, kitten.
* *Vowel-consonant-e syllable:* A consonant and a final silent *e* follow a single vowel which represents a long sound—for example, cake.

SCOPE AND SEQUENCE CHART

Grapho-Phonic Elements		Book Chapters
Phonogram syllable	ing (ing) king	1
Vowel combination syllable	oo ($\overline{oo}$) moon	2
Open syllable	a (ā), e (ē), i (ī), o (ō), u (ū)	3
Vowel y in open syllable	y (ī) fly	4
Closed syllable	a (ă), e (ĕ), i (ĭ), o (ŏ), u (ŭ)	5
Vowel-consonant-e syllable	a-e (ā), e-e (ē), i-e (ī), o-e (ō), u-e (ū)	6
Vowel combination syllable	ay (ā) day	7
Vowel combination syllable	ee (ē) seeds	8
Vowel combination syllable	ow (ō) grow	9
Vowel combination syllable	ea (ē) wheat	10
Vowel y that ends two-syllable words	y (ē) penny	11
Phonogram syllable	igh (ī) night	12
Vowel combination syllable	oa (ō) goat	13
Phonogram syllable	old (ōld) gold	14
Vowel combination syllable	ai (ā) rain	15
R-controlled syllable	ar (ar) star	16
R-controlled syllable	or (or) corn	17
R-controlled syllable	er (er) spider	18
R-controlled syllable	ir (er) birthday	19
R-controlled syllable	ur (er) turtle	20
Vowel combination syllable	oo (ŏo) cookies	21
Vowel combination syllable	ow (ow) owl	22
Vowel combination syllable	ou (ow) house	23
Vowel combination syllable	oy (oy) boy	24
Vowel combination syllable	oi (oy) noise	25
Vowel combination syllable	aw (aw) straw	26
Vowel combination syllable	au (aw) daughter	27
Vowel combination syllable	ou ($\overline{oo}$) soup	28
Final syllable	consonant-le fable	29
Final syllable	tion (shun) immigration	30
Consonant sound	g (j) George, magic, stingy	31
Consonant sound	c (s) Frances, Cinderella, fancy	32
Consonant sound	qu (kw) quilt	33
Consonant sound	x (ks) fox	34

- *Vowel combination syllable:* Two successive vowels (1) represent a single sound that may be represented by either vowel alone: *Vowel digraph*—for example, d<u>ay</u>, s<u>ee</u>ds, gr<u>ow</u>ing, wh<u>ea</u>t, g<u>oa</u>t, r<u>ai</u>n; or (2) represent a sound that begins at or near the position where the first vowel is articulated and moves or glides toward the position where the second vowel is articulated: *Diphthong*—for example, <u>ow</u>l, h<u>ou</u>se, b<u>oy</u>, n<u>oi</u>se, or *irregular diphthong*—m<u>oo</u>n, c<u>oo</u>kies, str<u>aw</u>, d<u>au</u>ghter, s<u>ou</u>p.
- *R-controlled vowel syllable:* An *r* follows a single vowel which represents a sound different from the sound represented by the vowel when followed by other consonant letters—for example, st<u>ar</u>, c<u>orn</u>, spid<u>er</u>, b<u>ir</u>thday, t<u>ur</u>tle.
- *Final syllable:* A group of vowel and consonant letters that occur as a unit at the end of words—for example, *Consonant-le*, fab<u>le</u>, and *tion*, immigra<u>tion</u>.
- *Phonogram syllable:* A vowel sound combined with one or more consonant sounds which, when a consonant sound (or sounds) is added—single consonant(s), consonant blend(s), or consonant digraph(s)—in initial and/or final position(s) comprise common words. Most phonograms must have consonant(s) added to become words—for example, <u>k</u>ing or <u>n</u>i<u>ght</u>. Some are words that become other words with the addition of consonant(s)—<u>g</u>old.

1   ing   king

BOOK LIST

Kings

King Bidgood's in the Bathtub, Audrey Wood, illustrated by Don Wood (San Diego: Harcourt Brace Jovanovich, 1985). The king *won't* get out of the bathtub, and he invites everyone in to join him—to battle, eat, fish, and dance! Finally, a young page solves the problem. He pulls the plug! Caldecott Honor Book.

Where the Wild Things Are, Maurice Sendak (New York: Harper & Row, 1963). Mischievous Max returns home from his adventures as king in the land of the Wild Things with a new understanding of belonging and love.

Mister King, Raija Siekkinen, translated from the Finnish by Tim Steffa, illustrated by Hannu Taina (Minneapolis, Minn.: Carolrhoda Books, Inc., 1986). In this modern fable, a lonely king who hasn't a single subject does not enjoy his beautiful house and kingdom until a huge cat arrives at his door. Winner of the Biennale of Illustrations Bratislava (BIB) Grand Prix award for illustrations.

The King's Flower, Mitsumasa Anno (New York: Philomel Books, 1976). A king, in this modern fable, demands that everything he owns be enormous until he discovers, in nature, a power greater than his own and learns that bigger is not always better.

Hungry Things and Word Play

The Hungry Thing, Jan Slepian and Ann Seidler, illustrated by Richard E. Martin (New York: Scholastic, 1967). A Hungry Thing arrives unexpectedly and baffles all of the townspeople except a little boy when he asks to eat shmancakes (with syrup), tickles (dill or sour), feetloaf, hookies, gollipops, foodles, smello, and boop with a smacker.

The Hungry Thing Returns, Jan Slepian and Ann Seidler, illustrated by Richard E. Martin (New York: Scholastic, 1990). The Hungry Thing returns with his daughter, who confounds the adults at school when she asks for flamburgers, bellyjeans, blownuts, crackeroni and sneeze, harshfellows, gubble bum, and a trip to the mathboom.

The Hungry Thing Goes to a Restaurant, Jan Slepian and Ann Seidler, illustrated by Elroy Freem (New York: Scholastic, 1992). It's the waiter and waitress's confusion this time when The Hungry Thing arrives with a mysterious sack and orders bapple moose, spoonadish, benchflies with smetchup, hopsickles, silk snakes, and born on the slob.

The Surprise Party, Pat Hutchins (New York: Young Readers Press, 1969). Rabbit's "I'm having a party tomorrow" becomes "hoeing the parsley tomorrow," and a chain of misunderstandings results as each of his friends hears and passes the invitation a little differently.

The Cat Who Wore a Pot on Her Head, Jan Slepian and Ann Seidler, illustrated by Richard E. Martin (New York: Scholastic, 1980). With a pot on her head to escape the noise of her busy family, Bendemolena the cat can't tell if her mother said to put the "fish on to bake," "bish in the lake," or "soap in the cake."

-Ing Action Words

Champions, Rebel Williams, illustrated by George Ford (Bothell, Wash.: Thomas C. Wright, Inc., 1990). A simple, repetitive pattern text with illustrations shows Olympic champions in action—running a race, jumping over bars, swimming laps, diving competitively, lifting weights, and throwing the javelin.

The Chick and the Duckling, Mirra Ginsburg, translated from the Russian of V. Suteyev, illustrated by José Aruego and Ariane Dewey (New York: The Trumpet Club, 1972). All is well in this repetitive pattern book when the chick does everything the duckling does—"taking a walk," "digging a hole"—until the duckling goes swimming. After its dramatic rescue by the duckling, the chick learns their differences.

I Was Walking Down the Road, Sarah E. Barchas, illustrated by Jack Kent (New York: Scholastic, 1975). In this classic predictable book, a girl catches animals as she is busy doing a variety of activities, including "working," "jumping," "cleaning," "sweeping," "eating," and "reading." Then she lets them go.

I Went Walking, Sue Williams, illustrated by Julie Vivas (San Diego: Harcourt Brace Jovanovich, 1989). A boy goes walking and, true to the cumulative nature of the story, collects the farm animals of different colors he sees who have been looking at him.

Brown Bear, Brown Bear, What Do You See?, Bill Martin, Jr., illustrated by Eric Carle (New York: Henry Holt and Company, 1967, 1983). Collages illustrate this cumulative tale in which children look at a mother and a collection of brightly colored animals that all look at each other.

Polar Bear, Polar Bear, What Do You Hear?, Bill Martin, Jr., illustrated by Eric Carle (New York: Henry Holt and Company, 1991). Martin and Carle's companion to *Brown Bear, Brown Bear, What Do You See?* features zoo animals that hear each other make characteristic noises and children in costume who imitate the sounds and actions of the animals.

Busy Day: A Book of Action Words, Betsy and Giulio Maestro (New York: Crown Publishers, Inc., 1978). The activities of an elephant and a clown throughout a day at the circus—from waking to sleeping—illustrate single *-ing* verbs.

Five Little Monkeys Jumping on the Bed, Eileen Christelow (New York: Clarion Books, 1989). Christelow's interpretation of this familiar counting rhyme—a cumulative story in reverse—has a humorous surprise ending. When the monkeys finally fall asleep, their mother jumps on the bed!

Sing a Song of Sixpence, illustrated by Tracey Campbell Pearson (New York: Dial Books for Young Readers, 1985). Watercolor, ink, and gouache paintings of the antics of the plump, rosy-cheeked inhabitants of the king's palace bring life and humor to the familiar rhyme. Music for the song is included.

The Napping House, Audrey Wood, illustrated by Don Wood (San Diego: Harcourt Brace Jovanovich, 1984). In this cumulative story, everyone except a flea is sleeping— "snoring granny, dreaming child, dozing dog, snoozing cat, slumbering mouse"—until the flea "bites the mouse, who scares the cat, who claws the dog. . . ."

Wind, Ron Bacon, illustrated by Philippa Stichbury (New York: Scholastic, 1984). Illustrated rhyming text invites readers to "feel the wind blowing" in a variety of contexts— sky, sea, beach, meadow, and city street.

Love Is Walking Hand in Hand, Charles M. Schulz (San Francisco: Determined Productions, Inc., 1965). Peanuts cartoon characters in action—"tickling," "wishing," "sharing," and "not nagging"—illustrate the meaning of love according to Schulz.

Happiness Is a Warm Puppy, Charles M. Schulz (New York: Random House, 1987). Snoopy, Charlie Brown, Linus, Lucy, and friends express their individual interpretations of happiness in this companion to *Love Is Walking Hand in Hand* by the same author.

Walking Is Wild, Weird and Wacky, Karen Kerber (Kansas City, Mo.: Landmark Editions, Inc., 1981). A twelve-year-old writer and illustrator celebrates action words with alliteration, including "Sauntering like a snail is sluggish" and "Treading like a turtle is tiring."

Millions of Eels, Howard Small, illustrated by Ulco Glimmerveen (New York: Scholastic, 1989). "Floating," "hatching," "drifting," "changing," "growing," "becoming," "swimming," "climbing," "wriggling," "squeezing," "sliding," "hunting," "escaping," "returning," "breeding," "floating": Realistic illustrations and simple text introduce the life cycle of the freshwater eel. Includes map and glossary of terms.

Have You Seen Birds?, Joanne Oppenheim, illustrated by Barbara Reid (New York: Scholastic, 1986). Clay collage illustrations combined with poetic text show birds in action in a variety of habitats through the seasons: "screeching, splashing, tapping, drilling, trilling, strutting, paddling, diving, and soaring."

MOTIVATION AND EXTENSION ACTIVITIES

Kings

1. Students and teacher explore the illustrations and note patterns as they read *King Bidgood's in the Bathtub*, *The Napping House*, and *Where the Wild Things Are*. Wood uses light and color to convey the passing of time in *King Bidgood's in the*

Bathtub and to show the change of atmosphere and of weather from rainy to sunny in *The Napping House*. Sendak's illustrations in *Where the Wild Things Are* become larger and larger and culminate in three sets of two-page illustrations without text in the land of the Wild Things.

2. The teacher casually uses a few large props before he or she reads *The King's Flower*. The teacher pretends to write a note on a piece of large chart paper that he or she has prepared with large writing and uses a large pencil made from a paper towel roll and oaktag.

3. After they listen to or read *The King's Flower*, students plant a tulip bulb. They record their observations of its growth with words and/or pictures in a log book.

Hungry Things and Word Play

4. Students make up their own names for foods using rhymes as in *The Hungry Thing*, *The Hungry Thing Returns*, and *The Hungry Thing Goes to a Restaurant*. Individually or as a collaborative group project, they create a restaurant menu that lists and pictures their foods. The teacher creates a similar menu and brings in corresponding foods. He or she acts as waitress/waiter, and students order and eat their choices. The teacher brings in a favorite recipe—for "Snueberry Luffins," for example (which he or she has rewritten from a recipe for blueberry muffins). Students help bake and eat them.

5. The books *The Surprise Party* and *The Cat Who Wore a Pot on Her Head* extend word play beyond the rhymes of *The Hungry Thing*, *The Hungry Thing Returns*, and *The Hungry Thing Goes to a Restaurant* and include words that differ by one or a few sounds (phonemes) in positions other than the initial. Students and teacher explore the transformations together.

6. As they read *The Surprise Party*, students and the teacher discuss how easily rumors can be spread, as when Rabbit's "I'm having a party tomorrow" becomes "hoeing the parsley tomorrow" and a chain of misunderstandings results as each of his friends hears and passes the invitation a little differently.

Students experience this phenomenon as they play the game of "Telephone," in which they pass a message in whispers from one person to the next, and it often becomes misunderstood and confused (and comical when it is revealed at the end of the turn).

Students read and discuss other books in which misunderstandings result in rumors, including *Did You Say, "Fire"?* by Cowley (see Activity 4 in Chapter 6, vowel-consonant-e cake) and in versions of the "Henny Penny" story: *Henny Penny* by Zimmerman, "Chicken Licken" in *The Stinky Cheese Man and Other Fairly Stupid Tales* by Scieszka, *Chicken Little* by Kellogg, and *Foolish Rabbit's Big Mistake* by Martin (see Activity 6 in Chapter 11, y penny).

-ing Action Words

7. Students and teacher compare and contrast patterns and details in *I Went Walking*, *Brown Bear, Brown Bear, What Do You See?*, and *Polar Bear, Polar Bear, What Do You Hear?*.

8. The music for the song of *Sing a Song of Sixpence* is included in the back of the book. Students and teacher join voices and sing the book (and eat bread and honey, if they don't have a recipe for blackbird pie handy!).

9. Before they listen to or read *The Napping House*, students brainstorm and the teacher records as many words as they can that mean "sleeping" (synonyms) and end

with *-ing*. As appropriate, the teacher gives clues to help students come up with a variety. For example, for *napping* the teacher (1) acts out a clue, such as pretends to hold an imaginary blanket and suck his or her thumb, or (2) gives a verbal clue, such as "Babies and cats often sleep during the day. When they do, they are. . . ." The teacher introduces or reviews the dictionary and the thesaurus as resource books.

10. Students act out the plot sequences in the books that follow traditional patterns. **The Napping House** is a cumulative story, **Five Little Monkeys Jumping on the Bed** is a cumulative story in reverse, and **Where the Wild Things Are** follows a quest or home-adventure(s)-home pattern.

11. As the teacher prepares to read aloud **Wind**, he or she turns on several fans in the room that are positioned to blow items around—papers, curtains, pages of books, and students' hair, for example. After sharing the book, students and teacher create a book that follows the pattern of **Wind** and describes the actions of the wind in the classroom context. For example,

> Feel the wind blowing,
> Whisking papers on the floor.
>
> Feel the wind blowing,
> Messing up our hair. . . . and so on

The teacher records ideas on (chart) paper as students offer them. Students illustrate them.

12. After they listen to or read **Love Is Walking Hand in Hand** and **Happiness Is a Warm Puppy**, students tell about what they enjoy doing for fun, using *-ing* words, or they write and illustrate a *Fun Is* book that follows the pattern from the Schulz books and fill in blanks to complete *-ing* verbs on each page:

> Fun is _____ing _____ .
> Fun is _____ing _____ . . . . and so on

Student responses might include, for example, "Fun is *slid*ing *in the snow*" or "Fun is *eat*ing *ice cream cones*."

13. Individually or as a group, students brainstorm as many synonyms as they can for walking or other actions—running, sleeping (see the foregoing Activity 9), or jumping, for example—after they listen to or read **Walking Is Wild, Weird and Wacky**. Then they say or write and illustrate their own alliterative sentences for each word.

Ambitious students and teachers create an Alliterative Alphabet Action Book with an action for each letter of the alphabet. For example, students write

> Ambling is adventurous and aggravating.
> Bouncing is bubbly and boingy.
> Climbing is clunky and crunchy.
> Digging is dirty and dangerous. . . . and so on

Published alliterative alphabet books include the following:

A My Name Is Alice, Jane Bayer, illustrated by Steven Kellogg (New York: The Trumpet Club, 1984).

A Is for Angry: An Animal and Adjective Alphabet, Sandra Boynton (New York: Workman Publishing, 1983, 1987).

Aster Aardvark's Alphabet Adventures, Steven Kellogg (New York: Morrow, 1987).

Faint Frogs Feeling Feverish & Other Tantalizing Tongue Twisters, Lilian Obligado (New York: Puffin Books, 1983).

A Beastly Circus, Peggy Parish, illustrated by Peter Parnall (New York: Simon & Schuster, 1969).

Dr. Seuss's ABC, Dr. Seuss (New York: Random House, 1963).

While they are focusing on initial sounds in words and after they listen to or read Obligado's *Faint Frogs Feeling Feverish & Other Tantalizing Tongue Twisters*, students try to say tongue twisters from *Tongue Twisters*, written by Charles Keller and illustrated by Ron Fritz (New York: Simon & Schuster, 1989), and *Six Sick Sheep: 101 Tongue Twisters*, written by Joanna Cole and Stephanie Calmenson and illustrated by Alan Tiegreen (New York: Scholastic, 1993).

14. Students research and make clay models of a favorite bird and its habitat in a specific season after they listen to (or read) *Have You Seen Birds?*.

15. By turns, students select pages that show actions from any of the books in the "-Ing Action Words" section of the Word List, including the books they or other students have written (the foregoing Activities 11, 12, and 13). They do not show the page, and they give clues for others to guess the action. They describe the action and/or illustration verbally or act out or draw clues. If they draw clues, they use words or pictures that are different from those in the books. Players confirm or revise/correct their responses by looking at the selected page.

16. Students and the teacher locate on a map and/or globe the places/cultures (depicted or of origin) in the books read in this chapter—for example, Finland (*Mister King*).

TEACHER REFERENCE

Cloze Sentences

One-Syllable Words

Cloze Sentences 1

1. The <u>king</u> is the husband of the queen.
2. A <u>ring</u> is a thing you wear on your finger.
3. A bird with a broken <u>wing</u> cannot fly.
4. A <u>sting</u> or bite from a bee can swell up.
5. You need a ball of <u>string</u> to fly a kite.
6. <u>Ding</u> is the sound when a bell rings.

Cloze Sentences 2

1. A gift can be a <u>thing</u> you give to someone as a present.
2. You can <u>sing</u> a song.

3. I <u>bring</u> my lunch to school in a bag.

4. The doctor gave me a <u>sling</u> to wear for my broken arm.

5. You have to <u>swing</u> your bat to hit the ball in baseball.

6. <u>Spring</u> is the season after winter and before summer.

Dictations (Cloze)

1. A clock by your bed can <u>ring</u> to get you up if you set the <u>thing</u>.

2. In the <u>spring</u>, a bird had a nest made out of <u>string</u>. It had a broken <u>wing</u> in a <u>sling</u> so it did not fly or <u>sing</u>.

3. If you <u>swing</u> at it, an ant or a bee can <u>sting</u> you! It is not a good <u>thing</u> to do.

4. The <u>king</u> had a red <u>ring</u>. It was a big <u>thing</u> to the <u>king</u>, but did he have to <u>sing</u> about it all of the time?

ing (ing) king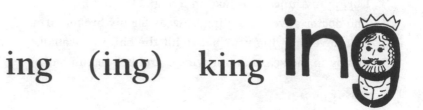

d	br
k	sl
r	spr
s	st
w	sw
	str
	th

Name _____ Date _____

Word List 1

ing   (ing)   king   **ing**

ding   **bring**

king   **sling**

ring   **spring**

sing   **sting**

wing   **swing**

                      string

                      thing

Name _____ Date _____

ing (ing) king

Write a word from the Word List to complete each sentence.

1. The _____ is the husband of the queen.

2. A _____ is a thing you wear on your finger.

3. A bird with a broken _____ cannot fly.

4. A _____ or bite from a bee can swell up.

5. You need a ball of _____ to fly a kite.

6. _____ is the sound when a bell rings.

Name _____ Date _____

Cloze Sentences 1

ing   (ing)   king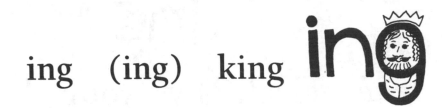

1. A gift can be a _____ you give to someone as a present.

2. You can _____ a song.

3. I _____ my lunch to school in a bag.

4. The doctor gave me a _____ to wear for my broken arm.

5. You have to _____ your bat to hit the ball in baseball.

6. _____ is the season after winter and before summer.

Name _____ Date _____

Cloze Sentences 2

ing

1. A clock by your bed can _____ to get you up if you set the _____.

2. In the _____, a bird had a nest made out of _____. It had a broken _____ in a _____ so it did not fly or _____.

3. If you _____ at it, an ant or a bee can _____ you! It is not a good _____ to do.

4. The _____ had a red _____. It was a big _____ to the _____, but did he have to _____ about it all of the time?

Name _____ Date _____

Dictations

2 oo moon

BOOK LIST

The Moon

Goodnight Moon, Margaret Wise Brown, illustrated by Clement Hurd (New York: Harper & Row, 1947). In rhyming verse, a young rabbit says goodnight to things in his bedroom (shown in black and white) as the room (pictured in color) darkens as night progresses.

Papa, Please Get the Moon for Me, Eric Carle (New York: Scholastic, 1986). Fold-out illustrations take the reader beyond the book's dimensions in this fantasy, in which a girl's father climbs a ladder to get the moon for her.

Happy Birthday, Moon, Frank Asch (New York: Simon & Schuster Books for Young Readers, 1982). Soft, luminous illustrations complement the story of a bear who, in his attempt to befriend the moon, talks with his own echo and devises a clever plan to give the moon a birthday gift.

Mooncake, Frank Asch (New York: Scholastic, 1983). Bear builds a rocket out of junk to find out what the moon tastes like; however, when he awakens he finds not the moon but a wintry surprise—mooncake!

Moongame, Frank Asch (New York: Scholastic, 1984). When the moon disappears behind a cloud during a game of hide and seek with him, Bear mistakes it for a series of familiar objects.

Grandfather Twilight, Barbara Berger (New York: Philomel Books, 1984). Poetic in text and illustration, the simple tale follows Grandfather Twilight, who, every evening, releases the moon into the sky from an infinite strand of pearls.

Anansi the Spider: A Tale from the Ashanti, Gerald McDermott (New York: Holt, Rinehart & Winston, 1972). Two related tales about Anansi the trickster include a quest, in which Anansi is saved in six trials through the individual talents of his six sons, and a *pourquoi* (how or why) tale of how the moon came to be in the sky. Caldecott Honor Book.

"Owl and the Moon" in **Owl At Home**, Arnold Lobel (New York: Scholastic, 1975). In a collection of five stories, Owl is alone at home, but he is entertained by the winter wind, bumps in his bed, sad thoughts, a challenge to himself, and his new friend—the moon. In "Owl and the Moon," Owl attempts to make friends with the moon but does not really understand its ways.

The Moon Seems to Change: A Let's-Read-and-Find-Out Book, Franklyn M. Branley, illustrated by Barbara and Ed Emberley (New York: HarperCollins, 1960, 1987). Easy-to-read text, illustrations, and diagrams explain the phases of the earth's moon and key vocabulary. Includes illustrated instructions for an experiment to show moon phases using an orange and a flashlight.

What the Moon Is Like: A Let's-Read-and-Find-Out Book, Franklyn M. Branley, illustrated by True Kelley (New York: HarperCollins, 1963, 1986). Photographs, drawings, and a map illustrate easy-to-read text that describes the physical properties of the moon.

Moon Rope/Un lazo a la luna: A Peruvian Folktale, Lois Ehlert, translated into Spanish by Amy Prince (San Diego: Harcourt Brace Jovanovich, 1992). Written in English and Spanish, this adaptation of a Peruvian *pourquoi* legend tells the adventures of mole and fox as they climb to the moon on a grass rope ladder and explains why moles live underground and a fox's face is in the moon.

Why the Sun and the Moon Live in the Sky: An African Folktale by Elphinstone Dayrell, illustrated by Blair Lent (New York: Scholastic, 1968). Characters in this *pourquoi* tale wear costumes in the story of a visit from the water and his people that crowds the sun and his wife, the moon, out of their house on earth and forces them to live in the sky.

Wait Till the Moon Is Full, Margaret Wise Brown, illustrated by Garth Williams (New York: HarperCollins, 1948, 1976). A little raccoon has to wait for the moon to progress through its phases until it is full before his mother will let him venture into the night.

Owl Moon, Jane Yolen, illustrated by John Schoenherr (New York: Scholastic, 1987). The paintings and verbal imagery in this book invite readers to accompany a girl and her father on a moonlit winter night owling adventure. Caldecott Award Book.

The Whales' Song, Dyan Sheldon, illustrated by Gary Blythe (New York: Scholastic, 1990). Lilly learns about the magic of the whales in her grandmother's lap, and she dreams, offers her gift into the sea, and waits. One night, by moonlight, the whales return a gift: They sing her name.

Papagayo: The Mischief Maker, Gerald McDermott (San Diego: Harcourt Brace Jovanovich, 1980, 1992). This *pourquoi* tale explains moon phases. Papagayo, the parrot, annoys the nocturnal animals during the day, but he becomes their hero one night when his noisy plan saves their beloved thinning moon from the teeth of the hungry moondog.

Dragon Kite of the Autumn Moon, Valerie Reddix, illustrated by Jean and Mou-Sien Tseng (New York: Lothrop, Lee & Shepard Books, 1991). By Chinese tradition, each year Grandfather and Tad-Tin make and fly a kite and cut its string to release their troubles on Kite Day, but this year, with Grandfather seriously ill and unable to help him make a kite, Tad-Tin chooses to fly and release his special dragon kite, made by Grandfather to celebrate Tad-Tin's birth, and its magic touches and heals Grandfather.

Many Moons, James Thurber, illustrated by Louis Slobodkin (San Diego: Harcourt Brace Jovanovich, 1943, 1970). In this modern fable, when none of the wise members of the King's court can think of a way to get the moon for the ill Princess Lenore, it is the jester and Princess Lenore herself who show real wisdom. Caldecott Award Book.

MOTIVATION AND EXTENSION ACTIVITIES

1. In ***Goodnight Moon***, the colored illustrations of the room become progressively darker as it becomes later. Students compare and contrast the ways light and color are used to show the passage of time and change in the atmosphere or environment in this book and in ***King Bidgood's in the Bathtub*** and ***The Napping House***, both by Wood (Chapter 1, ing king). The teacher challenges students to find the mouse, who appears in a different place in each illustration of the room.

2. ***Papa, Please Get the Moon for Me*** is a fictional introduction to the phases of the moon. The moon gradually diminishes in size as the little girl's father waits for it to be small enough to carry back to his daughter. After it disappears completely, it begins to grow again before her eyes. ***The Moon Seems to Change: A Let's-Read-and-Find-Out Book*** is a nonfiction resource book that explains the phases of the moon with easy-to-read text, illustrations, and diagrams.

Students and the teacher discuss the similarities and differences between the fiction and nonfiction introductions to the phases of the earth's moon that they have read. They explore the phases of the moon by following the illustrated instructions in ***The Moon Seems to Change: A Let's-Read-and-Find-Out Book*** to complete an experiment using an orange and a flashlight. They observe and record for a month the locations and apparent changes of the moon in relationship to a familiar landscape. Students use clay, small rocks, and other materials to sculpt a moon landscape in relief map or diorama format. They use the information they know or learn from ***What the Moon Is Like: A Let's-Read-and-Find-Out Book*** and other resource books and materials.

3. After they listen to or read ***Papa, Please Get the Moon for Me***, students explore and experiment with fold-out and pop-up illustrations.

- They make fold-out, pop-up, and push, pull, and turn books using as a guide ***How to Make Pop-Ups*** by Joan Irvine, illustrated by Barbara Reid (New York: Morrow Junior Books, 1987).

- They look at other books with pop-up illustrations. Jan Pienkowski has created several. Among them are ***Oh My, a Fly*** (Chapter 4, y fly) and ***Dinnertime***, ***Little Monsters***, ***Small Talk***, and ***Doorbell***. In ***New at the Zoo: A Mix and Match Pop-Up Book*** by Kees Moerbeek (Los Angeles: Intervisual Communications, 1989), readers mix up pictures of tops and bottoms and written attributes of zoo animals in a pop-up book to create new creatures, such as "monbra" and "zekey" from monkey and zebra.

- The teacher extends this theme and the accompanying word play and experimentation with the introduction of two flip books: ***Croc-gu-phant: A Mini-Flip-Flap Book*** and ***Por-gua-can: A Mini-Flip-Flap Book*** by Sara Ball (West Germany:

Ars Edition, 1985). In these books, readers mix tops, middles, and bottoms of animals and the syllables of their three-syllable names to make new animals. Other books that feature the mixed-up attributes of animals are listed in Activity 18 of this chapter.

4. The repetitive echo pattern of the text of *Happy Birthday, Moon* supports students as they read Bear's echo (in oral cloze) immediately after the teacher reads Bear's part aloud.

5. Students discover the seasonal pattern of *Mooncake* using clues from the text and illustrations.

6. Students and the teacher share "mooncake" (lime sherbet or pistachio ice cream) after they share the book *Mooncake*.

7. With Bear's rocket in *Mooncake* as inspiration, students try their hand at inventions using a collection of junk that the teacher sets out for exploration. (Science museums and landfill areas often have recycling areas that are wonderful sources for treasure hunters.) The teacher reads aloud several books in which children discover creative uses for common objects:

A Flower Pot Is Not a Hat, Martha Moffett, illustrated by Susan Perl (New York: E. P. Dutton & Co., Inc., 1972).

What Can You Do with a Shoe?, Beatrice Schenk de Regniers (New York: Harper & Row, 1955).

Christina Katerina & the Box, Patricia Lee Gauch, illustrated by Doris Burn (New York: Coward, McCann & Geoghegan, Inc., 1971).

8. Students and teacher accept the invitation at the end of *Moongame*: "Then everyone played hide and seek."

9. Before students and the teacher read *Grandfather Twilight*, the teacher passes around a string/necklace of pearls for students to explore.

10. There is a striking contrast between McDermott's use of color in the two tales in *Anansi the Spider: A Tale from the Ashanti*. A change from rose to blue backgrounds defines the transition between the two tales. Students and teacher discuss the effects of this technique. Students generate titles for each tale.

11. The prologue to *Anansi the Spider: A Tale from the Ashanti* provides background information about oral tradition, the Ashanti culture of West Africa, and Anansi the "mischief maker." A map locates the home of the people who gave Anansi to the world.

Students and teacher locate West Africa on a large world map and globe. They pin a piece of string from a copy of the book cover (or one drawn by students) to the appropriate location on the map. They create a bulletin board display to which they add as they read and share books together.

12. Students experiment with repeating designs like those in *Anansi the Spider: A Tale from the Ashanti* using geometric shapes cut from paper for pasting onto poster board or from sponges dipped into paint.

13. Students, family/community members, friends, and/or teachers who speak and read Spanish read aloud *Moon Rope/Un lazo a la luna: A Peruvian Folktale*.

14. Introductory material for **Moon Rope/Un lazo a la luna: A Peruvian Folktale** provides background information about folk literature and the Peruvian culture, from which this tale comes. Ehlert based her collage illustrations on "ancient Peruvian textiles, jewelry, ceramic vessels, sculpture, and architectural detail" and used the food, animals, and colors important to that culture in her pictures and designs.

After they listen to or read **Moon Rope/Un lazo a la luna: A Peruvian Folktale** and the teacher shares this background information, students and the teacher experiment with collage pictures and designs using colored and metallic paper.

15. Students make and wear costumes influenced by African cultures like those worn by the characters in **Why the Sun and the Moon Live in the Sky: An African Folktale by Elphinstone Dayrell** and present a play of the tale.

16. Students and teacher listen to the tape of **Owl Moon** (available from Scholastic) and practice their owl calls.

17. Students and teacher make noise. They join in the animals' chanting and accompany themselves with rhythm instruments (student or commercially made) as the teacher or students read aloud **Papagayo: The Mischief Maker**.

18. "Is the moon a rabbit?" asks the little raccoon in **Wait Till the Moon Is Full**. Is the moon "round and flat like a coin," "twice as big as this palace," "molten copper," or "green cheese," as members of the king's court and his daughter, Princess Lenore, in **Many Moons** offer? As students and teacher discuss these descriptions of the moon, the teacher introduces or reviews figurative language, which is used to compare the unknown or less known with the familiar, with examples such as "The moon is like a pie in the sky" (simile), "The moon is green cheese" (metaphor), and "The man in the moon" (personification).

- Students tell and/or write and illustrate what the moon looks like to them. They complete phrases:

   The moon is like _____ . (for similes)

   The moon is as _____ . (for similes)

   The moon is _____ . (for metaphors)

   The moon is a _____ . (for personification).

- Students read **The Littlest Dinosaur**, by Bernard Most (San Diego: Harcourt Brace Jovanovich, 1989), in which Most introduces the littlest dinosaurs and describes their size compared to common objects.

- Students explore books that feature similes, including **Quick as a Cricket**, by Audrey Wood, illustrated by Don Wood (Singapore: Child's Play, 1982), and the following, which focus on the mixed-up attributes of animals:

   Baby Monkey, Sheila K. Hollander (Glenview, Ill.: Scott, Foresman and Company, 1971, 1976).

   I Wish that I Had Duck Feet, Theo. LeSieg, illustrated by B. Tobey (New York: Random House, 1965).

   The Mixed-Up Chameleon, Eric Carle (New York: Scholastic, 1975, 1984).

   Monkey Face, Frank Asch (New York: Parents' Magazine Press, 1977).

What Kind of Bird Is That?, Mirra Ginsburg, adapted from a Russian story by V. Suteyev, illustrated by Giulio Maestro (New York: Crown Publishers, Inc.).

You Look Ridiculous Said the Rhinoceros to the Hippopotamus, Bernard Waber (Boston: Houghton Mifflin Co., 1966).

♦ Students tell and/or illustrate an "I Am As . . ." book, following the pattern of *Quick as a Cricket*.

♦ After they listen to or read the mixed-up animal books and *If I Ran the Circus* and *If I Ran the Zoo*, by Seuss (and *New at the Zoo, Croc-gu-phant: A Mini-Flip-Flap Book*, and *Por-gua-can: A Mini-Flip-Flap Book* from Activity 3 in this chapter), students invent and draw their own mixed-up animals that combine the attributes of several animals. They do not share their drawings with anyone until they complete the following game activity.

   In pairs, by turns, students describe the drawing they have made to a partner without showing it. They say, for example, "It is as tall as a giraffe." "It has ears like an elephant." The partner draws each part of the animal described until the originator decides he or she has completed the description. Partners then trade roles and repeat the same procedure. Partners compare the original drawings to the directed copies and discuss the process they have shared. They comment about the importance of including details in a description and about the usefulness of the techniques, such as figurative language, that compare a new or less known thing to another, more familiar thing.

   (See the following for additional books and activities that feature figurative language: Activity 12 in Chapter 4, y fly; Activity 13 in Chapter 13, oa goat; Activities 12 and 13 in Chapter 16, ar star; Activity 10 in Chapter 22, ow owl; Activity 12 in Chapter 29, consonant-le fable; and Activity 8 in Chapter 32, c Frances Cinderella fancy.)

♦ Students and the teacher make their own colorful versions of the mixed-up chameleon with reusable stickers and two-page chameleon illustration that accompanies the text in *The Mixed-up Chameleon Sticker Book*, by Eric Carle (New York: Scholastic, 1993).

19. Students and the teacher locate on a map and/or globe the places/cultures (depicted or of origin) in the books read in this chapter, including West Africa/Ghana (*Anansi the Spider: A Tale from the Ashanti*), Peru (*Moon Rope/Un lazo a la luna*), Southeastern Nigeria (*Why the Sun and the Moon Live in the Sky*), New England in the United States (*Owl Moon*), world oceans (*The Whales' Song*), rainforest and jungle areas (*Papagayo: The Mischief Maker*), and Taiwan and China (*Dragon Kite of the August Moon*).

Cloze Sentences

One-Syllable Words

Cloze Sentences 1

1. The <u>moon</u> shines in the sky at night.
2. At a <u>zoo</u> you can see animals like monkeys in cages.
3. You can say "<u>boo</u>" to try to scare someone.
4. I wear a <u>boot</u> on each foot when I go sledding in the winter.
5. You can use a <u>tool</u> like a hammer to make things.
6. A <u>cool</u> day is more cold than it is hot.

Cloze Sentences 2

1. A plane can <u>zoom</u> up into the sky.
2. <u>Moo</u> is the sound a cow makes.
3. You can <u>shoot</u> a gun or a bow and arrow.
4. Do not run <u>too</u> fast, or you can trip and fall.
5. She said "<u>shoo</u>" to scare away the fly.
6. A <u>coo</u> is the soft sound a dove makes.

Dictations (Cloze)

1. I lost my <u>tooth</u> when I bumped it on a <u>stool</u>.
2. Use the <u>broom</u> to sweep the mud off your <u>boot</u>.
3. At the <u>zoo</u> a man fed a baby monkey some <u>food</u> with a <u>spoon</u>.
4. In the <u>cool</u> <u>moon</u>light I heard a dove <u>coo</u> and a cow <u>moo</u>, too.

oo ($\overline{oo}$) moon

b	b	t
c	c	l
m	m	n
sh	sh	t
t	t	l
z	z	m

Name _____ Date _____

Word List 1

oo ($\overline{oo}$) moon

boo	boot
coo	cool
moo	moon
shoo	shoot
too	tool
zoo	zoom

Name _____ Date _____

oo ($\overline{oo}$) moon OO

Write a word from the Word List to complete each sentence.

1. The _____ shines in the sky at night.

2. At a _____ you can see animals like monkeys in cages.

3. You can say "_____" to try to scare someone.

4. I wear a _____ on each foot when I go sledding in the winter.

5. You can use a _____ like a hammer to make things.

6. A _____ day is more cold than it is hot.

Name _____ Date _____

Cloze Sentences 1

oo (o͞o) moon OO

Write a word from the Word List to complete each sentence.

1. A plane can _____ up into the sky.

2. _____ is the sound a cow makes.

3. You can _____ a gun or a bow and arrow.

4. Do not run _____ fast, or you can trip and fall.

5. She said "_____" to scare away the fly.

6. A _____ is the soft sound a dove makes.

Name _____ Date _____

© 1995 by Cynthia Conway Waring

Cloze Sentences 2

OO

1. I lost my _____ when I bumped it on a _____.

2. Use the _____ to sweep the mud off your _____.

3. At the _____ a man fed a baby monkey some _____ with a _____.

4. In the _____ _____ light I heard a dove _____ and a cow _____, _____.

Name _____ Date _____

Dictations

3   Open Syllable   go

BOOK LIST

Go!

Oh, A-Hunting We Will Go, John Langstaff, illustrated by Nancy Winslow Parker (New York: Macmillan Publishing Company, 1974). Hunters in this humorous version of the familiar folk song round up animals and put them in rhyming containers—a snake in a cake, a goat in a boat, a fish in a dish, and a bear in his underwear! Includes music for piano and guitar accompaniment.

What Game Shall We Play?, Pat Hutchins (New York: Greenwillow Books, 1990). When Duck and Frog cannot decide what game to play, they go to find friends for advice and, though they are unaware, play a series of games of hide and seek which are observed by Owl overhead, who wisely suggests a game of hide and seek in which he is "it."

Little Fox Goes to the End of the World, Ann Tompert, illustrated by John Wallner (New York: Scholastic, 1976). While she sews her a new jacket, Little Fox's sensitive mother actively engages with her daughter as she tells about her adventures during an imaginary trip to the end of the world.

The Runaway Bunny, Margaret Wise Brown, illustrated by Clement Hurd (New York: Harper & Row, 1942, 1970, 1972). A young rabbit considers running away but decides to stay at home with his loving mother after he proposes destinations and she describes her plans to be with him wherever he goes.

Mama, Do You Love Me?, Barbara M. Joosse, illustrated by Barbara Lavallee (New York: Scholastic, 1991). A young child's mother responds to her series of questions with assurances of her unfailing love. The text and detailed illustrations of the story and a section following contain information about the native Arctic people—the Inuit or Eskimos.

Shoes from Grandpa, Mem Fox, illustrated by Patricia Mullins (New York: The Trumpet Club, 1989). When Jessie outgrows her clothes, Grandpa offers to buy her new shoes, and each member of her extended family promises to buy a piece of clothing to go with them in this rhyming cumulative story.

1. Students sing, create a dance, form a parade, or act out the events in sequence to dramatize *Oh, A-Hunting We Will Go*.

2. By turns, students select an animal and its fate from *Oh, A-Hunting We Will Go* and act out or draw it for others to guess.

3. The addition of verses, as in *Oh, A-Hunting We Will Go*, is common in folk literature and music. Students add and illustrate new rhyming verses for the song. They create verses for the animals in the book or for animals they choose. Possible verses for animals from the book might include fox in socks, lamb in jam, goat in a coat, bear on a stair, whale in the mail, snake in a lake, mouse in a blouse, pig in a fig, skunk in a trunk, armadillo in a willow, fish in a wish(bone), and Brontosaurus in (the stomach of) a Tyrannosaurus (Rex).

A group of writers compile new verses into a collaborative book and share them, or individual students write and illustrate their own collections and read or sing them aloud to others.

Writers may benefit from some rhyming inspiration. The teacher and/or students, with support, read aloud and share books that feature rhyming and word play, including the following:

- *On a Cold, Cold Day*, Andrea Butler, illustrated by Robert Avitabile (Crystal Lake, Ill.: Rigby Inc., 1988). In this short book with a supportive pattern and illustrations, animals keep warm on a cold day by wearing clothing that rhymes with their names and, in the end, a little boy wears all of the garments.

- *Carrot/Parrot* and *Mitten/Kitten*, Jerome Martin (New York: The Trumpet Club, 1991). As readers lift a flap on each page of these colorful books, they change the initial letter of a word that describes a picture and reveal a new rhyming word that labels a picture, which is part of the original picture.

- *See You Later Alligator . . . A First Book of Rhyming Word-Play*, Barbara Strauss and Helen Friedland, illustrated by Tershia d'Elgin (New York: The Trumpet Club, 1987). In a collection of rhyming good-byes, a series of animals is pictured in locations and involved in activities that rhyme with their names, including a porcupine at a mine and fleas on skis.

- *The Missing Tarts*, B. G. Hennessy, illustrated by Tracey Campbell Pearson (New York: Scholastic, 1989). After the knave steals her tarts, the Queen of Hearts asks a number of well-known nursery rhyme characters for help to find them, and they give answers that rhyme with their names.

- *Squeeze a Sneeze*, Bill Morrison (Boston: Houghton Mifflin Company, 1977). The book presents several illustrated rhyming nonsense verses (including "Take a snail for a sail in a polka dot pail") and invites readers to join in the word play by thinking of their own.

- *This Old Man: A Musical Counting Book*, illustrated by Tony Ross (New York: Macmillan Publishing Company, 1990). With the pull of a tab, readers hear the tune as they read and sing the familiar rhyming counting song about the old man who played "knick-knack" on items shown in the humorous illustrations—the last of which is a full-page pop-out.

* **This Old Man**, illustrated by Carol Jones (Boston: Houghton Mifflin Company, 1990). Each verse of the well-known song is introduced on one page with a cut-out hole that reveals, for readers to predict, part of the illustration on the next page, which includes the corresponding item on which the old man played "nick nack."

After they read/sing both versions of the "This Old Man" song—**This Old Man: A Musical Counting Book** and **This Old Man**—students (individually or as contributors to a group collaborative book) create and illustrate their own rhymes for each number. Rhyming words for each number in the counting song include one (drum, thumb, sun, bun), two (shoe, stew, dew, glue), three (knee, bee, flea, key), four (door, floor, core [of an apple], four [on a sports shirt]), five (hive, as I drive, five [on a sports shirt]), six (sticks, Kix® [cereal], picks [hair or guitar], six [on a sports shirt]), seven (heaven, seven [on a sports shirt], eleven [on a sports shirt]), eight (gate, skate, plate, date [fruit or on a calendar]), nine (line, nine [on a sports shirt], pine, stein [mug], tine [of a fork], vine, wine), ten (hen, den, men, pen), eleven (heaven, seven [on a sports shirt], eleven [on a sports shirt]), and twelve (elf, shelf, shelves, himself).

4. After they read and share **Oh, A-Hunting We Will Go**, the teacher distributes a scavenger hunt list to individual or pairs/groups of students who "A-Hunting Will Go" for common rhyming objects and containers to hold them. Students with different reading strengths and abilities work together as partners or a team, and/or the list is in a rebus or rebus-and-word format for emerging and beginning readers. Players collect the objects and containers from throughout the school. The list might include

1. a flag in a bag
2. sand in your hand
3. a pup (toy or picture) in a cup
4. number 2 in a shoe
5. a rock in a sock
6. a goat (toy or picture) in a coat
7. a bat in a hat
8. number 8 in a plate
9. a can in a pan
10. a flute in a boot
11. socks in a box
12. this list in your fist.

5. The teacher extends the exploration of rebus messages (introduced in Activity 4) by reading aloud and/or supporting students as they read other books that contain rebuses, including the following (listed in alphabetical order by title):

"I Can't" Said the Ant, Polly Cameron (New York: Scholastic, 1961).

It's a Perfect Day, Abigail Pizer (New York: HarperCollins, 1990).

The Real Mother Goose Picture Word Rhymes, illustrated by Blanche Fisher Wright (New York: Checkerboard Press, 1916, 1944, 1987).

The Rebus Treasury, Jean Marzollo, illustrated by Carol Devine Carson (New York: Dial Books for Young Readers, 1986).

Rooster's Off to See the World, Eric Carle (New York: Scholastic, 1972).

The Secret Birthday Message, Eric Carle (New York: HarperCollins, 1971).

They create and share their own rebus and rebus-and-word messages and/or books.

6. Students listen to or read *Moongame* (Chapter 2, oo moon) before or after they listen to or read *What Game Shall We Play?*, and they, too, play hide and seek.

7. After they read and share *Little Fox Goes to the End of the World* and *The Runaway Bunny*, students and the teacher tell and/or write and illustrate other places a character might go on an imaginary journey. They describe each of the character's adventures and the response of a sensitive and supportive parent to each proposed destination.

8. The mothers in *Little Fox Goes to the End of the World*, *The Runaway Bunny*, and *Mama, Do You Love Me?* are remarkably sensitive and supportive and are able to assure their children of the unfailing quality of their love and the security of their relationship even when their children attempt to challenge them. Students and the teacher discuss this theme common to the three books. They compare and contrast the mothers in the three books with parents (some of whom are more sensitive and supportive than others) in other books which the teacher reads aloud, including *Alexander and the Terrible, Horrible, No Good, Very Bad Day* by Viorst (Chapter 7, ay day); *Peter's Chair* by Keats (Chapter 9, ow growing); *Little Bear* by Minarik (Chapter 19, ir birthday, and Chapter 29, ou soup); *Noisy Nora* by Wells (Chapter 25, oi noise); *Mean Soup* by Everitt (Chapter 28, ou soup); *A Bargain for Frances*, *Bedtime for Frances*, *A Birthday for Frances*, *Best Friends for Frances*, *Bread and Jam for Frances*, and *A Baby Sister for Frances* by Hoban (Chapter 32, c Frances Cinderella fancy).

9. An umiak (whalebone boat covered with animal skin similar to but larger than a kayak) is referred to in the text and pictured in the story and on the cover of *Mama, Do You Love Me?*. Students and the teacher learn more about umiaks and about the Inuit tradition of recording stories and adventures on umiak paddles and other wooden items as they read the "Picture Story (The Arctic)" chapter in *Kid Pix around the World: A Multicultural Computer Activity Book*, by Barbara Chan (Reading, Mass.: Addison-Wesley Publishing Company, 1993). The book contains essays that provide background information about twenty cultures around the world and detailed, step-by-step instructions that show children how to do drawing and painting activities using "Kid Pix™" computer software. Presented cultures are marked on a world map in the front of the book.

Students record an Arctic or Inuit adventure and adventures of their own on an umiak paddle using their computer and following the suggestions in *Kid Pix around the World: A Multicultural Computer Activity Book*.

10. In *Shoes from Grandpa*, Jessie outgrows her clothes and is offered a collection of fancy new ones to go with the shoes from Grandpa by members of her extended family. She politely but clearly presents her own wish for a simple pair of jeans.

Students and the teacher share their own experiences with outgrowing clothing and important items and compare and contrast them with those of Jessie in *Shoes from*

Grandpa and of characters in other books. (See Activity 8 in Chapter 9, *ow growing*, for additional books and an activity.)

11. Students and the teacher locate on a map and/or globe the places/cultures (depicted or of origin) of the books read in this chapter, including northern Alaska in the United States (***Mama, Do You Love Me?***) and the Inuit culture in the Arctic—Siberia, Alaska, Canada, and Greenland ["Picture Story (The Arctic): in ***Kid Pix around the World: A Multicultural Computer Activity Book***].

TEACHER REFERENCE

Cloze Sentences

One-Syllable Words

Cloze Sentences 1

1. I said "<u>no</u>" when I did not want to go.
2. The box was <u>so</u> big I could not lift it.
3. <u>We</u> all went on the trip—my Mom, my Dad, and I.
4. <u>I</u> ate the cake all by myself!
5. I <u>go</u> on a green light, and I stop on a red light.
6. My mother told me that <u>she</u> can't come to my baseball game.
7. I said "<u>hi</u>" to the new student in our class when he came in the room.

Cloze Sentences 2

1. "<u>Ho, ho, ho</u>" is what Santa Claus says.
2. My mom told <u>me</u> that I can go to the birthday party.
3. I said you may have <u>a</u> piece of cake but not two!
4. I went to see my uncle. <u>He</u> is my Dad's brother.
5. Where can my dog <u>be</u>? He has been gone all day!
6. A <u>pro</u> gets money to do his or her job.
7. If you get the <u>flu</u> you can be very sick.

Dictations (Cloze)

1. <u>She</u> said <u>hi</u> to <u>me</u> when <u>she</u> got up to <u>go</u>.
2. <u>No</u>, <u>I</u> cannot <u>go</u> <u>so</u> fast on <u>a</u> bike.
3. Santa Claus can <u>go</u> "<u>Ho, ho, ho</u>."
4. Can <u>he</u> <u>be</u> the only one to <u>go</u> on <u>a</u> trip? Can't <u>I</u> <u>go</u>?

Open Syllable   go

$\bar{a}$	$\bar{e}$	$\bar{i}$	$\bar{o}$	$\bar{u}$
	b		g	fl
	h	h	h	
	m		n	
	sh		pr	
	w		s	

Name _____ Date _____

Word List 1

Open Syllable   go

ā	ē	ī	ō	ū
a	be	I	go	flu
	he	hi	ho	
	me		no	
	she		pro	
	we		so	

Name _____   Date _____

Open Syllable go

Write a word from the Word List to complete each sentence.

1. I said "_____" when I did not want to go.

2. The box was _____ big I could not lift it.

3. _____ all went on the trip—my Mom, my Dad, and I.

4. _____ ate the cake all by myself!

5. I _____ on a green light, and I stop on a red light.

6. My mother told me that _____ can't come to my baseball game.

7. I said "_____" to the new student in our class when he came in the room.

Name _____ Date _____

© 1995 by Cynthia Conway Waring

Cloze Sentences 1

Open Syllable   go

Write a word from the Word List to complete each sentence.

1. "_____, _____, _____" is what Santa Claus says.

2. My mom told _____ that I can go to the birthday party.

3. I said you may have _____ piece of cake but not two!

4. I went to see my uncle. _____ is my Dad's brother.

5. Where can my dog _____? He has been gone all day!

6. A _____ gets money to do his or her job.

7. If you get the _____ you can be very sick.

Name _____   Date _____

Cloze Sentences 2

1. _____ said _____ to _____ when she got up to _____.

2. _____, I cannot _____ _____ fast on _____ bike.

3. Santa Claus can _____ " _____, _____, _____."

4. Can _____ _____ the only one to _____ on _____ trip? Can't _____ _____?

Name _____ Date _____

Dictations

4 y fly

BOOK LIST ══════════════════════════════════════

Fly into Action

What Can Fly?, Lucy Lawrence, illustrated by Lucinda Hunnam (Crystal Lake, Ill.: Rigby, 1989). This short book with repeated pattern and supportive illustrations contrasts pairs of animals pictured on opposite pages that can and cannot fly.

Would You Like to Fly?, Rebel Williams, illustrated by Don Baker (Bothell, Wash.: The Wright Group, 1990). Following a predictable pattern, this book poses the question in the title on each page about a variety of vehicles that fly.

Why Can't I Fly?, Rita Golden Gelman, illustrated by Jack Kent (New York: Scholastic, 1976). Minnie the monkey asks why she can't fly and courageously but unsuccessfully follows the suggestions of a series of flying animals. She does fly, in the end, carried into the sky on a blanket by her advisors.

"The Kite" in *Days with Frog and Toad*, Arnold Lobel (New York: Harper & Row, 1979). In the book, Frog and Toad learn about and celebrate the benefits of friendship—together, alone, and "alone together." In "The Kite," Frog offers suggestions and encouragement as Toad attempts to fly a kite while some robins interject criticism until Toad flies the kite far above the jeering birds.

Bear's Bargain, Frank Asch (New York: Scholastic, 1985). Two friends benefit from a bargain when Bear teaches Little Bird to be big with a pumpkin they grow from seed and Little Bird shows Bear how to fly with a kite they make.

Fly and Other Insect Stories

The Frog and the Fly, Leslie Wood (Oxford, England: Oxford University Press, 1985). Brief text describes the detailed illustrations, which show the short adventure of a fly who ingeniously escapes capture by a frog.

Fantail, Fantail, Margaret Mahy, illustrated by Bruce Phillips (New York: Richard C. Owen Publishers, Inc., 1984). Fantail the bird is offered a variety of food it does not like but eagerly eats a fly in this repetitive pattern book with supportive pictures.

Animal Clues: A Game for Two or More Players, David Drew (Crystal Lake, Ill.: Rigby, 1987). Patterned text that describes colored photographs of parts of animals' bodies and presents information about their habitats provides readers with clues to the identity of animals (including insects and a spider) revealed in a labeled photograph of the complete animal on the following page.

Mystery Monsters: A Game for Two or More Players, David Drew (Crystal Lake, Ill.: Rigby, 1987). Written clues and enlarged colored photographs of a body part challenge readers to guess the animal (including insects and a spider) presented in its entirety in a labeled photograph at the end of the book.

Old Black Fly, Jim Aylesworth, illustrated by Stephen Gammell (New York: Scholastic, 1992). In this colorful rhyming book with a refrain, during one day Old Black Fly does twenty-six irritating things—one for each letter of the alphabet—until someone stops him with a "swat."

I Know an Old Lady, Rose Bonne, illustrated by Abner Graboff, music by Alan Mills (New York: Scholastic, 1961). Text and illustrations combine to record the events that comprise the well-known and fatal adventure of the old lady who swallowed a fly. Includes music for the song.

There Was an Old Lady Who Swallowed a Fly, illustrated by Pam Adams (Restrop Manor, England: Child's Play, 1973). Cut-out shapes reveal text and illustrations that show the chain of events of the traditional song.

I Know an Old Lady Who Swallowed a Fly, Nadine Bernard Westcott (Boston: Little, Brown and Company, 1980). Humorous Westcott illustrations show in detail the old lady's attempts to deal with her increasingly serious plight after she accidentally swallows a fly. Includes music for the English folk song.

Oh My, a Fly!, Jan Pienkowski (Los Angeles: Price Stern Sloan, Inc., 1986). In this mini-pop-up book small enough to be held in one hand, three-dimensional animals dramatize the traditional song.

The Very Busy Spider, Eric Carle (New York: Scholastic, 1984). A spider repeatedly answers that she is too busy spinning her web when animal friends invite her to join their activities, but she's not too busy to catch a fly for dinner.

The Mixed-Up Chameleon, Eric Carle (New York: Scholastic, 1975, 1984). Discontent with its life, a chameleon wishes to become like a number of zoo animals and takes on a combination of their attributes, but when it becomes hungry it wishes to become itself once again so it can catch a fly.

A Fly Went By, Mike McClintock, illustrated by Fritz Siebel (New York: Random House, 1958, 1986). Colorful illustrations and rhyming text combine to reveal the story of a series of misunderstandings that result in a chain of animals—from a fly to a hunter—running away from each other.

Grasshopper on the Road, Arnold Lobel (New York: Harper & Row, 1978). Adventurous Grasshopper sets out on a journey along a road and meets a variety of insect characters who are involved in the details of their own lives.

I Spy

Each Peach Pear Plum, Janet and Allan Ahlberg (New York: Penguin Books, 1978). In this highly supportive rhyming book, readers spy nursery rhyme characters in the illustrations on each page and predict the next character(s)—partially revealed in the picture—from a rhyming clue.

Wacky Wednesday, Theo. LeSieg, illustrated by George Booth (New York: Random House, 1974). In this rhyming counting book, readers locate in the illustrations the increasing number of strange things a boy sees one unusual day.

Eye Spy: A Mysterious Alphabet, Linda Bourke (New York: The Trumpet Club, 1991). Words with multiple meanings for each letter of the alphabet are illustrated on each two-page spread in four frames. The first three frames show one meaning, and the fourth shows another meaning and provides a picture clue to the words beginning with the next letter of the alphabet on the following page.

I Spy: A Book of Picture Riddles, photographs by Walter Wick, riddles by Jean Marzollo, design by Carol Devine Carson (New York: Scholastic, 1992). Rhyming riddles challenge readers to spy objects that are part of a complex collection of items presented by theme and photographed in color.

Look!: The Ultimate Spot-the-Difference Book, illustrated by April Wilson, nature notes by A. J. Wood (New York: The Trumpet Club, 1990). Animals and vegetation in natural habitats around the world are pictured in companion illustrations which differ in twelve ways. A guide at the book's end highlights the differences and provides information about the elements depicted in the setting.

MOTIVATION AND EXTENSION ACTIVITIES

Fly into Action

   1. After they read **What Can Fly?**, students illustrate additional pairs of animals that can and cannot fly and write about them following the pattern of the book. They make individual or collaborative group books and share them with others.
   2. Before or after students read **Would You Like to Fly?**, the teacher reads aloud three books about imaginary and spiritual flying journeys: **Tar Beach** and **Aunt Harriet's Underground Railroad in the Sky** by Ringgold and **Abuela** by Dorros.
   In **Tar Beach**, by Faith Ringgold (New York: Scholastic, 1991), Ringgold's "Tar Beach" story quilt was adapted and combined with text and paintings in a book about Cassie's fantasy flight of the spirit amid the stars above New York City from the rooftop of her apartment building (Tar Beach). In **Aunt Harriet's Underground Railroad in the Sky**, by Faith Ringgold (New York: Crown Publishers, Inc., 1992), which contains background information about Harriet Tubman and the Underground Railroad (including a short bibliography of further readings and a map of routes), Cassie and her brother Be Be (from **Tar Beach**, by the same author) learn about slavery—and freedom—while they are flying aboard a fantasy train on the Underground Railroad, whose conductor is Harriet Tubman. (See Activity 13 in Chapter 16, ar star, and Activities 8 and 9 in Chapter 33, qu quilt, for activities related to the two books.)

In *Abuela*, by Arthur Dorros and illustrated by Elisa Kleven (New York: The Trumpet Club, 1991), a girl describes in Spanish and English the travels around New York City she shares with her abuela (grandmother) and an imaginary adventure she would like to take with her if they could fly above all of their favorite places. Students who do not understand or speak Spanish make predictions about the meaning of Spanish words as they listen to or read *Abuela*. They confirm or revise/correct their hypotheses by reading on in the story and by consulting the list of Spanish words, phrases, and sentences in the glossary at the back of the book, which includes definitions and pronunciations.

Students and the teacher compare and contrast the four books about flying. They discuss, draw, act out/mime, sing, and/or dance where they would go if they could fly and how they would fly—in their own bodies or aboard a vehicle that can fly.

3. Before or after they read **"The Kite" in *Days with Frog and Toad***, students and the teacher share (tell and/or write and illustrate) about time(s) they may have attempted to fly a kite (successfully or unsuccessfully). If weather, time, and resources permit, they make and fly kites. (See Activity 6 in Chapter 31, g George magic stingy, for other books that feature kite flying.)

4. As they explore the "Fly into Action" theme, the teacher reads aloud *The Fantastic Flying Journey*, a fictional adventure written by naturalist and conservationist Gerald Durrell and illustrated by Graham Percy (New York: Simon & Schuster, 1987). In the book, Uncle Lancelot and his grand niece and two grand nephews fly around the world in a hot air balloon in search of Uncle Lancelot's brother, Perceval, and Lancelot teaches the children about the animals, vegetation, and land indigenous to the places they visit.

Fly and Other Insect Stories

5. The teacher introduces and reviews the concept of words with multiple meanings (homographs) as he or she presents books for the "Fly and Other Insect Stories" unit, in which *fly* is a noun—in contrast to its function as a verb in the "Fly into Action" unit. (The concept that a word can represent more than one meaning, rather than the specific term *homograph*, is an understanding that is useful to readers.)

6. With support, as appropriate, students play the games related to the books and presented on the back covers of *Animal Clues: A Game for Two or More Players* and *Mystery Monsters: A Game for Two or More Players*. They write and illustrate their own "Animal Clues" and/or "Mystery Monsters" book(s) following the pattern of the book(s) they have read and share them with others.

7. As the teacher reads aloud *Old Black Fly*, he or she hesitates for students to read aloud the "Shoo fly! Shoo fly! Shooo" refrain that follows each event.

8. After they read *There Was an Old Lady Who Swallowed a Fly*, students make their own cut-out books that represent—in words and pictures—the events in order as they occur in the song.

9. After they read (and sing) several versions of the "Old Lady Who Swallowed a Fly" story and song—*I Know an Old Lady*, *There Was an Old Lady Who Swallowed a Fly*, *I Know an Old Lady Who Swallowed a Fly*, and *Oh My, a Fly!*—students and the teacher identify and discuss the similarities and differences among the books. They choose a favorite version and identify the criteria on which they based their selection. They dramatize the events depicted through movement, dance, song, music, and/or drama/puppetry.

10. After they read **Oh My, a Fly!**, students and the teacher extend their exploration of pop-up books. (See Activity 3 in Chapter 2, oo moon.)

11. Students dramatize the story of **The Very Busy Spider**—as actors, dancers, mimists, or puppeteers. They investigate the techniques used to produce the book, including the folded pages and the raised web that the spider weaves as the story progresses. They use similar folding techniques to create pictures and/or books and glue and string or yarn to create raised webs. They discuss the use of onomatopoeia (words that are similar to or contain the sound made—the buzz of a bee, for example—to represent vividly the sounds that characters, objects, and actions make) to represent the sounds of the animals in **The Very Busy Spider**. (See Activity 9 in Chapter 7, ay day, Activity 23 in Chapter 22, ow owl, and Activity 1 in Chapter 25, oi noise, for books and activities that feature onomatopoeia.)

12. In **The Mixed-Up Chameleon**, the chameleon wishes to be like several animals he sees at the zoo. Students and the teacher explore the use of similes in **The Mixed-Up Chameleon** and in other books. (See Activity 18 in Chapter 2, oo moon, Activity 13 in Chapter 13, oa goat, Activities 12 and 13 in Chapter 16, ar star, Activity 10 in Chapter 22, ow owl, Activity 12 in Chapter 29, consonant-le fable, and Activity 8 in Chapter 32, c Frances Cinderella fancy, for books and activities that feature figurative language, including similes.)

13. The teacher reads aloud **Stick-in-the-Mud Turtle** by Hoban and **Franklin Fibs** by Bourgeois (see Chapter 20, ur turtle), and the teacher and the students make and eat a traditional shoo-fly pie and compare and contrast it to the shoo-fly pie and fly pie in the respective books.

I Spy

14. As they share **Eye Spy: A Mysterious Alphabet**, students and the teacher review the concept of words with multiple meanings (homographs) and homophones as well as a strategy that combines the use of picture and initial letter cues to predict. (Students may need support with some words which may not be part of their experience or vocabulary.)

15. In addition to finding the objects identified by the rhyming riddles that accompany each two-page photograph in **I Spy: A Book of Picture Riddles**, students and the teacher respond to the challenges at the book's end to locate a frog in each photograph, to match presented supplementary riddles with their corresponding photographs, and to write their own rhyming riddles for pictures.

16. After they read the books suggested for the "I Spy" unit, students create their own "I Spy" books. They follow formats from the books, or they design their own.

They make a simple patterned "I Spy" book using paper held lengthwise with the left-hand third folded over.

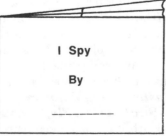

They fill in the provided blanks on the folded-over third of the page with information that directs the reader to look for an item in the picture they draw on the right-hand section of the page (that is exposed).

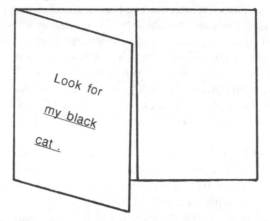

They fill in blanks in the center section of the page that provide the reader with clues about the location of the item. The reader lifts the left-hand section (which has been folded over) to confirm his or her prediction or to obtain more clues to aid in the search for the item.

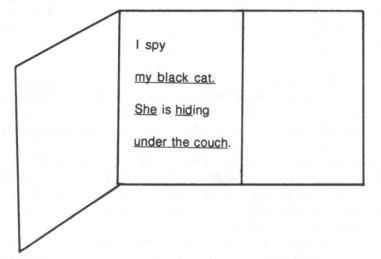

17. Students and the teacher locate on a map and/or globe the places/cultures (depicted or of origin) in the books read in this chapter, including New York City, New York in the United States (***Tar Beach***); routes of the Underground Railroad (***Aunt Harriet's Underground Railroad in the Sky***); London in England; the English Channel; France; the Pyrenees Mountains in Spain; the Mediterranean Ocean; the Sahara Desert, the Zambesi River, and the tropical rainforest in Africa; the Indian Ocean; the Red Desert and Ayers Rock in Australia; the Pacific Ocean; the North Pole; North America; Mexico; and the Amazon River, Andes Mountains, Argentina, and Patagonia in South America (***The Fantastic Flying Journey***); England (***I Know an Old Lady***, ***There Was an Old Lady Who Swallowed a Fly***, ***I Know an Old Lady Who Swallowed a Fly***, and ***Oh My, A Fly!***); South Asia; northern Europe; the rainforests of Australia

and New Guinea; the Red Sea between Africa and Asia; the tropical grasslands of the southern African savanna—from the Atlantic Ocean to the Indian Ocean; the rainforests of the Amazon River from the mountains of Peru to the Atlantic Ocean in northern Brazil; volcanic springs and Mount Fuji in Japan; the mountains of Australasia; the Sonoram Desert in Mexico; the Indian and Pacific Oceans; the Rocky Mountains from New Mexico to the Yukon; and the rainforests of central Africa and the Zaire (Congo) River (***Look!: The Ultimate Spot-the-Difference Book***).

TEACHER REFERENCE

Cloze Sentences

One-Syllable Words

Cloze Sentences 1

1. If you are <u>shy</u>, you may not like to meet people.
2. If you <u>cry</u>, you may be very sad.
3. If you catch a lot of fish, you may <u>fry</u> them in a pan and eat them for lunch.
4. If a pen is <u>my</u> pen, it belongs to me.
5. If a jet is in the <u>sky</u>, it can fly over me.

Cloze Sentences 2

1. If a pond is <u>dry</u>, it has no water in it.
2. If a jet can <u>fly</u>, it can go up in the sky.
3. If you hire a <u>spy</u> (like 007, James Bond), you may get help to solve a crime.
4. If you <u>try</u> to do something one time and can't, <u>try</u> one more time.
5. If you say "<u>by</u>," you are going to go away.

Dictations (Cloze)

1. You can <u>try</u> to <u>fly</u> <u>by</u> <u>my</u> home on a jet in the <u>sky</u>.
2. A <u>spy</u> can be <u>sly</u> and <u>spry</u>, but she cannot be <u>shy</u>, too.
3. Can you <u>pry</u> open a <u>dry</u> bit of two-<u>ply</u> rope?
4. <u>Why</u> do you <u>try</u> to <u>spy</u> on me? When you do I am so <u>shy</u> that I <u>cry</u>.

y (ī) fly

b	**m**
cr	**sh**
dr	**sk**
fl	**sp**
fr	**tr**

Name _____ Date _____

Word List 1

y (ī) fly

by	**my**
cry	**shy**
dry	**sky**
fly	**spy**
fry	**try**

Name _____ Date _____

Word List 2

y (ī) fly

Write a word from the Word List to complete each sentence.

1. If you are _____, you may not like to meet people.

2. If you _____, you may be very sad.

3. If you catch a lot of fish, you may _____ them in a pan and eat them for lunch.

4. If a pen is _____ pen, it belongs to me.

5. If a jet is in the _____, it can fly over me.

Name _____ Date _____

Cloze Sentences 1

y (ī) fly

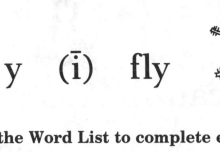

Write a word from the Word List to complete each sentence.

1. If a pond is _____ , it has no water in it.

2. If a jet can _____ , it can go up in the sky.

3. If you hire a _____ (like 007, James Bond), you may get help to solve a crime.

4. If you _____ to do something one time and can't, _____ one more time.

5. If you say "_____ ," you are going to go away.

Name _____ Date _____

Cloze Sentences 2

1. You can _____ to _____ _____ _____ home on a jet in the _____.

2. A _____ can be _____ and _____, but she cannot be _____, too.

3. Can you _____ open a _____ bit of two-_____ rope?

4. _____ do you _____ to _____ on me? When you do I am so _____ that I _____.

Name _____ Date _____

Dictations

5 Closed Syllable   cats and kittens

BOOK LIST

Cats and Kittens

Cat on the Mat, Brian Wildsmith (Oxford, England: Oxford University Press, 1982). In a brief story of a cat who scares away the animals who join her so she can have a mat to herself, the one line of text on each page differs by one word—the name of each animal intruder.

Have You Seen My Cat?, Eric Carle (New York: Scholastic, 1987). Two repeated lines and illustrations tell the story of a boy who travels around the world to look for his lost cat and is disappointed that the variety of cats (wild and domesticated) people show him are not his until he finds his cat and the reason she has been missing—a litter of kittens.

Cats and Kittens (Glenview, Ill.: Scott, Foresman and Company, 1971, 1976). Sentences that accompany black and white photographs on facing pages describe a variety of ways in which the habits of cats and kittens are alike.

Greedy Cat, Joy Cowley, illustrated by Robyn Belton (New York: Richard C. Owen Publishers, Inc., 1983). In this predictable book with a repetitive pattern, every time Mum and Katie go shopping, Greedy Cat eats all of what is in the shopping bag until Mum develops a plan and buys a pot of hot pepper.

Greedy Cat Is Hungry, Joy Cowley, illustrated by Robyn Belton (New York: Richard C. Owen Publishers, Inc., 1988). In this book with predictable, repetitive text, hungry Greedy Cat sits in front of the refrigerator to beg for food and everyone in the family calls him greedy except Katie, who feeds him—a whole string of sausages.

Mac and Tab, Barbara W. Makar (Cambridge, Mass.: Educators Publishing Service, 1968, 1977, 1985). In a flash of anger, Tab the cat eats his friend, Mac the rat, who ate his food while he napped.

Mac Is Safe, Barbara W. Makar (Cambridge, Mass.: Educators Publishing Service, 1968, 1977, 1985). In this sequel to ***Mac and Tab*** by the same author, Tab the cat goes to the vet, who operates to remove Mac, the rat, from his stomach. In the end, the two friends are reunited.

Fur, Jan Mark, illustrated by Charlotte Voake (New York: J. B. Lippincott, 1986). Readers of this short book wonder why thin Kitty is getting fat and acting strangely, making nests throughout the house, until they see the contents of her favorite nest—a litter of five kittens.

Tiger Is a Scaredy Cat, Joan Phillips, illustrated by Norman Gorbaty (New York: Random House, 1986). It is not unusual for cats to be afraid of dogs, trucks, vacuum cleaners, and the dark, as Tiger the cat is, but he is also afraid of mice until he returns a baby mouse to its parents and braves all of his fears.

Tom's Cat, Charlotte Voake (New York: Harper & Row, 1986). Tom keeps hearing noises and thinks it's his cat but always finds that the source is a family member, until he hears a "meow" from the living room and finds his cat, who has torn the springs out of a chair.

The Fat Cat: A Danish Folktale, Jack Kent (New York: Scholastic, 1971). In this cumulative tale, a cat goes on a spree and eats the old woman who owns him and, one or a few at a time, sixteen others until a woodcutter puts a stop to his eating, cuts open his stomach, and releases everyone.

The Farmyard Cat, Christine Anello, illustrated by Sharon Thompson (Gosford, New Zealand: Ashton Scholastic, 1987). When she falls from the henhouse fence, the cat starts a chain reaction that results in several angry farm animals chasing her, but she outsmarts them all when she stops suddenly and they fall over each other.

Cats and Mice, Rita Golden Gelman, illustrated by Eric Gurney (New York: Scholastic, 1978). A few words and comical illustrations present scenes in a contest of wits between cats and mice at a picnic, in which the mice are ahead until the final episode (when the cats outwit the mice with a plan).

The Cat and the Bird in the Hat, Norman Bridwell (New York: Scholastic, 1964). Near-sighted Spats the cat finds a hat that belongs to a bird, and neither of them wants to relinquish possession, but with the help of Milly they learn to share the hat and appreciate each other's positive qualities and develop a friendship in the process.

The Fire Cat, Esther Averill (New York: Harper & Row, 1960). Pickles the cat realizes his wish to do big and important things when he leaves his home in a yard between apartment buildings and becomes an active member of the city's fire department.

Scruffy, Peggy Parish, illustrated by Kelly Oechsli (New York: HarperCollins, 1988). Todd learns about the care of cats and about the animal shelter when he and a kitten choose each other as Todd's birthday gift from his parents.

MOTIVATION AND EXTENSION ACTIVITIES

1. At the beginning of the unit, students and the teacher brainstorm and record on one chart with the heading "True" (1) what they know (or think they know) to be true about cats (They catch mice, rats, chipmunks, and other small rodents. They are curious. They sleep a lot during the day and take cat naps. They clean themselves and their

kittens with their tongues.) and (2) what they wonder about or would like to learn about them (How do cats use their whiskers? What are some of the different kinds of cats and where did they come from originally? Are the tame [domesticated] cats we have as pets related to wild cats like lions and tigers? How do cats purr? If a male cat is called a tom, what is a female cat called? How long do cats usually live? Do cats really have nine lives? Why do cats' backs arch and why does their fur stand on end when they are angry or frightened?). On a second chart with the heading "Not True or False," students and the teacher record things that are not true about real cats that cat characters in books do (Make friends with rats and/or mice. Talk. Dance. Ride a motorcycle. Eat people.).

The teacher uses this opportunity to introduce or review the terms *nonfiction* (which he or she adds under the heading "True" on the first chart) and *fiction* (which he or she adds under the heading "Not True or False" on the second chart). (The teacher points out that *false* and *fiction* begin with the same letter to students who need a mnemonic device to remember the terms.)

Throughout the unit, students and the teacher verify or revise/correct and add information to the lists using the books suggested in this chapter and resource books and materials. They use the following informational books written for children and illustrated with drawings or photographs:

Kittens Are Like That, Jan Pfloog (New York: Random House, 1976, 1983).

All Kinds of Cats, Carolyn L. Burke and Jerome C. Harste (School Book Fairs, Inc., 1983).

How Kittens Grow, Millicent E. Selsam, photographs by Esther Bubley (New York: Scholastic, 1973).

How Kittens Grow, Millicent E. Selsam, photographs by Neil Johnson (New York: Scholastic, 1973, 1992).

Cats and Kittens: Learning About Animals (New York: Modern Publishing, 1985).

The Kids' Cat Book, Tomie dePaola (New York: The Trumpet Club, 1979).

Listen to Your Kitten Purr, Lilo Hess (New York: Scholastic, 1980).

Students learn about the nerves in cats' whiskers, which help them feel their way around objects as they hunt at night, and share cat riddles and jokes in the chapter entitled "The Cat's Whiskers" in *Scientific Eye: Exploring the Marvels of Science*, by Adam Hart-Davis (New York: Sterling Publishing Co., Inc., 1989).

Students and the teacher discover a possible origin of the belief or saying that cats have nine lives and whether it is true as they read "A Cat Has Nine Lives" in *Animal Fact/Animal Fable*, written by Seymour Simon and illustrated by Diane de Groot (New York: Crown Publishers, Inc., 1979), a resource about animals that provides factual information in an unusual and engaging format. The colorfully and accurately illustrated book presents scientific observations about the behavior of a variety of animals. For each animal, a true or false statement is presented on a right-hand page, and the reader guesses whether it is a fact or a fable (fiction) and turns the page to find out.

In their study of wild animal relatives of domesticated cats, students use, as one resource, the following issues of **Zoobooks** magazine (Wildlife Education, Ltd., 930 Washington Street, San Diego, Calif. 92103). Published monthly, **Zoobooks** magazines provide current information about groups of animals through brief text and colored photographs and diagrams with captions. Issues about wild cats include the following: "Big Cats" (1981 and March 1992, vol. 9, no. 6), "Cheetahs" (August 1990, vol. 7, no. 11), "Lions" (June 1989, vol. 6, no. 9), "Little Cats" (April 1986, vol. 2, no. 7), and "Tigers" (October 1987, vol. 5, no. 1, and July 1992, vol. 9, no. 10).

2. Throughout the unit and during their research, students and the teacher generate two lists of words (adjectives) and phrases that describe cats. On one chart, they list words and phrases that describe the attributes and features of real cats. On a second chart, they list words and phrases that describe fictional cat characters in the books they read or listen to in this unit. They compare and contrast them.

3. Students use what they know and learn about the attributes and features of cats as they act out with costumes and/or masks, make and use puppets to dramatize, or create a dance or movements for the stories in this unit. They choose background music that represents each character to be played at appropriate times during the play/puppet show/dance/movements.

4. Throughout the unit, students listen to books read aloud selected from the large number of picture books that feature cats as characters, including the following (listed alphabetically by author's last name):

Traveling to Tondo: A Tale of the Nkundo of Zaire, Verna Aardema, illustrated by Will Hillenbrand (New York: Scholastic, 1991). (See Chapter 29, consonant-le fable.)

Who Is the Beast?, Keith Baker (New York: The Trumpet Club, 1990).

Spider Cat, Nicola Bayley (London, England: Walker Books Ltd., 1984).

The Case of the Cat's Meow, Crosby Bonsall (New York: Harper & Row, 1965).

Annie and the Wild Animals, Jan Brett (Boston: Houghton Mifflin Company, 1985). (See Chapter 15, ai rain, and Chapter 17, or corn.)

Cross-Country Cat, Mary Calhoun, illustrated by Erick Ingraham (New York: Mulberry Books, 1979).

High Wire Henry, Mary Calhoun, illustrated by Erick Ingraham (New York: William Morrow and Company, Inc., 1991).

Wednesday Is Spaghetti Day, Maryann Cocca-Leffler (New York: Scholastic, 1990). (See Chapter 7, ay day.)

Garfield (collections), Jim Davis (New York: Ballantine Books).

Bonjour, Mr. Satie, Tomie dePaola (New York: Scholastic, 1991).

My Cat Beany, Jane Feder, illustrated by Karen Gundersheimer (New York: Alfred A. Knopf, 1979).

A Cat Called Kite, Mem Fox, illustrated by K. Hawley (Auckland, New Zealand: Ashton Scholastic, 1985).

Millions of Cats, Wanda Gag (New York: Coward, McCann & Geoghegan, Inc., 1928, 1956).

Cat Goes Fiddle-i-fee, Paul Galdone (New York: Clarion Books, 1985).

Puss in Boots, Paul Galdone (New York: Scholastic, 1976).

Hello, Cat You Need a Hat, Rita Golden Gelman, illustrated by Eric Gurney (New York: Scholastic, 1979).

The Old Woman Who Lived in a Vinegar Bottle, Rumer Godden, illustrated by Mairi Hedderwick (London: Macmillan Children's Books, 1972). (See Chapter 23, ou house, and Chapter 31, g George magic stingy.)

Lazy Lion, Mwenye Hadithi and Adrienne Kennaway (New York: The Trumpet Club, 1990).

The Christmas Day Kitten, James Herriot, illustrated by Ruth Brown (New York: St. Martin's Press, 1976, 1986).

Moses the Kitten, James Herriot, illustrated by Peter Barrett (New York: St. Martin's Press, 1974, 1984).

Oscar, Cat-about-Town, James Herriot (New York: St. Martin's Press, 1990).

Lucky's Choice, Susan Jeschke (New York: Scholastic, 1987).

Whiskers & Rhymes, Arnold Lobel (New York: Greenwillow Books, 1985).

Sam, Bangs & Moonshine, Evaline Ness (New York: The Trumpet Club, 1966).

Koko's Kitten, Francine Patterson, photographs by Ronald H. Cohn (New York: Scholastic, 1985).

Koko's Story, Francine Patterson, photographs by Ronald H. Cohn (New York: Scholastic, 1987).

Hubert's Hair-Raising Adventure, Bill Peet (Boston: Houghton Mifflin Company, 1959).

Mrs. Katz and Tush, Patricia Polacco (New York: Bantam Books, 1992).

The Tale of Tom Kitten, Beatrix Potter (New York: Frederick Warne & Co., Inc., 1907, 1935).

Puss in Boots, Susan Saunders, illustrated by Elizabeth Miles (New York: Scholastic, 1989).

The Cat in the Hat, Dr. Seuss (New York: Random House, 1957).

The Cat in the Hat Comes Back, Dr. Seuss (New York: Random House, 1958).

The Cat Who Wore a Pot on Her Head, Jan Slepian and Ann Seidler, illustrated by Richard E. Martin (New York: Scholastic, 1980). (See Chapter 1, ing king.)

Do Not Open, Brinton Turkle (New York: E. P. Dutton, 1981).

The Tenth Good Thing about Barney, Judith Viorst, illustrated by Erik Blegvad (New York: The Trumpet Club, 1971).

5. As they read and discuss the books suggested for this unit, students and the teacher share stories they know or have heard about cats. They create three-dimensional figures of the cat characters in their stories (from a variety of materials) to use as props as they present their tales. As they share the cat stories from their experiences, the teacher introduces or reviews the concept of folk tales—within families, communities, and cultures.

6. As they read *Have You Seen My Cat?*, students and teacher guess, from the information in the illustrations, the places around the world that the boy visits as he looks for his missing cat.

7. Students tell and/or write their own version of the "Greedy Cat" story after they read *Greedy Cat*. They substitute characters for Mum and Katie and foods of their choice that Greedy Cat eats and, in the end, an equivalent to Mum's pot of pepper.

8. After they read *Mac and Tab*, students and the teacher compile a number of episodes that could be added to give the story a happy ending. The teacher introduces or reviews the concept of sequel, and students and the teacher expand their episodes into a sequel to *Mac and Tab*. The teacher introduces the published sequel to *Mac and Tab*, *Mac Is Safe*, written by the same author, Barbara W. Makar, and explains that it is based on a story written by a boy, Mark Bouthot, from East Templeton, Massachusetts. Students and the teacher read *Mac Is Safe* and compare and contrast it to the sequels they have told and/or written.

9. Students and the teacher stop their previewing of *Fur* at the page before the kittens are first shown in the illustrations, and they make and revise predictions about the reasons for Kitty's behavior as they read up to that point. They confirm or revise/correct their hypotheses as they complete the book.

10. Students differentiate Tiger and Baby Mouse's voices in *Tiger Is a Scaredy Cat* by reading their dialogue aloud with expression.

11. After they determine the pattern of *Tom's Cat*, students guess what the source of each noise really is, and they read on to confirm or revise/correct their predictions.

12. As actors, puppeteers, dancers, or mimists, students dramatize the cumulative nature and pattern of *The Fat Cat: A Danish Folktale*. They tell and/or write text for the final illustration, in which the woodcutter is bandaging the Fat Cat's stomach after everyone has jumped out.

13. Readers keep score, orally or on a written scoreboard, of the points earned after

each chapter or episode of the contest between the cats and the mice in **Cats and Mice**. They decide on the winners in the end and give the reasons/criteria on which they based their decision.

14. Students compare and contrast stories, including **Scruffy** and **Emmett's Pig** (see Chapter 19, ir birthday), about children who receive pets for their birthday.

15. Students and teacher share riddles and jokes about cats in books of riddles, including the following:

Cat's out of the Bag!: Jokes about Cats, Sharon Friedman and Irene Shere, illustrated by Joan Hanson (Minneapolis: Lerner Publications Company, 1986).

It's Raining Cats and Dogs: Cat and Dog Jokes, Charles Keller, illustrated by Robert Quackenbush (New York: Pippin Press, 1988).

When readers (and listeners) engage in the word play involved in riddles and jokes, in addition to their knowledge of the subject matter, they use what they know about relationships between/among words (synonyms, antonyms, homophones, homographs, homonyms, and analogies) and about the nuances, associations, and subtleties of language. They call on their understanding of figurative language (similes, metaphors, and personification), idiomatic and proverbial expressions, and literary allusions to interpret the words and language of the clues and answers beyond the literal level. Students for whom the word play of riddles and jokes is difficult benefit from many supported experiences with activities involving them and from having strategies for solving them made explicit by peers and the teacher. It often is helpful for students to hear others talk through their thinking or problem-solving process.

Some students learn more about solving riddles and jokes through the process of creating their own. They use the information they have or discover by reading or listening to the books about cats (in this unit), or they research an area of interest and/or knowledge and become the community expert. They dictate or write and illustrate riddles and/or jokes on cards or in a book (as an individual project or as a collaborative project as part of a group) and share them with others. They give clues and additional information as necessary and useful for those guessing.

Riddles and jokes related to familiar subjects are easier for students and, whenever possible, they are best related to a unit of study. (See Activity 16 in Chapter 17, or corn, Activity 10 in Chapter 26, aw straw, and Activity 11 in Chapter 28, ou soup, for examples of activities focusing on word play related to thematic units.)

Students and the teacher use the sound clues of homophones to solve riddles together in **Eight Ate: A Feast of Homonym Riddles**, by Marvin Terban and illustrated by Giulio Maestro (New York: Clarion Books, 1982).

16. Students and the teacher discuss the idiomatic expressions "To let the cat out of the bag," "raining cats and dogs," "to play a cat-and-mouse game," and "cat burglar" introduced in the books of cat riddles and jokes (**Cat's Out of the Bag!: Jokes about Cats**, by Friedman and Shere, and **It's Raining Cats and Dogs: Cat and Dog Jokes**) and other idiomatic expressions and traditional sayings related to cats, including "a catty person," "Has the cat got your tongue?" "the cat's pajamas," "There's more than one way to skin a cat," "cat on a hot tin roof," and "Curiosity killed the cat." Students extend their exploration of idiomatic expressions by reading and discussing other books that feature them.

- They learn about a possible origin of the idiomatic expression "to let the cat out of the bag" and of other idioms in *In a Pickle and Other Funny Idioms*, by Marvin Terban and illustrated by Giulio Maestro (New York: Clarion Books, 1983).

- They listen to (or read) "Story Number Two: The Trip" in *George and Martha Round and Round: Five Stories about the Best of Friends*, by James Marshall (Boston: Houghton Mifflin Company, 1988), in which the idiomatic expression "raining cats and dogs" is used to describe the weather (page 14). (See the "George and Martha" unit in Chapter 31, g George magic stingy, for additional "George and Martha" books and activities.)

- They read three books by Fred Gwynne in which a girl imagines literally the statements she hears adults make that involve idiomatic expressions: *The King Who Rained* (New York: Prentice-Hall Books for Young Readers, 1970), *A Chocolate Moose for Dinner* (New York: The Trumpet Club, 1976), and *A Little Pigeon Toad* (New York: The Trumpet Club, 1988).

- Students listen to or read books from the "Amelia Bedelia" series by Peggy Parish, in which Amelia Bedelia, the maid, interprets words literally and misses the nuances of language.

Together, students and the teacher tell and/or write and illustrate idiomatic expressions, including those related to cats. On a piece of paper held lengthwise and divided in half from top to bottom, they draw first—on the left—a picture of the literal meaning (as Maestro in *In a Pickle and Other Funny Idioms* by Terban or the girl in the Gwynne books might do) and second—on the right—a picture of the idiomatic/figurative meaning. They bind a set of phrases contributed by a group of students and the teacher into individual or group books.

17. Students and the teacher play a cumulative listening and memory game from colonial times in the United States, "The Minister's Cat." By turns, players repeat aloud the responses that have preceded theirs and add their own response, which describes a cat using a single word (adjective) that begins with the next consecutive letter of the alphabet. For example, at the sixth turn of the game the response might be, "The minister's cat is agile, bouncy, cute, dreamy, energetic, and furry."

As an individual project or a collaborative group project, students make and illustrate an adjective alphabet book about the Minister's Cat.

18. As they discuss relationships between domesticated/tame/pet cats and their wild cat relatives, students learn about traditional beliefs in China about the ability of tigers, through magic powers, to provide protection and about a tradition in some Chinese families of making clothing in the shape of tigers to protect their children.

Students follow the directions to make tiger slippers on their computer presented in "Tiger Slippers (China)" in *Kid Pix around the World: A Multicultural Computer Activity Book*, by Barbara Chan (Reading, Mass.: Addison-Wesley Publishing Company, 1993). The book contains essays that provide background information about twenty cultures around the world and detailed, step-by-step instructions that show children how to do drawing and painting activities using "Kid Pix" computer software. Presented cultures are marked on a world map in the front of the book.

19. Students and the teacher locate on a map and/or globe the places/cultures (of origin or depicted) in the books read in this chapter, including East Templeton, Massachusetts in the United States (*Mac Is Safe*); Denmark (*The Fat Cat: A Danish*

Folktale); Egypt (*All Kinds of Cats* and *The Kids' Cat Book*); Siam, Burma, and Persia (*Cats and Kittens: Learning About Animals* and *The Kids' Cat Book*); the Isle of Manx in the Irish Sea (*The Kids' Cat Book*); Cornwall in England (*The Kids' Cat Book*); Japan (*The Kids' Cat Book*); the Himalayan Mountains in Tibet (*The Kids' Cat Book*); Maine in the United States (*The Kids' Cat Book*); Baghdad in Iraq (*Listen to Your Kitten Purr*); Zaire (*Traveling to Tondo: A Tale of the Nkundo of Zaire*); Africa (*Lazy Lion*); England (*The Old Woman Who Lived in a Vinegar Bottle*); Paris in France (*Bonjour, Mr. Satie*); Yorkshire in England (*The Christmas Day Kitten*, *Moses the Kitten*, and *Oscar, Cat about Town*); San Francisco, California in the United States (*Koko's Kitten* and *Koko's Story*); the Lake Country in England (*The Tale of Tom Kitten*); and China ["Tiger Slippers (China)" in *Kid Pix around the World: A Multicultural Computer Activity Book*].

TEACHER REFERENCE

Cloze Sentences

One-Syllable Words

Cloze Sentences 1

1. The sun can be <u>red</u> when it sets.
2. I got <u>up</u> at ten o'clock.
3. You can<u>not</u> run in class.
4. A pig that is <u>fat</u> is not thin.
5. Tell Dad I will get <u>him</u> lunch when I get back.
6. I had my lunch in a big <u>bag</u>.
7. I get <u>hot</u> when I sit in the sun.
8. A dog can sit up and <u>beg</u> to get food.

Cloze Sentences 2

1. We can ask Dad to go shopping with <u>us</u>.
2. My cat had a <u>nap</u> when it sat on my lap.
3. If you swing the bat and get a hit, then <u>run</u> as fast as you can.
4. I can <u>rip</u> my pants on a tack if I sit on it.
5. It is Mom's <u>job</u> to get the trash to the dump.
6. I <u>met</u> a man at the shop when I went with my dad and mom.
7. Ask <u>if</u> you can go shopping with us.

Dictations

1. <u>Tom has</u> a <u>dog that is</u> as <u>big</u> as <u>his cat</u>. <u>It has</u> a <u>big pen</u> to <u>run in</u> with <u>him and</u> a <u>red dish that it gets fed in</u>. <u>Tom has lots</u> of <u>fun</u> with <u>his</u> cat and <u>his dog</u>.

2. <u>If</u> you <u>hand us</u> the <u>pot</u>, we <u>can mend it</u>. <u>Yes, then</u> we <u>can dig up</u> the <u>sod and</u> plant a <u>shrub in</u> the <u>pot</u>. <u>It will not</u> be a <u>big job</u>.

Closed Syllable

cats and kittens

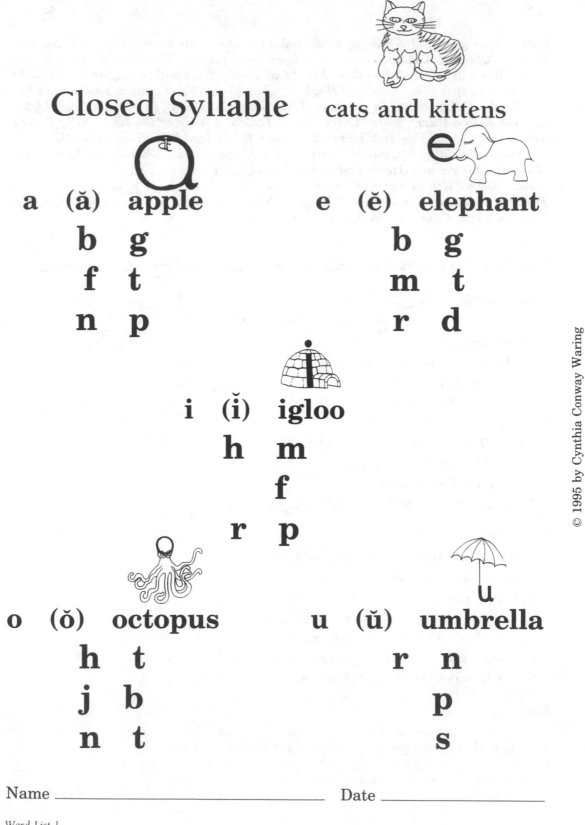

a (ă) apple

b	g
f	t
n	p

e (ĕ) elephant

b	g
m	t
r	d

i (ĭ) igloo

h	m
	f
r	p

o (ŏ) octopus

h	t
j	b
n	t

u (ŭ) umbrella

r	n
	p
	s

Name _____ Date _____

Word List 1

Closed Syllable   cats and kittens

a (ă) **apple**
    bag
    fat
    nap

e (ě) **elephant**
        beg
        met
        red

i (ǐ) **igloo**
        him
        if
        rip

o (ǒ) **octopus**
        hot
        job
        not

u (ŭ) **umbrella**
        run
        up
        us

Name _____ Date _____

Closed Syllable   cats and kittens

Write a word from the Word Lists to complete each sentence.

1. The sun can be _____ when it sets.

2. I got _____ at ten o'clock.

3. You can _____ run in class.

4. A pig that is _____ is not thin.

5. Tell Dad I will get _____ lunch when I get back.

6. I had my lunch in a big _____ .

7. I get _____ when I sit in the sun.

8. A dog can sit up and _____ to get food.

Name _____ Date _____

Cloze Sentences 1

Closed Syllable   cats and kittens

Write a word from the Word Lists to complete each sentence.

1. We can ask Dad to go shopping with _____ .

2. My cat had a _____ when it sat on my lap.

3. If you swing the bat and get a hit, then _____ as fast as you can.

4. I can _____ my pants on a tack if I sit on it.

5. It is Mom's _____ to get the trash to the dump.

6. I _____ a man at the shop when I went with my dad and mom.

7. Ask _____ you can go shopping with us.

Name _____ Date _____

Cloze Sentences 2

6 Vowel-Consonant-e

Syllable cake

BOOK LIST ════════════════════════════════

Cakes and Pancakes

Pancakes for Breakfast, Tomie dePaola (San Diego: Harcourt Brace Jovanovich, 1978). In this wordless picture book, a woman is interrupted repeatedly as she attempts to make pancakes because she runs out of ingredients and then her pets overturn them, so she invites herself to the neighbors' and eats their pancakes.

Did You Say, "Fire"?, Joy Cowley, illustrated by Penny Newman (New York: Richard C. Owen Publishers, Inc., 1987). When a mouse smells the smoke from a birthday cake, it panics and starts a rumor of fire that is passed on from animal to animal until fire fighters and even the television camera crew come to investigate.

Oh, A-Hunting We Will Go, John Langstaff, illustrated by Nancy Winslow Parker (New York: Macmillan Publishing Company, 1974). Hunters in this humorous version of the familiar folk song round up animals and put them in rhyming containers—a snake in a cake, a goat in a boat, a fish in a dish, and a bear in his underwear! Includes music for piano and guitar accompaniment.

The Cake That Mack Ate, Rose Robart, illustrated by Maryann Kovalski (Boston: Little, Brown and Company, 1986). In this cumulative story, the excitement builds as more and more ingredients are added to a cake for a birthday, but the cake is ruined when Mack, the dog, sneaks in and eats it before the party.

Jake Baked the Cake, B. G. Hennessy, illustrated by Mary Morgan (New York: Penguin Books, 1990). This rhyming book follows the people preparing for and involved in a wedding and shows Jake, the baker, at different stages of making and decorating the four-tiered wedding cake.

The Pancake, Anita Lobel (New York: Bantam Doubleday Dell Publishing Group, Inc., 1978). In this cumulative tale that follows the pattern of the "Gingerbread Man" story, to escape being eaten by seven hungry children, a pancake jumps out of the pan and rolls away from the children's mother and an increasing number of other hungry characters until a pig tricks and eats it.

The Wolf's Chicken Stew, Keiko Kasza (New York: The Trumpet Club, 1987). Rather than make chicken stew from the hen as she is, a wolf decides to fatten her up by putting pancakes, doughnuts, and cake on her porch, but he finds he can't eat her when her thankful chicks smother him with kisses and call him "Uncle Wolf."

Hedgehog Bakes a Cake, Maryann Macdonald, illustrated by Lynn Munsinger (New York: Bantam Doubleday Dell Publishing Group, Inc., 1990). Hedgehog begins to make a cake and, one at a time, his friends stop by, offer advice, and make a mess of his batter and kitchen. When alone again, Hedgehog cleans the kitchen, starts over, bakes the cake, and, finally, shares it with his friends. Includes recipe for Hedgehog's Yellow Cake.

Pancakes, Pancakes!, Eric Carle (New York: Scholastic, 1990). Jack gets the ingredients so his mother can make pancakes for breakfast—flour at the mill, an egg from the henhouse, milk from the cow, butter from the churn, firewood from the woods, and jam from the cellar.

Mooncake, Frank Asch (New York: Scholastic, 1983). Bear builds a rocket out of junk to find out what the moon tastes like; however, when he awakens he finds not the moon but a wintry surprise—mooncake!

Journey Cake, Ho!, Ruth Sawyer, illustrated by Robert McCloskey (New York: The Viking Press, 1953). A singing Journey Cake made by an old woman takes Johnny, the hired boy, and the animals that chase it full circle and back to the farm of the old woman and her husband in this version of the "Gingerbread Man" story from the southern United States.

Cloudy with a Chance of Meatballs, Judi Barrett, illustrated by Ron Barrett (New York: Scholastic, 1978). A modern tall tale inspired by a pancake is told by Grandpa about a town whose food was conveniently supplied from the sky until the weather took a "turn for the worse" and made the town uninhabitable.

Thunder Cake, Patricia Polacco (New York: Philomel Books, 1990). A girl's Babushka (grandmother) helps her overcome her fear of thunderstorms by teaching her how to gather the ingredients, make Thunder Cake, and put it in the oven between the first clap of thunder and the arrival of the storm. Includes the recipe for Thunder Cake.

MOTIVATION AND EXTENSION ACTIVITIES

1. Throughout the unit, students read and/or listen to books about cakes and pancakes. See Chapter 19, ir birthday, for books and activities related to birthday cakes and pancakes.

2. Students tell, dictate, and/or write the text to correspond with the illustrations of the wordless picture book *Pancakes for Breakfast*.

3. Before or after they read or listen to *Pancakes for Breakfast*, *The Pancake*, *The Wolf's Chicken Stew*, *Pancakes, Pancakes!*, and/or *Cloudy with a Chance of Meatballs*, students follow the recipe in *Pancakes for Breakfast* to make pancakes and invite the neighbors (or friends) to join them in eating them.

4. As they read *Did You Say, "Fire"?*, students and the teacher discuss how easily

rumors can be spread, especially when misunderstanding and panic are involved. They read and discuss other books in which misunderstandings result in rumors, including **The Surprise Party**, by Pat Hutchins (New York: Young Readers Press, 1969), in which Rabbit's "I'm having a party tomorrow" becomes "hoeing the parsley tomorrow" and a chain of misunderstandings results as each of his friends hears and passes the invitation a little differently (see Activity 5 in Chapter 1, ing king), and versions of the "Henny Penny" story (see Activity 36 in Chapter 11, y penny).

Students experience this phenomenon as they play the game of "Telephone," in which they pass a message in whispers from one person to the next, and it often becomes misunderstood and confused (and comical when it is revealed at the end of the turn).

5. After they read **Oh, A-Hunting We Will Go**, students, individually or as a group collaborative project, illustrate their own book entitled "A Snake in a Cake," which follows the same pattern as the book (in which hunters round up and hide in rhyming containers animals, people, and objects whose names include a vowel-consonant-e syllable).

The teacher prepares the cover with the title "A Snake in a Cake" and the pages of the book with the following:

On one side of the paper	On the reverse side of the paper
Oh, a-hunting we will go, A-hunting we will go; We'll catch _____	And hide _____ And then we'll let _____ go!

The teacher and/or students write the following rhyming information in the blanks, and the students illustrate each page and the cover. They compile the pages into a book and read it to peers and other audiences. One way students share their books is to cover the text (and/or illustrations) on the second page and have others guess the rhyming container and then uncover and read the text to confirm or revise/correct their predictions. For example,

Oh, a-hunting we will go,
    A-hunting we will go;

1. We'll catch <u>a dime</u>	And hide <u>it in slime</u>
	And then we'll let <u>it</u> go
		it
2.	a bone	it in a cone
		it
3.	a pine	it in wine
		it
4.	an ape	him in a cape
		him
5.	a coke	it in smoke
		it
6.	a wire	it in a tire
		it
7.	a rose	it in a hose
		it
8.	a man alive	him in a hive
		him

9.	a flake	on a rake it
10.	a porcupine	her in a mine , her
11.	a gnome	him in my home him
12.	a whale	her on a scale her
13.	a tike	him on a bike him
14.	a bride	her on a slide her

6. The cumulative story **The Pancake** follows a pattern similar to the familiar traditional story of the "Gingerbread Man," and **Journey Cake, Ho!** is a version of the "Gingerbread Man" story from the South in the United States.

Students read **The Gingerbread Man**, illustrated by Karen Schmidt (New York: Scholastic, 1967, 1985), a cumulative tale in which a gingerbread man escapes the oven and runs away from a boy, an old man and woman, farmers, a bear, and a wolf and is tricked and eaten by a fox. They also read "The Stinky Cheese Man" in **The Stinky Cheese Man and Other Fairly Stupid Tales**, by Jon Scieszka and illustrated by Lane Smith (New York: Viking, 1992). The book contains eleven humorous modern retellings of well-known traditional tales; in "The Stinky Cheese Man," a lonely old woman makes a man out of stinky cheese and when he jumps out of the oven and runs away no one chases him because of his awful smell—not even the fox, at the end, so he just falls apart in the river! (The modern and often humorous versions of the stories often provide older readers with the motivation to read and discuss traditional tales.)

Students and the teacher discuss the similarities and differences among the four versions of the "Gingerbread Man" story suggested for this unit. They dramatize—as actors, mimists, dancers, and/or puppeteers—the cumulative nature of the tales.

7. Trying not to make a mess of the kitchen/cooking area, students follow the recipe for Hedgehog's Yellow Cake in **Hedgehog Bakes a Cake** (not the advice of friends who might drop by and offer it) and share it with their friends (and teacher!).

8. As they listen to or read **Mooncake**, students discover the seasonal pattern of the book using clues from the text and illustrations. They share "mooncake" (lime sherbet or pistachio ice cream) after they share the book.

9. Students and the teacher tell stories about their experiences in thunder and lightning storms and share the ways they have coped with their fears of thunder and lightning as they follow the recipe for Thunder Cake in **Thunder Cake**. They frost the cake and decorate it with strawberries, set the table with tablecloth and dishes, and eat Thunder Cake in a room with the lights dimmed. They imagine that it is a rainy day and they can hear rain on the roof and windows and thunder in the background and can see flashes of lightning light up the sky.

10. Students and the teacher locate on a map and/or globe the places/cultures (depicted or of origin) in the books read in this chapter, including New England in the United States (**Pancakes for Breakfast**); France and Spain (**Jake Baked the Cake**);

the southern United States (*Journey Cake, Ho!*); and Russia and Michigan in the United States (*Thunder Cake*).

TEACHER REFERENCE ════════════════════════════════════

Cloze Sentences

One-Syllable Words

Cloze Sentences 1

1. A <u>plane</u> can fly in the sky.
2. My mom has a big <u>smile</u> when she is not sad.
3. A <u>bone</u> is the thing my dog likes to bite on best.
4. Dogs like to <u>chase</u> cats.
5. I broke a <u>plate</u> when it was my job to wipe the dishes.
6. I like to jump <u>rope</u> for fun.
7. I can tell <u>time</u> if I look at a clock.

Cloze Sentences 2

1. A <u>stove</u> with a fire in it can make us hot.
2. The big mom cat had five <u>cute</u> kittens.
3. The sun can <u>shine</u> on us if the fog lifts.
4. If you cannot sing a <u>tune</u>, you can hum it.
5. The bride was not <u>late</u> to the wedding. She got to it on time.
6. I can <u>drive</u> a truck if it is not too big.
7. I hope you will be <u>here</u> at snack time so you will not miss the cupcakes.

Cloze Sentences 3

1. A <u>cube</u> of ice can make a drink like Coke® cold.
2. It is <u>rude</u> to call a kid names.
3. The <u>eve</u> is the time of day before you go to bed.
4. My dad's <u>snore</u> woke me up.
5. I made a <u>cake</u> with frosting, and then we ate it.

Multisyllable Words

6. A <u>cupcake</u> is a cake that you make the size of a cup.
7. A <u>pancake</u> is a cake that you make in a pan.

Dictations

1. <u>Pete</u> and <u>Dave</u> <u>made</u> a <u>trade</u>. Pete gave Dave a <u>plane</u> in a <u>crate</u> and a <u>crane</u> that <u>shines</u> in the sun. <u>Dave</u> gave <u>Pete</u> a <u>cute</u> <u>mule</u> and <u>nine</u> <u>miles</u> of <u>rope</u>!

2. There was a <u>fire</u> in <u>Pete's</u> <u>cute</u> <u>frame</u> <u>home</u> in the <u>lane</u>. The <u>flames</u> <u>made</u> a <u>hole</u> in the <u>pine</u> on the <u>side</u> of the <u>drive</u>. I <u>hope</u> the <u>gate</u> to the <u>home</u> is <u>safe</u>. Did a <u>pipe</u> or a <u>fire</u> in the <u>stove</u> <u>make</u> the <u>blaze</u>?

Vowel-Consonant-e Syllable   cake

a (ā) -   e (ē) -   i (ī) -
  ch s   v   dr v
   l t   h r   sh n
  pl n   sm l
  pl t   t m

o (ō) -   u (ū) -
  b n   c b
  r p   c t
 sn r   r d
 st v   t n

       c k
    cupc k
    panc k

Name _____ Date _____

Word List 1

Vowel-Consonant-e Syllable cake

a (ā) -
chase
late
plane
plate

e (ē) -
eve
here

i (ī) -
drive
shine
smile
time

o (ō) -
bone
rope
snore
stove

u (ū) -
cube
cute
rude
tune

cake
cupcake
pancake

Name _____ Date _____

Word List 2

Vowel-Consonant-e Syllable cake

Write a word from the Word List to complete each sentence.

1. A _____ can fly in the sky.

2. My mom has a big _____ when she is not sad.

3. A _____ is the thing my dog likes to bite on best.

4. Dogs like to _____ cats.

5. I broke a _____ when it was my job to wipe the dishes.

6. I like to jump _____ for fun.

7. I can tell _____ if I look at a clock.

Name _____ Date _____

Cloze Sentences 1

Vowel-Consonant-e Syllable cake

Write a word from the Word List to complete each sentence.

1. A _____ with a fire in it can make us hot.

2. The big mom cat had five _____ kittens.

3. The sun can _____ on us if the fog lifts.

4. If you cannot sing a _____ , you can hum it.

5. The bride was not _____ to the wedding. She got to it on time.

6. I can _____ a truck if it is not too big.

7. I hope you will be _____ at snack time so you will not miss the cupcakes.

Name _____ Date _____

Cloze Sentences 2

Vowel-Consonant-e Syllable cake

Write a word from the Word List to complete each sentence.

1. A _____ of ice can make a drink like Coke® cold.

2. It is _____ to call a kid names.

3. The _____ is the time of day before you go to bed.

4. My dad's _____ woke me up.

5. I made a _____ with frosting, and then we ate it.

6. A _____ is a cake that you make the size of a cup.

7. A _____ is a cake that you make in a pan.

Name _____ Date _____

Cloze Sentences 3

7   ay   day

BOOK LIST ══════════════════════════════════════

Memorable Days

Today Is Monday, illustrated by Eric Carle (New York: Philomel Books, 1993). In this picture book of the well-known cumulative song with Carle's brightly colored collage illustrations, animals eat a different food each day of the week and invite the world's children to eat them all on Sunday. Music and full lyrics for the song are included at the end of the book.

Today Is Monday: A Song Book and Wall Frieze, illustrated by Susan Baum (New York: HarperCollins, 1992). The book folds out into a wall frieze with, for each day of the week, an illustration on one side and the song's lyrics on the reverse. Includes music for the song.

Our Teacher, Miss Pool, Joy Cowley, illustrated by Diane Perham (New York: Richard C. Owen Publishers, Inc., 1983). After her car breaks down, Miss Pool, an elementary school teacher, must go to school using a different means of transportation every day until she fixes her car at the end of the week.

My Bike, Craig Martin (New York: Richard C. Owen Publishers, Inc., 1982). In this cumulative story with supportive colored photographs, a boy rides his bike in increasing numbers of locations each day for a week, until he crashes on Sunday.

The Very Hungry Caterpillar, Eric Carle (New York: Scholastic, 1969). After it hatches from its egg, a caterpillar eats through a different food each day of the week until it develops an upset stomach and, when it recovers, creates a cocoon and transforms into a butterfly.

When the TV Broke, Harriet Ziefert, illustrated by Mavis Smith (New York: Penguin Group, 1989). Each day of the week that the television is gone for repair, Jeffrey (previously an avid viewer) discovers productive activities to replace his viewing, and when the TV is fixed he finds he is too busy to watch it.

Cookie's Week, Cindy Ward, illustrated by Tomie dePaola (New York: Scholastic, 1988). Cookie, the curious cat, has misadventures each day of the week that result in messes all around the house.

One Monday Morning, Uri Shulevitz (New York: Macmillan Publishing Company, 1967). In this cumulative story with a surprise ending, a boy entertains himself in his apartment on a rainy day by using his imagination to create an adventure for each day of the week.

It's a Perfect Day, Abigail Pizer (New York: HarperCollins, 1990). In this combination word-and-rebus cumulative book, animals on a farm celebrate a perfect day with characteristic activities and noises.

Wacky Wednesday, Theo. LeSieg, illustrated by George Booth (New York: Random House, 1974). In this rhyming counting book, readers locate in the illustrations the increasing number of strange things a boy sees one unusual day.

More Spaghetti, I Say!, Rita Golden Gelman, illustrated by Jack Kent (New York: Scholastic, 1977). Her friend Freddy is upset with Minnie, the monkey, when all she wants to do all day is eat spaghetti, but the tables are turned when she gets a stomachache and he tries the spaghetti!

More Spaghetti, I Say!, Rita Golden Gelman, illustrated by Mort Gerberg (New York: Scholastic, 1992). Gelman's original text has been interpreted with Gerberg's illustrations and larger, bold type for this story of Minnie, the monkey, who is too busy to play because she eats spaghetti all day in a variety of settings and ways.

Wednesday Is Spaghetti Day, Maryann Cocca-Leffler (New York: Scholastic, 1990). While her owners are away at school and work each Wednesday, Catrina the cat and her friends prepare, eat, and clean up the mess from a fancy spaghetti lunch.

The Snowy Day, Ezra Jack Keats (New York: The Viking Press, 1962). Keats's bright collage illustrations and appealing text create a classic story of a small boy's adventures after a snowfall in the city. Caldecott Award Book.

Imogene's Antlers, David Small (New York: Scholastic, 1985). The day that Imogene wakes up and discovers that she has grown antlers, everyone reacts to the amazing sight, and the next day Imogene discovers that the antlers have vanished and have been replaced by a peacock's tail!

Nana Upstairs & Nana Downstairs, Tomie dePaola (New York: Penguin Books, 1973). As a little boy, Tommy enjoyed his Sunday visits with Nana Upstairs and Nana Downstairs, and it is a great loss when his great grandmother and, later, his grandmother die; but falling stars appear to Tommy as their kisses and help him deal with his grief.

The Wednesday Surprise, Eve Bunting, illustrated by Donald Carrick (New York: The Trumpet Club, 1989). Anna's grandmother comes to babysit every Wednesday night, and while her parents are away Anna and her grandmother work on an important surprise for Anna's father's birthday: Anna teaches her grandmother how to read.

Alexander and the Terrible, Horrible, No Good, Very Bad Day, Judith Viorst, illustrated by Ray Cruz (New York: Scholastic, 1972). Alexander has one of those days in which it seems that everything goes wrong for him only, and his mother assures him that bad days are part of life and cannot be escaped by running away—even to Australia.

Alexander, Who Used to Be Rich Last Sunday, Judith Viorst, illustrated by Ray Cruz (New York: Scholastic, 1978). Alexander's grandparents visit one Sunday and give him and his two brothers each a dollar, and it doesn't take him long—bit by bit—to spend or lose all of his money.

Aunt Flossie's Hats (and Crab Cakes Later), Elizabeth Fitzgerald Howard, illustrated by James Ransome (New York: Clarion Books, 1991). When Susan and her sister Sarah visit their great-great-aunt Flossie on a Sunday afternoon, they enjoy the stories she tells (inspired by the hats in her collection) and a special meal of crab cakes.

The Crack-of-Dawn Walkers, Amy Hest, illustrated by Amy Schwartz (New York: Penguin Group, 1984). Sadie and her brother alternate Sundays with their grandfather, who takes them on early morning walks to share their special places in the city.

Chicken Sunday, Patricia Polacco (New York: Scholastic, 1992). A girl remembers Sundays with her friends and their mother, Miss Eula, and a special Easter when they made pysanky eggs to earn money to buy Miss Eula a hat she had admired.

On the Day You Were Born, Debra Frasier (San Diego: Harcourt Brace Jovanovich, 1991). In poetic prose the sun, the moon, the stars, and the earth and its elements and inhabitants greet a child on the day of its birth. The book contains background information about migrating animals, earth, sun, moon, stars, gravity, tides, rain, trees, and the color of people's skin.

MOTIVATION AND EXTENSION ACTIVITIES

1. Students and the teacher write their own versions of ***Today Is Monday*** (Carle) and/or ***Today Is Monday: A Song Book and Wall Frieze*** (Baum). They substitute their personal food favorites, and they sing their own versions and the traditional versions of the song to the tune included at the back of the two books.

2. Before or after they read ***Our Teacher, Miss Pool***, students read ***Where Is Miss Pool?***, written by Joy Cowley and illustrated by Diane Perham (New York: Richard C. Owen Publishers, Inc., 1987), in which a search around school for her locates the missing Miss Pool at home sick with a cold.

3. After they read ***Our Teacher, Miss Pool***, students write a story about their own teacher (or person of their choice) following the pattern of the book. They substitute the name of the person and the means of transportation they select.

4. Students share (tell and/or write and illustrate) their own versions of ***My Bike***. They follow the cumulative pattern of the book and describe where they ride (or might ride) a bike each day of the week.

5. Students use a story pattern and flap-book and cut-paper technique similar to those used in ***The Very Hungry Caterpillar*** and write their own personalized "The Very Hungry (Student's Name)" book, in which they are the hungry character who eats enormous amounts of the foods of their choice.

6. After they read and discuss ***When the TV Broke***, students and the teacher tell and/or write and illustrate as many things as they can think of that they do (or could

do) if the TV becomes broken in their homes. (Students and teachers who do not have a television tell what they do rather than watch TV.)

7. Students and the teacher discuss their interpretations of the ending of **One Monday Morning**. They share (tell and/or write and illustrate) how they entertain themselves on a rainy day. (See Chapter 15, ai rain, for additional activities related to rain and snow.)

8. After they read **It's a Perfect Day**, students and the teacher further explore rebus and rebus-and-word messages as they read and/or listen to other books that contain them. (See Activity 5 in Chapter 3, open syllable go, for suggested books and activities.)

9. Students and the teacher discuss the use of onomatopoeia (words that are similar to or contain the sound made—the buzz of a bee, for example—to represent vividly the sounds that characters, objects, and actions make) to represent the sounds of the animals as they read **It's a Perfect Day**. (See Activity 11 in Chapter 4, y fly, Activity 23 in Chapter 22, ow owl, and Activity 1 in Chapter 25, oi noise, for books and activities that feature onomatopoeia.)

10. After they read **Wacky Wednesday**, students create their own book in which readers locate items that do not fit in the illustrations. (See Chapter 4, y fly, for additional books that invite readers to spy elements in the illustrations of books and Activity 16 in that chapter for an activity that involves student-created "I Spy" books.)

11. Students and the teacher compare and contrast the interpretations by two illustrators of Gelman's story of Minnie the monkey's passion for spaghetti—**More Spaghetti, I Say!** (Kent and Gerberg). They discuss the page lay-outs and the print size of the two versions and consider the effect of these (and other variables) on ease of reading and enjoyment. They select a favorite version and discuss the criteria on which they based their choice.

12. With **Wednesday Is Spaghetti Day** and **More Spaghetti, I Say!** (Kent and Gerberg), students and the teacher read, sing, and/or listen to other books in which spaghetti is featured, including the following: (1) **On Top of Spaghetti**, by Tom Glazer and illustrated by Tom Garcia (New York: Doubleday & Company, Inc., 1982), a humorous parody of the traditional song "On Top of Old Smokey" which shows the adventures and misadventures of a meatball that rolls from the top of a plate of spaghetti after a sneeze and in which music for the song complements text/lyrics on each page, and (2) **Cloudy with a Chance of Meatballs**, by Judi Barrett and illustrated by Ron Barrett (New York: Scholastic, 1978), a modern tall tale inspired by a pancake and told by Grandpa about a town whose food was conveniently supplied from the sky until the weather took a "turn for the worse" and made the town uninhabitable.

13. The teacher prepares **The Snowy Day** with oaktag or heavy paper covering the illustration and text on page 31. Students listen to or read the book through page 30 and share (tell and/or write and illustrate) an ending for the story from that point. They then remove the paper mask from page 31 and resume listening or reading and compare and contrast their endings with the one Keats has given his story.

14. Students and the teacher make snow-scene collages inspired by the illustrations in **The Snowy Day**. (See Activity 25 in Chapter 15, ai rain, for art activities that incorporate techniques used by illustrators of books that feature a snow or rain theme.)

15. As they read and discuss **Nana Upstairs & Nana Downstairs**, **The Wednesday Surprise**, **Aunt Flossie's Hats (and Crab Cakes Later)**, **The Crack-of-Dawn Walkers**, and **Chicken Sunday**, students and the teacher share (tell and/or write and

illustrate) about times they share(d) with their grandparent(s), great aunt(s) and/or uncle(s), other special relative(s) and/or friend(s), or other important special people. (See Activities 4 and 5 in Chapter 16, ar star, for additional activities related to *Nana Upstairs & Nana Downstairs*.)

16. Before or after they read *Alexander and the Terrible, Horrible, No Good, Very Bad Day*, students and the teacher tell and/or write and illustrate about the worst day(s) they have ever had. They discuss ways they have coped with such days (and people who may have helped them). They listen to or read *Mean Soup*, by Everitt, in which Horace's mother helps him deal with a bad day by making mean soup, and they make a pot of "mean soup." (See Activity 7 in Chapter 28, ou soup.)

17. As they read *Alexander, Who Used to Be Rich Last Sunday*, students use actual dollar bills and coins to determine the total amount of money each of Alexander's brothers has at the beginning of the book and to enact the events that result in his losing or spending all of the dollar his grandparents give him.

Students and the teacher share (tell and/or write and illustrate) how they have lost and/or spent money unwisely and about ways in which they, like Alexander, have tried to make or obtain money. (It may be helpful for students or the teacher to bring in and explain the function of bus and subway tokens for students who are unfamiliar with them.) They extend their understanding of money, buying power, and relationships between coins and bills as they read and discuss *If You Made a Million*, by David M. Schwartz and illustrated by Steven Kellogg (New York: Scholastic, 1989), and *How Much Is a Million*, by David M. Schwartz and illustrated by Steven Kellogg (New York: Scholastic, 1985).

18. After they read *Chicken Sunday*, students and the teacher read *The Egg Tree*, by Katherine Milhous (New York: Macmillan Publishing Company, 1950, 1978), about decorating eggs in an additional culture. In this Caldecott Award Book, Grandmom teaches her grandchildren how to decorate eggs with traditional designs to decorate an Easter egg tree. Students follow directions in *The Egg Tree* to decorate eggs and make an egg tree using the traditional designs and method described.

Students make traditional Ukrainian pysanky eggs using chicken or duck eggs and/ or on their computer following the directions in "Pysanky (Ukraine)" in *Kid Pix around the World: A Multicultural Computer Activity Book*, by Barbara Chan (Reading, Mass.: Addison-Wesley Publishing Company, 1993). The book contains essays that provide background information about twenty cultures around the world and detailed, step-by-step instructions that show children how to do drawing and painting activities using "Kid Pix" computer software. Presented cultures are marked on a world map in the front of the book.

Dyeing the eggs in these activities provides background experiences for Activity 10 in Chapter 13, oa goat, in which students experiment with dyeing wool.

19. Before or after they listen to or read *On the Day You Were Born*, students and the teacher share (tell and/or write and illustrate) stories they have heard about the day they were born. They discuss oral tradition—within families and cultures. (See Activities 24 and 25 in Chapter 19, ir birthday, for related activities.)

20. Students and the teacher locate on a map and/or globe the places/cultures (depicted or of origin) in the books read in this chapter, including Baltimore, Maryland in the United States (*Aunt Flossie's Hats (and Crab Cakes Later)*); Berkeley, California in the United States and Russia and the Ukraine (*Chicken Sunday*); Berks County and Quakerstown, Pennsylvania in the United States (*The Egg Tree*); and the Ukraine

["Pysanky (Ukraine)" in *Kid Pix around the World: A Multicultural Computer Activity Book*].

TEACHER REFERENCE

Cloze Sentences

One-Syllable Words

Cloze Sentences 1

1. You <u>stay</u> here if you do not go away.
2. <u>Gray</u> is the name of black plus white.
3. <u>Play</u> time is a fun time to do games.
4. <u>Hay</u> is dry grass.
5. You <u>pay</u> with cash or a check when you get a thing at a store.
6. In the <u>day</u> the sun may shine, and we are not in bed.
7. A big hen may <u>lay</u> a lot of eggs.
8. A <u>stray</u> dog or cat has no home.
9. <u>Say</u> your name if you are here.

Multisyllable Words

Cloze Sentences 2

1. <u>Sunday</u> is the day before Monday.
2. An <u>ashtray</u> is a thing you may use if you smoke.
3. On the <u>runway</u> a plane will land soon.
4. <u>Friday</u> is the last day of school in the week.
5. A <u>payment</u> can be cash or a check for a thing you get at a store.
6. A <u>playful</u> kitten likes to play and have fun.
7. <u>Daytime</u> is the time when the sun is up and we are awake.
8. If you <u>repay</u> me, then you pay me back.
9. A <u>hayloft</u> is a spot where hay is kept.

Dictations

1. A <u>stray</u> dog is here to <u>stay</u> and <u>play</u> with us in the <u>hay(loft)</u>.
2. Did <u>Jay's</u> mom <u>say</u> that he can <u>stay</u> and <u>play</u> <u>relay</u> in the <u>spray</u> of the hose on this hot <u>day</u>?
3. <u>Today</u> is the <u>day</u> <u>Ray</u> has to <u>pay</u> for the <u>gray</u> <u>clay</u> on the <u>tray</u> he got on <u>Friday</u>.
4. On <u>Sunday</u> and <u>Friday</u> <u>Jay</u> can swim and dive with <u>Ray</u> in the <u>bay</u>.
5. <u>Today</u> and <u>Sunday</u> a <u>stray</u> dog can <u>play</u> on the <u>runway</u>, but on <u>Friday</u> the jets <u>may</u> hit him on the <u>way</u>.

ay (ā) day

d		ashtr	
gr		d	time
h		Frid	
l		h	loft
p		p	ment
pl		pl	ful
s		rep	
st		runw	
str		Sund	

Name _____ Date _____

© 1995 by Cynthia Conway Waring

Word List 1

ay (ā) day **ay**

day	ashtray
gray	daytime
hay	Friday
lay	hayloft
pay	payment
play	playful
say	repay
stay	runway
stray	Sunday

Name _____ Date _____

ay (ā) day

Write a word from the Word List to complete each sentence.

1. You _____ here if you do not go away.

2. _____ is the name of black plus white.

3. _____ time is a fun time to do games.

4. _____ is dry grass.

5. You _____ with cash or a check when you get a thing at a store.

6. In the _____ the sun may shine, and we are not in bed.

7. A big hen may _____ a lot of eggs.

8. A _____ dog or cat has no home.

9. _____ your name if you are here.

Name _____ Date _____

Cloze Sentences 1

ay (ā) day

Write a word from the Word List to complete each sentence.

1. _____ is the day before Monday.

2. An _____ is a thing you may use if you smoke.

3. On the _____ a plane will land soon.

4. _____ is the last day of school in the week.

5. A _____ can be cash or a check for a thing you get at a store.

6. A _____ kitten likes to play and have fun.

7. _____ is the time when the sun is up and we are awake.

8. If you _____ me, then you pay me back.

9. A _____ is a spot where hay is kept.

Name _____ Date _____

Cloze Sentences 2

8   ee   seeds   ee

BOOK LIST ════════════════════════════════════

Seeds

Pumpkin Pumpkin, Jeanne Titherington (New York: Scholastic, 1986). This short book with large type, brief text, and detailed illustrations follows a pumpkin seed through stages of growth from the time Jaime plants it until he carves a jack-o'-lantern and harvests seeds for the following spring.

The Carrot Seed, Ruth Krauss, illustrated by Crockett Johnson (New York: Harper & Row, 1945). A boy plants a carrot seed and tends it faithfully in spite of his family's lack of encouragement when it is slow to sprout, and his patience is rewarded when he harvests an enormous carrot.

Titch, Pat Hutchins (New York: Macmillan Publishing Company, 1971). Titch, the youngest of three children, finds that everything he has is the smallest, but he watches with pride as his small seed grows into a plant taller than his siblings.

Bear's Bargain, Frank Asch (New York: Scholastic, 1985). Two friends benefit from a bargain when Bear teaches Little Bird to be big with a pumpkin they grow from seed and Little Bird shows Bear how to fly with a kite they make.

A Seed Is a Promise, Claire Merrill, illustrated by Susan Swan (New York: Scholastic, 1973). This short, illustrated factual book identifies seeds in daily life, presents the processes of fertilization and growth and means of dispersion of seeds, and describes simple experiments that demonstrate properties of seeds.

All about Seeds: Do-It-Yourself Science, Melvin Berger, illustrated by Anna DeVito (New York: Scholastic, 1992). This easy-to-read book with detailed illustrations and diagrams describes simple activities and experiments that encourage observation of the properties, needs, ways of growth and travel, and uses of seeds. Includes a recipe for granola that uses a variety of seeds.

The Tiny Seed, Eric Carle (New York: Scholastic, 1987). Beginning in autumn, the book records the travel and different fates of a group of flower seeds—one of which, a tiny seed, survives to grow into a large flower which releases its seeds the following autumn to complete the cycle.

"Summer," in *Four Stories for Four Seasons*, Tomie dePaola (New York: Simon & Schuster, 1977). This book presents the adventures of four friends—Missy Cat, Master Dog, Mistress Pig, and Mister Frog—during each of the four seasons. In "Summer," each friend plants a garden that fits his or her likes and personality, including Master Dog, who plants a bone garden.

This Year's Garden, Cynthia Rylant, illustrated by Mary Szilagyi (New York: Macmillan Publishing Company, 1984). Lyrical text and richly colored illustrations combine to record the yearly cycle through the seasons of an extended family's vegetable garden.

The Empty Pot, Demi (New York: The Trumpet Club, 1990). The aged Emperor finds only one child worthy as his successor when he gives each child in the land a seed to plant and Ping, alone, appears before him with an empty pot—for all of the seeds had been cooked.

Jamie O'Rourke and the Big Potato: An Irish Folktale, Tomie dePaola (New York: Scholastic, 1992). Tomie dePaola captures the Irish storyteller's voice in his story of lazy Jamie O'Rourke, who never has to work again after he plants a seed he is given by a leprechaun and it grows into a giant potato.

Pettranella, Betty Waterton, illustrated by Ann Blades (Toronto, Ontario: Douglas & McIntyre Ltd., 1980). When her family immigrates to Canada, Pettranella promises her grandmother, who stays behind, that she will plant the seeds her grandmother gives her when they get to their new home.

Georgia Music, Helen V. Griffith, illustrated by James Stevenson (New York: Mulberry Books, 1986). When she plays her grandfather's harmonica and captures the sounds of his favorite insects and birds, a girl discovers a way to bring the joy of her grandfather's garden to him in the city apartment he shares with her and her mother.

The King's Flower, Mitsumasa Anno (New York: Philomel Books, 1976). A king, in this modern fable, demands that everything he owns be enormous until he discovers in nature a power greater than his own and learns that bigger is not always better.

Miss Rumphius, Barbara Cooney (New York: Penguin Books Inc., 1982). Fueled by her own adventurous nature, Alice Rumphius travels and lives by the sea and, inspired by her grandfather's advice, does "something to make the world more beautiful" when she plants lupine seeds throughout the countryside around her home.

SEEDS Pop-Stick-Glide, Patricia Lauber, photographs by Jerome Wexler (New York: Crown Publishers, Inc., 1981). In this nonfiction resource book, detailed close-up black and white photographs and text present a variety of ways in which seeds travel or are distributed and provide a brief introduction to the properties, fertilization, and growth of seeds.

Three Tales of Three

Goldilocks and the Three Bears

Deep in the Forest, Brinton Turkle (New York: E. P. Dutton & Co., Inc., 1976). A bear cub, in this wordless picture-book version of the "Goldilocks and the Three Bears" story, visits the cabin of a family of three people—mother, father, and little girl—samples their porridge, tries out their chairs and breaks the smallest, and romps on their beds.

When Goldilocks Went to the House of the Bears, illustrated by Jenny Rendall (New York: Scholastic, 1986). The traditional story of "Goldilocks and the Three Bears" is made easy to read with a refrain combined with repeated words and a rhyming pattern.

The Three Bears, Paul Galdone (New York: Clarion Books, 1972). Print size in the text of Galdone's version of "Goldilocks and the Three Bears" shows the ascending order of the three bears and their possessions in the well-known tale of a girl's adventures as an intruder in the house of a bear family.

Goldilocks and the Three Bears, Jan Brett (New York: G. P. Putnam's Sons, 1987). Borders that frame the illustrations provide additional details in Brett's retelling of the traditional tale of Goldilocks's visit and misadventures at the bear family's home while they take a walk as their porridge cools.

Goldilocks and the Three Bears, James Marshall (New York: Scholastic, 1988). Mischievous Goldilocks, in Marshall's humorous retelling of the story, defies her parents' warning and wanders through the forest and into the home of the three bears. Caldecott Honor Book.

Three Little Kittens

Three Little Kittens, Paul Galdone (New York: Clarion Books, 1986). Large, bold text complements Galdone's double-page illustrations of the familiar nursery rhyme about three kittens who find their lost mittens, dirty them as they eat pie, and wash them to please their mother.

Three Little Kittens, illustrated by Lilian Obligado (New York: Random House, 1974). Obligado's illustrations capture the expressions of the three kittens and their mother as they experience a range of feelings along with their adventures and misadventures in the well-known nursery rhyme.

The Three Little Pigs

The Three Little Pigs: A British Folk Tale, (Glenview, Ill.: Scott, Foresman and Company, 1971, 1976). This easy-to-read version contains the basic plot and familiar refrains of the traditional tale of the ill-fated attempts of a wolf to blow down the three pigs' houses of straw, sticks, and bricks and eat the three pigs.

Three Little Pigs and the Big Bad Wolf, Glen Rounds (New York: The Trumpet Club, 1992). Bold text highlights key words in the well-known folk tale of a wolf's pursuit of three pigs in their houses of straw, sticks, and bricks and the triumph of the last pig, who outsmarts the wolf.

The Three Little Pigs, Paul Galdone (New York: Clarion Books, 1970). In Galdone's version of the traditional story, only the third little pig, who built his house of bricks, survives—by his wits and courage—the threats of a wolf that eats his siblings (who make their houses of straw and sticks).

The Three Little Pigs, James Marshall (New York: Scholastic, 1989). Marshall's playful illustrations and colorful language combine to create a humorous retelling of the story of the pigs, who build houses of straw, sticks, and brick and are pursued by a hungry wolf (who eats all but the third pig, who outwits him).

The True Story of the 3 Little Pigs by A. Wolf, Jon Scieszka, illustrated by Lane Smith (New York: Scholastic, 1989). The wolf from the "Three Little Pigs" story tries to clear his name as he tells *his* side of the story, in which he claims he was framed and a cold caused him to sneeze and accidentally blow the pigs' houses down.

The Three Little Wolves and the Big Bad Pig, Eugene Trivizas, illustrated by Helen Oxenbury (New York: Margaret K. McElderry Books, 1993). In this humorous retelling of the familiar "Three Little Pigs" story with a contemporary setting, the animals' roles are reversed and the Big Bad Pig resorts to modern tools and technology to destroy the houses of the three "cuddly little wolves" made of bricks, cement, and metal; but all ends happily when the pig is transformed by the wolves' fourth house—made of fragrant flowers.

MOTIVATION AND EXTENSION ACTIVITIES

Seeds

1. After they read **Pumpkin Pumpkin**, students read **Jack-o'-Lantern**, by Miriam Frost and illustrated by Steven Hauge (Bothell, Wash.: The Wright Group, 1990), a book of eight pages in which children carve six pumpkins that express different emotions and, in the end, make them into a pumpkin pie.

Students act out and/or draw their own jack-o'-lanterns to accompany each page of **Jack-o'-Lantern** that show the emotions on the faces described by the adjectives in the text: happy, sad, scared, mad, silly, and sleepy. They dramatize for others to guess and compile a list of words that describe (adjectives) other emotions a jack-o'-lantern could show and draw jack-o'-lantern faces that show them. They dictate/write text following the pattern of the book and compile their illustrations into an individual or group collaborative book.

Students and the teacher draw on paper a plan/draft for a jack-o'-lantern that shows an emotion and then carve it from a pumpkin. Students describe (orally and/or in writing) and illustrate steps to follow to carve a pumpkin into a jack-o'-lantern. They then follow their own or another student's directions to carve a jack-o'-lantern and verify or revise/correct the steps and details during the process. Students and the teacher make and eat a pumpkin pie made from the contents of their own pumpkins or from canned pumpkin. They bake and eat the pumpkin seeds.

2. Students plant their own pumpkin and carrot seeds after they read **Pumpkin Pumpkin**, **The Carrot Seed**, and **Jack-o'-Lantern**.

The teacher prepares a basket (or box) with the following: flower pots; small rocks; potting soil; cups, drinking glasses, and spoons; packet(s) of pumpkin and carrot seeds; water in a container; wooden craft or popsicle sticks; and pens and/or markers (for labeling the sticks).

The teacher presents the basket and the following letter to the student(s), who read it and follow the directions as independently of the teacher as possible. (For some students, the teacher adds illustrations as clues at key points or writes the letter as a rebus-and-word message.)

Dear _____,

Today we are going to plant pumpkin seeds and carrot seeds. See if the things we need are in the basket.

We will need:

1. 2 pots
2. rocks
3. potting soil
4. a cup, a glass, and a spoon to fill the pots with potting soil
5. a packet of pumpkin seeds
6. a packet of carrot seeds
7. water
8. sticks
9. pens

To plant the seeds:

1. Put rocks on the bottom of the pots.
2. Fill the pots with potting soil.
3. Make holes for the seeds.
4. Put the seeds in the holes.
5. Put potting soil on top of the seeds.
6. Water the seeds.
7. Write "pumpkin" or "carrot" on the sticks.
8. Put the sticks in the pots.

From,
(Teacher's Name)

After they plant their pumpkin and carrot seeds, students record their observations of their growth with words and/or pictures in a log book. The teacher writes the following directions for the log book for students to follow on a regular basis (every few days):

1. Check the plants.
2. Water the plants (if needed).
3. Write the date in the log.
4. Make a sketch of the plants.
5. Then write or tell what you see. What is happening to the plants? Are the plants growing?

   3. The teacher asks students to consider the following: "If wishes came from planting seeds, which three wishes would you pick? Which three seeds would you plant?" Students and the teacher design, illustrate, and label seed packets for three kinds of "wish seeds." They then share (tell and/or write and illustrate) about their lives before and after they planted their wish seeds and had their wishes granted. (See Activity 6 in Chapter 14, old gold, for an activity related to wishes and the book *The Three Wishes* by Salzman.)

   4. Starting with the illustrations on the title page of *Titch*, students predict and then confirm or revise/correct the pattern the book follows. (Items are introduced according to size, with Titch's always the smallest.)

   5. Students read (or listen to) *You'll Soon Grow into Them, Titch*, another book about Titch by Hutchins. In the book, as Titch, the youngest in his family, tires of having to grow into his siblings' hand-me-downs, his parents buy him new clothes and present him with a baby brother to whom he can pass on his outgrown clothes. (See Activity 8 in Chapter 9, ow grow, for an activity related to the book.)

   6. Students and the teacher compile a list of the seeds that are part of their daily lives as they read *A Seed Is a Promise* and *All about Seeds: Do-It-Yourself Science*. They collect and display as many examples as they can.

   7. Students observe the properties, needs, process of growth, means of dispersion, and uses of seeds as they complete the activities and experiments described in *A Seed Is a Promise* and *All about Seeds: Do-It-Yourself Science*. They follow the recipe in *All about Seeds: Do-It-Yourself Science* to make granola using a variety of seeds. They extend the discussion of seeds (including wheat, rice, and corn) as major sources of food for people in different cultures around the world introduced in *All about Seeds: Do-It-Yourself Science*. (See Chapter 10, ea wheat, and Chapter 17, or corn.)

   8. As they read **"Summer"** in *Four Stories for Four Seasons*, students and the teacher share (tell and/or write and illustrate) about the kind of garden they would plant (or have planted) that shows something about their likes and personality; or, in a group, they each write about and/or illustrate a garden that reflects their likes and personality without indicating their identity and others try to match gardens and people.

   9. In "A Note about the Story" preceding *Jamie O'Rourke and the Big Potato: An Irish Folktale*, Tomie dePaola describes his Irish grandfather, a dramatic storyteller, from whom he first heard the story, and some of the qualities of the oral storytelling tradition in his family. Students and the teacher share about storytellers among their family and/or friends and discuss oral tradition and folklore from their own families, cultures, and experiences. They invite storytellers (special people from among family, friends, acquaintances, and/or professionals) to share stories and folklore with them and their peers and teachers through live or taped presentations.

10. Jamie O'Rourke is given a magic seed by a leprechaun that grows into a giant pratie (potato) in *Jamie O'Rourke and the Big Potato: An Irish Folktale*. Students and the teacher compare and contrast this element of the story with a similar episode in *Jack and the Beanstalk* by Faulkner. (See Chapter 10, ea wheat.)

11. In *Jamie O'Rourke and the Big Potato: An Irish Folktale*, the townspeople join together to dig up the giant potato when Jamie cannot harvest it himself. Students and the teacher compare and contrast this motif in the book with similar sequences in the cumulative stories *The Great Big Enormous Turnip*, by Tolstoy, and *The Enormous Watermelon*, by Parkes and Smith. (See Chapter 9, ow grow.)

12. Students and/or teachers who have immigrated from another country or culture (or know someone who has) share (tell and/or write and illustrate) about something they were given from their previous home to take to their new one, like the seeds that Pettranella's grandmother gave her to take to Canada in *Pettranella*. (See Chapter 30, tion immigration, for additional activities related to immigration.)

13. Before or after they read *Georgia Music*, students and/or the teacher bring in harmonicas for others to explore. Those who play the instrument make insect and bird sounds familiar to them like the sounds the girl made for her grandfather.

14. After they listen to (or read) *The King's Flower*, students follow directions to plant a tulip bulb (or other flower bulb, such as paperwhite narcissus). The teacher prepares a basket (or box) with the following: a clear glass container; small rocks; cups, drinking glasses, and spoons; flower bulbs (for forcing); water in a container; wooden craft or popsicle sticks; and pens and/or markers (for labeling the sticks).

The teacher presents the basket and the following letter to the student(s), who read it and follow the directions as independently of the teacher as possible. (For some students, the teacher adds illustrations as clues at key points or writes the letter as a rebus-and-word message.)

Dear _____,

Today we are going to plant bulbs. See if the things we need are in the basket.

We will need:

1. a glass pot
2. rocks
3. a cup, a glass, and a spoon to fill the pot with rocks
4. bulbs
5. water
6. sticks
7. pens

To plant the bulbs:

1. Fill half of the glass pot with rocks.
2. Set the bulbs on top of the rocks.
3. Put the rocks up to the top of the bulbs.

---

4. Water the bulb so that just the bottom is wet.

5. Write "bulbs" on the stick.

6. Put the stick in the glass pot.

From,

(Teacher's Name)

After they plant the flower bulbs, students record their observations of their growth with words and/or pictures in a log book. (See Activity 2 in this chapter for directions for students to follow in their log books.) Students compare and contrast the growth of their seeds and the bulbs (if they have planted both). (See Activity 2 in Chapter 1, ing king, for an additional activity related to *The King's Flower*.)

15. The teacher or students bring in a lupine plant to explore (and/or lupine seeds to plant) before or after they read *Miss Rumphius*.

16. Before or after they read *Miss Rumphius*, students and the teacher share (tell and/or write about and illustrate) two important things they might want to do (or have done) in their lives and they describe the third important thing, according to Miss Rumphius's grandfather: what they might do (or have done) to "make the world more beautiful."

Three Tales of Three

17. At the beginning of the unit, students brainstorm stories (beast tales) they know that have three major animal characters. If they have difficulty thinking of the more familiar tales, the teacher gives clues: Goldilocks and the _____ (Three Bears), "_____ lost their mittens" (The Three Little Kittens), and/ or The wolf said "I'll huff and I'll puff" and _____ said "Not by the hair of my chinny chin chin" (The Three Little Pigs).

Students and the teacher discuss the repetition of some numbers as a pattern or motif in traditional literature, often the number three. In the three tales in this unit, there are three main animal characters. Traditional tales that contain a number motif may also feature characters who receive three wishes, meet three challenges or perform three tasks, or surmount three trials.

If students suggest the "Three Blind Mice" story, they compare and contrast the interpretations with the musical score of John W. Ivimey's text for the song from Mother Goose by two illustrators: *The Complete Story of the Three Blind Mice*, illustrated by Paul Galdone (New York: The Trumpet Club, 1987), and *The Adventures of the Three Blind Mice*, illustrated by Nola Langner (New York: Scholastic, 1965). If they suggest the "Three Billy Goats Gruff" story, they compare and contrast four versions of the folk tale. (See Chapter 13, oa goat.)

18. Students tell and/or write the story for the wordless book *Deep in the Forest*.

19. Students and the teacher compare and contrast traditional versions of the "Goldilocks and the Three Bears" story with Turkle's *Deep in the Forest*, in which the intruder is a bear cub in the home of three people.

20. Students and the teacher compare and contrast different versions of each of the three well-known traditional tales in the unit. The modern and often humorous versions of the stories (including Marshall's and Scieszka's) often provide older students with motivation to read and discuss traditional tales.

21. Students dramatize the stories in the unit. They read them with expression and differentiate individual character voices, act them out in a play with props and masks/costumes, and/or present them as puppet plays.

22. Students and the teacher consider Galdone and/or Marshall as an "Illustrator Under Study" as they read the books they illustrated from the unit.

23. As they read **Goldilocks and the Three Bears**, students and the teacher explore the use of borders in the illustrations. They extend their consideration of this technique in other books by Brett and in books by Vera B. Williams. (See Activity 9 in Chapter 15, ai rain.)

24. Students and the teacher explore the physical properties of straw. (See Activities 1 and 2 in Chapter 26, aw straw.) They then experiment, in the role of the wolf, with attempting to blow down small three-dimensional models of the pigs' houses—made of straw, sticks, and bricks (or Lego® blocks). They huff, and they puff, and . . . they describe the results (orally and/or in writing) of their experiment and compare and contrast them to the experiences of the wolf in the "Three Little Pigs" stories suggested for this unit: **The Three Little Pigs: A British Folk Tale**, **Three Little Pigs and the Big Bad Wolf**, **The Three Little Pigs** (Galdone and Marshall), and **The True Story of the 3 Little Pigs by A. Wolf**.

25. After they read **The True Story of the 3 Little Pigs by A. Wolf** and **The Three Little Wolves and the Big Bad Pig**, students and the teacher discuss the "Three Little Pigs" folk tale as told traditionally from a point of view sympathetic to the three pigs contrasted with these versions of the story told from the point of view of the wolf or with characters' roles reversed. They retell/rewrite and illustrate a familiar folk/fairy tale from the point of view of a character different from the original or from the principal(s) or reverse characters' roles. They discuss points of view expressed by students/teachers involved in real-life or staged (role-played) incidents in which they have been active participants or observers.

In the beginning of **The True Story of the 3 Little Pigs by A. Wolf**, the wolf expresses his thoughts about why wolves may have become considered "big and bad" characters in books. Students and the teacher consider the stereotypical portrayal of wolves and foxes in childrens' books and folk/fairy tales. (See Activity 2 in Chapter 34, x fox.)

26. Students and the teacher locate on a map and/or globe the places/cultures (depicted or of origin) in the books read in this chapter, including China (**The Empty Pot**); Ireland (**Jamie O'Rourke and the Big Potato: An Irish Folktale**); Manitoba in Canada (**Pettranella**); Georgia and Baltimore, Maryland in the United States (**Georgia Music**); Maine in the United States (**Miss Rumphius**); and England [**The Three Little Pigs: A British Folk Tale**, **Three Little Pigs and the Big Bad Wolf**, **The Three Little Pigs** (Galdone, Marshall), **The True Story of the 3 Little Pigs by A. Wolf**, and **The Three Little Wolves and the Big Bad Pig**].

TEACHER REFERENCE ═══

Cloze Sentences

One-Syllable Words

Cloze Sentences 1

1. If you <u>speed</u> on a bike, then you go fast.

2. A <u>bee</u> can sting you if it gets mad.

3. I like to plant <u>seeds</u> in the spring.

4. May I <u>meet</u> you at the store so I can go shopping with you?

5. When it is hot, I sleep with just a <u>sheet</u> on my bed.

6. I like <u>sweet</u> things like cake and candy.

7. If you make a <u>speech</u>, then you say a lot.

Cloze Sentences 2

1. I <u>feed</u> my cat food from a can.

2. You can <u>sweep</u> with a broom.

3. A pine <u>tree</u> can have cones on it.

4. He shot a <u>deer</u> when he went hunting.

5. I brush my <u>teeth</u> before I go to bed.

6. <u>Three</u> is the same as 2 add on 1.

7. The <u>sheep</u> ate the grass on the hill.

8. My boots keep my <u>feet</u> dry.

Multisyllable Words

Cloze Sentences 3

1. <u>Fifteen</u> is the same as 5 add on 10.

2. I like to sip <u>rootbeer</u> on a hot day.

3. A <u>cheerful</u> classmate is not sad a lot of the time.

4. <u>Sixteen</u> is the same as 10 add on 6.

5. I got a <u>canteen</u> to put things to drink in when we go camping.

6. We tested the <u>deepness</u> of the pool before we went diving.

7. <u>Nineteen</u> is the same as 10 add on 9.

8. I got a <u>speeding</u> ticket for driving too fast.

9. We made a <u>beeline</u> from class to lunch so we were not late.

Dictations

1. I have <u>three</u> jobs. I <u>need</u> to <u>feed</u> my cat, <u>sweep</u>, and brush my <u>teeth</u>. Then I am <u>free</u> to go to <u>sleep</u>.

2. <u>Lee</u> will <u>meet</u> <u>three</u> men on the <u>street</u> in his <u>green</u> <u>jeep</u>. It will <u>cheer</u> him up to <u>sweep</u> up the <u>street</u> at top <u>speed</u>. Last <u>week</u> <u>Lee</u> had to <u>steer</u> his <u>jeep</u> so he did not hit a <u>deer</u> and a <u>sheep</u> in the <u>street</u>.

3. I had a bad day! I lost <u>three</u> <u>teeth</u>, bit my <u>cheek</u>, and got wet <u>feet</u>. Then I had to make a <u>speech</u> in front of <u>fifteen</u> students. When I made a <u>beeline</u> home to <u>meet</u> you, I was <u>speeding</u> and got a ticket!

ee (ē) seeds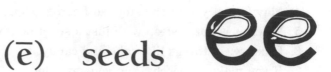

b		b	line
d	r	cant	n
f	d	ch	rful
f	t	d	pness
m	t	fift	n
s	ds	ninet	n
sh	p	rootb	r
sh	t	sixt	n
sp	ch	sp	ding
sp	d		
sw	p		
sw	t		
t	th		
thr			
tr			

Name _____ Date _____

Word List 1

ee (ē) seeds

bee	beeline
deer	canteen
feed	cheerful
feet	deepness
meet	fifteen
seeds	nineteen
sheep	rootbeer
sheet	sixteen
speech	speeding
speed	
sweep	
sweet	
teeth	
three	
tree	

Name _____ Date _____

ee (ē) seeds ℰℯ

Write a word from the Word List to complete each sentence.

1. If you _____ on a bike, then you go fast.

2. A _____ can sting you if it gets mad.

3. I like to plant _____ in the spring.

4. May I _____ you at the store so I can go shopping with you?

5. When it is hot, I sleep with just a _____ on my bed.

6. I like _____ things like cake and candy.

7. If you make a _____, then you say a lot.

Name _____ Date _____

Cloze Sentences 1

ee (ē) seeds

Write a word from the Word List to complete each sentence.

1. I _____ my cat food from a can.

2. You can _____ with a broom.

3. A pine _____ can have cones on it.

4. He shot a _____ when he went hunting.

5. I brush my _____ before I go to bed.

6. _____ is the same as 2 add on 1.

7. The _____ ate the grass on the hill.

8. My boots keep my _____ dry.

Name _____ Date _____

Cloze Sentences 2

ee (ē) seeds

Write a word from the Word List to complete each sentence.

1. _____ is the same as 5 add on 10.

2. I like to sip _____ on a hot day.

3. A _____ classmate is not sad a lot of the time.

4. _____ is the same as 10 add on 6.

5. I got a _____ to put things to drink in when we go camping.

6. We tested the _____ of the pool before we went diving.

7. _____ is the same as 10 add on 9.

8. I got a _____ ticket for driving too fast.

9. We made a _____ from class to lunch so we were not late.

Name _____ Date _____

Cloze Sentences 3

9   ow   grow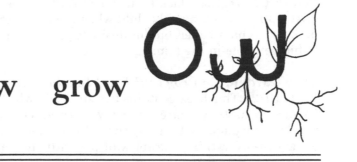

BOOK LIST

Growing

The Great Big Enormous Turnip, Alexei Tolstoy (Glenview, Ill.: Scott, Foresman and Company, 1971, 1976). In this cumulative tale, when an old man plants a turnip it grows so large that he must call members of his family and their pets to help him pull it up. Includes background information about turnips and lyrics and musical score for "The Turnip Song."

The Enormous Watermelon, Brenda Parkes and Judith Smith, illustrated by Mary Davy (Crystal Lake, Ill.: Rigby Education, 1986). In this cumulative story, Old Mother Hubbard plants a small seed which grows into an enormous watermelon, and she needs to call nursery-rhyme characters to help her pull it up. The flap format reveals a picture clue to the next character she will call in the series.

Down by the Bay: Raffi Songs to Read, illustrated by Nadine Bernard Westcott (New York: Crown Publishers, Inc., 1987). Between rhyming refrains, two children in Westcott's humorous illustrations astound their mother with animals in outrageous contexts that rhyme with their names.

You'll Soon Grow into Them, Titch, Pat Hutchins (New York: William Morrow & Company, Inc., 1983). As Titch, the youngest in his family, tires of having to grow into his siblings' hand-me-downs, his parents buy him new clothes and present him with a baby brother to whom he can pass on his outgrown clothes.

Shoes from Grandpa, Mem Fox, illustrated by Patricia Mullins (New York: The Trumpet Club, 1989). When Jessie outgrows her clothes, Grandpa offers to buy her new shoes, and each member of her extended family promises to buy a piece of clothing to go with them in this rhyming cumulative story.

Growing Vegetable Soup, Lois Ehlert (San Diego: Harcourt Brace & Company, 1987). Giant text and word labels for all items pictured combine with Ehlert's brilliant illustrations to show the stages of growth and tools used as a child and father grow vegetables and make soup. Includes recipe for vegetable soup.

The Giving Tree, Shel Silverstein (New York: Harper & Row, 1964). A boy's loyal and generous friend, the tree who loves him, has a gift to offer him at every stage of his life.

Peter's Chair, Ezra Jack Keats (New York: Harper & Row, 1967). At first, Peter resists giving up his place as only child when the cradle and crib he has outgrown are painted pink for his baby sister, but his desire to paint his small chair for her marks his transition to his new role in the family.

"The Garden," in ***Frog and Toad Together***, Arnold Lobel (New York: Harper & Row, 1971, 1972). This book contains five stories in which Frog and Toad celebrate the joys of friendship as they share everyday experiences and their fears and dreams. In "The Garden," inspired by Frog's garden, Toad plants his own garden and finds it hard work as he does everything (except wait patiently) to make the seeds start to grow.

Grandpa's Too-Good Garden, James Stevenson (New York: Greenwillow Books, 1989). Grandpa tells Louie and Mary Ann a humorous tall tale about the adventures he and Uncle Wainey shared as children when their garden grew to giant proportions.

MOTIVATION AND EXTENSION ACTIVITIES

1. Students and the teacher continue to explore the theme of "seeds and growing" (introduced in Chapter 8, ee seeds) as they read, respond to, and discuss the books in this chapter.

2. Before or after they read ***The Great Big Enormous Turnip***, students and the teacher examine a raw turnip and sample cooked turnip. They discuss the background information that follows the story and their own knowledge and experience with turnips. They sing "The Turnip Song" at the back of the book.

3. Students and the teacher join Old Mother Hubbard, Humpty Dumpty, Little Miss Muffet, Jack and Jill, and Wee Willy Winky, who "all sat down to eat" a watermelon in ***The Enormous Watermelon***. They enjoy a seed-spitting contest—*outside!*

4. As actors, dancers, mimists, and/or puppeteers, students dramatize the cumulative nature and pattern of ***The Great Big Enormous Turnip*** and ***The Enormous Watermelon***.

5. In ***Jamie O'Rourke and the Big Potato: An Irish Folktale***, by Tomie dePaola (see Chapter 8, ee seeds), the townspeople join together to dig up the giant potato when Jamie cannot harvest it. Students and the teacher compare and contrast this motif in the book with similar sequences in the cumulative stories ***The Great Big Enormous Turnip*** and ***The Enormous Watermelon***.

6. Starting with the words (adjectives) from ***The Great Big Enormous Turnip*** and ***The Enormous Watermelon***, students and the teacher compile a list of words that mean the same or nearly the same as (synonyms) *big, great,* and *enormous*. The teacher introduces or reviews the dictionary and the thesaurus as resource books. Students and the teacher read and discuss ***The King's Flower***, by Mitsumasa Anno (Chapter 1, ing king), a modern fable in which a king demands that everything he owns be enormous until he discovers in nature a power greater than his own and learns that bigger is not always better.

7. Students and the teacher sing the tune for the song included at the back of the book as they read ***Down by the Bay: Raffi Songs to Read***. They create and illustrate additional rhyming verses and compile them into individual or collaborative group books. (See Activity 3 in Chapter 3, open syllable go, for additional books and activities that feature rhyming.)

8. Before or after they read *You'll Soon Grow into Them, Titch*, *Shoes from Grandpa*, and *Peter's Chair*, students and the teacher share (tell and/or write and illustrate) what they do when they outgrow their clothes or other items. If several family members, friends, or community agencies/organizations are part of their recycling chain, they draw and label a diagram showing the journey of one piece of clothing or hand-me-down/along item.

9. After they read *Growing Vegetable Soup*, students illustrate and label the items, tools, and actions listed in each step of the recipe on the back of the book (as Ehlert does in the book). They make individual recipes or they compile their individual parts into one group collaborative recipe. They verify and/or revise/correct details, steps, and sequence as they follow their illustrated recipe to make vegetable soup. Then they eat the soup.

10. Peter's mother and father in *Peter's Chair* are patient and supportive as Peter learns to come to terms with an important time of change and transition in his life. Students and the teacher compare and contrast Peter's parents and parents (some of whom are more sensitive than others) in other books. (See Activity 2 in Chapter 32, c Frances Cinderella fancy, for a list of suggested books.) They share (tell and/or write and illustrate) about a time of change and transition in their lives (including the birth or adoption of a sibling, the remarriage of a parent.)

11. Students make finger puppets for the characters in **"The Garden" in *Frog and Toad Together*** (Frog, Toad, and the narrator) and present a puppet show of the story. They draw the characters on paper (and the narrator, in the likeness of the person narrating) and glue or sew them onto fingers that have been cut from old gloves or mittens, and they make simple props and scenery based on information from the illustrations and text of the story.

Students edit or rewrite the story as a play. They indicate parts by writing the names of characters in the margin or by underlining each part with a different color (Frog—green, Toad—brown, and narrator—another color). They omit the words that indicate speakers—for example, "said Frog," "asked Toad." One student (using three different voices and the puppets to differentiate the characters), a student and the teacher, or several students read the parts to present the play.

12. To support some students, the teacher and student(s) alternate reading the narrative text and the characters' dialogue (in the cartoon "bubbles") in *Grandpa's Too-Good Garden*.

13. After they read *Grandpa's Too-Good Garden* by James Stevenson, students and the teacher read and discuss other tall tales—modern and modern interpretations of traditional tales—including the following:

Also by James Stevenson:

"Could Be Worse!" (New York: Penguin Books, 1977).

The Great Big Especially Beautiful Easter Egg (New York: Scholastic, 1983).

We Hate Rain! (New York: Greenwillow Books, 1988). (See Chapter 15, ai rain.)

By Steven Kellogg:

Johnny Appleseed: A Tall Tale (New York: Scholastic, 1988).

Paul Bunyan: A Tall Tale (New York: William Morrow & Company, 1984).

Pecos Bill: A Tall Tale (New York: Scholastic, 1986).

By Judi Barrett and illustrated by Ron Barrett:

Cloudy with a Chance of Meatballs (New York: Atheneum, 1978).

By Ezra Jack Keats:

John Henry: An American Legend (New York: Scholastic, 1965).

Students create their own tall tale "Would You Rather" book (individual or collaborative book) patterned after *Would you rather . . .*, by John Burningham (New York: Thomas Y. Crowell, 1978), in which readers are challenged to select one of several fantastic choices pictured in which they could become tall tale characters. Students and the teacher discuss the concept of large size as it relates to tall tales and in conjunction with their discussion related to Activity 6 in this chapter.

14. Students and the teacher locate on a map and/or globe the places/cultures (depicted or of origin) in the books read in this chapter, including Russia (*The Great Big Enormous Turnip*); Leominster and Longmeadow in Massachusetts, the Allegheny Mountains, Pennsylvania, Ohio, Lake Erie, Indiana, Illinois, Missouri, the Rocky Mountains, and California in the United States (*Johnny Appleseed: A Tall Tale*); Maine, the Appalachian Mountains, the St. Lawrence River, the Great Lakes, Vermont, the Great Plains, the Rocky Mountains, Texas, Arizona, the Grand Canyon, and California in the United States (*Paul Bunyan: A Tall Tale*); New England, Texas, the Arctic Circle, the Grand Canyon, and California in the United States (*Pecos Bill: A Tall Tale*); and the Atlantic and Pacific Oceans (*John Henry*).

TEACHER REFERENCE

Cloze Sentences

One-Syllable Words

Cloze Sentences 1

1. The <u>snow</u> was three feet deep, and we had fun jumping in the drifts.
2. I hope the wind will <u>blow</u> so I can fly my kite.
3. My mom <u>throws</u> the ball to me so I can catch it.
4. I <u>grow</u> plants from seeds.
5. It takes skill to drive a big truck in a <u>low</u> tunnel.

Cloze Sentences 2

1. My job at home is to <u>mow</u> the grass when it needs it.
2. We may see a big black <u>crow</u> flying in the sky while we plant the seeds.
3. I can <u>show</u> you the way to lunch when I go.
4. A brook may <u>flow</u> fast in the spring.
5. I sit in the <u>row</u> of desks in front of you in math class.

Cloze Sentences 3

1. The wind was <u>blowing</u> the snow into deep drifts.
2. The sun was <u>yellow</u> until it set, and then it was a deep red.
3. With his bow and <u>arrow</u> he shot a deer.
4. If you <u>follow</u> me, I will show you the way to my home.
5. We had fun <u>throwing</u> snowballs until we hit a window and broke it.
6. When I jump rope in the sun, I can see my <u>shadow</u> jump rope too.
7. It had <u>snowed</u> while I was sleeping, and when I woke up the trees had white caps on them.
8. On the <u>lowest</u> branch of the tree I put my chickadee and jay feeder so I can fill it with seeds and not have to use a ladder.
9. If you look out a <u>window</u> on a day when it is snowing, you can see a lot of white flakes.

Dictations

1. You can <u>grow</u> grass in a <u>row</u> and <u>mow</u> it <u>low</u> but not in the <u>snow</u>!
2. The <u>crow</u> had <u>flown</u> nine miles when the <u>snow</u> began to <u>blow</u>.
3. The bandit jumped from the <u>window</u>, and the cop <u>followed</u> him. He ran fast and kept <u>low</u>. The <u>yellow</u> moon cast his <u>shadow</u> as he went. He ran like an <u>arrow</u>, but he was too <u>slow</u> to <u>throw</u> off the cop.

ow (ō) grow

bl	arr
cr	bl ing
fl	foll
gr	l est
l	shad
m	sn ed
r	thr ing
sh	wind
sn	yell
thr s	

Name _____ Date _____

ow (ō) grow

blow	arrow
crow	blowing
flow	follow
grow	lowest
low	shadow
mow	snowed
row	throwing
show	window
snow	yellow
throws	

Name _____ Date _____

Word List 2

ow (ō) grow

Write a word from the Word List to complete each sentence.

1. The _____ was three feet deep, and we had fun jumping in the drifts.

2. I hope the wind will _____ so I can fly my kite.

3. My mom _____ the ball to me so I can catch it.

4. I _____ plants from seeds.

5. It takes skill to drive a truck in a _____ tunnel.

Name _____ Date _____

Cloze Sentences 1

ow (ō) grow

Write a word from the Word List to complete each sentence.

1. My job at home is to _____ the grass when it needs it.

2. We may see a big black _____ flying in the sky while we plant the seeds.

3. I can _____ you the way to lunch when I go.

4. A brook may _____ fast in the spring.

5. I sit in the _____ of desks in front of you in math class.

Name _____ Date _____

ow (ō) grow

Write a word from the Word Lists to complete each sentence.

1. The wind was _____ the snow into deep drifts.

2. The sun was _____ until it set, and then it was a deep red.

3. With his bow and _____ he shot a deer.

4. If you _____ me, I will show you the way to my home.

5. We had fun _____ snowballs until we hit a window and broke it.

6. When I jump rope in the sun, I can see my _____ jump rope too.

7. It had _____ while I was sleeping, and when I woke up the trees had white caps on them.

8. On the _____ branch of the tree I put my chickadee and jay feeder so I can fill it with seeds and not have to use a ladder.

9. If you look out a _____ on a day when it is snowing, you can see a lot of white flakes.

Name _____ Date _____

10 ea wheat

BOOK LIST ══

Wheat and Beans

The Little Red Hen: A Favorite Folk-Tale, illustrated by J. P. Miller (Racine, Wis.: Western Publishing Company, Inc., 1954). After a duck, goose, cat, and pig refuse to help her plant, tend, reap, grind, and bake the wheat into bread, the hen refuses their offer to help her eat it and she eats it all herself.

The Little Red Hen, illustrated by Lucinda McQueen (New York: Scholastic, 1985). In McQueen's version of the story, it is a gossiping goose, a vain cat, and a sleepy dog who answer "Not I" when the hen asks for help with the wheat and who must watch as she eats all the bread she bakes.

The Little Red Hen, Paul Galdone (New York: Clarion Books, 1973). Three lazy animals—cat, dog, and mouse—learn their lesson and become good helpers around the house after the hen gives them none of the cake she made because they had refused to help her with the wheat.

"Not Now!" Said the Cow, Joanne Oppenheim, illustrated by Chris Demarest (New York: Bantam Doubleday Dell Publishing Group, Inc., 1989). In this cumulative tale, a variation of the "Little Red Hen" story, a crow asks a series of friends to help him plant some corn seed. In turn, they answer no in their own ways that rhyme with their names.

Jack and the Beanstalk, illustrated by Matt Faulkner (New York: Scholastic, 1965, 1986). The supportive text and Faulkner's detailed illustrations make this an easy-to-read version of the traditional tale of Jack's adventures in the land of the giant, which he enters by climbing a beanstalk grown from magic beans.

"The Little Red Hen" and "Jack's Bean Problem," in ***The Stinky Cheese Man and Other Fairly Stupid Tales***, Jon Scieszka, illustrated by Lane Smith (New York: Viking, 1992). This book contains eleven humorous modern retellings of well-known traditional tales. "The Little Red Hen" appears throughout the book and meets her demise at its end, made into a sandwich out of the bread she baked and eaten by a giant. In "Jack's Bean Problem," Jack tells an endless story to prevent the giant from grinding Jack's bones into bread.

Jack and the Beanstalk, Steven Kellogg (New York: The Trumpet Club, 1991). Characteristic Kellogg illustrations accompany this adaptation of the classic English tale which combines vocabulary true to its origin and contemporary humor.

MOTIVATION AND EXTENSION ACTIVITIES

1. At the beginning of the unit, students and the teacher explore stalks of wheat and beanstalks. They experiment with the hand-threshing process for wheat and snap green beans by hand. They compile (and illustrate) a list of wheat and bean forms and products and assemble as many items on their list as possible for display during the unit.

2. After they read the three versions of the "Little Red Hen" story—*The Little Red Hen: A Favorite Folk-Tale* (Miller), *The Little Red Hen* (McQueen), and *The Little Red Hen* (Galdone)—students and the teacher discuss similarities and differences in the books: the characters; the details, steps, and sequence in the process from planting to eating the wheat; the food the Little Red Hen baked using the wheat; and the ending of the story. They select their favorite version and identify the criteria on which they based their choice. They dramatize their favorite version of the story. They read it with expression and with voices that identify individual characters, act it out in a play, create and present movements or a dance, or present a puppet show.

3. Students bake and eat their own loaves of bread. (Those who say "Not I" during the process are excluded from eating it!)

4. *"Not Now!" Said the Cow* is a cumulative tale, based on the "Little Red Hen" story, in which a crow asks a series of animals to help him plant some corn seed and, like the Little Red Hen, he eats the popcorn he had grown and popped—all by himself. (See Activity 4 in Chapter 17, or corn, for an activity related to the book.) Students and the teacher compare and contrast the two stories.

5. After they read the "Little Red Hen" stories—*The Little Red Hen: A Favorite Folk-Tale* (Miller), *The Little Red Hen* (McQueen), and *The Little Red Hen* (Galdone)—students and the teacher discuss a theme or implied moral/lesson of the story: Those who do not work do not eat. They compare and contrast this story with two versions of an Aesop's fable with a similar theme and moral/lesson that is read aloud: "The Ants and the Grasshopper" in *The Aesop for Children*, illustrated by Milo Winter (Chicago: Rand McNally & Co., 1919, 1947) and "The Grasshopper and the Ants" in *Aesop's Fables Retold in Verse*, Tom Paxton, illustrated by Robert Rayevsky (New York: William Morrow & Company, Inc., 1988). (See Chapter 29, consonant-le fable, for additional books and activities related to fables.)

Students listen to *Frederick*, a Caldecott Honor Book by Leo Lionni (New York: The Trumpet Club, 1967), read aloud. In the book, Frederick, the mouse, gathers colors and images during the fall while the other mice gather food, and when the food supply is depleted near the end of winter it is Frederick's poetry that nourishes them. Students suggest themes and lessons/morals for *Frederick* and discuss the ways in which the story is similar and different from the aforementioned Little Red Hen stories and Aesop's fables.

6. As oral interpreters, actors, and/or puppeteers, students dramatize *Jack and the Beanstalk*. They interpret individual character voices as they read the story, act it out in a play, or present a puppet show.

7. The motif of a person given a magic seed by a magical being is common in traditional folk tales. The magic seed often provides for the person's basic needs to be met for the rest of his or her life. (See Activity 7 in Chapter 14, old gold, for an activity related to this motif and theme.)

In *Jack and the Beanstalk*, Jack is given magic beans by an old man in exchange for the family's old cow, and they grow into the beanstalk that enables his mother and him to live without working for the rest of their lives. Similarly, in *Jamie O'Rourke and the Big Potato: An Irish Folktale*, by Tomie dePaola (New York: Scholastic, 1992), a leprechaun gives lazy Jamie a magic seed that grows into a giant pratie (potato), and he never has to work again.

Students listen to or read *Jamie O'Rourke and the Big Potato: An Irish Folktale* and identify the motif in the two tales and compare and contrast the two stories. (See Activities 9, 10, and 11 in Chapter 8, ee seeds, for additional activities related to *Jamie O'Rourke and the Big Potato: An Irish Folktale*.)

8. Students listen to or read "The Little Red Hen" and "Jack's Bean Problem" in *The Stinky Cheese Man and Other Fairly Stupid Tales* and discuss the way Scieszka has woven the two stories into the book. The modern and often humorous versions of the stories often provide older readers with motivation to read and discuss traditional tales.

9. Students and the teacher locate on a map and/or globe the places/cultures (depicted or of origin) in the books read in this chapter, including England (*Jack and the Beanstalk*), Greece ("The Ants and the Grasshopper" in *The Aesop for Children* and "The Grasshopper and the Ants" in *Aesop's Fables Retold in Verse*); and Ireland (*Jamie O'Rourke and the Big Potato: An Irish Folktale*).

TEACHER REFERENCE

Cloze Sentences

One-Syllable Words

Cloze Sentences 1

1. A <u>flea</u> is an insect that likes to stay on dogs and cats.
2. Ice <u>cream</u> cones are fun to eat!
3. <u>Meat</u> can be beef, ham, hot dogs, or chicken.
4. A <u>beach</u> is a strip of sand by the shore of the sea.
5. With my <u>ears</u> I can hear you.
6. You may see a <u>seal</u> and a seagull near the sea.

Cloze Sentences 2

1. A <u>scream</u> can be a yell for help.
2. <u>East</u> is on a side of a state and is not on the west side.
3. A <u>year</u> has twelve months.
4. The Little Red Hen planted <u>wheat</u>, and then she picked it and took it to the mill.
5. I like to eat green <u>beans</u> with my meal.

Multisyllable Words

Cloze Sentences 3

1. I put my tea in a <u>teacup</u>, and then I drink it while it is hot.
2. You may eat a <u>peanut</u> butter and jelly or jam sandwich for lunch.
3. When you are within <u>earshot</u> you can hear me.

4. You may see a <u>seagull</u> fly in the sky near the sea.

5. <u>Screaming</u> is the same as yelling.

6. If you are <u>fearless</u>, you are not scared of things.

7. I use a <u>teaspoon</u> to mix the milk in my coffee before I drink it.

8. The windows in the bathroom kept <u>steaming</u> up when I was taking a bath.

Dictations

1. We had <u>cream</u> of <u>wheat</u> and one <u>peach</u> to <u>eat</u> as a <u>treat</u>.

2. <u>Jean</u> <u>treated</u> Mr. <u>Bean</u> to a <u>cheap</u> <u>meal</u> at a <u>clean</u> spot <u>near</u> the <u>beach</u>. It was not a <u>feast</u> in the <u>least</u>! <u>Each</u> of them had <u>lean meat</u>, a bag of <u>peanuts</u>, and a <u>steaming</u> <u>teacup</u> of <u>spearmint</u> <u>tea</u> with a <u>teaspoon</u> of <u>cream</u>.

3. I did <u>hear</u> with my own <u>ears</u> of the theft of a <u>peach</u>, <u>cream</u> of <u>wheat</u>, and <u>bleach</u> at the store <u>near</u> me, so I <u>beat</u> it to the <u>beach</u> by way of the <u>stream</u>.

4. The <u>meat</u> was <u>cheap</u> at the store, but the man <u>cheated</u> <u>Jean</u> by <u>sneaking</u> in some fat. That <u>treatment</u> did not <u>mislead</u> <u>fearless</u> <u>Jean</u>! She was not <u>pleased</u>, so she will not shop at that store one more time. I hope that it <u>teaches</u> the man that it does not pay to <u>cheat</u>!

ea (ē) wheat

b__ch	__rshot
b__ns	f__rless
cr__m	p__nut
__rs	s__gull
__st	scr__ming
fl__	st__ming
m__t	t__cup
scr__m	t__spoon
s__l	
wh__t	
y__r	

Name _____ Date _____

Word List 1

ea (ē) wheat

beach	earshot
beans	fearless
cream	peanut
ears	seagull
east	screaming
flea	steaming
meat	teacup
scream	teaspoon
seal	
wheat	
year	

Name _____ Date _____

Word List 2

ea (ē) wheat

Write a word from the Word List to complete each sentence.

1. A _____ is an insect that likes to stay on dogs and cats.

2. Ice _____ cones are fun to eat!

3. _____ can be beef, ham, hot dogs, or chicken.

4. A _____ is a strip of sand by the shore of the sea.

5. With my _____ I can hear you.

6. You may see a _____ and a seagull near the sea.

Name _____ Date _____

Cloze Sentences 1

ea (ē) wheat

Write a word from the Word List to complete each sentence.

1. A _____ can be a yell for help.

2. _____ is on a side of a state and is not on the west side.

3. A _____ has twelve months.

4. The Little Red Hen planted _____, and then she picked it and took it to the mill.

5. I like to eat green _____ with my meal.

Name _____ Date _____

Cloze Sentences 2

ea (ē) wheat

Write a word from the Word List to complete each sentence.

1. I put my tea in a _____ , and then I drink it while it is hot.

2. You may eat a _____ butter and jelly or jam sandwich for lunch.

3. When you are within _____ you can hear me.

4. You may see a _____ fly in the sky near the sea.

5. _____ is the same as yelling.

6. If you are _____ , you are not scared of things.

7. I use a _____ to mix the milk in my coffee before I drink it.

8. The windows in the bathroom kept _____ up when I was taking a bath.

Name _____ Date _____

Cloze Sentences 3

11   y   penny

BOOK LIST

Penny Stories

Henny Penny, H. Werner Zimmermann (New York: Scholastic, 1989). Amusing water-color illustrations and easy-to-read large print combine to tell the familiar cumulative story of a hen who, after she is hit on the head by an acorn, passes on her panic about the sky falling to an increasing collection of friends and leads them, on the way to tell the king, to an untimely end in the fox's cave.

"Chicken Licken," in *The Stinky Cheese Man and Other Fairly Stupid Tales*, Jon Scieszka, illustrated by Lane Smith (New York: Viking, 1992). In one of eleven humorous modern retellings of well-known traditional tales, Henny Penny becomes Chicken Licken, who, with her friends, meets her demise on the way to tell the President that "the sky is falling"—not in the fox's cave, but when the book's Table of Contents falls on them.

Chicken Little, Steven Kellogg (New York: The Trumpet Club, 1985). Kellogg's story is a modern, humorous retelling of the traditional tale with a contemporary setting and police rather than a king. In the end, the plotting and poultry-loving fox villain is sentenced to prison and a vegetarian diet, and the hen tells her grandchildren the story under an oak tree she plants (from the acorn, of course).

Foolish Rabbit's Big Mistake, Rafe Martin, illustrated by Ed Young (New York: G. P. Putnam's Sons, 1985). In possibly the oldest known Henny Penny story, animal after animal heeds rabbit's hysterical cries that "the earth's breaking up!" and follows him as he runs for his life until a wise lion reassures them and teaches them a lesson.

Picking Peas for a Penny, Angela Shelf Medearis, illustrated by Charles Shaw (New York: Scholastic, 1990). This rhythmic counting rhyme tells the story, first told to the author by her mother, of a three-generational family who pick peas in the heat of a summer day during the Depression of the 1930s in the United States.

Penny and the Four Questions, Nancy E. Krulik, illustrated by Marian Young (New York: Scholastic, 1993). Penny learns about friendship when she shares the reading of the four questions at her family's Passover Seder and the *afikomen* and gift with a girl who has recently immigrated to the United States from Russia.

Teeny Tiny Stories

The Teeny Tiny Woman, Jane O'Connor, illustrated by R. W. Alley (New York: Random House, 1986). The words *teeny tiny* are used to describe everything in the woman's life, including a bone that she brings home from a graveyard and that provides her with a teeny tiny scary adventure with the bone's owner—a ghost.

Teeny Tiny, Jill Bennett, illustrated by Tomie dePaola (New York: The Trumpet Club, 1985). A teeny tiny cat and a teeny tiny dog and several ghosts join the teeny tiny woman in Bennett's retelling of the traditional tale, which is illustrated with the muted colors of dePaola's drawings.

The Teeny Tiny Woman: A Folktale, Margot Zemach (New York: Scholastic Book Services, 1965). Zemach's version of the folktale is teeny tiny—only 4¼" by 4¼"—small enough to fit one hand of the most teeny tiny reader. Two-color drawings, in red and purple, illustrate the tale.

MOTIVATION AND EXTENSION ACTIVITIES

Penny Stories

1. Students and the teacher read dramatically the parts of the characters with individual character voices in the "Henny Penny Stories": ***Henny Penny***, **"Chicken Licken"** in ***The Stinky Cheese Man and Other Fairly Stupid Tales***, ***Chicken Little***, and ***Foolish Rabbit's Big Mistake***. They choose one word (adjective) that describes the voice that they have used for each character. The teacher (or students) writes the words so that students can discover the pattern: two-syllable words that end with y ($\bar{e}$). Students offer, for example,

In the "Henny Penny" stories:

Henny Penny—whiny

Cocky Locky—braggy

Ducky Lucky—quacky

Goosey Loosey—honky

Turkey Lurkey—gobbly

Foxy Loxy—raspy

In Foolish Rabbit's Big Mistake:

the foolish rabbit—scaredy

the first bear—sleepy

the second bear—munchy

the elephant—rumbly

the snake—hissy

the lion—growly

2. The modern, humorous versions of stories such as the **"Chicken Licken"** in ***The Stinky Cheese Man and Other Fairly Stupid Tales*** (by Jon Scieszka) and ***Chicken Licken*** (by Steven Kellogg) retellings of "Henny Penny" stories often provide older readers with motivation to read and study the traditional tales. Students and the

teacher compare and contrast the traditional and modern versions. They tell and/or write and illustrate their own modern versions of the "Henny Penny" story or other traditional tales.

3. In a note from the author, Rafe Martin identifies *Foolish Rabbit's Big Mistake* as one of hundreds of traditional Jataka tales from India that have been presented (through oral tradition and the arts) for almost 2500 years. This story may be the oldest "Henny Penny" story known. Students and the teacher compare and contrast this story with the traditional and modern "Henny Penny" stories they have read.

4. On the page of *Foolish Rabbit's Big Mistake* that introduces the snake, characters are described as "screaming rabbits," "moaning bears," "trumpeting elephants," and a "hissing" snake. On the next page they are described as "running," "screeching," and "panting." Students and the teacher think of and write other *ing* words that could describe characters in the book, including the wise lion: roaring, growling, thinking, reassuring, questioning, insisting, yawning, and sleeping.

5. Students and the teacher tell and/or write and illustrate stories of unfounded fears they may have had. They compare and contrast them with the fears of characters in the "Henny Penny" stories they have read.

6. Students and the teacher discuss examples they may know from real life of the passing of rumors and mob hysteria similar to those read about in the "Henny Penny" stories. Students experience this phenomenon as they play the game of "Telephone," in which they pass a message from one person to the next, and it often becomes misunderstood and confused (and comical when it is revealed at the end of the turn). They read and discuss other books in which misunderstandings result in rumors, including *The Surprise Party* by Hutchins (see Activity 6 in Chapter 1, *ing king*) and *Did You Say, "Fire"?* by Cowley (see Activity 4 in Chapter 6, vowel-consonant-e syllable *cake*).

7. Students and the teacher read aloud *Picking Peas for a Penny* and clap their hands, tap their feet, or use rhythm instruments to mark the near-rap beat.

8. Students and the teacher locate the period of the Depression of the 1930s in the United States, depicted in *Picking Peas for a Penny*, on a time line. They create a large time line in the classroom on which they mark books from different periods in history and to which they add during units of study.

9. In *Picking Peas for a Penny*, Grandfather gives the children a penny for each pound of peas they pick, and the girl is able to buy "candy, gum, and caramel corn" and a bottle of soda for 5 cents. The teacher provides additional information to help students develop an understanding about the difference between the amount a penny could buy during the Depression in the United States and currently. Students and the teacher compare the cost of food, cars, homes, clothing, and other items familiar to the students during the two periods in history. If possible, they explore magazine and newspaper advertisements from different periods in time in the United States.

The teacher reads aloud *Immigrant Girl* by Harvey (see Chapter 30, *tion immigration*), and students and the teacher discuss how much a few pennies could buy in New York City in 1910. (A movie at the nickelodeon cost 5 cents, and a pretzel or a roasted sweet potato cost 3 cents.)

10. Students and the teacher explore the buying power of a penny today in the United States.

   ♦ The teacher provides a large jar of pennies and the other coins and bills needed to complete the following activity. Together, students and the teacher show the number of pennies in a nickel (5), a dime (10), a quarter (25), a half dollar (50), a dollar—bill and coin—(100), $5.00 (500), $10.00 (1000), and $50.00 (5000). They discuss typical items that can be purchased for each amount of money.

♦ Students and the teacher bring in items that can be purchased for a penny, including penny candy and a penny's worth of bulk items: nails, washers, screws, rice, beans, peas, lentils, raisins, flour, etc.

♦ Students and the teacher extend their understanding of money, buying power, and relationships between coins and bills as they read and discuss *If You Made a Million*, by David M. Schwartz and illustrated by Steven Kellogg (New York: Scholastic, 1989), and *How Much Is a Million*, by David M. Schwartz and illustrated by Steven Kellogg (New York: Scholastic, 1985).

11. Before or after they read *Penny and the Four Questions*, the teacher shows students nesting toys and/or dolls, like the one Penny's new friend, Natasha, brought with her from Russia.

12. As they read *Penny and the Four Questions*, students and teachers who share Passover Seder with their family and friends share (tell and/or write about and illustrate) their experiences.

13. Students and the teacher discuss the different ways the word *penny*, a word with multiple meanings, is used in the unit: as part of a rhyming name for a hen in *Henny Penny* and *Chicken Little*, as the name of a coin in *Picking Peas for a Penny*, and as a girl's name in *Penny and the Four Questions*.

Teeny Tiny Stories

14. Students and the teacher choose their favorite version of the "Teeny Tiny" stories—*The Teeny Tiny Woman* (O'Connor, Zemach) and *Teeny Tiny*. They identify the criteria on which they based their selection.

15. Students and the teacher locate on a map and/or globe the places/cultures (of origin or depicted) in the books read in this chapter, including India (*Foolish Rabbit's Big Mistake*) and Russia (*Penny and the Four Questions*).

TEACHER REFERENCE ═══════════════════════════════════

Cloze Sentences

Multisyllable Words

Cloze Sentences 1

1. When it is <u>misty</u>, it is hazy and foggy.
2. If a man is <u>nasty</u>, then he is mean.
3. I like to sit in a <u>shady</u> spot by a tree on a hot day.
4. On a <u>windy</u> day it is very breezy and I can fly a kite.
5. My cat is so <u>lazy</u> that all she will do is eat and sleep!
6. The frog felt <u>slimy</u> to me when I picked it up at the pond.
7. I cannot hike on a <u>stony</u> path with bare feet.

Cloze Sentences 2

1. <u>Fifty</u> is the same as 5 times 10.
2. I like to ride my black and white <u>pony</u> when I have the time.
3. You are <u>thrifty</u> if you can save a lot of cash.
4. <u>Twenty</u> is the same as 10 times 2.
5. His truck is <u>shiny</u> when he rubs wax on it and then wipes it off with a clean cloth.
6. If you have <u>plenty</u>, then you have lots and lots to share.
7. The <u>baby</u> wore a bib when he ate his lunch.

Cloze Sentences 3

1. My mom has a <u>ruby</u> ring that is deep red.
2. With a <u>penny</u> you can get a tenth as much as you can get with a dime.
3. A <u>tiny</u> puppy is not big, and I can pick it up in my hand.
4. Your <u>duty</u> is to do the things needed for your job.
5. If you feel <u>happy</u>, then you do not feel sad.
6. If my home gets <u>dusty</u>, then I need to sweep and clean it.

Dictations

1. It was a damp and <u>misty</u> day. The wind had a <u>nasty</u> sting. <u>Betsy</u> was not <u>lazy</u>. It was her <u>duty</u> to get <u>hefty</u> logs and make a fire in a <u>shady</u> and <u>stony</u> spot. The fire was <u>smoky</u>, but <u>Betsy</u> was <u>cozy</u>.

2. <u>Henry</u> will tell the <u>jury</u> that he had kept his <u>tiny</u>, <u>shiny</u> <u>ruby</u> ring and <u>plenty</u> of cash in a <u>tidy</u> safe, but that a <u>nasty</u> bandit had stolen them in a <u>shady</u> theft. It will be the <u>duty</u> of the <u>jury</u> to tell if the man on the bench did take <u>Henry's</u> things.

3. On a <u>windy</u>, <u>frosty</u> day a <u>tiny</u> <u>lady</u> went on a <u>twenty</u>-mile ride on a <u>bony</u> and <u>lazy</u> <u>pony</u> that was not much more than a <u>baby</u>. The <u>lady</u> was a bit <u>shaky</u> as she rode on a <u>bumpy</u>, <u>stony</u> path. Then a snake in the <u>slimy</u> moss on the path scared the <u>pony</u>, and it went <u>crazy</u>. The <u>lady</u> landed with a <u>nasty</u> plop on the <u>dusty</u> path and was not <u>happy</u>.

y (ē) penny

dust	bab
fift	dut
happ	laz
mist	pon
nast	rub
penn	shad
plent	shin
thrift	slim
twent	ston
wind	tin

Name _____ Date _____

Word List 1

y (ē) penny

dusty	baby
fifty	duty
happy	lazy
misty	pony
nasty	ruby
penny	shady
plenty	shiny
thrifty	slimy
twenty	stony
windy	tiny

Name _____ Date _____

Word List 2

y   (ē)   penny

Write a word from the Word List to complete each sentence.

1. When it is _____ it is hazy and foggy.

2. If a man is _____ , then he is mean.

3. I like to sit in a _____ spot by a tree on a hot day.

4. On a _____ day it is very breezy and I can fly a kite.

5. My cat is so _____ that all she will do is eat and sleep!

6. The frog felt _____ to me when I picked it up at the pond.

7. I cannot hike on a _____ path with bare feet.

Name _____   Date _____

Cloze Sentences 1

y (ē) penny

Write a word from the Word List to complete each sentence.

1. _____ is the same as 5 times 10.

2. I like to ride my black and white _____ when I have the time.

3. You are _____ if you can save a lot of cash.

4. _____ is the same as 10 times 2.

5. His truck is _____ when he rubs wax on it and then wipes it off with a clean cloth.

6. If you have _____, then you have lots and lots to share.

7. The _____ wore a bib when he ate his lunch.

Name _____ Date _____

Cloze Sentences 2

y (ē) penny

Write a word from the Word List to complete each sentence.

1. My mom has a _____ ring that is deep red.

2. With a _____ you can get a tenth as much as you can get with a dime.

3. A _____ puppy is not big, and I can pick it up in my hand.

4. Your _____ is to do the things needed for your job.

5. If you feel _____, then you do not feel sad.

6. If my home gets _____, then I need to sweep and clean it.

Name _____ Date _____

Cloze Sentences 3

12 igh night

Stories of the Night

Goodnight Moon, Margaret Wise Brown, illustrated by Clement Hurd (New York: Harper & Row, 1947). In rhyming verse, a young rabbit says goodnight to things in his bedroom (shown in black and white) as the room (pictured in color) darkens and night progresses.

I Hear a Noise, Diane Goode (New York: E. P. Dutton, 1988). One night a child and his mother are whisked out his bedroom window by a monster who takes them home. The adventure is short lived: The monster's mother scolds it and makes it take them back!

King Bidgood's in the Bathtub, Audrey Wood, illustrated by Don Wood (San Diego: Harcourt Brace Jovanovich, 1985). The king *won't* get out of the bathtub, and he invites everyone in to join him—to battle, eat, fish, and dance! Finally, a young page solves the problem. He pulls the plug! Caldecott Honor Book.

Good-Night Owl, Pat Hutchins (New York: The Trumpet Club, 1972). One by one, the daytime animals in this cumulative story make noise that keeps Owl awake during the day, but in the end he achieves his goal of revenge when he screeches at night and awakens them.

Jesse Bear, What Will You Wear?, Nancy White Carlstrom (New York: Scholastic, 1986). Detailed illustrations provide clues to meaning in this predictable rhyming book that follows Jesse Bear and his family from morning to night of a busy day.

Grandfather Twilight, Barbara Berger (New York: Philomel Books, 1984). Poetic in text and illustration, this simple tale follows Grandfather Twilight, who releases the moon into the sky every evening from an infinite strand of pearls.

Franklin in the Dark, Paulette Bourgeois, illustrated by Brenda Clark (New York: Scholastic, 1986). Franklin is afraid of the dark and of being in small, cramped places, and Franklin is a turtle! When he learns from other animals and his mother that they have their own fears, he is more comfortable sleeping in his shell—with his night light on!

Wait Till the Moon Is Full, Margaret Wise Brown, illustrated by Garth Williams (New York: HarperCollins, 1949, 1976). A little raccoon has to wait for the moon to progress through its phases until it is full before his mother will let him venture into the night.

The Old Woman and Her Pig, illustrated by Paul Galdone (New York: McGraw-Hill, 1960). In this classic cumulative tale, the old woman worries that she won't get home the night her pig refuses to jump over the stile. No one she asks will help until she feeds the cat, which begins a chain of events that forces the pig to jump.

"Strange Bumps," in ***Owl at Home***, Arnold Lobel (New York: Scholastic, 1975). In a collection of stories, Owl is alone at home, but he is entertained by the winter wind, bumps in his bed, sad thoughts, a challenge to himself, and his new friend—the moon. In "Strange Bumps," in bed at night Owl is frightened by two bumps under the blankets that mysteriously move every time his legs move.

Porcupine's Pajama Party, Terry Webb Harshman, illustrated by Doug Cushman (New York: Harper & Row, 1988). When he invites his friends Owl and Otter to sleep at his house, Porcupine discovers that being together makes everything more fun— making cookies, watching a scary movie on TV, and being scared in the dark.

No Bath Tonight, Jane Yolen, illustrated by Nancy Winslow Parker (New York: Harper & Row, 1978). All week a little boy convinces everyone not to make him take a bath— everyone, that is, except his grandmother, who arrives with her love magic and, together, they make kid tea—in the bathtub!

Bedtime for Frances, Russell Hoban, illustrated by Garth Williams (New York: Harper & Row, 1960). In a series of episodes, little Frances the badger and her wise parents successfully deal with a common childhood fear—night noises and sights.

Dashiel and the Night, Larry Callen, illustrated by Leslie Morrill (New York: E. P. Dutton, 1981). Dashiel's powerful dream about fireflies that light his way through the night gives him the courage to face and conquer his fear of the dark and come to know the night and its noises as a friend.

The Goodnight Circle, Carolyn Lesser, illustrated by Lorinda Bryan Cauley (San Diego: Harcourt Brace Jovanovich, 1984). In a series of goodnight scenes, the daytime forest animals and their young go to sleep. The circle continues with good mornings to nocturnal animals as they wake up and is completed when the first daytime animal awakens.

MOTIVATION AND EXTENSION ACTIVITIES ════════════════════════════

　　1. Students tell and/or write and illustrate ***I Hear a Noise*** from the point of view of the little monster, who tells one of his or her friends who wasn't there about his or her adventure.
　　2. Students make masks and/or costumes or puppets and act out the tale of ***King Bidgood's in the Bathtub***.
　　3. As students read the rest of the text of ***Wait Till the Moon Is Full***, the teacher reads and sings the song that mother sings to the little raccoon which is more challenging reading.
　　4. Students and the teacher share about times they have had to wait. They discuss how they felt while they were waiting, whether anything made the waiting easier, and

how they felt when the desired event happened or the end of waiting finally arrived. They compare and contrast their experiences to those of the little raccoon in *Wait Till the Moon Is Full*. (See Activity 10 in Chapter 19, ir birthday, for an activity related to waiting and anticipating.)

5. Many traditional cumulative stories belong to a category which might be considered static cumulative tales: a pattern in which there is the simple adding or accumulating of a collection of characters or other elements. In contrast, *Goodnight Owl* follows a dynamic cumulative tale pattern: a pattern in which characters accumulate (who typically attempt to achieve a common goal) and an event or final character causes an action that involves the characters (and typically provides positive movement toward or fulfillment of the goal of the protagonists or negative movement toward or fulfillment of the goal of the antagonist). Owl, in *Goodnight Owl*, achieves his goal of revenge on the daytime animals who kept him awake during the day when he screeches and wakes them up at night.

The Old Woman and Her Pig follows a variation of the classic dynamic cumulative tale with a chain reaction or dominoes pattern: a pattern in which a series of characters are added who respond negatively to the desired outcome of the central character. Then an event stops the negative cycle and reverses it toward a positive outcome and begins a chain reaction, like falling dominoes, that achieves the desired outcome of the protagonist. In *The Old Woman and Her Pig*, the old woman wants to get home with the pig she bought at the market. The pig and a series of additional characters refuse to help her reach her goal. An event—she feeds the cat—stops the negative cycle and initiates a positive one. In the end, the pig jumps the stile and the woman gets home that night.

Students and the teacher explore the cumulative patterns in *Good-Night Owl* and *The Old Woman and Her Pig* and in other books that follow similar patterns.

- As they listen to or read the books, students identify the goals of the characters, list their responses in order as they appear, and draw and label an illustration or diagram that shows the pattern of the book(s). For example, the following diagram is for *The Old Woman and Her Pig*:

pig(no) + dog(no) + stick(no) + fire(no) + water(no) + ox(no) + butcher(no) + rope(no) + rat(no) + cat(if, then)

(The old woman feed the cat.)   ***EVENT***

pig(yes) + dog(yes) + stick(yes) + fire(yes) + water(yes) + ox(yes) + butcher(yes) + rope(yes) + rat(yes) + cat(yes)

- Students make masks and/or costumes or puppets and props (and scenery) and dramatize the cumulative pattern and nature of the tales.
- Students and the teacher compare and contrast the stories in this chapter with other cumulative tales they read that follow the three different patterns: static cumulative tales, dynamic cumulative tales, and dynamic cumulative tales variation with a chain reaction or dominoes pattern.
- Students and the teacher compare and contrast three stories that are a dynamic cumulative tales variation with a chain reaction or dominoes pattern:

    The Old Woman and Her Pig by Galdone (this chapter)

    Why Mosquitoes Buzz in People's Ears: A West African Tale by Aardema (Chapter 22, ow owl)

    One Fine Day by Hogrogian (Chapter 34, x fox).

6. Before or after they share **No Bath Tonight**, students and the teacher brew loose tea in a teapot, sample the tea, and examine and "read" the tea leaves in their emptied cups, as Jeremy's grandmother does after she finishes drinking her tea.

7. At the end of **No Bath Tonight**, Jeremy's grandmother pretends to be able to read in his "kid tea" Jeremy's past—and his future, which includes "a walk in the park," "an ice cream soda," and "a long, long story at bedtime." Students wash their hands in the sink and make "kid tea." Then the teacher pretends to read their past—and their future, which includes a walk outside, an ice cream soda, and a long, long read-aloud story.

8. Students and the teacher tell and/or write and illustrate about their fears of noises and sights of the night and/or of the dark. They tell how they cope(d) with or conquer(ed) them and whether there are/were any things or people that help(ed) them or give/gave them courage. They compare and contrast their experiences with those of the characters in **I Hear a Noise**, **Franklin in the Dark**, "Strange Bumps" in **Owl at Home**, **Porcupine's Pajama Party**, **Bedtime for Frances**, and **Dashiel and the Night**.

9. Students and the teacher tell and/or write and illustrate in sequence the steps/ events in the routines or traditions they follow to get ready for bed at night and to get ready for school (or other destination) in the morning.

10. After they listen to or read **The Goodnight Circle**, students explore other books—fiction and nonfiction resources—that have information about the habits of daytime and nocturnal animals. They use, as one resource, the "Night Animals" issues of **Zoobooks** magazine (February 1987, vol. 3, no. 5, and January 1991, vol. 8, no. 4) published by Wildlife Education, Ltd., 930 Washington Street, San Diego, California 92103. Published monthly, **Zoobooks** magazines provide current information about groups of animals through brief text and colored photographs and diagrams with captions.

TEACHER REFERENCE

Cloze Sentences

One-Syllable Words

Cloze Sentences 1

1. When my boots got too <u>tight</u>, I got a bigger size.
2. We <u>might</u> go camping with you, but we may not have time.
3. We <u>light</u> the fire in the stove to heat my home.
4. A <u>high</u> branch on a tree is not low. It is up near the top.
5. In the <u>fight</u> he got mad and hit his classmate.
6. <u>Night</u> is the time when the sky is not light and we sleep.

Cloze Sentences 2

1. My home is on the <u>right</u>-hand side of the street, and his is on the left.
2. A <u>bright</u> lamp shines a lot of light in the room.
3. My <u>sight</u> is helped when I put on my glasses to drive.

4. She ran off in <u>fright</u> when she was scared by the big dog.

5. My <u>flight</u> by plane to Boston leaves at nine o'clock tonight.

Multisyllable Words

Cloze Sentences 3

1. To see in the bright <u>sunlight</u> he wore sunglasses to the beach.

2. We have <u>daylight</u> each day when the sun is shining in the sky.

3. A thing that happens <u>nightly</u> happens each night.

4. <u>Twilight</u> is the time of day right after the sun sets.

5. In the play we shine a <u>spotlight</u> on the actress when she makes a speech.

6. <u>Tonight</u> you need to go right to bed. Last night you stayed up too late!

7. A bright flash of <u>lightning</u> woke me up last night.

8. In the <u>moonlight</u> the moon is so bright that we can see at night as well as we can see in daylight.

Dictations

1. The <u>twilight</u> makes me <u>sigh</u> with <u>delight</u>! From this hill I can see the last of the <u>daylight</u> as the sun sets from way up <u>high</u>. I will stay here to see the <u>moonlight</u> <u>tonight</u>.

2. Today in the <u>daylight</u> the <u>sunlight</u> was too <u>bright</u> when I drove. It helped my <u>sight</u> to have my sunglasses on. <u>Tonight</u> we <u>might</u> go to the play in the <u>moonlight</u>. I just hope that the street <u>lights</u> and the <u>spotlights</u> will not be too <u>bright</u>!

3. He jumped from bed last <u>night</u> when the <u>sight</u> of a <u>bright</u> flash of <u>lightning</u> gave him a <u>fright</u>. He ran <u>right</u> into my bedroom and held <u>tight</u> to my hand when the <u>sight</u> of the <u>lightning</u> scared him.

4. The <u>sight</u> of two men in a <u>fight</u> can be a <u>fright</u>. It lasted all <u>night</u> by <u>moonlight</u>, but as a hint of <u>daylight</u> lit up the sky the men gave big <u>sighs</u> and gave up the <u>fight</u>.

igh   (ī)   night igh

br	t	dayl	t
f	t	l	tning
fl	t	moonl	t
fr	t	n	tly
h		spotl	t
l	t	sunl	t
m	t	ton	t
n	t	twil	t
r	t		
s	t		
t	t		

Name _____ Date _____

Word List 1

igh (ī) night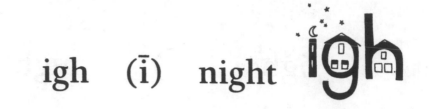

bright	**daylight**
fight	**lightning**
flight	**moonlight**
fright	**nightly**
high	**spotlight**
light	**sunlight**
might	**tonight**
night	**twilight**
right	
sight	
tight	

Name _____ Date _____

Word List 2

igh (ī) night

Write a word from the Word List to complete each sentence.

1. When my boots got too _____ , I got a bigger size.

2. We _____ go camping with you, but we may not have time.

3. We _____ the fire in the stove to heat my home.

4. A _____ branch on a tree is not low. It is up near the top.

5. In the _____ he got mad and hit his classmate.

6. _____ is the time when the sky is not light and we sleep.

Name _____ Date _____

Cloze Sentences 1

igh (ī) night

Write a word from the Word List to complete each sentence.

1. My home is on the _____ -hand side of the street, and his is on the left.

2. A _____ lamp shines a lot of light in the room.

3. My _____ is helped when I put on my glasses to drive.

4. She ran off in _____ when she was scared by the big dog.

5. My _____ by plane to Boston leaves at nine o'clock tonight.

Name _____ Date _____

Cloze Sentences 2

igh (ī) night igh

Write a word from the Word List to complete each sentence.

1. To see in the bright _____ he wore sunglasses to the beach.

2. We have _____ each day when the sun is shining in the sky.

3. A thing that happens _____ happens each night.

4. _____ is the time of day right after the sun sets.

5. In the play we shine a _____ on the actress when she makes a speech.

6. _____ you need to go right to bed. Last night you stayed up too late!

7. A bright flash of _____ woke me up last night.

8. In the _____ the moon is so bright that we can see at night as well as we can see in daylight.

Name _____ Date _____

13 oa goat

BOOK LIST

Goats and Sheep

The Three Billy Goats Gruff: A Norwegian Folktale, illustrated by Ellen Appleby (New York: Scholastic, 1984). In turn, the three billy goats—from youngest to oldest—cross a bridge under which a mean troll lives, and the first two are able to convince him to wait for the last and largest goat, who puts an end to him.

The Three Billy Goats Gruff, P. C. Asbjornsen and J. E. Moe, taken from the translation of G. W. Dasent, illustrated by Marcia Brown (San Diego: Harcourt Brace Jovanovich, 1957, 1985). On their way to the hillside to eat, three billy goats outwit a hungry troll who lives under the bridge they must cross. They convince him to let the smaller two pass by, and the third and largest goat tosses the troll into the river.

The Three Billy Goats Gruff, Paul Galdone (New York: Clarion Books, 1973). The details and perspective of Galdone's illustrations capture the drama of the story of three billy goat brothers who outsmart the ugly troll by persuading him to wait to eat the third goat, who is the largest and strong enough to toss the troll into the river.

The Three Billy Goats Gruff: A Norwegian Folk Tale with Woodcuts, Susan Blair (New York: Scholastic, 1963). Blair's detailed woodcut illustrations interpret the well-known story of three billy goats who use their wits and their largest brother's strength to outsmart and overcome the troll so that they can pass over his bridge on their way to the hillside to eat.

The Rough, Gruff Goat Brothers Rap, Bernice and Jon Chardiet, illustrated by J. C. Suares (New York: Scholastic, 1993). The Chardiets' contemporary interpretation of the traditional "Three Billy Goats Gruff" story, with the troll as the keeper of a toll bridge, is told in rhyme and set to rap rhythm with background music and chorus on a companion audio tape.

"Charlie Needs a Cloak," Tomie dePaola (New York: Scholastic, 1973). One of Charlie the shepherd's sheep—a mischievous rascal—tries to thwart him at each step of the process as Charlie makes a new cloak from its wool. In a wordless subplot, an industrious mouse secretly stores some of Charlie's possessions in its stump for the winter. Contains a glossary of key vocabulary.

Pelle's New Suit, Elsa Beskow, translated by Marion Letcher Woodburn (New York: Harper & Row). When he outgrows his old suit, Pelle shears his lamb and barters his labor with family and townspeople, who complete parts of the process to make him a new wool suit.

A New Coat for Anna, Harriet Ziefert, illustrated by Anita Lobel (New York: Scholastic, 1986). After World War II, Anna's mother has no money to buy her a new coat, but she trades family treasures with the farmer for wool, with a woman to spin it, and with a tailor to make it, and with Anna she dyes the coat red with berries.

When Sheep Cannot Sleep: The Counting Book, Satoshi Kitamura (New York: Farrar, Straus and Giroux, 1986). When Wooly the sheep suffers from insomnia, he takes a walk and counts increasing numbers of objects until, finally, he counts his family and friends and falls asleep.

Gregory, the Terrible Eater, Mitchell Sharmat, illustrated by José Aruego and Ariane Dewey (New York: Scholastic, 1980). Gregory the goat worries his parents when he refuses to eat the cans, boxes, and bottle caps they offer him and prefers to eat fruits and vegetables, but—with the help of Dr. Ram and a plan of their own—mother and father goat help their family reach a mealtime compromise.

The Goat in the Rug, as told to Charles L. Blood and Martin Link by Geraldine, illustrated by Nancy Winslow Parker (New York: Macmillan Publishing Company, 1976). Geraldine the goat describes each step in the process of making her mohair into a Navaho rug—clipping, washing and drying, carding, spinning, dyeing, and weaving. Contains a glossary of vocabulary with diagrams.

Annie and the Old One, Miska Miles, illustrated by Peter Parnall (Boston: Little, Brown and Company, 1971). Though she tries at first to stop time and her mother's weaving to prevent her beloved grandmother's approaching death, Annie is able to understand the legacy she shares with past and future generations as she takes her grandmother's stick and begins to weave.

Coal Mining Communities

The Rag Coat, Lauren Mills (Boston: Little, Brown and Company, 1991). Children in a small Appalachian coal mining town learn the meaning of community when The Quilting Mothers make Minna a coat from their cloth rags so that she can attend school.

When I Was Young in the Mountains, Cynthia Rylant, illustrated by Diane Goode (New York: Penguin Books, 1982). A woman shares childhood memories of daily life with her extended family in a coal mining community in the Appalachian Mountains. Caldecott Honor Book.

Appalachia: The Voices of Sleeping Birds, Cynthia Rylant, illustrated by Barry Moser (San Diego: Harcourt Brace Jovanovich, 1991). Rylant's text and Moser's paintings create a quiet portrait of the people of the Appalachian Region—through the days and seasons of their lives in the mountains.

In Coal Country, Judith Hendershot, illustrated by Thomas B. Allen (New York: Alfred A. Knopf, 1987). Full-page illustrations in pastels and charcoal complement each page of text, which depicts life through the seasons of a coal miner's family in Ohio in the 1930s.

MOTIVATION AND EXTENSION ACTIVITIES

Goats and Sheep

1. Throughout the "Goats and Sheep" unit, students and the teacher gather and record information that they know or discover about goats and sheep as they read suggested books for this unit or consult resource books, encyclopedias, or dictionaries. They record information on a data matrix like the one that follows, and they compare and contrast the two animals. If time and opportunity permit, they take a field trip to collect data about goats and sheep.

	GOATS	SHEEP
Products	Milk, cheese, wool, meat, leather	Meat, wool for cloth, pelts for fur, milk, cheese
Where they live	On land with thin growth not good enough for sheep or cattle	Pastures, hills
What they look like	Long beard on chin	No beard
	Short tail turns up	Tail turns down
	Horns are hollow and grow up, not to sides	Horns grow to sides
	Smaller than sheep (100 to 120 pounds)	Bigger than goats
	Hair is straight	Wool is sometimes curly
What they eat	Grass and shrubs	Grass and shrubs
	Do not eat tin cans or trash	
	Do lick off labels of cans to eat the glue	
Males called	Rams	Rams
Females called	Nannies or does	Ewes
Babies and young called	Kids	Lambs

2. The troll in three of the four versions of the "Three Billy Goats Gruff" story suggested for this unit (all but the Galdone version) is described using similes—for example, "with eyes as big as saucers and a nose as long as a poker." The teacher introduces/reviews figurative language, particularly similes, and explains its function to compare the unknown to the familiar. He or she provides a fire poker and saucers for

students to examine and then reads aloud the foregoing description of the troll *before* students preview, read, or listen to any of the versions of the "Three Billy Goats Gruff" story. Students visualize the troll and draw him. They later refer to their drawing as they evaluate the accuracy of the illustrations of the troll in each of the three versions that contain the foregoing description.

3. The words that the troll speaks in Brown's version of **The Three Billy Goats Gruff** are written in italics, but twice in the text his words "Very well! Be off with you" are not placed in italics. Observant readers use their detective skills to identify the two places in the text where the troll's words are not in italics.

4. The "Three Billy Goats Gruff" stories follow the common pattern in traditional literature of repetition of numbers and events, especially three. Students and the teacher consider other stories that contain this motif. (See Activity 17 in Chapter 8, ee seeds.)

5. While they read, students and the teacher discuss, compare, and contrast the illustrations in the four versions of the "Three Billy Goats Gruff" story suggested for this unit. Students choose their favorite illustrations for the tale, and they make puppets for and present a shadow puppet play of that version. They identify the criteria on which they based their selection. They make puppets for each character and for the narrator (in the likeness of the person narrating). They draw characters in the style of the favored illustrator and glue them onto chopsticks, craft or popsicle sticks, or pencils. They make the theater by draping a single thickness of cloth over two chairs of equal height, and they place a light source—a flashlight or lamp (a high-intensity lamp that is movable works well)—4″ to 6″ behind the cloth screen and the puppets. Puppeteers sit behind the chairs and hold the puppets so that the bottoms of the characters' feet when walking are at the level of the chair.

6. Students listen to the audio tape of **The Rough, Gruff Goat Brothers Rap** (available through Scholastic) as they read along in the book. (Contemporary versions of stories often provide older readers with motivation to read and discuss traditional folk tales.)

7. As they read the four books in this unit about the process involved in preparing wool for use in garments or a rug—**"Charlie Needs a Cloak," Pelle's New Suit, A New Coat for Anna**, and **The Goat in the Rug**—students predict and then verify or revise/correct their predictions of the steps and sequence that characters in the books follow.

8. Students make hypotheses about the pattern of **When Sheep Cannot Sleep: The Counting Book** without looking at the chart on the last page of the book. They count groups of objects to confirm or revise their hypotheses.

9. While they read **Gregory, the Terrible Eater**, students and the teacher discuss healthy food (people food) and junk food (goat food) as they are presented in the book. Students then sort items presented in a picnic basket into the following two categories and match word label cards the teacher has prepared for each item. In effect, they create both a three-dimensional and a two-dimensional outline. Finally, students eat some of the healthy food, if they choose. Items in each category include the following:

Healthy or People Food	*Junk or Goat Food*
plum	soap
cupcake	sock
carrot	tin can

Healthy or People Food	Junk or Goat Food
potato chips	string
green string beans	spool
ice cream cone	ring
grapes	yo-yo
egg	dime
dates	clay
milk	napkin
peach	rug
	spoon
	bag
	stick
	fan
	tape
	stone (rock)
	toothbrush
	sunglasses
	globe

Students and the teacher discuss the food of real goats and challenge the accuracy of the premise that goats eat trash on which *Gregory, the Terrible Eater* is based. They use resource books and materials to research what goats eat. As one resource, they read "Goats Will Eat Almost Anything," in *Animal Fact/Animal Fable*, Seymour Simon, illustrated by Diane de Groat (New York: Crown Publishers, Inc., 1979), which provides factual information in an unusual and engaging format. The colorfully and accurately illustrated book presents scientific observations about the behavior of a variety of animals. For each animal, a true or false statement is presented on a right-hand page, and the reader guesses whether it is a fact or a fable (fiction) and turns the page to find out. According to the entry in *Animal Fact/Animal Fable*, goats chew tin can labels to reach the glue but do not eat the metal cans, and they prefer to eat (as does Gregory goat) fruit, vegetables, grass, and plant leaves. Students and the teacher also discuss what is considered healthy and junk food for people.

10. During the "Goats and Sheep" unit, students compare and contrast samples of goat hair and sheep wool. They experiment with hand spinning with raw wool/hair and hand weaving and crocheting with wool yarn. They dye wool/hair using natural dyes (nuts, berries, tea) and commercially available dyes. They compare and contrast the dyeing process with wool with dyeing eggs. (See Activity 18 in Chapter 7, ay day.)

Coal Mining Communities

11. Pelle in *Pelle's New Suit*, Anna in *A New Coat for Anna*, and Minna in *The Rag Coat* learn about the strength of family and community as they draw on their resources to obtain the clothing they need. Students and the teacher discuss this theme common to the three books.

12. After they read **The Rag Coat**, students and the teacher extend their study of quilts. (See Chapter 33, qu quilt, for suggested books and activities.)

13. The teacher reads aloud the sentence on page 13 of Rylant and Moser's **Appalachia: The Voices of Sleeping Birds** that describes the night: "Night in these houses is thick, the mountains wear heavy shawls of fog, and giant moths flap at the porch lights while cars cut through the dark hollows like burrowing moles." Students visualize and/or draw/paint/dramatize the images (literal and/or figurative) that the descriptions (which use figurative language—personification and similes) evoke. (See Activity 18 in Chapter 2, oo moon, Activity 12 in Chapter 4, y fly, Activities 12 and 13 in Chapter 16, ar star, Activity 10 in Chapter 22, ow owl, Activity 12 in Chapter 29, consonant-le fable, and Activity 8 in Chapter 32, c Frances Cinderella fancy, for additional books and activities that feature figurative language.)

14. After they listen to or read **In Coal Country**, students experiment with pastels and charcoal drawings. The teacher suggests a subject: a four-page or four-quadrant illustration of students' hometowns through the seasons.

15. Students and the teacher locate on a map and/or globe the places/cultures (depicted or of origin) in the books read in this chapter, including Norway (**The Three Billy-Goats Gruff: A Norwegian Folktale**, **The Three Billy Goats Gruff** (Brown and Galdone), **The Three Billy-Goats Gruff: A Norwegian Folk Tale with Woodcuts**, and **The Rough, Gruff Goat Brothers Rap**); Sweden (**Pelle's New Suit**); Europe (**A New Coat for Anna**); Navaho culture and Window Rock, Arizona in the United States (**The Goat in the Rug** and **Annie and the Old One**); coal mining communities in the Appalachian Mountains of Tennessee and West Virginia in the United States (**The Rag Coat**, **When I Was Young in the Mountains**, and **Appalachia: The Voices of Sleeping Birds**); and coal mining communities in Ohio in the United States (**In Coal Country**).

TEACHER REFERENCE ═══════════════════════════════════

Cloze Sentences

One-Syllable Words

Cloze Sentences 1

1. Please use <u>soap</u> to clean your hands before you eat.
2. I like to eat <u>toast</u> with jam while it is still hot from the toaster.
3. You may have <u>roast</u> beef with gravy at a meal.
4. I was glad I had on a thick <u>coat</u> and not a thin jacket when I went sledding.
5. You can <u>float</u> on a raft on a lake or a pond.
6. An <u>oak</u> is a tree that can grow to be big.
7. You can <u>coast</u> down a hill on your bike.

Cloze Sentences 2

1. A <u>goat</u> is an animal that likes to eat trash, tin cans, and coats.
2. A <u>toad</u> is a lot like a frog.
3. I can <u>loan</u> you a dime if you pay it back.

4. A <u>boat</u> is fun to row on a lake.
5. A <u>road</u> means nearly the same as a street.
6. I <u>groan</u> and moan when I feel sick.
7. A <u>coach</u> can help and teach a team.
8. I had a sore <u>throat</u> when I was sick last week.

Multisyllable Words

Cloze Sentences 3

1. When we hear the dog <u>groaning</u> in his sleep, we can tell that he is having a bad dream or he is sick.
2. I <u>toasted</u> my sandwich in the toaster before I ate it.
3. He was <u>coasting</u> on his bike all the way from the top of the hill.
4. When a lot of traffic blocks the <u>roadway</u>, it takes us a long time to get home.
5. We have fun <u>floating</u> on rafts on the lake on a hot day.

Dictations

1. <u>Joan</u> went fishing on the <u>coast</u>. She heard a lot of <u>toads</u> <u>croak</u> on the <u>foaming</u> sand as she got a <u>load</u> of fish.
2. Pat heard <u>moaning</u> and <u>groaning</u> <u>floating</u> up the <u>road</u>. There was a <u>goat</u> on the side of the <u>road</u> with a trap on its <u>throat</u>. <u>Joan</u> went by <u>boat</u> to the <u>coast</u> to get help.
3. Jim was <u>floating</u> a <u>load</u> of <u>soap</u> by the <u>coast</u> on <u>board</u> a <u>boat</u> that Tom had <u>loaned</u> him. When the <u>boat</u> got to land he sent the <u>soap</u> by <u>coach</u>.
4. Sam was <u>floating</u> by the <u>coast</u> in his <u>boat</u>. When the wind came up the sea began to <u>roar</u> and <u>foam</u>, and Sam <u>groaned</u>. He did not <u>loaf</u> but got his <u>oars</u> and went to the <u>coast</u> that was his <u>goal</u>.

oa (ō) goat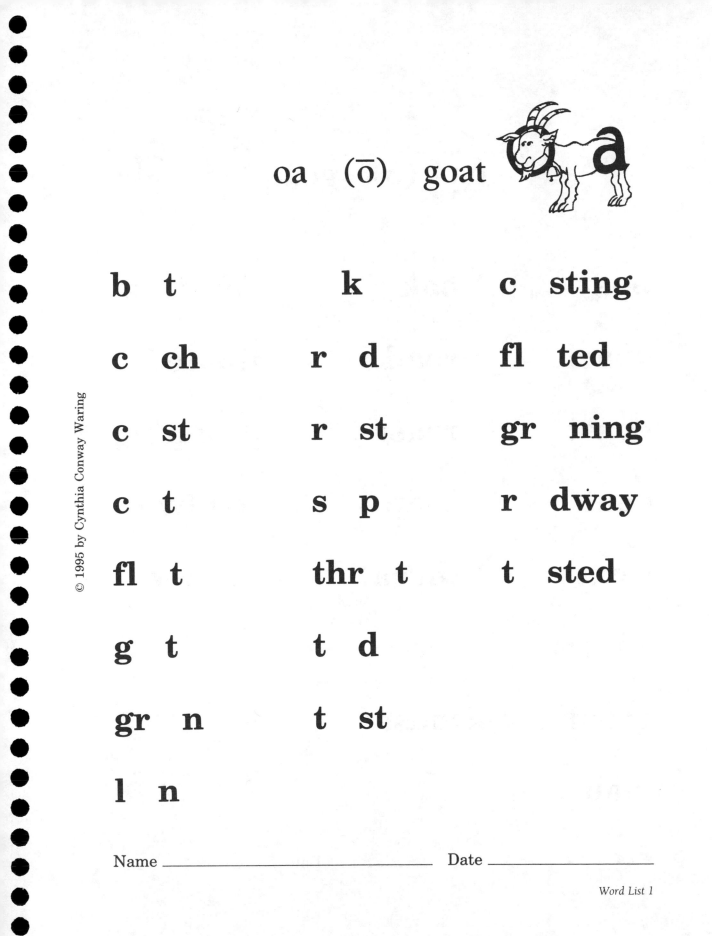

b t   k   c sting

c ch   r d   fl ted

c st   r st   gr ning

c t   s p   r dway

fl t   thr t   t sted

g t   t d

gr n   t st

l n

Name _____ Date _____

oa (ō) goat

boat	oak	coasting
coach	road	floated
coast	roast	groaning
coat	soap	roadway
float	throat	toasted
goat	toad	
groan	toast	
loan		

Name _____ Date _____

Word List 2

oa (ō) goat

Write a word from the Word List to complete each sentence.

1. Please use _____ to clean your hands before you eat.

2. I like to eat _____ with jam while it is still hot from the toaster.

3. You may have _____ beef with gravy at a meal.

4. I was glad I had on a thick _____ and not a thin jacket when I went sledding.

5. You can _____ on a raft on a lake or a pond.

6. An _____ is a tree that can grow to be big.

7. You can _____ down a hill on your bike.

Name _____ Date _____

Cloze Sentences 1

oa (ō) goat

Write a word from the Word List to complete each sentence.

1. A _____ is an animal that likes to eat trash, tin cans, and coats.

2. A _____ is a lot like a frog.

3. I can _____ you a dime if you pay it back.

4. A _____ is fun to row on a lake.

5. A _____ means nearly the same as a street.

6. I _____ and moan when I feel sick.

7. A _____ can help and teach a team.

8. I had a sore _____ when I was sick last week.

Name _____ Date _____

oa (ō) goat

Write a word from the Word List to complete each sentence.

1. When we hear the dog _____ in his sleep, we can tell that he is having a bad dream or he is sick.

2. I _____ my sandwich in the toaster before I ate it.

3. He was _____ on his bike all the way from the top of the hill.

4. When a lot of traffic blocks the _____ , it takes us a long time to get home.

5. We have fun _____ on rafts on the lake on a hot day.

Name _____ Date _____

14 old gold

BOOK LIST

Gold

The Pot of Gold: An Irish Folk Tale (Glenview, Ill.: Scott, Foresman and Company, 1971, 1976). When a man marks the tree where an elf's gold is buried with a scarf and goes home to get a shovel, he makes the elf promise he won't take the scarf off the tree, and he doesn't. The elf outsmarts the man and marks *every* tree with an identical scarf!

King Midas and the Golden Touch, Al Perkins, illustrated by Haig and Regina Shekerjian (New York: Scholastic, 1969, 1973). In his insatiable desire for gold, King Midas wishes that everything he touches turns to gold, but he discovers that he is not happy because he cannot eat or drink. When he turns his beloved daughter into a golden statue, he asks to have the golden touch reversed.

King Midas and the Golden Touch, Freya Littledale, from the tale by Nathaniel Hawthorne, illustrated by Daniel Horne (New York: Scholastic, 1989). King Midas gains wisdom and finds that he loves his daughter more than gold when, given the golden touch, he turns her into gold and discovers that riches do not make him happy if it means losing her.

The Three Wishes, M. Jean Craig, illustrated by Yuri Salzman (New York: Scholastic, 1968, 1986). Granted three wishes by the fairy whose tree home he spares, a woodcutter wastes the first two in haste and anger but uses the last out of love for his wife.

Peter and the North Wind: Retold from the Norse Tale The Lad Who Went to the North Wind, Freya Littledale, illustrated by Troy Howell (New York: Scholastic, 1971, 1988). After it blows their flour away, Peter goes to the North Wind to get the flour back and receives a magic cloth that gives food, a magic goat that makes gold, and a magic stick that hits at command and protects him from an innkeeper who tries to steal Peter's magic objects.

The Magic Tablecloth, the Magic Goat, and the Hitting Stick, Freya Littledale, illustrated by Alfred Olschewski (New York: Scholastic, 1971, 1972). Olschewski's illustrations interpret Littledale's text for the "Peter and the North Wind" story of the North Wind's provision for the basic needs of a poor boy and his mother through three magic objects—a cloth, a goat, and a stick.

The Frog Prince, Edith H. Tarcov, illustrated by James Marshall (New York: Scholastic, 1974). A princess agrees to allow a frog to become her companion if he retrieves her golden ball from his well, but she is surprised when he comes to the castle to claim his reward and even more surprised when he turns into a prince.

Lazy Jack, Tony Ross (New York: The Trumpet Club, 1986). In a classic noodlehead story, Lazy Jack follows his mother's advice but always at the wrong time; however, Jack's foolishness is rewarded when he makes a sad princess laugh, wins her hand in marriage, and never has to work again.

The Golden Goose, Susan Saunders, illustrated by Isadore Seltzer (New York: Scholastic, 1987). Aided by an old man's magic, a young man named Simpleton is rewarded for his kindness with a golden goose and the hand of the princess in marriage in this noodlehead story.

The Frog Prince Continued, Jon Scieszka, illustrated by Steve Johnson (New York: The Trumpet Club, 1991). In Scieszka's humorous sequel to the "Frog Prince" story, the prince, tired of living *unhappily* ever after with the princess, looks for a witch who will turn him back into a frog. When his plan fails, he gratefully returns home and kisses the princess, and they both turn into frogs and hop away happily ever after.

Clever Tom and the Leprechaun: An Old Irish Story, Linda Shute (New York: Scholastic, 1988). When a leprechaun shows him the bush where his gold is buried, Tom marks it with his garter and makes the leprechaun promise that he will not remove the garter while he gets a shovel, but the leprechaun keeps his promise *and* tricks Tom: He ties a garter to *every* bush in the field! Source notes provide background information for the story.

The Frog Prince, adapted from the retelling by the Brothers Grimm by Paul Galdone (New York: McGraw-Hill, 1975). A princess unwittingly releases a prince from the spell that turned him into a frog when she allows him to become her companion after he recovers her golden ball from his well.

"Clever and Vainglorious Kings," in *D'Aulaires' Book of Greek Myths*, Ingri and Edgar Parin D'Aulaires (Garden City, N.Y.: Doubleday & Company, Inc., 1962). In one of the collected Greek myths in this book, King Midas is granted a wish as a reward for an act of kindness and receives the golden touch. Though rich, he is not happy because he cannot eat or drink and his daughter is but a golden statue; therefore, he asks to have the wish revoked.

The Chocolate Touch, Patrick Skene Catling (New York: Bantam Doubleday Dell Publishing Group, Inc., 1952, 1979). A modern-day Midas, John Midas, receives the chocolate touch from a magic candy store and, like his traditional counterpart, learns that some things—like family and friends—are more important than his beloved chocolate.

MOTIVATION AND EXTENSION ACTIVITIES

1. At the beginning of the unit, students and the teacher explore gold in as many forms as possible—in items made of gold and in photographs in resource books and materials. They compile a list of uses for gold and locate on a map and globe places in the world where gold has been found.

2. Students and the teacher compare and contrast *The Pot of Gold: An Irish Folk Tale* and *Clever Tom and the Leprechaun: An Old Irish Story*. They discuss the ways in which the two books are the same and different and consider the ways in which a story may be made easier to read for beginning readers, as with *The Pot of Gold: An Irish Folk Tale*. They identify the elements of the story that have been retained in the shortened version and any elements that have been omitted. They discuss how the story has been affected by the changes. Students and the teacher choose their favorite version and indicate the criteria on which they based their selection.

3. After they read the two versions of the *King Midas and the Golden Touch* (Perkins, Galdone) suggested for this unit, students and the teacher compare and contrast the two books. They identify the differences and similarities between the two versions and choose a favorite based on the text and a favorite based on the illustrations. They discuss whether they chose the same or different versions depending on whether the text or illustrations were the basis for the selection, and they identify the specific criteria they used within each category.

The teacher explains the origin of the "King Midas and the Golden Touch" story in Greek myth and reads aloud "Clever and Vainglorious Kings" in *D'Aulaires' Book of Greek Myths* about King Midas. They discuss the similarities and differences among the three versions of the story suggested for this unit.

4. There are points in the Littledale version of *King Midas and the Golden Touch* where Horne's illustrations do not match the text. Students identify those points and consider how well the text and illustrations complement each other in this book to communicate the author's intended meaning.

The places in the book at which illustrations and text do not correspond include the following: First, the illustration in which King Midas takes a sip of coffee from his cup does not show the saucer that is referred to in the text, and the illustration, two pages before, shows King Midas with a mug rather than a cup in the same breakfast scene. Second, the illustration facing the text in which King Midas turns Marigold into a golden statue (and all of the illustrations of her) shows her with straight hair whereas the text refers to her "brown curls." Third, the text refers to King Midas running down a "path" to the river, but the illustration facing the text shows no path. Finally, the last scene shows *one* of Marigold's children in King Midas's lap, yet the text reads "Marigold's *children* sat in his lap."

5. After they read and respond to Littledale's version of *King Midas and the Golden Touch*, students and the teacher reread it and compile a list of compound words. There are many! Compound words as they occur for the first time from the beginning of the book include *upon, anything, Marigold, butterflies, himself, forever, sunrise, bedside, sunbeam, footstool, fingertips, handkerchief, birthday, breakfast, pancakes, strawberries, become, nothing, outside*.

6. There is a film version of the "King Midas and the Golden Touch" story (available from Rabbit Ears Productions, Inc., Westport, Connecticut). After they read the two book versions of the story suggested for this unit—*King Midas and the Golden Touch*

(Perkins, Littledale)—students and the teacher view the film version and compare and contrast the story presented in different media.

7. As they read *The Three Wishes*, students and the teacher share (tell and/or write about and illustrate) what they would wish if they had three wishes. (See Activity 3 in Chapter 8, ee seeds, for an activity that involves "wish seeds.")

The motif of wishes that have been magically granted but used unwisely—in haste, greed, or anger—is common in traditional literature. Students and the teacher discuss this motif in *The Three Wishes* and in other books, including *The Magic Fish* (Littledale), *The Magic Fish Rap* (Chardiet), *The Fisherman & His Wife* (Grimm), *The Old Woman Who Lived in a Vinegar Bottle* (Godden), *The Stone-Cutter: A Japanese Folk Tale* (McDermott), *The Magic Tree: A Tale from the Congo* (McDermott), *Strega Nona: An Old Tale* (dePaola), and *Sylvester and the Magic Pebble* (Steig). (See Activity 4 in Chapter 31, g George magic stingy, for an activity related to the magic wish motif.)

The Three Wishes also contains the motif of number (three) common in folk tales. Students and the teacher discuss other books with this motif. (See the "Three Tales of Three" unit in Chapter 8, ee seeds, for suggested books and activities.)

8. The themes in traditional folk literature frequently convey the needs, desires, and hopes of the common people who, often oppressed by those with wealth and power, express their wishes to have met their basic needs for food, money, and protection. In *Peter and the North Wind: Retold from the Norse Tale The Lad Who Went to the North Wind* and *The Magic Tablecloth, the Magic Goat, and the Hitting Stick*, Peter and his poor mother live in poverty until the North Wind gives them three magical items that provide for their basic needs—food, money, and protection—for the rest of their lives. Students and the teacher discuss other books with this common theme, including *Jack and the Beanstalk* (Faulkner) and *Jamie O'Rourke and the Big Potato: An Irish Folktale* (dePaola). (See Activity 7 in Chapter 10, ea wheat.) This theme is also expressed in *Lazy Jack*. Though by different means, Jack never needs to work again after he marries the princess. (See Activity 11 in this chapter.)

9. Olschewski's illustrations for Littledale's text of the "Peter and the North Wind" story, *The Magic Tablecloth, the Magic Goat, and the Hitting Stick*, predate Howell's by over fifteen years. Students and the teacher select their favorite illustrations and identify the criteria on which they based their choice. They discuss possible reasons for having a text interpreted by a different illustrator for a second publication after a number of years elapses.

10. Students and the teacher compare and contrast the two versions of *The Frog Prince* (by Tarcov and Galdone) suggested for this unit and choose the version they prefer, identifying the criteria on which they based their selection. They discuss their response to the attitude of disgust with which the princess treats the frog throughout the story (to the point of throwing him against the wall) and the reaction to her in the ending by the frog-turned-prince, who greets her kindly with a smile and marries her the next day. They discuss whether they feel that the princess retains her attitude toward the prince throughout Scieszka's modern sequel to the "Frog Prince" story, *The Frog Prince Continued*, and how they think her attitude might change after she is turned into a frog.

11. The motif of a suitor winning the hand of a sad princess by making her laugh is common in traditional folk tales and particularly in the humorous noodlehead (or numbskull) stories.

Students and the teacher identify and discuss this motif in books that contain it, including the two suggested for this unit: *Lazy Jack* and *The Golden Goose*.

12. As they listen to or read *Clever Tom and the Leprechaun: An Old Irish Story*, students who are not familiar with the vocabulary make predictions about the meanings of the words they may not know in this Irish tale (piggin, brogue, traipsed, peat bog, boliaun, garter). They confirm or revise/correct their hypotheses by reading on in the story and/or using the preceding context and accompanying illustrations (and referring to the source notes at the end of the book for an explanation and pronunciation of *boliaun*).

13. As they listen to or read *The Chocolate Touch*, students eat chocolate coins wrapped in gold foil (available for Chanukah and Christmas). They compare and contrast Catling's contemporary version of the "King Midas and the Golden Touch" story with the traditional versions suggested for this unit: *King Midas and the Golden Touch* (by Perkins and Littledale) and "Clever and Vainglorious Kings" in *D'Aulaires' Book of Greek Myths*. They discuss the ways in which the principal character in each of the four stories appears to be changed by his experiences and seems to be different at the end of the stories. Students and the teacher share (tell and/or write about and illustrate) the thing, like King Midas's gold and John Midas's chocolate, that they love to have and the corresponding "touch" they might be tempted to wish for.

14. Students and the teacher locate on a map and/or globe the places/cultures (depicted or of origin) in the books read in this chapter, including Ireland (*The Pot of Gold: An Irish Folk Tale* and *Clever Tom and the Leprechaun: An Old Irish Story*); Greece (*King Midas and the Golden Touch* (Perkins and Littledale) and "Clever and Vainglorious Kings" in *D'Aulaires' Book of Greek Myths*); Norway (*Peter and the North Wind: Retold from the Norse Tale The Lad Who Went to the North Wind* and *The Magic Tablecloth, the Magic Goat, and the Hitting Stick*); and Germany [*The Frog Prince* (Tarcov and Galdone)].

TEACHER REFERENCE

Cloze Sentences

One-Syllable Words

Cloze Sentences 1

1. This glass can <u>hold</u> three cups of milk.
2. When it is <u>cold</u>, I put on my coat, hat, mittens, and boots.
3. My ring is made of <u>gold</u>, and it shines when I clean it.
4. I <u>sold</u> my home last week, and I will get a big check for lots of money this week!
5. We <u>fold</u> clean clothes before we put them away.
6. She was <u>bold</u> when she bravely saved the cat's life by getting it down from a tree.
7. I hope my mom will not <u>scold</u> me for making that mistake. I did not mean to rip my coat!

Cloze Sentences 2

1. He needed to go shopping for a new coat. His <u>old</u> coat was too small.
2. She <u>told</u> us to stand in line until the bell rings at the beginning of lunch.

3. Green or gray <u>mold</u> may grow on food if it is not kept cold or put in a refrigerator or freezer.

Multisyllable Words

4. If my home is <u>unsold</u> at the end of this week, I will try to sell it for less.
5. A tale that is <u>retold</u> is told more than one time.
6. The sun was a <u>golden</u> yellow when it rose today.
7. She <u>boldly</u> went up to the cook and asked for more food.

Cloze Sentences 3

1. The sandwich became green and <u>moldy</u> when I left it in the picnic basket too long.
2. The man was <u>scolding</u> his dog for running across the street into traffic.
3. I <u>folded</u> my clean sheets to make them fit on the shelf.
4. The <u>oldest</u> man in this state is a hundred years old.
5. You'd better keep <u>holding</u> onto your dog's leash so he will not run into the road.
6. I felt the <u>coldness</u> as soon as I left my home, and I was glad I had on a thick coat.

Dictations

1. I <u>told</u> Mr. <u>Gold</u> to get the <u>mold</u> off the panes of glass before he <u>sold</u> his home.
2. Take the <u>old</u> <u>gold</u> cloth that I <u>sold</u> you and <u>hold</u> it. Then I will help you <u>fold</u> it.
3. That <u>old</u> man was so <u>bold</u>! He <u>told</u> the cop not to <u>scold</u> him for speeding!
4. The <u>old</u> lady did try to <u>hold</u> the <u>old</u>, <u>golden</u> cat, but he was <u>bold</u> and ran away. She <u>scolded</u> him and <u>told</u> him to come back.
5. The sky was <u>golden</u> at sunrise as the <u>old</u> man went <u>boldly</u> into the <u>coldness</u> to go camping and fishing. He had his <u>oldest</u> tent <u>folded</u> into a pack. It was a bit <u>moldy</u> from being stored, but he did not care as he set off, <u>holding</u> his fishing rod in his hand.

old (ōld) gold old

b	b	ly
c	c	ness
f	f	ed
g	g	en
h	h	ing
m	m	y
		est
s	uns	
sc	sc	ing
t	ret	

Name _____ Date _____

Word List 1

old　(ōld)　gold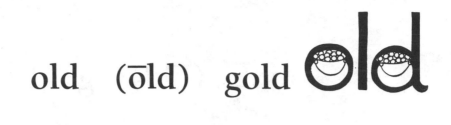

bold	**boldly**
cold	**coldness**
fold	**folded**
gold	**golden**
hold	**holding**
mold	**moldy**
old	**oldest**
sold	**unsold**
scold	**scolding**
told	**retold**

Name _____ Date _____

old (ōld) gold **old**

Write a word from the Word List to complete each sentence.

1. This glass can _____ three cups of milk.

2. When it is _____, I put on my coat, hat, mittens, and boots.

3. My ring is made of _____, and it shines when I clean it.

4. I _____ my home last week, and I will get a big check for lots of money this week!

5. We _____ clean clothes before we put them away.

6. She was _____ when she bravely saved the cat's life by getting it down from a tree.

7. I hope my mom will not _____ me for making that mistake. I did not mean to rip my coat!

Name _____ Date _____

Cloze Sentences 1

old (ōld) gold **old**

Write a word from the Word List to complete each sentence.

1. He needed to go shopping for a new coat. His _____ coat was too small.

2. She _____ us to stand in line until the bell rings at the beginning of lunch.

3. Green or gray _____ may grow on food if it is not kept cold or put in a refrigerator or freezer.

4. If my home is _____ at the end of this week, I will try to sell it for less.

5. A tale that is _____ is told more than one time.

6. The sun was a _____ yellow when it rose today.

7. She _____ went up to the cook and asked for more food.

Name _____ Date _____

© 1995 by Cynthia Conway Waring

Cloze Sentences 2

old (ōld) gold old

Write a word from the Word List to complete each sentence.

1. The sandwich became green and _____ when I left it in the picnic basket too long.

2. The man was _____ his dog for running across the street into traffic.

3. I _____ my clean sheets to make them fit on the shelf.

4. The _____ man in this state is a hundred years old.

5. You'd better keep _____ onto your dog's leash so he will not run into the road.

6. I felt the _____ as soon as I left my home, and I was glad I had on a thick coat.

Name _____ Date _____

Cloze Sentences 3

15 ai rain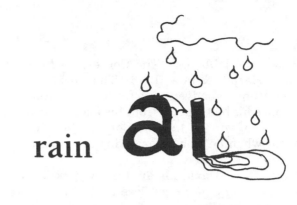

BOOK LIST

Rain and Snow

Peter Spier's Rain, Peter Spier (New York: The Trumpet Club, 1982). Spier captures the outdoor and indoor adventures and discoveries of a brother and sister during a day and night of rain in this wordless picture book with watercolor and ink illustrations.

Noah's Ark, Peter Spier (New York: Doubleday & Company, Inc., 1977). Realistic details in the ink and watercolor illustrations distinguish this version of the traditional story of the Ark, Noah, his family, and the animals before, during, and after the Flood. Caldecott Award Book.

Rainy Day Dream, Michael Chesworth (New York: Farrar, Straus and Giroux, 1992). In this wordless picture book, watercolor illustrations invite the reader to travel along with a boy who is swept on a fantasy rainy-day adventure as he holds onto the handle of his umbrella.

Rain, Donald Kalan, illustrated by Donald Crews (New York: Mulberry Books, 1978). Simple, bold illustrations and a few words (often in the colors they name) describe familiar parts of the environment during a rain shower. Repeated lines of the word *rain* appear in diagonal streams across the page during the storm.

When Will It Snow?, Syd Hoff, illustrated by Mary Chalmers (New York: Harper & Row, 1971). Mother tries to reassure Billy when he repeatedly asks if it soon will snow. Neither characters nor readers are disappointed at the book's end.

The Snowy Day, Ezra Jack Keats (New York: The Viking Press, 1962). Keats's bright collage illustrations and appealing text create a classic story of a small boy's adventures after a snowfall in the city. Caldecott Award Book.

Mooncake, Frank Asch (New York: Scholastic, 1983). Bear builds a rocket out of junk to find out what the moon tastes like; however, when he awakens he finds not the moon but a wintry surprise—mooncake!

A Letter to Amy, Ezra Jack Keats (New York: Harper & Row, 1968). A misunderstanding about his friend Amy's invitation to his party nearly lost in the rain almost ruins Peter's birthday, but all ends well when Amy and her parrot arrive in time for the cake and Peter's secret wish.

"Down the Hill" and "The Corner," in *Frog and Toad All Year*, Arnold Lobel (New York: Harper & Row, 1976). This book is a collection of stories about Frog and Toad's friendship and adventures through the seasons. In "Down the Hill," Frog convinces Toad to leave his bed and confront his fears of sledding but does not succeed in changing Toad's opinion of winter. In "The Corner," to cheer up Toad on a rainy day, Frog tells a story about when he looked for spring around a literal corner.

Snow Lion, David McPhail (New York: Parents Magazine Press, 1982). To escape the heat of the jungle, Lion flees to the hills where he discovers snow. When it melts as he attempts to take it back to his friends, Lion comes to understand the characteristics of snow.

We Hate Rain!, James Stevenson (New York: Greenwillow Books, 1988). When his grandchildren complain about a rainy day, Grandpa tells a tall tale about the time it poured for a month when he and his brother were children and water filled the four stories of their house.

Mushroom in the Rain, Mirra Ginsburg, adapted from the Russian of V. Suteyev, illustrated by José Aruego and Ariane Dewey (New York: Aladdin Books, 1974). In this cumulative story, animal after animal—ant, butterfly, mouse, sparrow, and rabbit—squeeze under a mushroom for shelter until it stops raining. A wise frog tells the amazed animals the secret of how they could all fit: Mushrooms grow in the rain!

The Mitten: An Old Ukrainian Folktale, Alvin Tresselt, adapted from the version by E. Rachev, illustrated by Yaroslava (New York: Scholastic, 1964). A little boy drops an old mitten in the snow and larger and larger animals climb in to keep warm. When a tiny cricket tries to squeeze in, the mitten splits open and tosses everyone back into the snow.

The Mitten: A Ukrainian Folktale, Jan Brett (New York: Scholastic, 1989). In this retelling, when a boy drops into the snow one of the new mittens his grandmother has knitted for him, a parade of animals squeezes into and then explodes out of the packed mitten when a bear sneezes, and the boy brings home to his incredulous grandmother two mittens—one greatly stretched.

Annie and the Wild Animals, Jan Brett (Boston: Houghton Mifflin Company, 1985). When her cat disappears one snowy day, Annie puts out corn cakes to attract a new pet, but the moose, wildcat, bear, and stag that crowd her yard are not what she had hoped for. In spring, the animals return to their homes, as does Annie's cat—with three kittens!

The Snow Child: A Russian Folktale, Freya Littledale, illustrated by Barbara Lavallee (New York: Scholastic, 1978). A childless couple builds a child out of snow, and she magically comes alive—always to live with them in winter and to return to the land of snow and cold during the warm months.

The Snow Child: A Russian Tale, Freya Littledale, illustrated by Leon Shtainmets (New York: Scholastic, 1978). Shtainmets's illustrations interpret Littledale's retelling of the Russian tale with delicate line drawings and tones of blue that convey the fragile world of the "child of the snow."

Stopping by Woods on a Snowy Evening, Robert Frost, illustrated by Susan Jeffers (New York: E. P. Dutton, 1978). Black and white and pastel drawings illustrate the well-known poem about a traveler and horse on a snowy winter evening in the woods.

The Legend of the Bluebonnet: An Old Tale of Texas, Tomie dePaola (New York: G. P. Putnam's Sons, 1983). A little girl sacrifices her most valued possession to bring rain to save her people from drought and famine, and blue flowers grow from the scattered ashes of her treasured doll. This *pourquoi* story tells the origin of bluebonnet wildflowers.

Katy and the Big Snow, Virginia Lee Burton (Boston: Houghton Mifflin Company, 1943). Strong and persistent Katy, the snow plow, plows out the city of Geoppolis—section by section—when it is crippled by a large snowfall. Includes illustrated maps of the city's streets.

White Snow Bright Snow, Alvin Tresselt, illustrated by Roger Duvoisin (New York: Scholastic, 1947). The people and animals in a small town prepare for and experience a snowy winter, and they celebrate the arrival of spring at its end.

The Big Snow, Berta and Elmer Hader (New York: Scholastic, 1948, 1976). Woodland animals anticipate and plan for the coming of snow. Those not hibernating are fed through the winter by an old man and woman who live nearby. Caldecott Medal Winner.

Yagua Days, Cruz Martel, illustrated by Jerry Pinkney (New York: Scholastic, 1976). Friends and family tell Anan about "yagua days" as he is growing up in New York City, but he does not understand their enthusiasm until he visits family in Puerto Rico and, on a rainy day, slides down the hill into the river on his stomach on a yagua (the outer covering of a palm frond). Contains a list of Spanish words with pronunciations and definitions.

Bringing the Rain to Kapiti Plain: A Nandi Tale, Verna Aardema, illustrated by Beatriz Vidal (New York: Dial Books for Young Readers, 1981). In this cumulative tale, Ki-pat shoots an arrow through a rain cloud and ends the terrible drought that had killed the vegetation and forced the animals to leave Kapiti Plain.

Time of Wonder, Robert McCloskey (New York: The Viking Press, 1957). Foggy mornings, sunny days, starlit nights, and a dramatic hurricane—McCloskey's text and watercolor illustrations create the summer world of an island in Penobscot Bay in Maine. Caldecott Medal Winner.

The Black Snowman, Phil Mendez, illustrated by Carole Byard (New York: Scholastic, 1989). A *Kente*, a magic storytelling cloth from Africa, discarded as a rag on a city street transforms a snowman and the lives of the two boys who make him.

Rain Player, David Wisniewski (New York: Clarion Books, 1991). With the help of Jaguar, Quetzal, and the sacred water, Pik brings rain to his parched land and earns the name Rain Player when he challenges and defeats the rain god in *pok-a-tok*, a game of ball. The author's note includes information about the Maya culture.

The Rainbabies, Laura Krauss Melmed, illustrated by Jim LaMarche (New York: Lothrop, Lee & Shepard Books, 1992). In this quest tale, a childless couple endures trials of water, fire, earth, and material temptation to protect the twelve tiny rainbabies sent to them by Mother Moonshower and are rewarded with a full-sized daughter of their own.

"Pooh and Piglet Hunt" and "Surrounded by Water," in ***Winnie-the-Pooh***, A. A. Milne, illustrated by Ernest H. Shepard (New York: Dell Publishing Co., Inc., 1926, 1954). This book introduces the adventures of a boy, Christopher Robin, and his toy bear, who's come to life as Winnie-the-Pooh, and their friends Piglet, Eeyore, Kanga and Roo, and Rabbit. In "Pooh and Piglet Hunt," as Pooh and Piglet follow pawprints in the snow in pursuit of a Woozle (or Wizzle), a strange thing occurs. Each time they circle the area, the prints of a new animal appear. In "Surrounded by Water," Pooh proves himself a hero when he (and Christopher Robin aboard Christopher Robin's umbrella) rescues Piglet, who is stranded when rain floods the Forest.

"Pooh Builds a House," in ***The House at Pooh Corner: Stories of Winnie-the-Pooh***, A. A. Milne, illustrated by Ernest H. Shepard (New York: E. P. Dutton, 1928, 1956). This book contains more stories of Christopher Robin and Pooh's friends in the Forest and introduces Tigger. In "Pooh Builds a House," on a snowy day Pooh and Piglet make a house for Eeyore at Pooh's Corner, but there's a problem. They use sticks from Eeyore's house at the other end of the Forest to construct it!

MOTIVATION AND EXTENSION ACTIVITIES

1. At the beginning of the unit, students and the teacher brainstorm and record lists in two columns: (1) what they know (or think they know), and (2) what they would like to learn about rain (on one chart) and snow (on another chart). Throughout the unit, they verify or correct and add information to the list using the books suggested in this chapter and resource books and materials.

2. Students tell and/or write stories for the wordless books: ***Peter Spier's Rain***, ***Noah's Ark***, ***Rainy Day Dream***, and ***Rain***.

3. With Peter Spier as an "Illustrator under Study," students and the teacher discuss a collection of his books, including ***Peter Spier's Rain*** and ***Noah's Ark***. Some of his other books are (in alphabetical order by title) ***And So My Garden Grows***; ***Bored—Nothing to Do***; ***Crash! Bang! Boom!***; ***Dreams***; ***Fast-Slow, High-Low***; ***Gobble, Growl, Grunt***; ***Hurrah, We're Outward Bound!***; ***London Bridge Is Falling Down***; ***Of Dikes and Windmills***; ***Oh, Were They Ever Happy!***; ***People***; ***Peter Spier's Advent Calendar***; ***Peter Spier's Birthday Cake***; ***Peter Spier's Christmas***; ***The Book of Jonah***; ***The Erie Canal***; ***The Fox Went out on a Chilly Night*** (see Chapter 34, x fox); ***The Star-Spangled Banner***; ***Tin Lizzie***; ***To Market! To Market!***; and ***We the People***.

4. Students and the teacher read more about the adventures of Frog and Toad in

Frog and Toad All Year and in *Days with Frog and Toad*, *Frog and Toad Are Friends*, and *Frog and Toad Together* by Arnold Lobel.

5. The plots of *Mushroom in the Rain*, *The Mitten: An Old Ukrainian Folktale* (Tresselt), and *The Mitten: A Ukrainian Folktale* (Brett) follow a common repetitive and cumulative pattern. (See Activity 5 in Chapter 12, *igh night*, for a more complete discussion.) In each tale, character after character tries to fit into a small space; however, there are differences in the details. In *Mushroom in the Rain*, the animals are able to fit under the mushroom due to its unique characteristic—it grows. (This is a static cumulative pattern—the simple adding or accumulating of a collection of characters.) Characters in *The Mitten* tales are not as fortunate. In this latter variation, animal after animal squeezes in and a final character [the tiny cricket in *The Mitten: An Old Ukrainian Folktale* (Tresselt) or a final event (the mouse's whisker causes the bear to sneeze in *The Mitten: A Ukrainian Folktale*, by Brett] breaks the shelter apart, sending all of the creatures flying out. (This is a dynamic cumulative pattern, in which characters accumulate and attempt to achieve a common goal and an event causes an action involving the characters. Typically, in this type of pattern, the characters achieve their goal. In *The Mitten*, they do not.)

After they read the three books, students and the teacher explore and compare and contrast the patterns and details.

+ They list the characters that appear in each version of *The Mitten* and complete a Venn diagram showing which animals are common to both.

+ They draw a diagram of the pattern:

Mushroom in the Rain:

animal + animal . . . shelter grows = animal + animal

The Mitten:

animal + animal . . . + animal or event = animal   animal

+ As an individual or group project, students make props, puppets, and scenery out of paper, cloth, or other materials for puppet shows of the tales. They make animal puppets out of paper attached to wooden craft/popsicle sticks or pencils, hand puppets out of socks, or finger puppets from the fingers cut off old gloves. A child-size umbrella makes a fine mushroom. A small pillowcase is a good-size mitten for sock hand puppets; a potholder mitt is a more appropriate size for stick or finger puppets.

+ Students act out the story. They dramatize the events in the story in costume with a large, adult-size umbrella (a beach or golf umbrella work well) as the mushroom or a sleeping bag or sheet as the mitten.

6. Students and the teacher verify the premise that mushrooms grow in the rain in *Mushroom in the Rain* and further investigate the characteristics of mushrooms in resource books and materials.

7. Students and the teacher compare and contrast the illustrations in the two versions of *The Mitten*. They discuss the ways the illustrators have chosen to depict the Ukrainian culture and environment through the techniques they have used and details they have included—setting, animals, clothing, and houses.

8. Before or after they listen to or read **Annie and the Wild Animals**, students make and eat corn cakes.

9. Students and the teacher engage in a study of the use of borders in illustrations.

• They explore the borders in the illustrations of the two books by Brett in this unit— **The Mitten: A Ukrainian Folktale** and **Annie and the Wild Animals**—and in others she has illustrated, including **Berlioz the Bear** (New York: G. P. Putnam's Sons, 1991), **Goldilocks and the Three Bears** (New York: G. P. Putnam's Sons, 1987) (see Chapter 8, ee seeds), and **The First Dog** (New York: The Trumpet Club, 1988).

• They read and discuss a series of books by Vera B. Williams about a three-generational family in a city in the United States in which borders reflect the mood, events, and details of the illustrations and text they surround:

A Chair for My Mother, Vera B. Williams (New York: Scholastic, 1982).

Something Special For Me, Vera B. Williams (New York: Mulberry Books, 1983). (See Chapter 19, ir birthday.)

Music, Music for Everyone, Vera B. Williams (New York: Mulberry Books, 1984).

10. After they read **The Snow Child: A Russian Folktale**, by Freya Littledale and illustrated by Barbara Lavallee, and **The Snow Child: A Russian Tale**, by Freya Littledale and illustrated by Leon Shtainmets, students compare and contrast the interpretations by the two illustrators of the tale retold by the same author.

11. Students listen to or read **The Rainbabies** and compare and contrast this story of a childless couple (a common motif in traditional literature) with the story of the childless couple in the two versions of **The Snow Child** that they have read.

12. After they listen to or read **The Rainbabies**, students name the four trials in the childless couple's quest for a child.

13. As they listen to or read **Yagua Days**, students who do not understand or speak Spanish make predictions about the meaning of Spanish words with which they may be unfamiliar. They confirm or revise/correct their hypotheses by reading on in the story and by consulting the list of Spanish words from the story at the back of the book, which includes definitions and pronunciations.

14. Background information that accompanies **Bringing the Rain to Kapiti Plain: A Nandi Tale** explains that the tale was discovered by an anthropologist in Nandi, Kenya over seventy years before Aardema retold it. Aardema rewrote the story using a cumulative refrain pattern and the rhythm of the cumulative nursery rhyme **The House That Jack Built** (Chapter 23, ou house).

Students and the teacher discuss the similarities and differences between the two rhymes.

• They compare and contrast the pattern and rhythm of the two rhymes as they read and discuss the books.

• They clap their hands, stamp their feet, or use rhythm instruments to punctuate the rhythmic patterns as the teacher or other students read the two rhymes.

15. After they listen to or read *Time of Wonder*, students and the teacher share about storms. Orally or in writing, they describe and illustrate storms they have experienced and tell what they did during the storm and if they were frightened.

16. On several pages of *Time of Wonder*, McCloskey's preliminary pencil sketches for his watercolor paintings are visible (including a pail in a beach scene that he did not paint). Students search the illustrations to discover them.

17. Students write the message they would have written and put in a bottle if they had been stranded during a flood, as Piglet was in "Surrounded by Water" in *Winnie-the-Pooh*.

18. If the teacher presents "Pooh Builds a House" in *The House at Pooh Corner: Stories of Winnie-the-Pooh* as a read-aloud, students read and sing the snow song (that repeats in the story) as it appears. In individual shared reading, students read and sing the song in the book as the teacher hesitates (oral cloze). Students in a group read and sing chorally from a chart the teacher has prepared.

19. *The Pooh Party Book*, Virginia H. Ellison, illustrated by Ernest Shepard (New York: Dell Publishing Co., 1971), describes five parties with Winnie-the-Pooh story themes—a birthday party for Eeyore and a party for each season with directions for making invitations, decorations, refreshments (with recipes), favors and crafts, and games. Students and the teacher give "A Woozle-Wizzle Snow Party," as described in *The Pooh Party Book*.

20. Students and the teacher share more of the stories about Christopher Robin and Pooh in the companion books: *Winnie-the-Pooh* and *The House at Pooh Corner: Stories of Winnie-the-Pooh*.

21. If the weather permits, students and the teacher go outside and have rainy or snowy day adventures. They make tracks in the snow, as the characters do in *The Snowy Day, Mooncake*, and "Pooh and Piglet Hunt" in *Winnie-the-Pooh*.

22. Many of the books in this unit show animals and people preparing for and living with snow and rain (or drought). Students and the teacher discuss what they know about preparing for and coping with changes in weather from their own experiences, from reading the books in this chapter and from resource books and materials.

23. Students and the teacher explore snow and ice through simple science experiments from *Snow and Ice: A Science Is Fun Book*, Stephen Krensky, illustrated by John Hayes (New York: Scholastic, 1989). The book includes clear directions for making six-sided paper snowflakes.

24. Students and the teacher tell and/or write and illustrate what they like to do on a rainy or snowy day. (See Activity 7 in Chapter 7, ay day, for a related activity and book.)

25. Students and the teacher discuss the techniques used by illustrators as they read and share the books in this chapter. The teacher makes supplies available and demonstrates techniques as appropriate during the unit. Students experiment with the following techniques to make rain or snow scenes or for their own purposes:

- *Watercolor paints and watercolor paints and ink:* Students create pictures, designs, or scenes with watercolor paints or pen and ink and watercolor paints.

- *Crayon resist and watercolor paints:* Students draw figures, objects, or designs with crayon and paint foregrounds and backgrounds with watercolor paints.

- *Picture and word collages:* Students make collages in the style of those in *Rain*. They cut pictures and weather, color, or individual choice words out of magazines and newspapers and/or they (or the teacher) make strips of repeated words on the computer or typewriter and paste or glue them on a paper background. They make snow or rain scene collages inspired by the illustrations in *The Snowy Day* and *A Letter to Amy*. They make collages using computer art described in the "Collage (Around the World)" chapter of *Kid Pix around the World: A Multicultural Computer Activity Book*. (See the final activity in this list.)

* *Cartooning:* Students tell their own rainy or snowy day (or choice of theme) tall tales using words and pictures in cartoon frames, as Stevenson does in *We Hate Rain!*.

* *Illustrated borders:* Jan Brett's illustrations in *The Mitten: A Ukrainian Folktale* and *Annie and the Wild Animals* are surrounded by detailed borders that relate to the text and pictures on the page. In *The Mitten*, the borders also give clues about the event or animal that will appear on the next page. Students incorporate illustrated borders in their paintings and drawings.

* *Cut-paper technique:* In an author's note at the end of *Rain Player*, David Wisniewski describes the procedure he uses to achieve the three-dimensional effect. He uses a cut-paper technique to make the illustrations, which are then photographed with special lighting to provide shadows. Students make three-dimensional pictures, designs, and scenes using a cut-paper technique. If they choose, they make dioramas in shoeboxes, possibly showing the people, cultures, and physical environments (including vegetation and animals) from books in this unit. Students make paper snowflakes. *Snow and Ice: A Science Is Fun Book* contains easy-to-follow, step-by-step directions for making six-sided flakes.

* *Paint stamps:* Several of the collage illustrations in *The Snowy Day* are complemented by painted snowflakes applied with stamps. Students make their own stamps by cutting sponges or potatoes into snowflake shapes. They dip them into paint and apply them to paper.

* *Spatter paint:* Students draw or paint figures, objects, and the background of a scene on a piece of paper with crayon, colored pencil, markers, chalk, or paint and place it on the bottom of an open box. They spatter paint to represent rain or snow by tapping a brush that is filled with paint on the side of the box or on their free hand.

* *Computer art:* Students use "Kid Pix" or other computer drawing and painting programs to create rain and snow scenes. Students or the teacher read the "Winter (Switzerland)" chapter in *Kid Pix around the World: A Multicultural Computer Activity Book*, Barbara Chan (Reading, Mass.: Addison-Wesley Publishing Company, 1993) and experiment with the techniques for making snow and rain scenes that it suggests. The book contains essays that provide background information about twenty cultures around the world and detailed, step-by-step instructions that show children how to do drawing and painting activities using "Kid Pix" computer software. Presented cultures are marked on a world map in the front of the book.

26. Students and the teacher locate on a map and/or globe the places/cultures (of origin or depicted) in the books read in this chapter, including New York City in the United States (*A Letter to Amy* and *Yagua Days*); Russia (*Mushroom in the Rain* and *The Snow Child*); Ukraine (*The Mitten*); the Comanche culture and Texas in the United States (*The Legend of the Bluebonnet: An Old Tale of Texas*); Puerto Rico

(*Yagua Days*); Nandi in Kenya (***Bringing the Rain to Kapiti Plain: A Nandi Tale***); Penobscot Bay of Maine in the United States (***A Time of Wonder***); Western Africa and the Ashanti culture (***The Black Snowman***); Mexico, Belize, Honduras, Guatemala, and El Salvador (***Rain Player***); England ((***Winnie-the-Pooh*** and ***The House at Pooh Corner: Stories of Winnie-the-Pooh***); and Switzerland ["Winter (Switzerland)" in ***Kid Pix around the World: A Multicultural Computer Activity Book***].

TEACHER REFERENCE

Cloze Sentences

One-Syllable Words

Cloze Sentences 1

1. You can take a <u>train</u> ride.
2. You can <u>sail</u> on a ship.
3. You can <u>sprain</u> your leg.
4. You can have a <u>pain</u> in your neck.
5. You can <u>paint</u> your bike red.
6. You can send a bandit to <u>jail</u>.
7. You can step on a cat's <u>tail</u>.
8. You can use a <u>chain</u> to lock your bike.

Cloze Sentences 2

1. You can have a <u>stain</u> or spot on your jacket.
2. You can <u>gain</u> a lot and get fat.
3. You can use your <u>brain</u> to think, read, write, and do math.
4. You can have no <u>air</u> in a flat tire.
5. You can follow a <u>trail</u> to take a hike.
6. You can get wet in the <u>rain</u>.
7. You can trip on your way up or down the <u>stairs</u>.

Multisyllable Words

Cloze Sentences 3

1. I get a <u>haircut</u> when my hair gets too long.
2. A <u>painless</u> shot does not give you pain when you get it.
3. An <u>aircraft</u> is nearly the same as an airplane.
4. You have to send a letter <u>airmail</u> when you send it overseas.
5. A <u>rainbow</u>, at times, can be seen in the sky when the sun shines after it rains.
6. You can go <u>sailing</u> on a lake or on the sea on a sailboat.
7. <u>Daily</u> is when a thing happens each day.

Cloze Sentences 4

1. You can make a <u>complaint</u> if you get a thing at a store that you do not like.
2. What <u>remains</u> of a cake is what is left of it.
3. An <u>ailment</u> can be a sickness or an illness.
4. <u>Dairy</u> products include milk and cheese.
5. If we <u>remain</u> seated, then we stay seated and do not get up.
6. When you see what a can or a box <u>contains</u>, you see what is inside of it.
7. The <u>mailman</u> brings mail to mailboxes each day.

Dictations

1. <u>Gail</u> has <u>trained</u> her dog well. <u>Daily</u> it <u>waits</u> on its <u>chain</u> for the <u>mailman</u>, wags its <u>tail</u>, and does not <u>complain</u>.
2. I <u>complained</u> when I had to <u>wait</u> for the <u>train</u> in the <u>rain</u>, but when a <u>rainbow</u> <u>remained</u> in the sky after the <u>rain</u> stopped I felt that I had <u>gained</u> from the <u>waiting</u>.
3. Ted held up a <u>train</u>. When he <u>failed</u> to get away he was put in <u>jail</u>, but his pal was <u>waiting</u> to <u>aid</u> him with <u>bail</u> so he did not <u>remain</u> in <u>jail</u>.

ai (ā) rain

r			s	l
br	n		spr	n
ch	n		st	n
g	n		st	rs
j	l		t	l
p	n		tr	l
p	nt		tr	n
r	n			

Name _____ Date _____

Word List 1

ai (ā) rain

air	sail
brain	sprain
chain	stain
gain	stairs
jail	tail
pain	trail
paint	train
rain	

Name _____ Date _____

Word List 2

ai (ā) rain

Write a word from the Word List to complete each sentence.

1. You can take a _____ ride.

2. You can _____ on a ship.

3. You can _____ your leg.

4. You can have a _____ in your neck.

5. You can _____ your bike red.

6. You can send a bandit to _____ .

7. You can step on a cat's _____ .

8. You can use a _____ to lock your bike.

Name _____ Date _____

Cloze Sentences 1

ai (ā) rain

Write a word from the Word List to complete each sentence.

1. You can have a _____ or spot on your jacket.

2. You can _____ a lot and get fat.

3. You can use your _____ to think, read, write, and do math.

4. You can have no _____ in a flat tire.

5. You can follow a _____ to take a hike.

6. You can get wet in the _____ .

7. You can trip on your way up or down the _____ .

Name _____ Date _____

Cloze Sentences 2

ai (ā) rain

lment   h rcut

rcraft   m lman

rm l   p nless

compl nt   r nbow

cont ns   rem n

d ly   rem ns

d ry

Name _____ Date _____

ai (ā) rain

ailment   haircut

aircraft   mailman

airmail   painless

complaint   rainbow

contains   remain

daily   remains

dairy

Name _____ Date _____

Word List 4

ai (ā) rain

Write a word from the Word List to complete each sentence.

1. I get a _____ when my hair gets too long.

2. A _____ shot does not give you pain when you get it.

3. An _____ is nearly the same as an airplane.

4. You have to send a letter _____ when you send it overseas.

5. A _____, at times, can be seen in the sky when the sun shines after it rains.

6. You can go _____ on a lake or on the sea on a sailboat.

7. _____ is when a thing happens each day.

Name _____ Date _____

Cloze Sentences 3

ai (ā) rain

Write a word from the Word List to complete each sentence.

1. You can make a _____ if you get a thing at a store that you do not like.

2. What _____ of a cake is what is left of it.

3. An _____ can be a sickness or an illness.

4. _____ products include milk and cheese.

5. If we _____ seated, then we stay seated and do not get up.

6. When you see what a can or a box _____, you see what is inside of it.

7. The _____ brings mail to mailboxes each day.

Name _____ Date _____

Cloze Sentences 4

16   ar   star   **ar**

BOOK LIST

Stars and Travelers

All I Am, Eileen Roe, illustrated by Helen Cogancherry (New York: Scholastic, 1990). A young boy reflects about who he is—"child, friend, neighbor, helper, listener and thinker, artist, animal lover, singer, dancer" and "daydreamer" by day and "stargazer" by night—as he wonders who he will be.

Draw Me a Star, Eric Carle (New York: Philomel Books, 1992). This book tells of an artist's personal and professional journey as, from childhood to his later years, he finds and develops his talent. One special star (drawn like the one Carle's grandmother taught him to make as a child) takes him on a spiritual journey.

Nana Upstairs & Nana Downstairs, Tomie dePaola (New York: Penguin Books, 1973). As a little boy, Tommy enjoyed his Sunday visits with Nana Upstairs and Nana Downstairs, and it is a great loss when his great grandmother and, later, his grandmother die; but falling stars appear to Tommy as their kisses and help him deal with his grief.

How Many Stars in the Sky?, Lenny Hort, illustrated by James E. Ransome (New York: The Trumpet Club, 1991). A boy and his father deepen their special relationship one night when they drive through the city to the country so they can count and sleep under the stars together.

The Josefina Story Quilt, Eleanor Coerr, illustrated by Bruce Degen (New York: Harper & Row, 1986). Pa is reluctant to let Faith take her old pet hen, Josefina, in their covered wagon as they travel west in 1850, and her misadventures nearly cause Josefina's demise, but the hen proves her worth along the way. Faith records their journey in a patchwork quilt.

The Quilt Story, Tony Johnston, illustrated by Tomie dePaola (New York: G. P. Putnam's Sons, 1985). When her family travels west in a covered wagon, the quilt Abigail's mother made provides a warm and comforting familiarity. Many years later, one of Abigail's young relatives discovers the quilt in the attic, and it accompanies her, too, to a new home.

Watch the Stars Come Out, Riki Levinson, illustrated by Diane Goode (New York: E. P. Dutton, 1985). A little girl learns that she shares her great grandmother's traits— red hair, the love of a good story, and pleasure in watching the stars come out—as her grandmother tells the story her mother told of her immigration to the United States from Europe.

The Drinking Gourd: A Story of the Underground Railroad, F. N. Monjo, illustrated by Fred Brenner (New York: HarperCollins, 1970). Tommy learns about the Underground Railroad as he helps his father take a family with young children from their home to the next station. Includes lyrics to a traditional song and an author's note with historical background.

Follow the Drinking Gourd, Jeanette Winter (New York: Alfred A. Knopf, 1988). A family and friends brave danger and hardship to use the directions hidden in the words of a song they were taught by an old sailor to follow the Drinking Gourd (the Big Dipper) north, along the Underground Railroad, to Canada to escape slavery. Includes music for the song and background information about the story.

The Long Way to a New Land, Joan Sandin (New York: Harper & Row, 1981). Invited to join his uncle's family in America when drought causes famine in Sweden, Carl Erik's family immigrates by boat to the United States in 1868. A map at the beginning of the book shows their journey.

The Long Way Westward, Joan Sandin (New York: Harper & Row, 1989). The book continues the story of Carl Erik's family (from *The Long Way to a New Land* by the same author), emigrants from Sweden to the United States, as they leave New York City and travel west in "emigrant train cars" to Minnesota to join Carl Erik's uncle and his family. A map at the beginning of the book records their journey.

Going West, Jean Van Leeuwen, illustrated by Thomas B. Allen (New York: Dial Books for Young Readers, 1992). Seven-year-old Hannah's account encompasses four seasons as her pioneer family adventures across the plains of the United States in a covered wagon to make a new life and home on the western prairie.

I'm Terrific, Marjorie Weinman Sharmat, illustrated by Kay Chorao (New York: Holiday House, 1977). Jason Everett Bear tries out being "a brand new bear" when he finds that his boastful attitude and habit of giving himself stars for his accomplishments alienate his friends, and he learns that just being himself is "terrific."

Make Way for Ducklings, Robert McCloskey (New York: Penguin Books, 1941). In the classic story of legendary travelers, Mrs. Mallard proves her competence and the value of bringing up her children well when she leads her eight ducklings from an island in the Charles River to the Public Garden in Boston, Massachusetts. Caldecott Award Book.

Dakota Dugout, Ann Turner, illustrated by Ronald Himler (New York: Macmillan Publishing Company, 1985). As she tells her granddaughter about the isolated and often difficult pioneer life through the seasons in a sod house on the prairies of Dakota, a woman reflects on the parts of the simple life that she misses.

Nettie's Trip South, Ann Turner, illustrated by Ronald Himler (New York: Scholastic, 1987). In a letter to a friend, ten-year-old Nettie describes how her trip south—where she sees the daily realities of slavery, including a slave auction—changes her.

Tar Beach, Faith Ringgold (New York: Scholastic, 1991). Ringgold's "Tar Beach" story quilt was adapted and combined with text and paintings in this book about Cassie's fantasy flight of the spirit amid the stars above New York City from the rooftop of her apartment building (Tar Beach).

Aunt Harriet's Underground Railroad in the Sky, Faith Ringgold (New York: Crown Publishers, Inc., 1992). Cassie and her brother Be Be (from ***Tar Beach*** by the same author) learn about slavery—and freedom—while flying aboard a fantasy train on the Underground Railroad, whose conductor is Harriet Tubman. Contains background information about Harriet Tubman and the Underground Railroad, including a short bibliography of further readings and a map of routes.

Letting Swift River Go, Jane Yolen, illustrated by Barbara Cooney (Boston: Little, Brown and Company, 1992). Under the stars one night, a woman is able to find a peace with the loss and her memories of the Swift River Valley towns in western Massachusetts, where she had lived as a child until they were evacuated and flooded to create the Quabbin Reservoir between 1927 and 1946.

The Orphan Boy: A Maasai Story, Tololwa M. Mollel, illustrated by Paul Morin (New York: Clarion Books, 1990). In this *pourquoi* story, a star disappears from the sky and an orphan boy mysteriously appears to live with a childless old man, who learns the price of curiosity. His insatiable interest in the boy's secret powers betrays the boy's trust and sends him back to the sky as the planet Venus. Notes about the author contain information about the Maasai and the author's life in Kenya and Tanzania.

Sarah, Plain and Tall, Patricia MacLachlan (New York: Harper & Row, 1985). Sarah answers an advertisement and leaves her seaside home in Maine to adjust to her new life as wife and mother of a man and his two young children on the western prairie of the United States. Newbery Award Book.

MOTIVATION AND EXTENSION ACTIVITIES

1. The experiences of the characters in the books in this chapter represent different themes and several different kinds of journeys undertaken by travelers. At the beginning of the unit, the teacher explains and displays, as headings of charts, the following themes that describe different journeys. As they listen to or read each book in the chapter, students decide to which category it belongs, and the teacher or students write it under the appropriate heading. Students explain the thinking behind their responses.

Inner/Personal/Spiritual Journeys

All I Am, Draw Me a Star, Nana Upstairs & Nana Downstairs, How Many Stars in the Sky?, I'm Terrific, Make Way for Ducklings, Nettie's Trip South, Tar Beach, Letting Swift River Go, The Orphan Boy

Pioneers Traveling West in the United States during the Mid-1800s

The Josefina Story Quilt; The Quilt Story; The Long Way Westward; Dakota Dugout; Sarah, Plain and Tall

Following the Stars: The Underground Railroad

Follow the Drinking Gourd (Winter), Follow the Drinking Gourd (Monjo), Aunt Harriet's Underground Railroad in the Sky, Nettie's Trip South

Immigration: Traveling from One Culture to a New Culture

Watch the Stars Come Out, **The Long Way to a New Land** (Chapter 30, tion immigration, contains additional books and activities related to this theme.)

During discussion, students and the teacher establish the historical context and geographical setting of each book and explore available background information. They consider the hardships (physical and emotional) with which characters are confronted and how they respond. They relate the challenges to the environment and setting and discuss who or what supported characters during challenges. They compare and contrast the cultures depicted (or of origin) of the stories. They discuss the inner journeys of the characters in the books and focus on how and why characters change and on the ways in which they are different at the end of the book.

2. After they read or listen to **All I Am**, students and the teacher reflect about who they are and might be in the future.

+ They tell and/or illustrate a book following the repetitive pattern of Roe's book.

+ They discuss how their reflections about themselves might change during different periods of their lives and in response to different situations and circumstances as they change—for example, with the birth or adoption of a sibling; with the discovery of a new interest, talent, hobby, or challenge; when they move to a new home and/ or school; when they get a new pet; when they become/became adults; when they get/got married; or when they get/got a (new) job.

3. In a letter to readers, Carle tells how the rhyme his German grandmother said as she drew stars for him when he was a child and a dream he had as an adult gave him the idea for writing **Draw Me a Star**. The dream gave him the story's beginning and end and then, he shares, he wrote the middle.

+ Students and the teacher discuss what they think Carle considers the beginning, middle, and end of his story.

+ They share how they have gotten ideas for pieces they have written.

+ They discuss the talents they are discovering and developing.

+ They tell how people and/or events have inspired them to discover or develop their talents.

+ They make stars as they follow the sequence of steps and say the rhyme from Carle's grandmother.

4. After they read or listen to **Nana Upstairs & Nana Downstairs**, students and the teacher share about the death of a grandparent or other important person in their lives.

5. Students and the teacher tell about seeing falling stars. They compare and contrast their experiences and those of Tommy in **Nana Upstairs & Nana Downstairs**.

6. Students and the teacher compare and contrast the city and country settings of *How Many Stars in the Sky?*.

7. The boy and his father in *How Many Stars in the Sky?* wonder about and identify constellations and planets they see in the sky during the night and day (the sun).

♦ Students and the teacher learn more about stars, planets, and the sky as they read and explore resource books and materials and share experiences—stargazing field trips and/or visits to an observatory or planetarium. They read and discuss *Where Are the Stars during the Day?: A Book about Stars*, by Melvin and Gilda Berger, illustrated by Blanche Sims (Nashville, Tenn.: Ideals Publishing Corporation, 1993).

♦ They find constellations in the sky and make their own pictures of constellations on the wall with coffee cans and flashlights, as described in the resource book *The Sky Is Full of Stars: A Let's-Read-and-Find-Out Book*, Franklyn M. Branley, illustrated by Felicia Bond (New York: Harper & Row, 1981).

8. Reading Rainbow Library has produced a special edition of *Watch the Stars Come Out* written by Marsha Cohen, MaryAnn Gray, and Barbara A. McCall and illustrated by Kris Nielsen (New York: Reading Rainbow Gazette, Inc., 1987). It contains the full text and illustrations of the book, "behind the scenes" background information, and suggested activities to accompany the book.

Students and the teacher explore and discuss the background information and complete selected activities from the special edition after they share *Watch the Stars Come Out*. (See Activity 2 in Chapter 30, tion immigration, for an activity that encourages students to use critical thinking and evaluative skills to evaluate the accuracy and current validity of some of the information presented in the special edition.)

9. Students and the teacher sing the song "Follow the Drinking Gourd" in the two versions of *Follow the Drinking Gourd*. If they choose, they add gestures or actions to dramatize it.

10. Students and the teacher compare and contrast the two versions of *Follow the Drinking Gourd* (Monjo, Winter) and choose their favorite. They identify the criteria on which they based their choice. They read or listen to a third story about the Underground Railroad—*Sweet Clara and the Freedom Quilt*, by Deborah Hopkinson and illustrated by James Ransome (New York: Alfred A. Knopf, 1993)—in which, aided by the quilt onto which she sews a map pattern of the Underground Railroad, Clara is reunited with her mother and sister and, with them and a friend, escapes to freedom. (See Chapter 33, qu quilt.) Students and the teacher compare and contrast the experiences of the characters in the three books about the Underground Railroad.

11. After they read or listen to *Nettie's Trip South*, students and the teacher write a letter to a friend describing a trip or experience that changed them.

12. Much of the power of Turner's writing in *Nettie's Trip South* comes from her use of figurative language—Nettie uses metaphors and similes to compare the unknown to the familiar as she describes her new experiences to her friend Addie, to whom she writes a letter. Students and the teacher identify and discuss the figurative language in *Nettie's Trip South*. They visualize and/or draw/paint pictures of the images (literal and/or figurative) the descriptions evoke. Images include metaphor ("His face was so black and round and fierce, it could've been fired from a cannon in war") and similes: "Trees were like old men with tattered gray coats," "*Gone*, Addie, like a sack of flour

pushed across a store counter," "a man with a face like the oak in our yard, all twisted," "the sun like a warm hand," and "a black skin like a tight coat."

13. Ringgold's Cassie in *Aunt Harriet's Underground Railroad in the Sky* uses figurative language (metaphors and similes) to describe her fantasy journey. For example, she uses metaphors ("a sea of clouds" and "The steam from the falls formed a soft blanket that lifted me up") and similes: "the mountains looked like pieces of rock candy and the oceans like tiny cups of tea," "It was like watching a silent movie," "Then the woman conductor's voice came like a soft whisper in my ear," "Then Aunt Harriet's voice came streaming down my cheeks like a gust of wind," "Now the tears came streaming down my cheeks like rain," and "Niagara Falls looked like a giant tea party with a billion cups of steaming hot tea being poured to a resounding applause." Students and the teacher identify and discuss the figurative language (metaphors and similes) in *Aunt Harriet's Underground Railroad in the Sky*. They visualize and/or draw/paint pictures of the literal and/or figurative images the descriptions create.

14. Students and the teacher explore and/or reread other books that feature figurative language. (See Activity 18 in Chapter 2, oo moon, Activity 12 in Chapter 4, y fly, Activity 13 in Chapter 13, oa goat, Activity 10 in Chapter 22, ow owl, Activity 12 in Chapter 29, consonant-le fable, and Activity 8 in Chapter 32, c Frances Cinderella fancy.)

15. Students and the teacher learn more about the Maasai/Masai people and culture of *The Orphan Boy: A Maasai Story* as they share two additional picture books:

- *Masai and I*, Virginia Kroll, illustrated by Nancy Carpenter (New York: Four Winds Press, 1992), in which the author compares and contrasts the cultures of East Africa and the United States. In the book, a little girl from a city in the United States imagines what it would be like if she and a Masai girl from East Africa (about which she learns in school) were to change places.

- *Who's in Rabbit's House?: A Masai Tale*, Verna Aardema, illustrated by Leo and Diane Dillon (New York: The Dial Press, 1969, 1977), which is the retelling of a Masai folktale as a play performed by villagers in masks and costumes. In the play, Rabbit refuses the aid of a series of her friends, who offer to help her get a frightening intruder out of her house until frog, posing as a poisonous spitting snake, scares the creature—who turns out to be just a caterpillar.

16. Students, in masks and costumes, perform the play of *Who's in Rabbit's House?: A Masai Tale*.

17. Before or after they listen to or read *Sarah, Plain and Tall*, students have opportunities to look at and discuss photographs, drawings, and paintings of plains settings and ocean settings from the United States. They then create plains pictures with colored pencils and pictures of the sea with three colored pencils—blue, gray, and green—like the ones Sarah gives to Anna and Caleb (and to them all) when she returns home from the store at the end of the book.

18. Students and the teacher locate on a map and/or globe the places/cultures (depicted or of origin) in the books read in this chapter, including Germany (*Draw Me a Star*); California and the plains and prairies of the western United States (*The Josefina Story Quilt*, *The Quilt Story*, *The Long Way Westward*, *Going West, Dakota Dugout*, and *Sarah, Plain and Tall*); Europe and New York City in the United States (*Watch the Stars Come Out*); routes of the Underground Railroad in the United States [*The Drinking Gourd: A Story of the Underground Railroad* (Monjo) and *Follow*

the Drinking Gourd (Winter), ***Aunt Harriet's Underground Railroad in the Sky***, and ***Sweet Clara and the Freedom Quilt***]; Gothenbury in Sweden, Hull and Liverpool in England, and New York City in the United States (***The Long Way to a New Land***); New York City in New York, Philadelphia and Pittsburgh in Pennsylvania, Crestline in Ohio, Fort Wayne in Indiana, Chicago in Illinois, LaCrosse in Wisconsin, and St. Paul and Anoka in Minnesota in the United States (***The Long Way Westward***); Boston, Massachusetts in the United States (***Make Way for Ducklings***); Dakota in the United States (***Dakota Dugout***); Chesapeake Bay in the United States (***Nettie's Trip South***); New York City in the United States (***Tar Beach***); Quabbin Reservoir and the Swift River valley in western Massachusetts in the United States (***Letting Swift River Go***); and eastern Africa, Kenya, and Tanzania (***The Orphan Boy: A Maasai Story***).

TEACHER REFERENCE

Cloze Sentences

One-Syllable Words

Cloze Sentences 1

1. A <u>sharp</u> knife cuts better than a dull knife.
2. A thing that is <u>far</u> away is not nearby.
3. He wore a <u>scarf</u> around his neck on the day that it snowed.
4. I sent a get well <u>card</u> to my mom when she was sick.
5. He likes to play on the swings in the back <u>yard</u> behind his home.
6. I need to get a mattress that is <u>hard</u>. My old mattress is too soft.
7. She used red <u>yarn</u> to knit a pair of mittens and a scarf that matches.

Cloze Sentences 2

1. If I cannot drive my <u>car</u>, I ride the bus.
2. It is fun to make a wish on a <u>star</u> that is in the night sky.
3. I got a <u>jar</u> of grape jam at the store so I can make sandwiches.
4. He shared his candy <u>bar</u> with me, and I gave him a cupcake.
5. A <u>barn</u> can be the home of the animals on a farm.
6. <u>Tar</u> can be used to pave a street.

Multisyllable Words

Cloze Sentences 3

1. I <u>harvest</u> the food that I grow in my garden when it is ripe.
2. We need to <u>sharpen</u> this knife. It is too dull to cut well.
3. I plant seeds in my <u>garden</u> to grow the food I need to eat.
4. The sunset was <u>scarlet</u> last night. I have never seen such a bright red!
5. <u>Carpet</u> means nearly the same as rug.
6. He shot arrows at the <u>target</u> using the old bow his dad gave him.
7. The <u>artist</u> sold his paintings at the art show.

Dictations

1. Mrs. <u>Sharp</u>, the <u>farmer's</u> wife, woke up with a <u>start</u> when the dog began <u>snarling</u> in the <u>barn</u>. She <u>darted</u> to the <u>barn</u> in the <u>dark</u> to see why he was <u>barking</u>. It was just a <u>harmless barn</u> cat with <u>dark markings</u>!

2. Mr. <u>Star</u>, the <u>artist</u> that makes his home on the <u>farm</u>, just finished a painting of the <u>barn</u> with a <u>scarlet harvest</u> sunset behind it. He plans to take it to <u>market</u> and will try <u>hard</u> to sell it.

3. <u>Mark</u> had a <u>hard</u> day and was <u>starved</u>. He <u>started</u> to <u>harvest</u> his <u>garden</u> in the <u>farmyard</u>, but all that was ripe was a <u>scarlet</u> tomato. It was <u>smart</u> of him to make himself a sandwich with jam from a <u>jar</u> from the last grape <u>harvest</u>.

4. At <u>harvest</u> time, as the <u>farmer</u> was going to <u>market</u> to sell the things from his <u>garden</u>, a <u>spark</u> from lightning <u>started</u> a fire in the hayloft in the <u>barn</u>. He lost all that he had <u>harvested</u> in the <u>scarlet</u> flames. He even had to <u>discard</u> his <u>car</u> that he had <u>parked</u> <u>far</u> away from the <u>barn</u> on the <u>tar</u> driveway in the <u>yard</u>.

ar (ar) star **ar**

b		sc	f		tist
b	n	sh	p	c	pet
c		st		g	den
c	d	t		h	vest
f		y	d	sc	let
h	d	y	n	sh	pen
j				t	get

Name _____ Date _____

Word List 1

ar   (ar)   star   **ar**

bar	scarf	artist
barn	sharp	carpet
car	star	garden
card	tar	harvest
far	yard	scarlet
hard	yarn	sharpen
jar		target

Name _____ Date _____

Word List 2

ar   (ar)   star   **ar**

Write a word from the Word List to complete each sentence.

1. A _____ knife cuts better than a dull knife.

2. A thing that is _____ away is not nearby.

3. He wore a _____ around his neck on the day that it snowed.

4. I sent a get well _____ to my mom when she was sick.

5. He likes to play on the swings in the back _____ behind his home.

6. I need to get a mattress that is _____. My old mattress is too soft.

7. She used red _____ to knit a pair of mittens and a scarf that matches.

Name _____ Date _____

Cloze Sentences 1

ar (ar) star **ar**

Write a word from the Word List to complete each sentence.

1. If I cannot drive my _____ , I ride the bus.

2. It is fun to make a wish on a _____ that is in the night sky.

3. I got a _____ of grape jam at the store so I can make sandwiches.

4. He shared his candy _____ with me, and I gave him a cupcake.

5. A _____ can be the home of the animals on a farm.

6. _____ can be used to pave a street.

Name _____ Date _____

Cloze Sentences 2

ar (ar) star **ar**

Write a word from the Word List to complete each sentence.

1. I _____ the food that I grow in my garden when it is ripe.

2. We need to _____ this knife. It is too dull to cut well.

3. I plant seeds in my _____ to grow the food I need to eat.

4. The sunset was _____ last night. I have never seen such a bright red!

5. _____ means nearly the same as rug.

6. He shot arrows at the _____ using the old bow his dad gave him.

7. The _____ sold his paintings at the art show.

Name _____ Date _____

Cloze Sentences 3

17 or corn

BOOK LIST

Corn and Popcorn

The Popcorn Book (Glenview, Ill.: Scott, Foresman and Company, 1976). This short informational book with colored photographs details a simple experiment for growing popcorn seeds and observing plant parts. A second part pictures the planting and growing cycle of corn, and a diagram shows the corn growth cycle from seed to ear.

"Not Now!" Said the Cow, Joanne Oppenheim, illustrated by Chris Demarest (New York: Bantam Doubleday Dell Publishing Group, Inc., 1989). In this cumulative tale (a variation of the "Little Red Hen" story), a crow asks a series of friends to help him plant some corn seed. In turn, they answer no in their own ways that rhyme with their names.

Popcorn: A Frank Asch Bear Story, Frank Asch (New York: Parents' Magazine Press, 1979). Sam, the bear, invites his friends to a Halloween party, and they all bring popcorn. When Sam pops a gigantic pot full, the popcorn fills the house, and host and guests have no choice but to eat it.

Hill of Fire, Thomas P. Lewis, illustrated by Joan Sandin (New York: Harper & Row, 1971). A farmer in Mexico who is bored with the routine of his daily life finds excitement when a volcano erupts in his cornfield as he is plowing. The story is based on the Paricutin volcano, which erupted in a Mexican cornfield in 1943.

A Treeful of Pigs, Arnold Lobel, illustrated by Anita Lobel (New York: Scholastic, 1979). A farmer's wife creatively and humorously counters her lazy husband's series of excuses, and he finally changes his ways and helps her harvest the corn crop and tend the pigs.

Annie and the Wild Animals, Jan Brett (Boston: Houghton Mifflin Company, 1985). When her cat disappears one snowy day, Annie puts out corn cakes to attract a new pet, but the moose, wildcat, bear, and stag that crowd her yard are not what she had hoped for. In spring, the animals return to their homes, as does Annie's cat—with three kittens!

Kanahena: A Cherokee Story, Susan L. Roth (New York: St. Martin's Press, 1988). As she stirs the Kanahena (hominy or cornmeal mush) in her pot, an old woman tells a girl an old *pourquoi* and trickster tale about Kanahena and how the trickster Terrapin got the scars on his shell when he tricked some angry wolves. Includes a recipe for Kanahena.

The Popcorn Book, Tomie dePaola (New York: Holiday House, 1978). As brothers investigate the properties, history, and legends of popcorn, one reads and the other cooks; but they both eat it at the end. Contains interesting information about popcorn and recipes for two ways to make popcorn.

The Popcorn Dragon, Jane Thayer, illustrated by Lisa McGue (New York: Scholastic, 1953, 1989). Dexter, a young fire-breathing dragon, delights in his discovery that he can blow smoke, but the other animals shun him for showing off until he finds in a cornfield a way his talent connects him to friends: He makes popcorn for them.

Rain Player, David Wisniewski (New York: Clarion Books, 1991). With the help of Jaguar, Quetzal, and the sacred water, Pik brings rain to his parched land and earns the name Rain Player when he challenges and defeats the rain god in *pok-a-tok*, a game of ball. The author's note includes information about the Maya culture.

Annie and the Old One, Miska Miles, illustrated by Peter Parnall (Boston: Little, Brown and Company, 1971). Though she tries at first to stop time and her mother's weaving to prevent her beloved grandmother's approaching death, Annie is able to understand the legacy she shares with past and future generations as she takes her grandmother's stick and begins to weave.

Corn Is Maize: The Gift of the Indians, Aliki (New York: Thomas Y. Crowell Company, 1976). This book provides information about corn: planting and growing cycle; history of the discovery, cultivation, and use by native peoples in South, Central, and North America; its use in other cultures and times; and different kinds and uses. Includes directions for making a simple corn husk doll and wreath.

Pop Corn & Ma Goodness, Edna Mitchell Preston, illustrated by Robert Andrew Parker (New York: The Viking Press, 1969). The life of a couple in the rural United States is told through rhythmic text, which is unified by a rhyming alliterative phrase at the end of each line and a refrain. Caldecott Honor Book.

"The Popcorn Blizzard" and "The Giant Cornstalk," in **Paul Bunyan Swings His Axe**, Dell J. McCormick, illustrated by Leo Summers (New York: Scholastic Book Services, 1936, 1963). Separate chapters recount the tall tale episodes in the life of the legendary giant logger, Paul Bunyan—from his birth in Maine to his disappearance in Oregon. In "The Popcorn Blizzard," Paul saves his men from the heat of the plains with a blizzard from a barnful of corn he buys from a farmer. In "The Giant Cornstalk," Paul plants a corn kernel that grows into a cornstalk that just won't stop growing.

MOTIVATION AND EXTENSION ACTIVITIES

1. At the beginning of and throughout the unit, the teacher displays corn and corn products in as many forms as possible. The teacher might include corn on the cob/ear (edible and decorative varieties), husks, silk, tassels, stalks, kernels cut from the cob/ear, popcorn (unpopped kernels and popped), flakes or cereal, meal, cornstarch, syrup, oil, flour, chips, baby powder, glue, soap, and alcohol.

- Students tell (or discover) what is the same about the forms of corn. (They are all corn or come from corn.)
- Students and/or the teacher label all of the items in the display and make (and illustrate) a list.
- Throughout the unit, students and the teacher add items to the display and list.
- The teacher asks students to tell how the items are the same and different. Together, students and the teacher generate as many ways as they can to sort/categorize the items. Categories might include by function (including edible/cooking or nonedible/decorative, by color (yellow, white, blue, or multicolor and subcategories by shade—light, medium, dark), liquid or solid, traditional or modern forms, by size (small, medium, or large or comparisons: as big as a grain of sand, a pea, a pebble, a grape, etc.), by texture (coarse or smooth), and processed or unprocessed.
- Students and/or the teacher make labels for each category, sort the items in each of the ways, and make a list (with illustrations) of items for each category.
- Students and the teacher, by turns, choose an item and give clues for others to guess. For example, for corn syrup:

  > It's liquid.
  > It's a clear color.
  > You eat it or cook with it.
  > It's sweet.
  > It's in a bottle.

2. At the beginning of and throughout the unit, students and the teacher think of as many things as they can that can be made of corn or can be cooked/baked from corn. Items might include corncob pipe, corn husk doll, corn husk wreath, strings of popcorn for decorative purposes, strings of corn as jewelry, collage pictures, popcorn sculptures (**The Pooh Party Book** contains directions for popcorn sculptures as part of "A Woozle-Wizzle Snow Party"; see Activity 19 in Chapter 15, ai rain), tortillas, tacos, succotash, tamales, cornbread, corn cakes, muffins, popcorn balls, shepherd's pie, mush, chowder or soup, creamed corn, fritters, pudding, omelet, relish, scalloped corn, souffle, cornbread dressing, pancakes, waffles, pone, hominy grits, cornmeal quiche, cornmeal scrapple, corn sticks, chili, pizza, and polenta.

- At the beginning of the unit, students and the teacher brainstorm and make (and illustrate) a list.
- Throughout the unit, they add to the list using information from the books they read and share and resource books and materials. They explore the index in a variety of cookbooks as part of this activity.
- They make or cook/bake and eat as many items as practical from the list throughout the unit.

3. Students and the teacher follow the directions in **The Popcorn Book** (Scott, Foresman and Company) and grow a popcorn plant from a seed/kernel.

- They plant the seed.
- They record their observations of the seed's growth with words and/or pictures in a log book.
- They label the parts of the plant in their illustrations.
- They create a diagram with pictures and words that shows the corn growth cycle.

4. After they read and share *"Not Now!" Said the Cow*, the teacher asks students to help him or her do a job. The teacher asks a series of questions: Who will help me get out the popcorn popper?, Who will help me measure the popcorn?, Who will help me pour the popcorn into the popper?, Who will help me turn it on?, and so on. When it is popped, the teacher eats the popcorn—with helpers or all by himself or herself!

5. Each of the guests at Sam Bear's Halloween party in *Popcorn: A Frank Asch Bear Story* arrives with a different brand or kind of popcorn that goes with his or her costume. The ballerina has "Tip Toe Popcorn," the astronaut has "Space Dust Popcorn," and the devil has "Red Hot Popcorn," for example. Students and the teacher think of other Halloween costumes and popcorn brands that would go with them, and they tell and/or write and illustrate their ideas.

6. A plot that includes food overflowing a cooking pot and filling a house or town, as in *Popcorn: A Frank Asch Bear Story*, is common in traditional literature. *Strega Nona: An Old Tale*, a Caldecott Honor Book by Tomie dePaola (Englewood Cliffs, N.J.: Prentice-Hall, 1975), has a similar plot. After Strega Nona leaves and tells Big Anthony not to touch her pasta pot, he uses her magic chant to make it start making pasta but can't remember exactly how to make it stop. Pasta overflows the pot and house and fills the town until Strega Nona returns, stops the pot, and comes up with a perfect solution. She gives Big Anthony a fork! (See Chapter 31, g George magic stingy.) Students and the teacher share *Strega Nona: An Old Tale* by dePaola and *Popcorn: A Frank Asch Bear Story* and compare and contrast the plots of the two stories.

7. At the end of *A Treeful of Pigs*, the wife and farmer eat corn pudding and hot corn muffins. So do students and the teacher, who follow recipes and make their own.

8. Students and the teacher follow the recipe in *Kanahena: A Cherokee Story* and make and eat the oldest food of the Cherokee people.

9. Information about the book and author of *Kanahena: A Cherokee Story* explains that Roth made collage illustrations out of "natural materials, including leaves, grasses, cotton, and real cornmeal, along with colored paper." Students and the teacher experiment with making similar collage pictures of subjects of their choice using natural materials. They include corn in as many forms as possible.

10. As students and the teacher follow the two recipes for making popcorn, they discuss what they learned about popcorn from reading *The Popcorn Book* (Tomie dePaola). They contribute additional information they may know. The two recipes in the book use a pan—saucepan or frying pan. Students and the teacher use a hot air popcorn popper to make a third batch. They describe, compare, and contrast the three batches.

11. Following the directions at the end of *Corn Is Maize: The Gift of the Indians*, students and the teacher make corn husk dolls and wreaths.

12. Students and the teacher clap their hands, stamp their feet, or use rhythm instruments to mark the beat of the rhyming phases and refrain in *Pop Corn & Ma Goodness* as the teacher or students read it aloud.

13. After students listen to or read "The Popcorn Blizzard" and "The Giant Corn-stalk" in *Paul Bunyan Swings His Axe*, students and the teacher review and discuss legends and tall tales. They read (or reread) and tell and/or write more legends and tall tales. (See Activity 13 in Chapter 9, *ow grow*, for additional books and activities.)

14. Throughout the unit, students and the teacher discuss cultures around the world for whom corn is a staple of diet, including those depicted in books suggested for this unit: *Hill of Fire, A Treeful of Pigs, Kanahena: A Cherokee Story, The Rain Player, Annie and the Old One, Corn Is Maize: The Gift of the Indians*, and "The Popcorn Blizzard" and "The Giant Cornstalk" in *Paul Bunyan Swings His Axe*.

15. Using information from suggested books from this unit and resource books and materials, students and the teacher discuss uses of corn in different cultures.

16. Students and the teacher engage in "a-maize-ing" word play throughout the unit. The teacher models and encourages students to play with words—homophones, homographs, idioms, puns, and riddles.

- Students visualize and/or draw the literal meanings of statements related to the "Corn and Popcorn" unit. On a piece of paper held lengthwise and divided in half from top to bottom, they draw, first—on the left—a picture of the literal meaning (as Maestro in *In a Pickle and Other Funny Idioms* by Terban or the girl in the Gwynne books might do; see later in this list) and, second—on the right—a picture of the idiomatic/figurative meaning. They bind a set of phrases contributed by a group of students and the teacher into individual or group books. The statements might include the following:

> He spoke with a husky voice when he had a cold.
>
> Get busy. Don't fritter your time away.
>
> I'm all ears when you speak.
>
> It's a-maize-ing (amazing) to hear that!
>
> That's a corny joke.
>
> Ideas kept popping up at the meeting.
>
> That's a cornball idea.
>
> Reporting for duty, Kernel (Colonel), Sir!
>
> Shucks, I feel shy.
>
> The lion stalks his prey.
>
> Is that cornbread dressing? Give her/him some privacy.
>
> I don't like to watch movies with mush and kissing in them.
>
> Popcorn balls (bawls) when it's sad.
>
> I saw Ma and Pop Corn at the store.

- Students and the teacher extend their exploration and enjoyment of word play by sharing other books that feature it.

> They read three books by Fred Gwynne in which a girl imagines literally the statements she hears adults make that involve idiomatic expressions: *The King Who Rained* (New York: Prentice-Hall Books for Young Readers, 1970), *A Chocolate Moose for Dinner* (New York:

The Trumpet Club, 1976), and *A Little Pigeon Toad* (New York: The Trumpet Club, 1988).

Students listen to or read books from the "Amelia Bedelia" series by Peggy Parish in which Amelia Bedelia, the maid, interprets words literally and misses the nuances of language.

Students and the teacher challenge each other to homophone riddles in *Eight Ate: A Feast of Homonym Riddles*, by Marvin Terban, illustrated by Guilio Maestro (New York: Clarion Books, 1982).

They explore idioms in *In a Pickle and Other Funny Idioms*, by Marvin Terban, illustrated by Guilio Maestro (New York: Clarion Books, 1983).

They read other books and engage in additional activities that feature word play and idioms. (See Activities 15 and 16 in Chapter 5, closed syllable cats and kittens, Activity 10 in Chapter 26, aw straw, and Activity 11 in Chapter 28, ou soup.)

17. Students and the teacher locate on a map and/or globe the places/cultures (depicted or of origin) in the books read in this chapter, including Calabria in Italy (*Strega Nona: An Old Tale*); the state of Michoacan in Mexico (*Hill of Fire*); North America and the southern Appalachian Mountains in the United States (*Kanahena: A Cherokee Story*); Mayar culture in Mexico, Belize, Honduras, Guatemala, and El Salvador (*Rain Player*); Mexico, South, Central, and North America, and the landing sites of Christopher Columbus in the "New World" (*Corn Is Maize: The Gift of the Indians*); North Dakota, the Mississippi River, the plains of the United States, the Grand Canyon and the Colorado River, the Rocky Mountains, the Pacific Ocean and coast, and the Golden Gate Bridge in San Francisco in California in the United States ("The Popcorn Blizzard" in *Paul Bunyan Swings His Axe*); and the Rocky Mountains, the Puget Sound in Oregon, Old Faithful Geyser in Yellowstone Park, and the Mississippi Valley in the United States ("The Giant Cornstalk" in *Paul Bunyan Swings His Axe*).

TEACHER REFERENCE

Cloze Sentences

One-Syllable Words

Cloze Sentences 1

1. You can ride a <u>horse</u> at a ranch.
2. You can pop a <u>cork</u> off the top of wine.
3. You can get wet in a <u>storm</u> when it rains or snows a lot.
4. You can eat <u>corn</u> on the cob.
5. You can use a <u>fork</u>, a knife, or a spoon when you eat.

Cloze Sentences 2

1. You can get a <u>thorn</u> in your hand if you pick a rose.
2. You can make the <u>horn</u> honk when you drive a car or a truck.

3. You can get your pants <u>torn</u> if you fall off your bike.

4. You can live in the <u>north</u>, south, east, or west.

5. You can play a <u>sport</u> like baseball or basketball.

6. You can sit on the <u>porch</u> in the front or the back of a home.

Multisyllable Words

Cloze Sentence 3

1. Each <u>morning</u> I get up before the sun rises, and it is still dark.

2. <u>Northwest</u> is between north and west.

3. A <u>doctor</u> may take care of you when you are sick.

4. A <u>hornet</u> came in the window last night, and it stung me on the arm.

5. An <u>actor</u> is a person who has a part in a play or a show.

6. If you <u>forget</u> the new teacher's name, you can ask him to repeat it for you.

7. You may use <u>cornmeal</u> to bake corn muffins.

8. I <u>forgave</u> my classmate when he asked me to forgive him.

9. It is <u>important</u> to look both ways before you cross the street.

Dictations

1. This <u>morning</u> we had a bad <u>storm</u> from the <u>northwest</u>. Branches <u>torn</u> from the trees by the wind landed on the <u>porch</u> roof. The <u>storm</u> was <u>short</u>, but I will not <u>forget</u> it!

2. <u>Norm</u> had such a bad lunch that he will not <u>forget</u> it <u>for</u> a long time! The menu did not have the <u>pork</u> chops he wanted to <u>order</u>, his <u>fork</u> had a bent tine, the <u>cork</u> was hard to get out of his wine, and he <u>scorched</u> his lips on his <u>corn</u> on the cob. He was a good <u>sport</u>, but he will not go back there <u>for</u> lunch!

3. During a bad <u>storm</u> a vet drove <u>north</u> to help a <u>horse</u> that was ill. It was <u>important</u> <u>for</u> him to get to the <u>horse</u> fast, but a <u>worn</u> spot on his car's tire gave way and he had a flat. The <u>horse</u> did get well, and the man who had called him <u>forgave</u> the <u>doctor</u> <u>for</u> being so late.

or (or) corn **or**

c k		act
c n	c	nmeal
f k		doct
h n	f	gave
h se	f	get
n th	h	net
p ch	imp	tant
sp t	m	ning
st m	n	thwest
th n		
t n		

Name _____ Date _____

Word List 1

or (or) corn

cork	actor
corn	cornmeal
fork	doctor
horn	forgave
horse	forget
north	hornet
porch	important
sport	morning
storm	northwest
thorn	
torn	

Name _____ Date _____

or   (or)   corn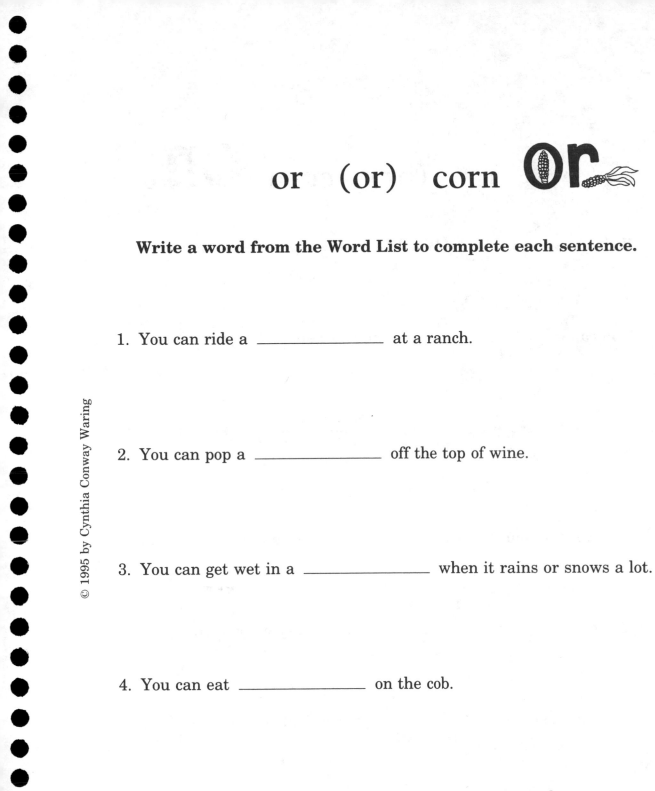

Write a word from the Word List to complete each sentence.

1. You can ride a _____ at a ranch.

2. You can pop a _____ off the top of wine.

3. You can get wet in a _____ when it rains or snows a lot.

4. You can eat _____ on the cob.

5. You can use a _____ , a knife, or a spoon when you eat.

Name _____   Date _____

or (or) corn **Or**

Write a word from the Word List to complete each sentence.

1. You can get a _____ in your hand if you pick a rose.

2. You can make the _____ honk when you drive a car or a truck.

3. You can get your pants _____ if you fall off your bike.

4. You can live in the _____, south, east, or west.

5. You can play a _____ like baseball or basketball.

6. You can sit on the _____ in the front or the back of a home.

Name _____ Date _____

or (or) corn Or

Write a word from the Word List to complete each sentence.

1. Each _____ I get up before the sun rises, and it is still dark.

2. _____ is between north and west.

3. A _____ may take care of you when you are sick.

4. A _____ came in the window last night, and it stung me on the arm.

5. An _____ is a person who has a part in a play or a show.

6. If you _____ the new teacher's name, you can ask him to repeat it for you.

7. You may use _____ to bake corn muffins.

8. I _____ my classmate when he asked me to forgive him.

9. It is _____ to look both ways before you cross the street.

Name _____ Date _____

Cloze Sentences3

18 er spider

BOOK LIST ═══

Anansi the Spider or Man: Trickster, Quest, and *Pourquoi* Tales

Anansi the Spider: A Tale from the Ashanti, Gerald McDermott (New York: Holt, Rinehart and Winston, 1972). Two related tales about Anansi the trickster include a quest, in which Anansi is saved in six trials through the individual talents of his six sons, and a *pourquoi* (how or why) tale of how the moon came to be in the sky. Caldecott Honor Book.

Anansi and the Moss-Covered Rock, Eric A. Kimmel, illustrated by Janet Stevens (New York: Scholastic, 1988). In this trickster tale, with the help of a magic, moss-covered rock, lazy but cunning Anansi the Spider tricks all of the animals in the forest out of their food until Little Bush Deer, who's been watching all the time, turns the tables and teaches Anansi a lesson.

Anansi Goes Fishing, Eric A. Kimmel, illustrated by Janet Stevens (New York: Holiday House, 1992). Anansi, the lazy and mischievous spider (from ***Anansi and the Moss-Covered Rock*** by the same author), returns in a combination trickster and *pourquoi* tale in which he tries to trick Turtle into going fishing for him, but wise Turtle outsmarts him. The story tells how spider webs began.

Anancy and Mr. Dry-Bone, Fiona French (New York: Scholastic, 1991). In this story based on Caribbean and African folk-tale characters, Anansi the man defeats Mr. Dry-Bone in a contest for Miss Louise's hand in marriage when he dresses up in animals' clothing and makes her laugh.

A Story a Story: An African Tale, Gail E. Haley (New York: Atheneum, 1970). This combination *pourquoi*, quest, and trickster tale tells how stories came to be told throughout the world. Anansi the Spider, who is neither young nor strong, uses his intelligence and trickery to accomplish three amazing tasks to buy the Sky God's stories. Caldecott Award Book.

Spider and the Sky God: An Akan Legend, Deborah M. Newton Chocolate, illustrated by Dave Albers (Mahwah, N.J.: Troll Associates, 1993). In this version of the *pourquoi/ quest/trickster* tale, Ananse the Spider, with direction from his wise wife, brings four things to the Sky God in payment for his stories, which Ananse now spins on the earth.

Anansi Finds a Fool: An Ashanti Tale, Verna Aardema, illustrated by Bryna Waldman (New York: Dial Books for Young Readers, 1992). In this trickster tale and fable, it is

Anansi the man who is found the fool in the end. Anansi's friend Bonsu cleverly takes advantage of Anansi's laziness and greed and turns his trickery back on him when Anansi tries to get Bonsu to do all the work of fishing.

Oh, Kojo! How Could You!: An Ashanti Tale, Verna Aardema, illustrated by Marc Brown (New York: The Trumpet Club, 1984). Lazy Anansi, the old man, tricks lazy Kojo, the young man, into trading gold for a dog, cat, and dove who appear useless; but they prove their value when they enable Kojo to receive, and later regain, a magic ring as a reward for an act of kindness. This *pourquoi* and trickster tale tells why the Ashanti people treat their cats better than their dogs.

"Anansi Rides Tiger," in ***Feathers and Tails: Animal Fables***, David Kherdian, illustrated by Nonny Hogrogian (New York: Philomel Books, 1992). This book is a collection of illustrated animal fables from cultures around the world. In "Anansi Rides Tiger," from West Africa, Anansi the Spider pretends to be ill to trick Tiger into letting him ride on his back with a saddle and bridle that Tiger, himself, supplies!

MOTIVATION AND EXTENSION ACTIVITIES

1. At the beginning of the unit, students and the teacher brainstorm and record on one chart with the heading "True" (1) what they know (or think they know) to be true about spiders: (They spin webs. They eat flies.) and (2) what they would like to learn about them: (Are they insects? Do they lay eggs?). On a second chart with the heading "Not True or False," they record things that are not true about real spiders that spider characters in books do: (Talk. Wear clothes.)

The teacher uses this opportunity to introduce or review the terms *nonfiction*, which he or she adds under the heading "True" on the first chart, and *fiction*, which he or she adds under the heading "Not True or False" on the second chart. (For students who need a mnemonic device to remember the terms, the teacher points out that *false* and *fiction* begin with the same letter.)

Throughout the unit, students and the teacher verify or correct and add information to the lists using the books suggested in this chapter and resource books and materials. They use, as one resource, the "Spiders" issue of ***Zoobooks*** magazine (March 1988, vol. 5, no. 6), published by Wildlife Education, Ltd., 930 Washington Street, San Diego, California 92103. Published monthly, ***Zoobooks*** magazines provide current information about groups of animals through brief text and colored photographs and diagrams with captions.

2. As an introduction to the motif or pattern of trickery (and particularly animal tricksters) in traditional literature, students and/or the teacher reread ***Kanahena: A Cherokee Story*** from the previous chapter (Chapter 17, or corn), which tells how the trickster Terrapin got the scars on his shell when he tricked some angry wolves. They also read ***Zomo the Rabbit: A Trickster Tale from West Africa***, by Gerald McDermott (San Diego: Harcourt Brace Jovanovich, 1992), a combination trickster and quest tale in which Zomo the Rabbit cleverly earns wisdom from the Sky God by accomplishing three tasks by tricking Big Fish, Wild Cow, and Leopard. Students and the teacher discuss animal trickster characters—the terrapin in ***Kanahena: A Cherokee Story*** and the rabbit trickster, Zomo, in ***Zomo the Rabbit: A Trickster Tale from West Africa***—

who are small, weak animals that trick larger and stronger animals and/or enemies or reach their goals by using their minds instead of might.

3. In an author's note in *Zomo the Rabbit: A Trickster Tale from West Africa*, McDermott explains the connection of Zomo, who originated in Hausaland, Nigeria, with trickster tales in the New World. In the Caribbean, Zomo is "Cunny Rabbit" or "Compere Lapin," and in the United States he is "Brer Rabbit."

Many cultures have animal trickster tales. In Africa it is Tortoise along with Anansi the Spider and Zomo the Rabbit. In the New World it is Anancy and Cunny Rabbit or Compere Lapin in the Caribbean; and in the United States it is Aunt Nancy and Brer Rabbit in the South, Coyote in the Southwest, and Raven in the Northwest.

Students and the teacher extend their study of trickster tales by reading books about New World Zomo the Rabbit or Anansi the Spider characters or other New World animal tricksters, including Coyote and Raven. (See the "How and Why: *Pourquoi* Tales from around the World" unit in Chapter 22, ow owl.)

4. Students and the teacher select activities related to *Anansi the Spider: A Tale from the Ashanti* from Motivation and Extension Activities 10 and 11 in Chapter 2, oo moon.

5. A theme of the first story, the quest, in *Anansi the Spider: A Tale from the Ashanti* is the value of individual gifts and talents and the need for contribution to the group or community (here it is the family) by every individual. The characters are not fully developed in the story; they are one dimensional—represented in text and illustrations (in a symbolic geometric design) by their particular talents. Students and the teacher discuss this theme and apply it to their own lives and the lives of others.

* They identify one (or several) gift or talent they possess. Then they design and illustrate a spider character in the style of the spider sons in *Anansi the Spider: A Tale from the Ashanti*, with a design on the body that represents each of their gifts or talents symbolically. They tell and/or write and illustrate how they could help someone or contribute to a group or community by using each gift or talent.

* They think about the person sitting next to them (to the left or right) and about a special talent or gift that person possesses. Then they tell and/or write and draw a picture showing that person using his or her talent to help others.

6. In the quest tale, the primary character (protagonist of hero/ine) is given a number of trials to endure, adventures to survive, or tasks to accomplish—often three. (See the "Number Three" unit in Chapter 8, ee seeds.) In some quest tales, the hero/ine is aided by a supernatural power by magic. After they read *Zomo the Rabbit: A Trickster Tale from West Africa* and *Anansi the Spider: A Tale from the Ashanti*, students and the teacher discuss the characteristics of quest tales.

7. Quest tales may also be considered home-adventure(s)-home story patterns. Students and the teacher extend their study of quest tales and further explore the home-adventure(s)-home story pattern.

* They read and discuss other stories that follow this common pattern in traditional literature, including *Zomo the Rabbit: A Trickster Tale from West Africa, Anansi the Spider: A Tale from the Ashanti, A Story a Story: An African Tale*, and *Spider and the Sky God: An Akan Legend* from this unit, and *Arrow to the Sun* by Gerald McDermott (Chapter 24, oy boy).

- They draw a diagram or story map to show the story shape of the quest tales they read. They show the movement of the primary character away from and returning to home and the trials, adventures, or tasks he or she accomplishes while away with a story diagram or map showing the quest of Anansi the Spider in *A Story a Story: An African Tale*.
- They tell and/or write and illustrate a third adventure of Anansi the Spider to follow the two in *Anansi the Spider: A Tale from the Ashanti*.
- They tell and/or write and illustrate their own quest/home-adventure(s)-home tales following the traditional story pattern.

8. After reading the book *Anansi the Spider: A Tale from the Ashanti*, students and the teacher watch the film by the same name (available from Weston Woods). They compare and contrast the story presented in the two media.

9. Before or after they read *Anansi and the Moss-Covered Rock*, students look for and examine moss-covered rocks (if they are available where they live or go to school).

10. As they read or listen to *Anansi and the Moss-Covered Rock*, students look for Little Bush Deer hiding in many of the illustrations.

11. The motif of a man winning the privilege of marrying a woman (often a princess) by making her laugh is common in traditional literature. Students and the teacher explore the motif as they read books that contain it, including *Anancy and Mr. Dry-Bone* in this chapter and *Lazy Jack* by Tony Ross (New York: The Trumpet Club, 1986). (See Activity 11 in Chapter 14, old gold, and Chapter 27, au daughter.)

12. In *A Story a Story: An African Tale*, Haley uses bold woodcut illustrations in nonprimary colors and African language patterns (including repetition), rhythms, and words (including onomatopoeia) to create a book to be read aloud. Students and the teacher explore the ways in which these elements work together in the book.

- They discuss the ways in which the text and illustrations convey and depict the African culture and complement each other in the tale.
- They move, walk, or dance to the story read aloud (with rhythm instruments).
- They view the film version of *A Story a Story: An African Tale* (available from Weston Woods), in which the background music is played exclusively on African instruments, and they look at and learn about African instruments (if available). They then use the African instruments and/or make simple instruments to accompany an oral reading presentation of the story.
- They explore and discuss the use of onomatopoeia (descriptive words that are similar to the sounds that characters and actions make—the buzz of a bee, for example) in this book and in other traditional African literature. (See Activity 23 in the "How and Why: *Pourquoi* Tales from around the World" unit in Chapter 22, ow owl.)

13. Students and the teacher compare and contrast the two versions of Anansi the Spider's quest for the Sky God's stories in *A Story a Story: An African Tale* and *Spider and the Sky God: An Akan Legend*.

14. Sections of *A Story a Story: An African Tale* and *Spider and the Sky God: An Akan Legend* give background information about the African people, *pourquoi* and trickster stories, traditional African storytelling, African language, and Anansi/Ananse stories in the New World. Students and the teacher discuss this background information

and compare and contrast it with other information they discover in other books in this unit and in resource books and materials. Students make masks and/or costumes and dramatize the adventures and story patterns in this unit by acting out selected books.

15. In the tales *A Story a Story: An African Tale* and *Spider and the Sky God: An Akan Legend*, before there were any stories on earth, all stories belonged to the Sky God (who, in *A Story a Story: An African Tale*, kept them next to him in a golden box). When Anansi earns the purchase price, the box is opened and the stories are dispersed throughout the world.

The story of "Pandora's Box (or Jar)" in *D'Aulaires' Book of Greek Myths*, Ingri and Edgar Parin d'Aulaire (New York: Doubleday & Company, Inc., 1962), is a Greek myth with a similar motif but less positive outcome. Out of curiosity, Pandora opens a jar from Zeus and unleashes Evil in the world, saving only Hope in the jar. Students and the teacher compare and contrast the two stories.

16. The motif of someone or something becoming stuck to another is common in traditional literature. In *A Story a Story: An African Tale* and *Spider and the Sky God: An Akan Legend*, it is Mmoatia the Fairy who is stuck to a gum doll. In the Brer Rabbit stories from the southern United States, characters are stuck to Tar Baby.

17. *Anansi Finds a Fool* is another version of the familiar African legend retold by Kimmel in *Anansi Goes Fishing*. Students and the teacher compare and contrast the two retellings.

18. *Oh, Kojo! How Could You!: An Ashanti Tale* and "Anansi Rides Tiger" in *Feathers and Tails: Animal Fables* are fables that involve Anansi, the trickster. Students and the teacher share more traditional and modern fables and explore this familiar form from traditional storytelling. (See the "Fables" unit in Chapter 29, consonant-le fable.)

19. Students and the teacher discuss the *pourquoi* tale pattern in books in this unit—*Anansi the Spider: A Tale from the Ashanti, Anansi Goes Fishing, A Story a Story: An African Tale, Spider and the Sky God: An Akan Legend*, and *Oh, Kojo! How Could You!: An Ashanti Tale*—and in other traditional and modern stories. (See the unit "How and Why: *Pourquoi* Tales from around the World" in Chapter 22, ow owl.)

20. Students and the teacher read and discuss trickster tales from different cultures and countries around the world.

21. Repetition is a common characteristic of traditional folk tales, and three is often the number of repetitions. (See the "Three Tales of Three" unit in Chapter 8, ee seeds.) There are often three central characters who face three trials or challenges, as in *The Three Little Pigs* (Chapter 8, ee seeds) or *The Three Billy Goats Gruff* (Chapter 13, oa goat). Repetition of character responses also recurs often in these tales: the "I'll huff and I'll puff" of the wolf and the "Not by the hair of my chinny chin chin" of the pigs in *The Three Little Pigs*, the "Oh, please don't take me. Wait . . ." of the goats and the "Who's that tramping over my bridge?" of the troll in *The Three Billy Goats Gruff*, or the "Fee fi fo fum" of Jack's giant in *Jack and the Beanstalk* (Chapter 10, ea wheat). In many African tales, words and phrases are repeated (typically three times) for emphasis or strength. Students and the teacher note this pattern as they read the books in this unit, other African tales, and other books from the folk-tale tradition.

22. With Gerald McDermott as an "Author/Illustrator under Study," students and the teacher read and discuss more of his books, including *Zomo the Rabbit: A Trickster Tale from West Africa* and *Anansi the Spider: A Tale from the Ashanti* from this

unit, *Papagayo: The Mischief Maker* (Chapter 2, oo moon, and Chapter 25, oi noise), and *Arrow to the Sun* (Chapter 24, oy boy).

23. With Verna Aardema as an "Author under Study," students and the teacher read and discuss more of her books, including *Anansi Finds a Fool: An Ashanti Tale* and *Oh, Kojo! How Could You!: An Ashanti Tale* from this unit, *Bringing the Rain to Kapiti Plain: A Nandi Tale* (Chapter 15, ai rain), *Who's in Rabbit's House: A Masai Tale* (Chapter 16, ar star, and Chapter 23, ou house), and *Why Mosquitoes Buzz in People's Ears* (in the "How and Why: *Pourquoi* Tales from around the World" unit in Chapter 22, ow owl).

24. Students and the teacher reflect on what they have learned about Anansi and his culture or origin during the unit. They discuss, for example, what words (adjectives) they might use to describe him, what motivates him, the source(s) of his strength, and the forces and elements in his culture that affect him and to which he responds. Students draw a picture (or an entire comic strip) of Anansi as a comic strip character in their culture at that time in history that reflects the aforementioned discussion.

25. Students and the teacher locate on a map and/or globe the places/cultures (depicted or of origin) in the books read in this chapter, including North America and the southern Appalachian Mountains (*Kanahena: A Cherokee Story*); Hausaland in Nigeria (*Zomo the Rabbit: A Trickster Tale from West Africa*); Akan and Ashanti culture and Ghana on the west coast of Africa *(Anansi the Spider: A Tale from the Ashanti, A Story a Story: An African Tale, Spider and the Sky God: An Akan Legend, Anansi Finds a Fool, Oh, Kojo! How Could You!: An Ashanti Tale*, and "Anasi Rides Tiger" in *Feathers and Tails: Animal Fables*; Africa *(Anansi and the Moss-Covered Rock* and *Anansi Goes Fishing)*, the Caribbean and Africa *(Anancy and Mr. Dry-Bone)*, and Greece (*D'Aulaires' Book of Greek Myths*).

TEACHER REFERENCE

Cloze Sentences

One-Syllable Words

Cloze Sentences 1

1. A <u>stern</u> teacher is very strict.
2. A <u>berth</u> is a bed on a train.
3. A <u>fern</u> is a green plant that grows in the forest.
4. I felt a <u>jerk</u> and a tug on my fishing line when I got a fish.
5. The <u>perch</u> was a twig that the bird sat on.
6. I will <u>serve</u> lemonade to each person who asks for a glass.
7. We traded writing tools. She gave me <u>her</u> pen, and I gave <u>her</u> mine.

Multisyllable Words

Cloze Sentences 2

1. A person's <u>sister</u> is a girl child of her or his mother and/or father.
2. I heard a crash of <u>thunder</u> just after I saw a flash of lightning.
3. In <u>November</u> we have a Thanksgiving feast.

4. A <u>lantern</u> was used long ago to light homes and is used today when camping.

5. Your <u>partner</u> is the person with whom you play, dance, read, or do your job.

6. I looked <u>under</u> the desk to see if the pen I dropped had rolled there.

7. I got a <u>blister</u> on my foot from running a long way.

8. I love to eat <u>lobster</u> that has just been taken fresh from a trap in the sea and is still in its shell.

9. If you don't put money in the parking <u>meter</u>, you may get a parking fine or ticket.

Cloze Sentences 3

1. <u>December</u> is the last month of the year.

2. Please <u>whisper</u>. If you talk, you may wake the baby.

3. A <u>carpenter</u> is a person who makes things from wood.

4. I <u>perspire</u> under my arms when I run a lot.

5. In <u>October</u> the leaves fall from the trees, and we trick or treat on Halloween.

6. <u>Yesterday</u> had to be Sunday. Today is Monday.

7. A <u>monster</u> is a scary thing that is big, ugly, and bad but not real.

8. In <u>September</u> school may begin after Labor Day.

9. A <u>spider</u> spins a web so that it can catch a fly to eat.

Dictations

1. In the <u>thunder</u> storm <u>yesterday</u> the <u>fisherman</u> and his <u>partner</u> used a <u>lantern</u> to check the <u>lobster</u> traps.

2. It is hard for me to get a <u>metered</u> parking spot by my job so I like being a <u>commuter</u> on the subway, and the <u>better</u> the <u>driver</u> the <u>safer</u> the trip!

3. Last <u>November</u> my <u>sister</u> and I took a train trip to visit my <u>partner's</u> <u>mother</u>. We <u>were</u> <u>served</u> lunch and <u>dinner</u>. <u>Later</u>, while we slept in the <u>upper</u> berths, we felt the <u>jerk</u> of the train <u>under</u> us <u>every</u> time the train went <u>faster</u>.

er (er) spider

b	th	blist	partn	
f	n	carpent	p	spire
h		Decemb	Septemb	
j	k	lant n	sist	
p	ch	lobst	spid	
s	ve	met	thund	
st	n	monst	und	
		Novemb	whisp	
		Octob	yest day	

Name _____ Date _____

er (er) spider

berth	blister	partner
fern	carpenter	perspire
her	December	September
jerk	lantern	sister
perch	lobster	spider
serve	meter	thunder
stern	monster	under
	November	whisper
	October	yesterday

Name _____ Date _____

Word List 2

er (er) spider

Write a word from the Word List to complete each sentence.

1. A _____ teacher is very strict.

2. A _____ is a bed on a train.

3. A _____ is a green plant that grows in the forest.

4. I felt a _____ and a tug on my fishing line when I got a fish.

5. The _____ was a twig that the bird sat on.

6. I will _____ lemonade to each person who asks for a glass.

7. We traded writing tools. She gave me _____ pen, and I gave _____ mine.

Name _____ Date _____

er (er) spider

Write a word from the Word List to complete each sentence.

1. A person's _____ is a girl child of her or his mother and/ or father.

2. I heard a crash of _____ just after I saw a flash of lightning.

3. In _____ we have a Thanksgiving feast.

4. A _____ was used long ago to light homes and is used today when camping.

5. Your _____ is the person with whom you play, dance, read, or do your job.

6. I looked _____ the desk to see if the pen I dropped had rolled there.

7. I got a _____ on my foot from running a long way.

8. I love to eat _____ that has just been taken fresh from a trap in the sea and is still in its shell.

9. If you don't put money in the parking _____, you may get a parking fine or ticket.

Name _____ Date _____

Cloze Sentences 2

er (er) spider **er**

Write a word from the Word List to complete each sentence.

1. _____ is the last month of the year.

2. Please _____. If you talk, you may wake the baby.

3. A _____ is a person who makes things from wood.

4. I _____ under my arms when I run a lot.

5. In _____ the leaves fall from the trees, and we trick or treat on Halloween.

6. _____ had to be Sunday. Today is Monday.

7. A _____ is a scary thing that is big, ugly, and bad but not real.

8. In _____ school may begin after Labor Day.

9. A _____ spins a web so that it can catch a fly to eat.

Name _____ Date _____

Cloze Sentences 3

19   ir birthday

Birthdays: Expectations and Anticipation, Celebration, and Disappointment

Did You Say, "Fire"?, Joy Cowley, illustrated by Penny Newman (New York: Richard C. Owen Publishers, Inc., 1987). When a mouse smells the smoke from a birthday cake, it panics and starts a rumor of fire that is passed on from animal to animal until fire fighters and even the television camera crew come to investigate.

Birthday Surprise, Louis Sabin, illustrated by John Magine (Mahwah, N.J.: Troll Associates, 1981). The story of a gift inside a series of nesting boxes and a visit by his friends that saves a birthday Sammy the skunk thought everyone had forgotten is told with simple, repetitive text consisting of only forty-nine different words and supportive illustrations.

The Cake That Mack Ate, Rose Robart, illustrated by Maryann Kovalski (Boston: Little, Brown and Company, 1986). In this cumulative story, the excitement builds as more and more ingredients are added to a cake for a birthday, but the cake is ruined when Mack, the dog, sneaks in and eats it before the party.

"Birthday Soup," in ***Little Bear***, Else Holmelund Minarik, illustrated by Maurice Sendak (New York: Harper & Row, 1957). This book is a collection of four stories about Little Bear and his sensitive Mother Bear, who is always nearby to support and enjoy him. In "Birthday Soup," when he thinks that Mother Bear has forgotten his birthday, Little Bear makes birthday soup to share with his friends, and Mother Bear arrives with the cake just in time for the party.

The Secret Birthday Message, Eric Carle (New York: HarperCollins, 1971). Tim finds a message in code that leads him to a surprise birthday gift—a puppy. Large picture-book pages contain cut-out geometric shapes that correspond to the word-and-rebus code.

Happy Birthday, Moon, Frank Asch (New York: Simon & Schuster Books for Young Readers, 1982). Soft, luminous illustrations complement the story of a bear who, in his attempt to befriend the moon, talks with his own echo and devises a clever plan to give the moon a birthday gift.

"The Hat," in ***Days with Frog and Toad***, Arnold Lobel (New York: Harper & Row, 1979). Frog and Toad learn about and celebrate the benefits of friendship—together, alone, and "alone together." In "The Hat," when the hat that Frog gives Toad for his birthday is too big for him, Frog shrinks it to fit, but Toad is convinced that his head grew larger because of the big thoughts he'd been thinking.

A Letter to Amy, Ezra Jack Keats (New York: Harper & Row, 1968). A misunderstanding about his friend Amy's invitation to his party nearly lost in the rain almost ruins Peter's birthday, but all ends well when Amy and her parrot arrive in time for the cake and Peter's secret wish.

Scruffy, Peggy Parish, illustrated by Kelly Oechsli (New York: HarperCollins, 1988). Todd learns about the care of cats and about the animal shelter when he and a kitten choose each other as Todd's birthday gift from his parents.

Night Noises, Mem Fox, illustrated by Terry Denton (New York: The Trumpet Club, 1989). One evening, as Lily dozes by the fire, only her dog is aware of the noises that announce the arrival of her large extended family and forty-seven friends, who surprise her with a ninetieth birthday party.

Waiting for Noah, Shulamith Levey Oppenheim, illustrated by Lillian Hoban (New York: Harper & Row, 1990). Noah listens intently as his grandmother recounts in detail the events of her day as she waited for his birth.

Arthur's Birthday, Marc Brown (New York: The Trumpet Club, 1989). Arthur and Muffy have a problem: Their friends can't come to both of their birthday parties at the same time. Then Arthur comes up with a creative solution.

Happy Birthday, Ronald Morgan!, Patricia Reilly Giff, illustrated by Susanna Natti (New York: Penguin, 1986). After a fight with his best friend, Ronald Morgan doesn't think his birthday wishes—for a classroom party, a best friend, and a puppy—will come true, but acts of kindness (including his own) produce reconciliation and a celebration.

George and Martha Tons of Fun: Five Stories about the Best of Friends, James Marshall (Boston: Houghton Mifflin Company, 1980). In this collection of five stories, hippos George and Martha get angry, get sick, get a funny picture taken, get hypnotized, get caught stealing cookies from the cookie jar, and get a birthday gift.

Emmett's Pig, Mary Stolz (New York: HarperCollins, 1959). Emmett's parents have a creative solution to his long-time wish to have a pig for a pet. On Emmett's birthday, they travel from their city apartment to a farm in the country, where little King Emmett awaits his master.

The Wednesday Surprise, Eve Bunting, illustrated by Donald Carrick (New York: The Trumpet Club, 1989). Anna's grandmother comes to babysit every Wednesday night, and while Anna's parents are away Anna and her grandmother work on an important surprise for Anna's father's birthday: Anna teaches her grandmother how to read.

Something Special for Me, Vera B. Williams (New York: Mulberry Books, 1983). In this second of three books about Rosa's three-generational family in a city in the United

States, when Rosa finds it difficult to select a birthday present worthy of the coins in the savings jar, she chooses an accordion like the one her grandmother played.

A Birthday for Frances, Russell Hoban, illustrated by Lillian Hoban (New York: Harper & Row, 1969). Birthdays are wonderful—unless they're your little sister Gloria's! Frances, the badger, struggles with jealousy and learns about giving.

Cranberry Birthday, Wende and Harry Devlin (New York: Macmillan Publishing Company, 1988). Everyone can have a secret birthday wish, even an old sea captain named Mr. Whiskers. A surprise party with his friends, a homemade cake, and the puppy he'd wanted save the birthday he had dreaded. The book includes a recipe for "Grandmother's Birthday Cake."

Lyle and the Birthday Party, Bernard Waber (Boston: Houghton Mifflin Company, 1966). Not only does Lyle the Crocodile have difficulty not being the birthday boy on Joshua's birthday, but it makes him sick enough to be hospitalized. In the end, Lyle experiences the benefits of giving—and receiving.

Magical Hands, Marjorie Barker, illustrated by Yoshi (Saxonville, Mass.: Picture Book Studio, 1989). Before he goes to work making barrels, William, the cooper, gives his three friends their wishes—to have their chores done for them by "magic" on their birthdays—and William's "magical hands" do not go unrewarded on his own birthday.

Dragon Kite of the Autumn Moon, Valerie Reddix, illustrated by Jean and Mou-sien Tseng (New York: Lothrop, Lee & Shepard Books, 1991). By Chinese tradition, each year Grandfather and Tad-Tin make and fly a kite and cut its string to release their troubles on Kite Day, but this year, with Grandfather seriously ill and unable to help him make a kite, Tad-Tin chooses to fly and release his special dragon kite, made by Grandfather to celebrate Tad-Tin's birth, and its magic touches and heals Grandfather.

"Eeyore Has a Birthday," in *Winnie-the-Pooh*, A. A. Milne, illustrated by Ernest H. Shepard (New York: Dell Publishing Co., Inc., 1926, 1954). This book introduces the adventures of a boy, Christopher Robin, and his toy bear, who's come to life as Winnie-the-Pooh, and their friends Piglet, Eeyore, Kanga and Roo, and Rabbit. "Eeyore Has a Birthday" is the bittersweet story of Winnie-the-Pooh and Piglet's attempts to cheer up their friend, gloomy Eeyore the donkey, by giving him a birthday party and gifts.

On the Day You Were Born, Debra Frasier (San Diego: Harcourt Brace Jovanovich, 1991). In poetic prose the sun, the moon, the stars, and the earth and its elements and inhabitants greet a child on the day of its birth. The book contains background information about migrating animals, earth, sun, moon, stars, gravity, tides, rain, trees, and the color of people's skin.

MOTIVATION AND EXTENSION ACTIVITIES ═══════════════════

1. Before or after they read *Birthday Surprise*, the teacher shows students nesting boxes or nesting toys to explore (like those Penny's friend brought with her from Russia in *Penny and the Four Questions* in Chapter 11, y penny).

2. Before or after they read *The Secret Birthday Message*, students and the teacher explore rebus and rebus-and-word messages and books. They read more books that contain rebuses. (See Activity 5 in Chapter 3, open syllable go, for a list of suggested books.) They create and share their own rebus and/or rebus-and-word messages and/or books.

3. As they read *Happy Birthday, Moon*, students complete Activity 4 in Chapter 2, oo moon.

4. After they read "The Hat" in *Days with Frog and Toad*, students and the teacher tell and/or write and illustrate about a birthday gift they gave or received that did not turn out as well as they had hoped and what they were able to do, if anything, to change the result or cope with the disappointment.

5. Birthdays and parties were nearly spoiled in *The Birthday Surprise*, "Birthday Soup" in *Little Bear*, *A Letter to Amy*, and *Happy Birthday, Ronald Morgan*. Students and the teacher tell and/or write and illustrate about a time their birthday or party (or that of someone they know) was almost ruined or turned out to be a disappointment. Then they tell and/or write about and illustrate the best birthday and party they ever had or attended.

6. After they read *A Letter to Amy*, students write invitations to a party—to a friend or the teacher asking them to eat snack or lunch with them or to read together; to an older student, a teacher from another classroom, or a family member asking them to visit the classroom to read with them or to see a class or individual project; to other students and teachers inviting them to "An Eeyore Birthday Party" (see Activity 23 in this chapter); or to whomever they desire to meet their own purposes. They refer to Activity 2 in this chapter if they choose to include rebuses with the words in their invitations.

7. Students read about birthday cakes as they read the books suggested for this unit (and about a variation—birthday pancakes—as they read *Scruffy* and *Emmett's Pig*). (See Chapter 6, vowel-consonant-e syllable cake, for additional books and activities related to cakes and pancakes.) Students and the teacher compare and contrast stories, including *Scruffy* and *Emmett's Pig*, about children who receive pets for their birthdays.

8. In *Arthur's Birthday*, Arthur's solution to the problem of having two birthday parties at the same time worked for Muffy, their friends and family, and him. Students and the teacher try to think of other solutions to the problem. They discuss the positive and negative aspects of each solution and decide whether each solution would work for all of the characters involved.

9. After they read *Happy Birthday, Ronald Morgan!*, *Emmett's Pig*, *Cranberry Birthday*, and *Magical Hands*, students and the teacher tell and/or write and illustrate about important birthday wishes that did or did not come true.

10. Waiting for important events, like a birthday or the birth of a grandchild (*Waiting for Noah*), is difficult. Students and the teacher share (tell and/or write and illustrate) about times they found/find it difficult to wait for something or someone. They create a list or handbook of things to do to make waiting for/anticipating birthdays (or other special events or occasions) easier.

11. After they read *Something Special for Me*, students and the teacher share experiences they may have had choosing birthday presents for themselves or for others.

12. "If you could have anything you wanted for your birthday . . .": Students and the teacher tell what they think they might select. The teacher may choose to limit the amount of money available for the gift by bringing in a jar with coins like the one in *Something Special for Me*.

13. Students and the teacher read the other two books by the same author about Rosa's family. The prequel to **Something Special for Me** is **A Chair for My Mother** (New York: Scholastic, 1982), in which Rosa, Mama, Grandma—and even Aunt Ida and Uncle Sandy—save their coins in a big jar to buy Mama a chair to rest in after work as a waitress at a diner. In the sequel, **Music, Music for Everyone** (New York: Mulberry Books, 1984), when Grandma is sick, Rosa thinks of a way to cheer her up and fill the empty coin jar, and the idea for Rosa and her friends to create the Oak Street Band is born.

14. In the three books about Rosa's family, **Something Special for Me**, **A Chair for My Mother**, and **Music, Music for Everyone**, the borders reflect the mood, events, and details of the illustrations and text they surround. If students are reading them for the first time, they explore the use of borders in William's books and in Jan Brett's books. (See Activity 9 in Chapter 15, ai rain.)

15. **A Birthday for Frances** is one of six books about Frances the badger, her wise parents, her little sister Gloria, and her friends. Students and the teacher read other Frances books and complete related activities, including singing her songs. (See the "Frances the Badger Stories" unit in Chapter 32, c Frances Cinderella fancy.)

16. After or as they read **The Secret Birthday Message, Happy Birthday, Ronald Morgan!, Emmett's Pig**, and **Cranberry Birthday**, students and the teacher share about their pets.

- They tell and/or write and illustrate about how they first received their pets.
- They share about whether they had to wait a long time, as many of the characters in the books do, to get the pet.
- They share pet stories. (This is a favorite discussion topic for most students—and teachers!)

17. **Cranberry Birthday** is set on Cape Cod, Massachusetts in the United States, where cranberries are grown, but a note that accompanies the recipe for "Grandmother's Birthday Cake" explains that cranberries are out of season at the time of Mr. Whiskers's birthday; therefore, the recipe in the book is for strawberry cake. The teacher or students bring in cranberries in several forms for sampling: raw berries, juice, sauce, relish, and bread. (They may choose to make their own sauce, relish, and bread as an extension of their exploration.) Students and the teacher follow the recipe in the book and make and eat "Grandmother's Birthday Cake."

18. The Devlins have written several books about Maggie, Grandmother, and Mr. Whiskers and their life on Cape Cod in Massachusetts. Students and the teacher share more books (and food made from the included recipes) in the series.

19. At some time, most people have to cope with being the person not having the birthday. Students and the teacher share their own experiences and feelings surrounding this common theme. They discuss ways they have dealt with it and compare and contrast their stories with Frances's in **A Birthday for Frances** and with Lyle's in **Lyle and the Birthday Party**.

20. The teacher or students bring in a wooden barrel to explore before students (or the teacher) read **Magical Hands**.

21. After they read or listen to **Magical Hands**, students and the teacher tell, act out, and/or write and illustrate about what their "magical hands" could do for their

friends and family on their birthdays. They share what chores they would wish done by "magic" on their birthdays (and everyday!).

22. Students and the teacher gather the props for reading "Eeyore Has a Birthday" in **Winnie-the-Pooh**—an empty but "Useful Pot to Keep Things In" with a birthday message in the style of Winnie-the-Pooh and Owl and a "small piece of damp rag" of a red balloon, of course!

23. Students and the teacher give "An Eeyore Birthday Party" as described in **The Pooh Party Book**, Virginia H. Ellison, illustrated by Ernest H. Shepard (New York: Dell Publishing Co., 1971). The book describes five parties with Winnie-the-Pooh story themes—a birthday party for Eeyore and a party for each season—and includes directions for making invitations, decorations, refreshments (with recipes), favors and crafts, and games.

24. After they read or listen to **Waiting for Noah, Dragon Kite of the Autumn Moon**, and **On the Day You Were Born**, students and the teacher tell all that they know or can find out about the day they were born. They bring in and share items that commemorate that day: baby books, hospital tags, newspaper clippings from the day, birth announcements, greeting cards and gift wrapping paper, photographs and/or videos, infant clothing, kites, and stories (and witnesses as guest speakers, if it can be arranged).

25. The first part of **On the Day You Were Born** is a poetic presentation of information about and images of elements of the natural world. The second part is a collection of nonfiction selections that provide background information about the same topics. Students and the teacher compare and contrast the way in which scientific information is communicated in the fiction and nonfiction portions of the book.

26. Students and the teacher locate on a map and/or globe the places/cultures (depicted or of origin) in the books read in this chapter, including New York City in the United States (**A Letter for Amy**); Australia (**Night Noises**); Cape Cod, Massachusetts, in the United States (**Cranberry Birthday**); and Taiwan and China (**Dragon Kite of the Autumn Moon**).

TEACHER REFERENCE ===

Cloze Sentences

One-Syllable Words

Cloze Sentences 1

1. The girl's <u>skirt</u> with the black belt was so long that it went below her knees.
2. The <u>third</u> student in line is after the second student in line.
3. <u>Birch</u> trees look different from other trees with their white bark.
4. I need to <u>stir</u> the pancake batter with a spoon while I heat up the pan.
5. The <u>first</u> thing I do each morning is shut off my alarm clock.
6. <u>Sir</u> is a name of respect used to speak to knights.
7. A <u>bird</u> was singing from the branch of a tree by my window.

Cloze Sentences 2

1. This <u>shirt</u> is too small for me. The sleeves are too short for my arms.
2. The <u>girl</u> sitting next to me is my sister.
3. I like to <u>twirl</u> my spaghetti on my fork before I eat it.

Multisyllable Words

Cloze Sentences 3

1. I was so <u>thirsty</u> that I drank three cups of punch.
2. On my <u>birthday</u> I have a big cake and get a lot of gifts.
3. If you put your <u>dirty</u> socks in the hamper, I will wash them.
4. The <u>whirlwind</u> from the wind storm got dust all over homes and stores.
5. <u>Thirty</u> is the same as 3 times 10.

Dictations

1. The <u>girl</u> saw that the <u>skirt</u> she had gotten for her <u>birthday</u> was <u>dirty</u>. The <u>firm</u> that made the <u>skirt</u> was <u>thirty</u> years old, but it did a careless job.

2. Mr. <u>Birch</u> went camping and hunting on his <u>birthday</u>. The <u>first</u> day he shot <u>thirty</u> <u>birds</u>, but by the <u>third</u> day he was so <u>thirsty</u> and his <u>shirt</u> and pants felt so <u>dirty</u> that he went home.

3. The <u>bird</u> in the <u>birch</u> tree got <u>dirty</u> in a <u>whirlwind</u> of dust that was <u>stirred</u> up by a wind storm. During the storm the <u>bird</u> did not <u>stir</u> but held <u>firm</u> to the branch it was sitting on. The <u>first</u> thing it did at the end of the storm was get a drink. All that dust made the <u>bird</u> <u>thirsty</u>!

ir (er) birthday

b ch   b thday

b d   d ty

f st   th sty

g l   th ty

sh t   wh lwind

s

sk t

st

th d

tw l

Name _____ Date _____

ir (er) birthday

birch	birthday
bird	dirty
first	thirsty
girl	thirty
shirt	whirlwind
sir	
skirt	
stir	
third	
twirl	

Name _____ Date _____

Word List 2

ir (er) birthday

Write a word from the Word List to complete each sentence.

1. The girl's _____ with the black belt was so long that it went below her knees.

2. The _____ student in line is after the second student in line.

3. _____ trees look different from other trees with their white bark.

4. I need to _____ the pancake batter with a spoon while I heat up the pan.

5. The _____ thing I do each morning is shut off my alarm clock.

6. _____ is a name of respect used to speak to knights.

7. A _____ was singing from the branch of a tree by my window.

Name _____ Date _____

ir (er) birthday

Write a word from the Word List to complete each sentence.

1. This _____ is too small for me. The sleeves are too short for my arms.

2. The _____ sitting next to me is my sister.

3. I like to _____ my spaghetti on my fork before I eat it.

Name _____ Date _____

Cloze Sentences 2

ir (er) birthday

Write a word from the Word List to complete each sentence.

1. I was so _____ that I drank three cups of punch.

2. On my _____ I have a big cake and get a lot of gifts.

3. If you put your _____ socks in the hamper, I will wash them.

4. The _____ from the wind storm got dust all over homes and stores.

5. _____ is the same as 3 times 10.

Name _____ Date _____

Cloze Sentences 3

20   ur   turtle

BOOK LIST ═══

Turtles, Terrapins, and Tortoises

Franklin in the Dark, Paulette Bourgeois, illustrated by Brenda Clark (New York: Scholastic, 1986). Franklin is afraid of the dark and of being in small, cramped places, and Franklin is a turtle! When he learns from other animals and his mother that they have their own fears, he is more comfortable sleeping in his shell—with his night light on!

Franklin Fibs, Paulette Bourgeois, illustrated by Brenda Clark (New York: Scholastic, 1991). When his friends boast about their abilities and Franklin the turtle tells a fib, he discovers that he is happier when he is honest about what he can do and that his friends like him just as he is.

Franklin Is Lost, Paulette Bourgeois, illustrated by Brenda Clark (New York: Scholastic, 1992). During a hide and seek game with his friends, Franklin the turtle is distracted and, in spite of his mother's warning, goes into the woods alone and gets lost. He is found—safe and contrite—in the end.

Hurry Up, Franklin, Paulette Bourgeois, illustrated by Brenda Clark (New York: Scholastic, 1986). As usual, Franklin the turtle is distracted on the way by his friends' invitations to play, and he (with a snail, to whom he offers a ride, on his back) has to hurry to be on time for his friend Bear's birthday party.

Little Turtle's Big Adventure, David Harrison, illustrated by J. P. Miller (New York: Random House, 1969, 1978). A little turtle is forced out of his pond home when people with bulldozers and steam shovels build a road. He survives the four seasons and tries out several locations before he finds a suitable new home.

Kanahena: A Cherokee Story, Susan L. Roth (New York: St. Martin's Press, 1988). As she stirs the Kanahena (hominy or cornmeal mush) in her pot, an old woman tells a girl an old *pourquoi* and trickster tale about Kanahena and how the trickster Terrapin got the scars on his shell when he tricked some angry wolves. Includes a recipe for Kanahena.

The Turtle and the Monkey: A Philippine Tale, Paul Galdone (New York: Clarion Books, 1983). Turtle tricks Monkey—not once, but three times—when she asks Monkey's help to plant a banana tree she found and Monkey greedily takes his portion—or more.

Anansi Goes Fishing, Eric A. Kimmel, illustrated by Janet Stevens (New York: Holiday House, 1992). Anansi, the lazy and mischievous spider (from ***Anansi and the Moss-Covered Rock*** by the same author), returns in a combination trickster and *pourquoi* tale in which he tries to trick Turtle into going fishing for him, but wise Turtle outsmarts him. The story tells how spider webs began.

Turtle Spring, Lillian Hoban (New York: Bantam Doubleday Dell Publishing Group, Inc., 1978). One spring day, the whole turtle family thinks the bump in the garden is a bomb, and no one does anything but think about it until ten baby turtles hatch from it.

Stick-in-the-Mud Turtle, Lillian Hoban (New York: Bantam Doubleday Dell Publishing Group, Inc., 1977). Everyone except Mr. Turtle (whom Mrs. Turtle calls "Stick-in-the-Mud Turtle") has to experience the negative side of the fancy life and material possessions of the new turtle family that moves into the pond neighborhood before they are again content with their own simple life.

The Tortoise and the Hare: An Aesop Fable, Janet Stevens (New York: Scholastic, 1984). In Stevens's humorous retelling of the familiar Aesop fable with a contemporary setting, Tortoise's friends help him train for the race and Hare wears jogging shorts and Tortoise wears running shoes.

The Hare and the Tortoise, Brian Wildsmith (Oxford, England: Oxford University Press, 1966). Characteristic full-page Wildsmith illustrations embellish this version of the famous race between the boastful Hare and the persevering Tortoise.

"The Hare and the Tortoise," in ***The Aesop for Children***, Milo Winter (Chicago: Rand McNally & Co., 1919, 1947, 1984). In Winter's terse retelling of the fable, the Hare takes a nap to show the Tortoise just how laughable his attempt is to challenge him in the race.

"The Tortoise and the Hare," in ***Aesop's Fables Retold in Verse***, Tom Paxton, illustrated by Robert Rayevsky (New York: Morrow Junior Books, 1988). In Paxton's retelling of the fable, in rhyming verse illustrated in rich natural tones, the Hare is his most prideful, boasting self and the Tortoise is his most determined.

"The Tortoise and the Hair," in ***The Stinky Cheese Man and Other Fairly Stupid Tales***, Jon Scieszka, illustrated by Lane Smith (New York: Viking, 1992). In "The Tortoise and the Hair," one of eleven humorous modern retellings of well-known traditional tales, the Hare challenges the Tortoise to run faster than the Hare can grow his hair.

The Foolish Tortoise, Richard Buckley, illustrated by Eric Carle (New York: Scholastic, 1985). Tired of being encumbered and slow, Tortoise takes off his shell in this rhyming story and fable and finds that he's far too vulnerable without its protection.

And Still the Turtle Watched, Sheila MacGill-Callahan, illustrated by Barry Mosher (New York: Dial Books for Young Readers, 1991). Carved out of rock by an old man to watch over the Delaware people, the turtle observes other people as they destroy the forest, cultivate the land, build cities, and blind and deface the turtle with spray paint. Finally, the turtle is restored and placed in a botanical garden (like the one in New York City which inspired this story).

MOTIVATION AND EXTENSION ACTIVITIES

1. At the beginning of the unit, students and the teacher brainstorm and record on one chart with the heading "True" (1) what they know (or think they know) to be true about turtles/terrapins/tortoises (They have shells. They move slowly.), and (2) what they would like to learn about them (Do they lay eggs? Do they have teeth? What do they eat?). On a second chart with the heading "Not True or False," they record things that are not true about real turtles/terrapins/tortoises that characters in books do (Talk. Wear clothes.).

The teacher uses this opportunity to introduce or review the terms *nonfiction*, which he or she adds under the heading "True" on the first chart, and *fiction*, which he or she adds under the heading "Not True or False" on the second chart. (For students who need a mnemonic device to remember the terms, the teacher points out that *false* and *fiction* begin with the same letter.)

Throughout the unit, students and the teacher verify or revise/correct and add information to the lists using the books suggested in this chapter and resource books and materials. They use, as one resource, the "Turtles" issues of *Zoobooks* magazine (1985 and May 1988, vol. 5, no. 8), published by Wildlife Education, Ltd., 930 West Washington Street, San Diego, California 92103. Published monthly, *Zoobooks* magazines provide current information about groups of animals through brief text and colored photographs and diagrams with captions.

2. The main characters in this chapter are called turtle, terrapin, and tortoise.

- Students and the teacher research whether the different names describe/label the same animal or different animals with subtle differences. They use dictionaries, encyclopedias, *Zoobooks* magazines (see the preceding Activity 1), and other resource books and materials in addition to the books suggested for this unit.

- Students and the teacher discover that tortoises live on dry land and turtles (or terrapins) in the water—freshwater turtles in ponds or rivers and sea turtles in oceans—and that they have many differences. They compare and contrast them and develop a data matrix that shows similarities and differences for attributes, including Habitat, What They Eat, Shell, Legs and Toes, Protection, Predators, Homes, Products. (See Activity 1 in the "Goats and Sheep" unit in Chapter 13, oa goat.)

- Throughout the unit and during their research, students and the teacher generate two lists of words (adjectives) and phrases that describe turtles/terrapins/tortoises. On one chart, they list words and phrases that describe the attributes of real turtles/terrapins/tortoises. On a second chart, they list words and phrases that describe the fictional turtle/terrapin/tortoise characters in the books they read in this unit. They compare and contrast them.

- Students use what they know and learn about the attributes and features of turtles/terrapins/tortoises as they act out with costumes and/or masks, make and use puppets to dramatize, dance, or create a dance or movements for the stories/fables in this chapter. They choose background music that represents each character to be played at appropriate times during the play/puppet show/dance/movements.

- Students generate and research names used interchangeably (and perhaps not accurately) to describe the same or similar animals, including rabbit, bunny, and hare; polliwog and tadpole; and donkey and ass.

3. Students and the teacher tell and/or write and illustrate about fears they may have or have had and how they cope(d) with or conquer(ed) them. They share whether there are/were things or people that help(ed) them or give/gave them courage. They compare and contrast their experiences with those of Franklin and the other animal characters in *Franklin in the Dark*. They discuss the specific fear of the dark or of the night that they might experience/have experienced and that of characters in books. (See Activity 8 in Chapter 12, igh night.)

4. In *Kanahena: A Cherokee Story* and *The Turtle and the Monkey: A Philippine Tale*, trickster Terrapin or Turtle outwits foes by insisting that he or she fears most as punishment being thrown into water, which, of course, is just where the amphibious trickster is most at home. Students and the teacher compare and contrast the similar stories from two different cultures. They discuss how the different physical settings of the two countries are depicted through the illustrations and the text. They make drawings or paintings that depict each setting and/or write stories/plays that occur in them.

5. It is because of her specific physical characteristics that Turtle needs to ask Monkey, who is more physically suited to the tasks, for help in *The Turtle and the Monkey: A Philippine Tale*. Monkey uses one of Turtle's attributes to her disadvantage (he turns her on her back), but Turtle triumphs when she uses another of her traits, of which Monkey is unaware (she is amphibious), to his disadvantage. Students and the teacher compare the attributes of the two animal characters and discuss how they contribute to the story.

6. *Anansi Goes Fishing* is the story of a classic match of African trickster versus African trickster as wise Turtle wins when he outsmarts lazy Anansi the Spider. Students and the teacher compare and contrast two versions of this story, in which the trickster, Anansi, himself is tricked: *Anansi Goes Fishing* and *Anansi Finds a Fool: An Ashanti Tale*. (See Activity 17 in Chapter 18, er spider.)

7. Would a turtle lay her eggs in a lettuce bed? Is it realistic that the mother turtle forgot that she buried the eggs? Do turtle eggs typically hatch in the fall, as Mrs. Turtle says she told the eggs to do? Or do they hatch in the spring? Students and the teacher use information from their research in this unit, their experience, and other reading to answer these and other questions about the way the habits and attributes of turtles, although fictionalized, are depicted in *Turtle Spring*.

8. As they read *Stick-in-the-Mud Turtle*, students and the teacher decide whether the habits and characteristics of turtles, although fictionalized, are depicted accurately based on what they have learned from their research, experience, and other reading. Do turtles live in mud holes near ponds, sunbathe, eat flies, and sit under lily pads?

9. Students and the teacher follow a recipe and make and eat a traditional shoo-fly pie and compare and contrast it to the shoo-fly pie in *Stick-in-the-Mud Turtle* and the fly pie in *Franklin Fibs*.

10. Students and the teacher compare and contrast the five versions of the "Tortoise and the Hare" fable in this unit. They each choose their favorite and give the criteria on which they based their selection.

11. The modern, humorous versions of fables such as ***The Tortoise and the Hare: An Aesop Fable***, by Stevens, and "The Tortoise and the Hair" in ***The Stinky Cheese Man and Other Fairly Stupid Tales***, by Scieszka, often provide older readers with motivation to read and study traditional literature. Students and the teacher compare and contrast the traditional and modern versions. They tell and/or write and illustrate their own modern versions of the "Tortoise and the Hare" fable or other traditional fables/ stories. (See Chapter 29, consonant-le fable.)

12. In some retellings of the "Tortoise and the Hare" fable, the moral is written and in others it is implied. Students and the teacher provide a moral for the versions that do not contain one. They each choose one moral for the fable that they prefer from among all of the suggested morals. They give reasons for their choice.

13. The authors of the five different versions of the "Tortoise and the Hare" fable use a number of different adjectives to describe the two characters. Students and the teacher add these descriptive words to the list of attributes they are compiling for Activity 2 of this chapter.

14. In ***Rachel and Obadiah*** by Turkle, a story set in a Quaker community on Nantucket Island off the coast of Massachusetts in the United States, Obadiah is the hare as he boasts that he can stop to eat blackberries and still catch up with and beat his little sister Rachel, the tortoise, in their race to tell the captain's wife that a ship has been sighted and collect the silver coin as a reward. Students and the teacher read ***Rachel and Obadiah***, by Brinton Turkle (New York: E. P. Dutton, 1978). They compare and contrast this story, which shares a common theme, with the "Tortoise and the Hare" fable retellings they read in this unit.

15. The tortoise in ***The Foolish Tortoise*** learns a lesson about who he is. The story may be seen as a modern fable with an implied moral. Students and the teacher generate morals for the story. Each of them chooses their preferred moral from among those generated and gives reasons for their choice.

16. Based on their knowledge of tortoises from research, experience, and reading, students evaluate whether a real tortoise could take off its shell, as the tortoise does in ***Franklin in the Dark*** and in ***The Foolish Tortoise***. They give reasons for their re- sponses. As one resource, they read "A Turtle Can Walk Out of Its Shell" in ***Animal Fact/Animal Fable***, Seymour Simon, illustrated by Diane de Groat (New York: Crown Publishers, Inc., 1979), which provides factual information in an unusual and engaging format. The colorfully and accurately illustrated book presents scientific observations about the behavior of a variety of animals. For each animal, a true or false statement is presented on a right-hand page, and the reader guesses whether it is a fact or a fable (fiction) and turns the page to find out.

17. The impact of the actions of people intruding on native peoples and animals and their environment is poignantly expressed in ***Little Turtle's Big Adventure*** and ***And Still the Turtle Watched*** and humorously told in ***Stick-in-the-Mud Turtle***. Stu- dents and the teacher discuss this theme and consider the impact of "progress/civilization" on the natural environment and its inhabitants as they read the three books from this unit. They read other books that focus on this theme, including the following two picture books:

♦ ***The Little House***, Virginia Lee Burton (Boston: Houghton Mifflin Company, 1942, 1969). Through the seasons and years, a little house, originally built in the country, watches the city grow closer and closer until she is surrounded by tall buildings, crowds of people, noise, and pollution. In the end, she is relocated to the country by the great-great-granddaughter of her first owner. Caldecott Award Book.

• ***The Land of Gray Wolf***, Thomas Locker (New York: Dial Books, 1991). Told by the character Running Deer, a young boy, and illustrated with Locker oil paintings, the book contrasts the ways of the native people who live in harmony with their natural environment and those of white settlers who ravage the land, force Running Deer's people onto a reservation, and move on—leaving the land to be reclaimed by the animals.

18. Turtles are part of the folklore and art of many cultures. Students and the teacher explore the turtle as an element in the "Dreamtime" pictures drawn by the Aborigine people of Australia. They read the "Dreamtime (Australia)" chapter in ***Kid Pix around the World: A Multicultural Computer Activity Book***, Barbara Chan (Reading, Mass.: Addison-Wesley Publishing Company, 1993) and paint a sea turtle "Dreamtime" design on their computer. The book contains essays that provide background information about twenty cultures around the world and detailed, step-by-step instructions that show children how to do drawing and painting activities using "Kid Pix" computer software. Presented cultures are marked on a world map in the front of the book.

19. Students and the teacher locate on a map and/or globe the places/cultures (depicted or of origin) in the books read in this chapter, including North America and the southern Appalachian Mountains (***Kanahena: A Cherokee Story***); the Philippines (***The Turtle and the Monkey: A Philippine Tale***); Africa (***Anansi Goes Fishing***); Ashanti culture and Ghana on the west coast of Africa (***Anansi Finds a Fool: An Ashanti Tale***); Greece (***The Tortoise and the Hare: An Aesop Fable***, ***The Hare and the Tortoise***, "The Hare and the Tortoise" in ***The Aesop for Children***, "The Tortoise and the Hare" in ***Aesop's Fables Retold in Verse***, and "The Tortoise and the Hair" in ***The Stinky Cheese Man and Other Fairly Stupid Tales***; the Quaker community on Nantucket Island off the coast of Massachusetts in the United States (***Rachel and Obadiah***); the Delaware River delta and New York City in the United States (***And Still the Turtle Watched***); North America (***The Land of Gray Wolf***); and Australia ["Dreamtime (Australia)" in ***Kid Pix around the World: A Multicultural Computer Activity Book***].

TEACHER REFERENCE

Cloze Sentences

One-Syllable Words

Cloze Sentences 1

1. I have a small <u>purse</u> that I keep in my pocketbook that holds my money.
2. I <u>hurt</u> my leg when I was running and I fell on the steps.
3. <u>Fur</u> keeps many animals like cats and dogs warm on cold days.
4. You can <u>burn</u> yourself on a hot stove if you are not careful.
5. The baby <u>burst</u> into tears when the doctor gave him a shot.
6. A long time ago a person had to <u>churn</u> by hand her or his own butter.

7. If you <u>turn</u> or twist a knob or push a button, you can turn on the TV.

8. The <u>nurse</u> at the hospital woke me up when it was time to take my pills.

9. The tall, white <u>church</u> was the biggest and oldest building in the town.

Multisyllable Words

Cloze Sentences 2

1. A <u>turtle</u> can pull its legs and head into its hard shell to protect itself.

2. <u>Saturday</u> is the first day of the weekend and the day before Sunday.

3. If you are not born with <u>curly</u> hair, you may curl your hair by setting it on curlers or by getting a permanent.

4. A <u>surprise</u> party is a party that is kept secret.

5. <u>Thursday</u> is the day before Friday.

6. A <u>sturdy</u> tree is a good tree to climb. It is strong and will not bend over.

7. Do not <u>disturb</u> a person who is sleeping.

Dictations

1. On <u>Saturday</u> the <u>church</u> <u>burned</u> down. As it was <u>burning</u>, flames <u>burst</u> from the windows and the roof, and thick smoke made it hard to see. A <u>sturdy</u> wall was <u>hurled</u> over by a blast inside, and a <u>nurse</u> and a fireman were badly <u>hurt</u>.

2. It was no <u>surprise</u> to us when Mr. <u>Burns</u> told us that he had <u>hurt</u> his leg in his fall at <u>church</u> last <u>Thursday</u>. It <u>disturbs</u> him that when he uses the <u>sturdy</u> cane that the <u>nurse</u> gave him he is as slow as a <u>turtle</u>.

3. By <u>surprise</u> on <u>Thursday</u> a man <u>burst</u> into a room at the <u>nursing</u> home and a <u>nurse</u> was <u>hurt</u> and had her <u>purse</u> stolen. The cops were <u>spurred</u> on to catch the <u>sturdy</u> fellow who had taken it. By <u>Saturday</u> they had gotten the <u>purse</u> and the man, who had <u>turned</u> himself in.

ur (er) turtle

b___n   c___ly

b___st   dist___b

ch___ch   Sat___day

ch___n   st___dy

___f   s___prise

h___t   Th___sday

n___se   t___tle

p___se

t___n

Name _____ Date _____

Word List 1

ur (er) turtle

burn	curly
burst	disturb
church	Saturday
churn	sturdy
fur	surprise
hurt	Thursday
nurse	turtle
purse	
turn	

Name _____ Date _____

Word List 2

ur (er) turtle

Write a word from the Word List to complete each sentence.

1. I have a small _____ that I keep in my pocketbook that holds my money.

2. I _____ my leg when I was running and I fell on the steps.

3. _____ keeps many animals like cats and dogs warm on cold days.

4. You can _____ yourself on a hot stove if you are not careful.

5. The baby _____ into tears when the doctor gave him a shot.

6. A long time ago a person had to _____ by hand her or his own butter.

7. If you _____ or twist a knob or push a button, you can turn on the TV.

8. The _____ at the hospital woke me up when it was time to take my pills.

9. The tall, white _____ was the biggest and oldest building in the town.

Name _____ Date _____

Cloze Sentences 1

ur   (er)   turtle **ur**

Write a word from the Word List to complete each sentence.

1. A _____ can pull its legs and head into its hard shell to protect itself.

2. _____ is the first day of the weekend and the day before Sunday.

3. If you are not born with _____ hair, you may curl your hair by setting it on curlers or by getting a permanent.

4. A _____ party is a party that is kept secret.

5. _____ is the day before Friday.

6. A _____ tree is a good tree to climb. It is strong and will not bend over.

7. Do not _____ a person who is sleeping.

Name _____ Date _____

© 1995 by Cynthia Conway Waring

Cloze Sentences 2

21   oo   cookies

BOOK LIST ==

Cookies and Friends

The Doorbell Rang, Pat Hutchins (New York: Mulberry Books, 1986). In this predict-able, repetitive book with a refrain, more and more people come to the door to share the cookies that Ma baked. When there is only enough left for one cookie each, the doorbell rings again and it's grandma—with more cookies!

"Cookies," in ***Frog and Toad Together***, Arnold Lobel (New York: Harper & Row, 1971, 1972). This book contains five stories in which Frog and Toad celebrate the joys of friendship as they share everyday experiences and their fears and dreams. In "Cookies," neither Frog nor Toad has enough willpower to stop eating Toad's freshly baked cookies. Newbery Honor Book.

"The Tea Party," in ***Penrod's Pants***, Mary Blount Christian, illustrated by Jane Dyer (New York: Macmillan Publishing Company, 1986). This book contains five stories about the friendship shared by Penrod Porcupine and his long-suffering pal, Griswold the Bear, who is able, again and again, to tolerate Penrod's irritating ways. In "The Tea Party," no matter what he does, Griswold cannot convince Penrod to be polite and leave the last cookie on the plate.

Porcupine's Pajama Party, Terry Webb Harshman, illustrated by Doug Cushman (New York: Harper & Row, 1988). When he invites his friends Owl and Otter to sleep at his house, Porcupine discovers that being together makes everything more fun—making cookies, watching a scary movie on TV, and being scared in the dark. In "Baking Cookies," the friends find that after they sample the dough while they make it, there's only enough left to make three cookies!

Two Good Friends, Judy Delton, illustrated by Giulio Maestro (New York: Crown Pub-lishers, Inc., 1974). The "Odd Couple" of animals, Duck (a neatness fanatic who doesn't cook) and his dear friend Bear (a wonderful but messy cook) discover that they each have gifts to celebrate and share.

If You Give a Mouse a Cookie, Laura Joffe Numeroff, illustrated by Felicia Bond (New York: Scholastic, 1985). In this ultimate "If . . . then" book, a boy sets off a circular chain of events, which exhausts him and may continue indefinitely, when he gives a cookie to a mouse.

If You Give a Moose a Muffin, Laura Joffe Numeroff, illustrated by Felicia Bond (New York: Scholastic, 1991). In this companion to *If You Give a Mouse a Cookie* by the same author, a boy starts a similar chain of events that may never stop when he gives a muffin to a hungry and artistic moose, who turns the house upside down with his enthusiasm.

"Split Pea Soup," in *George and Martha: Five Stories about Two Great Friends*, James Marshall (New York: Scholastic, 1972). This first book in the series introduces the friendship of two hippopotamuses, George and Martha, as they discover each other's likes, dislikes, and habits and they cheer each other on through some misadventures. In "Split Pea Soup," Martha makes split pea soup again and again until she and George confess that they don't like it and would rather eat chocolate chip cookies.

The Stingy Baker, Janet Greeson, illustrated by David LaRochelle (Minneapolis: Carolrhoda Books, Inc., 1990). In this *pourquoi* tale from the United States that explains one origin of the baker's dozen, a stingy baker learns generosity from a dissatisfied witch customer, who casts a spell on his shop and cookies, and from an angel, who breaks the spell.

MOTIVATION AND EXTENSION ACTIVITIES

1. Because of its theme, this unit naturally invites baking responses. There are a number of cookbooks written with inexperienced cooks in mind that provide detailed general instructions for cooking and baking and clearly presented and illustrated step-by-step recipes. Students and the teacher follow recipes for baking cookies as part of activities for this unit using the following cookbooks or from among their own sources and favorites.

The Cookie Lovers Cookie Cookbook, Prudence Younger (New York: The Trumpet Club, 1988), contains thirty-four cookie recipes for bar, drop, molded, cut-out, and easy no-bake cookies, cookie and ice cream sandwiches, and cookies for special occasions and gives instructions for giving a cookie party.

The Little Cooks: Recipes from around the World for Boys and Girls, Eve Tharlet (New York: UNICEF), contains thirty-six recipes for preparing food from countries around the world, a map of the world that locates the countries of origin, illustrations of children in the dress of their countries/cultures, information about healthy eating habits, and background information about the work of UNICEF. Cookie recipes include Mantecados (Cinnamon Cookies) from Morocco, Ful-Sudani (Peanut Macaroons) from the Sudan, Jam Cookies from Germany, and Betusutemeny (Letter Cookies) from Hungary.

Peter Rabbit's Natural Foods Cookbook, Arnold Dobrin, illustrated by Beatrix Potter (New York: Frederick Warne, 1977), is a collection of recipes, with illustrations by England's Beatrix Potter, for food that characters in her books would have liked to cook or eat (including a recipe for "Littletown-Farm Carrot Cookies").

Better Homes and Gardens Step-by-Step Kids' Cookbook, Linda Henry, Editor (Des Moines, Iowa: Meredith Corporation, 1985), is a beginner's guide with easy-to-cook and no-cook recipes that have numbered steps and colored photographs, including a recipe for "Chunky Chocolate Cookies" that look like the ones Toad baked in "Cookies" in *Frog and Toad Together*.

2. Traditionally, Swedish cooks used carved wooden cookie stamps to make designs on *pepparkakor* (ginger snap) cookies just before they were baked. Students and the teacher read the "Cookie Stamps (Sweden)" chapter and experiment with the techniques suggested for making similar cookie stamp designs on the computer in *Kid Pix around the World: A Multicultural Computer Activity Book*, Barbara Chan (Reading, Mass.: Addison-Wesley Publishing Company, 1993). The book contains essays that provide background information about twenty cultures around the world and detailed, step-by-step instructions that show children how to do drawing and painting activities using "Kid Pix" computer software. Presented cultures are marked on a world map in the front of the book.

The "Cookie Stamps (Sweden)" chapter contains a recipe for making the traditional Swedish *pepparkakor* ginger snap cookies. Students and the teacher make the cookies and follow the directions to use a cookie stamp or a fork to make designs before they bake them.

3. Before readers turn the pages in *The Doorbell Rang*, they guess or use concrete objects (or cookies!) to show how the dozen cookies that Ma baked are divided up differently each time more people come to share them.

4. The predictable plot and large number of characters make *The Doorbell Rang* a story that lends itself to being performed by a group of students or by individuals with puppets. Students act it out with props (some of which may need to be baked, of course!).

5. After reading "Cookies" in *Frog and Toad Together*, students and the teacher share stories (tell and/or write and illustrate) about a time when they found it difficult to stop eating cookies (or any other food) or lacked willpower to stop doing something.

6. Students and the teacher read more about the friendship and adventures of Frog and Toad in the other stories in *Frog and Toad Together* and *Frog and Toad All Year, Days with Frog and Toad*, and *Frog and Toad Are Friends*, by Arnold Lobel.

7. Students and the teacher read more about the adventures of Penrod Porcupine and Griswold Bear in other chapters of *Penrod's Pants* and in its sequel, *Penrod Again*, by Mary Blount Christian, illustrated by Jane Dyer (New York: Macmillan Publishing Company, 1987), in which their friendship deepens as they share their daily lives, the possibility of Penrod moving away, cramped quarters, and holiday gifts.

8. In "Baking Cookies" in *Porcupine's Pajama Party*, the friends sample raw cookie dough as they mix it. If the local ice cream store or supermarket carries it, students and the teacher sample cookie dough ice cream (safer to eat than cookie dough, which contains raw egg).

9. Together, students and the teacher create and illustrate an "If You Give a _____ a _____"—an "If . . . then" story patterned after *If You Give a Mouse a Cookie* and *If You Give a Moose a Muffin*.

- Groups of students create a class book together in round-robin fashion while sitting in a circle. Each person adds an event that logically follows the previous event. A recorder for the group writes down the ideas, which are later written in book form to be illustrated by students.

- Individual students and the teacher alternate turns to add events to the book, and one person acts as scribe or they take turns. They then illustrate the book.

- An individual student dictates the entire story to a scribe (another student or the teacher) or records ideas independently.

10. Students gather or make props and act out the sequence of events in the *If You Give a Mouse a Cookie* and/or *If You Give a Moose a Muffin* books or their own "If You Give a _____ a _____" stories.

11. If they are not full, students and the teacher make and eat muffins as they share *If You Give a Moose a Muffin*. Students and the teacher generate as many ways as they can think of that cookies and muffins are the same, on one chart, and different, on another chart. For example:

Same	*Different*
You can eat them.	You make cookies on a cookie sheet, but you make muffins in muffin tins.
They are made with flour.	
They have sugar in them.	Cookies are flat, but muffins are tall and rounded and fat.
You bake them.	
They look round when you look from the top.	

12. Students and the teacher locate on a map and/or globe the places/cultures (depicted or of origin) in the books read in this chapter, including Morocco, Sudan, Germany, and Hungary (*The Little Cooks: Recipes from around the World for Boys and Girls*); England (*Peter Rabbit's Natural Foods Cookbook*); and Sweden ["Cookie Stamps (Sweden)" in *Kid Pix around the World: A Multicultural Computer Activity Book*].

TEACHER REFERENCE ══════════════════════════════════

Cloze Sentences

One-Syllable Words

Cloze Sentences 1

1. The <u>crook</u> had a mask on when she robbed the bank.
2. We <u>stood</u> in line for such a long time when we were shopping that my legs got tired.
3. We looked under the <u>hood</u> of my car to see if the spark plugs looked all right.
4. A <u>book</u> is a good gift for a person who likes to read.
5. <u>Wool</u> from a sheep makes good knitted mittens or hats.
6. <u>Wood</u> needs to be chopped and split before it can be burned in a stove.
7. The <u>brook</u> was flowing over its banks after the big rainstorm.

Cloze Sentences 2

1. The <u>hook</u> in the hall is the spot where I hang my coat and hat.
2. After I <u>cook</u> dinner I serve the food and we all sit down to eat.

3. A <u>woof</u> from the car next to mine let me know that a dog was inside.

4. I got a blister on my left <u>foot</u> when I went on a long hike last week.

5. I <u>shook</u> the salad dressing to mix it up before I put it on my salad.

6. He got a <u>good</u> hit at the baseball game today—much better than the one he got yesterday.

7. Take a <u>look</u> at that amazing sunset!

Multisyllable Words

Cloze Sentences 3

1. She lost her <u>pocketbook</u>, which had all of her money and her checkbook in it.

2. The girl's <u>scrapbook</u> had tickets and score cards from every baseball game she had seen.

3. <u>Football</u> and soccer are two sports in which the feet are used to kick a ball to a goal.

4. It was hard for me to get the <u>fishhook</u> out of the fish's lip after I hooked it on my line.

5. <u>Cookies</u>—freshly baked and hot from the oven—are the best dessert that I know!

6. You can look in a <u>cookbook</u> to discover ways to cook food.

Dictations

1. After the <u>football</u> game we all <u>stood</u> in the kitchen as I made chocolate chip <u>cookies</u>. I had made the <u>cookies</u> so often that I did not need to <u>look</u> in my <u>cookbook</u>. The <u>cookies</u> must have been <u>good</u>! We ate them all.

2. It <u>looked</u> like a <u>good</u> day for fishing in the <u>brook</u>, so Mr. <u>Hood</u> <u>took</u> his rod and <u>fishhooks</u> and <u>stood</u> in the <u>wooded</u> spot by the <u>brook</u> that he liked best. His luck was <u>good</u> and he got a lot of fish to take home. He <u>took</u> a photo of them for his <u>scrapbook</u> and then <u>cooked</u> them up for his dinner.

3. At the <u>bookstore</u> I <u>stood</u> just a <u>foot</u> from a <u>crook</u> who <u>took</u> a <u>book</u> and a <u>scrapbook</u> and was trying to hide them in her <u>pocketbook</u> when the clerk <u>looked</u> her way. It was <u>good</u> that she did not get away with the theft, but it <u>shook</u> me up to see it happen.

oo (o͝o) cookies 🍪🍪

b k	h k	c kb k
br k	l k	c kies
c k	sh k	fishh k
cr k	st d	f tball
f t	w d	pocketb k
g d	w f	scrapb k
h d	w l	

© 1995 by Cynthia Conway Waring

Name _____ Date _____

oo (o͝o) cookies

book	hook	cookbook
brook	look	cookies
cook	shook	fishhook
crook	stood	football
foot	wood	pocketbook
good	woof	scrapbook
hood	wool	

Name _____ Date _____

oo (o͝o) cookies

Write a word from the Word List to complete each sentence.

1. The _____ had a mask on when she robbed the bank.

2. We _____ in line for such a long time when we were shopping that my legs got tired.

3. We looked under the _____ of my car to see if the spark
   plugs looked all right.

4. A _____ is a good gift for a person who likes to read.

5. _____ from a sheep makes good knitted mittens or hats.

6. _____ needs to be chopped and split before it can be burned
   in a stove.

7. The _____ was flowing over its banks after the big rainstorm.

© 1995 by Cynthia Conway Waring

Name _____ Date _____

Cloze Sentences 1

oo (o͝o) cookies

Write a word from the Word List to complete each sentence.

1. The _____ in the hall is the spot where I hang my coat and hat.

2. After I _____ dinner I serve the food and we all sit down to eat.

3. A _____ from the car next to mine let me know that a dog was inside.

4. I got a blister on my left _____ when I went on a long hike last week.

5. I _____ the salad dressing to mix it up before I put it on my salad.

6. He got a _____ hit at the baseball game today—much better than the one he got yesterday.

7. Take a _____ at that amazing sunset!

Name _____ Date _____

© 1995 by Cynthia Conway Waring

Cloze Sentences 2

oo (ŏŏ) cookies 🍪🍪

Write a word from the Word List to complete each sentence.

1. She lost her _____, which had all of her money and her checkbook in it.

2. The girl's _____ had tickets and score cards from every baseball game she had seen.

3. _____ and soccer are two sports in which the feet are used to kick a ball to a goal.

4. It was hard for me to get the _____ out of the fish's lip after I hooked it on my line.

5. _____—freshly baked and hot from the oven—are the best dessert that I know!

6. You can look in a _____ to discover ways to cook food.

© 1995 by Cynthia Conway Waring

Name _____ Date _____

Cloze Sentences 3

22   ow   owl

BOOK LIST ══════════════════════════════════════

Owls

Good-Night, Owl!; Pat Hutchins (New York: The Trumpet Club, 1972). One by one, the daytime animals in this cumulative story make noise that keeps Owl awake during the day, but in the end he achieves his goal of revenge when he screeches at night and awakens them.

The Strange Disappearance of Arthur Cluck, Nathaniel Benchley, illustrated by Arnold Lobel (New York: Harper & Row, 1967). In this easy-to-read mystery, Owl is the nighttime detective who helps Mrs. Cluck find her missing son, Arthur, after he disappears suddenly and the other chicks, who had vanished as mysteriously from the farm.

Owl at Home, Arnold Lobel (New York: Scholastic, 1975). In a collection of five stories, Owl is alone at home, but he is entertained by the winter wind, bumps in his bed, sad thoughts, a challenge to himself, and his new friend—the moon.

Porcupine's Pajama Party, Terry Webb Harshman, illustrated by Doug Cushman (New York: Harper & Row, 1988). When he invites his friends Owl and Otter to sleep at his house, Porcupine discovers that being together makes everything more fun—making cookies, watching a scary movie on TV, and being scared in the dark.

Owl Moon, Jane Yolen, illustrated by John Schoenherr (New York: Scholastic, 1987). The paintings and verbal imagery in this book invite readers to accompany a girl and her father on a moonlit winter night owling adventure. Caldecott Award Book.

Why Mosquitoes Buzz in People's Ears: A West African Tale, Verna Aardema, illustrated by Leo and Diane Dillon (New York: The Dial Press, 1975). In this cumulative *pourquoi* tale, the mosquito sets off a series of events that culminates in the death of one of Mother Owl's owlets, and she refuses to wake the sun until mosquito is punished. To this day, mosquitoes whine in people's ears to ask if everyone is still angry. Caldecott Award Book.

Owls in the Family, Farley Mowat (Boston: Little, Brown and Company, 1961). This eleven-chapter book tells the adventures of a boy and his dog and family, whose lives change dramatically after he saves and brings home two owls—Wol, from the top of a tree ravaged in a storm, and Weeps, from the bottom of an oil barrel.

How and Why: *Pourquoi* Tales from around the World

The Creation and Workings of the Elements of Nature

Anansi the Spider: A Tale from the Ashanti, Gerald McDermott (New York: Holt, Rinehart and Winston, 1972). Two related tales about Anansi the trickster include a quest, in which Anansi is saved in six trials through the individual talents of his six sons, and a *pourquoi* (how or why) tale of how the moon came to be in the sky. Caldecott Honor Book.

Arrow to the Sun: A Pueblo Indian Tale, Gerald McDermott (New York: The Viking Press, 1974). In this combination quest and *pourquoi* tale from a Pueblo myth, the Boy, the son of the Sun, is ridiculed on earth by his peers because he has no father, and he leaves to search for him. Made into an arrow, he travels to the Sun, proves himself by enduring four trials, is transformed and filled with the Sun's power, and returns to earth, where he is respected. Tells how the spirit of the Sun was brought to the earth. Caldecott Award Book.

Moon Rope/Un lazo a la luna: A Peruvian Folktale, Lois Ehlert, translated into Spanish by Amy Prince (San Diego: Harcourt Brace Jovanovich, 1992). Written in English and Spanish, this adaptation of a Peruvian *pourquoi* legend tells the adventures of mole and fox as they climb to the moon on a grass rope ladder and why moles live underground and a fox's face is in the moon.

Why the Sun and the Moon Live in the Sky: An African Folktale by Elphinstone Dayrell, illustrated by Blair Lent (New York: Scholastic, 1968). Characters in this *pourquoi* tale wear costumes in the story of a visit from the water and his people that crowds the sun and his wife, the moon, out of their house on earth and forces them to live in the sky.

How the Rooster Saved the Day, Arnold Lobel, illustrated by Anita Lobel (New York: Penguin Books, 1977). This *pourquoi* tale tells why the rooster crows to bring up the morning sun. To prolong the night's darkness that hides him as he steals, a robber tries to prevent the rooster from crowing, but the rooster tricks *him* into crowing.

How the Sun Was Brought Back to the Sky, Mirra Ginsburg, illustrated by José Aruego and Ariane Dewey (New York: Macmillan Publishing Co., Inc., 1975). When the sun is hidden by clouds for three days, in this *pourquoi* tale, five chicks set out to bring it back. With the help of friends and the moon, they find and clean the sun, and now it shines every day.

The Legend of the Indian Paintbrush, Tomie dePaola (New York: Scholastic, 1988). Not a warrior, Little Gopher develops his own gift. Guided by a dream, he paints the stories of his people with brushes he is given, which take root. This *pourquoi* tale tells how Indian Paintbrush flowers began.

The Legend of the Bluebonnet: An Old Tale of Texas, Tomie dePaola (New York: G. P. Putnam's Sons, 1983). A little orphaned girl sacrifices her most valued possession to bring rain to save her people from drought and famine, and blue flowers grow from the scattered ashes of her treasured doll. This *pourquoi* story tells the origin of bluebonnet wildflowers.

"The First Fire," in **Cherokee Animal Tales**, George F. Scheer, illustrated by Robert Frankenberg (New York: Holiday House, Inc., 1968). The collection of thirteen *pourquoi* tales from Cherokee storytellers explains the origin of fire and of the characteristics and features of animals and includes background information about the Cherokee people. In "The First Fire," only the Water Spider, of all the animals, is able to carry fire from the island where it was given by the lightning of the Thunders so that the animals can warm themselves.

Papagayo: The Mischief Maker, Gerald McDermott (San Diego: Harcourt Brace Jovanovich, 1980, 1992). This *pourquoi* tale explains moon phases. Papagayo, the parrot, annoys the nocturnal animals during the day, but he becomes their hero one night when his noisy plan saves their beloved thinning moon from the teeth of the hungry moon-dog.

The Orphan Boy: A Maasai Story, Tololwa M. Mollel, illustrated by Paul Morin (New York: Clarion Books, 1990). In this *pourquoi* story, a star disappears from the sky and an orphan boy mysteriously appears to live with a childless old man, who learns the price of curiosity. His insatiable interest in the boy's secret powers betrays the boy's trust and sends him back to the sky as the planet Venus. Notes about the author contain information about the Maasai and the author's life in Kenya and Tanzania.

The Behavior and Customs of People

Tikki Tikki Tembo, Arlene Mosel, illustrated by Blair Lent (New York: Scholastic, 1968). This *pourquoi* tale tells why the Chinese give their children short names rather than long ones. A treasured first son nearly drowns when his brother is not able to say his long name quickly in order to get help.

A Story a Story: An African Tale, Gail E. Haley (New York: Atheneum, 1970). This combination *pourquoi*, quest, and trickster tale tells how stories came to be told throughout the world. Anansi the Spider, who is neither young nor strong, uses his intelligence and trickery to accomplish three amazing tasks to buy the Sky God's stories. Caldecott Award Book.

Spider and the Sky God: An Akan Legend, Deborah M. Newton Chocolate, illustrated by Dave Albers (Mahwah, N.J.: Troll Associates, 1993). In this version of the *pourquoi*/ quest/ trickster tale, Ananse the Spider, with direction from his wise wife, brings four things to the Sky God in payment for his stories, which Ananse now spins on the earth.

The Stingy Baker, Janet Greeson, illustrated by David LaRochelle (Minneapolis: Carolrhoda Books, Inc., 1990). In this *pourquoi* tale from the United States that explains one origin of the baker's dozen, a stingy baker learns generosity from a dissatisfied witch customer, who casts a spell on his shop and cookies, and from an angel, who breaks the spell.

Oh, Kojo! How Could You!: An Ashanti Tale, Verna Aardema, illustrated by Marc Brown (New York: The Trumpet Club, 1984). Lazy Anansi, an old man, tricks lazy Kojo, the young man, into trading gold for a dog, cat, and dove, who appear useless; but they prove their value when they enable Kojo to receive, and later regain, a magic ring as a reward for an act of kindness. This *pourquoi* and trickster tale tells why the Ashanti people treat their cats better than their dogs.

"How the First Letter Was Written" and "How the Alphabet Was Made," in ***New Illustrated Just So Stories***, Rudyard Kipling, illustrated by Nicolas (New York: The Trumpet Club, 1912, 1952). This book is a collection of twelve *pourquoi* stories that explain the origin of the features or traits of animals and the custom of people using written language to communicate. In "How the First Letter Was Written," a little girl, Taffy, draws pictures on birch bark for a messenger to give to her mother so that she will send her father's spear; and in "How the Alphabet Was Made," Taffy associates the sounds her father makes with pictures and draws symbols to represent them.

Features and Traits of Animals

Lazy Lion, Mwenye Hadithi and Adrienne Kennaway (New York: The Trumpet Club, 1990). In this *pourquoi* tale, lazy Lion orders a variety of animals to make him a house, but he is dissatisfied with their efforts and even in heavy rain—when the animals take shelter in the homes they made—Lion does not find a house and wanders the African plain.

Kanahena: A Cherokee Story, Susan L. Roth (New York: St. Martin's Press, 1988). As she stirs the Kanahena (hominy or cornmeal mush) in her pot, an old woman tells a girl an old *pourquoi* and trickster tale about Kanahena and how the trickster Terrapin got the scars on his shell when he tricked some angry wolves. Includes a recipe for Kanahena.

The Loon's Necklace, William Toye, illustrated by Elizabeth Cleaver (Oxford, England: Oxford University Press, 1977). Torn and cut-out paper collages illustrate this *pourquoi* tale of how the loon got its markings. When Loon gives a blind old man his sight, he gives Loon his shell necklace, which breaks and scatters white flecks on the bird's black feathers.

The Rooster's Horns: A Chinese Puppet Play to Make and Perform, Ed Young with Hilary Beckett, illustrated by Ed Young (New York and Cleveland: William Collins & World Publishing Company in cooperation with the U.S. Committee for UNICEF, 1978). In the days when Rooster had horns, Dragon envied them and, with Worm's help, he tricked Rooster with flattery into letting him borrow them on a visit to Heaven. Every day at dawn, Rooster looks to Heaven for Dragon's return and crows for him to give back his horns. This *pourquoi* tale tells why the rooster crows at dawn and why worms fear roosters.

Why Mosquitoes Buzz in People's Ears: A West African Tale, Verna Aardema, illustrated by Leo and Diane Dillon (New York: The Dial Press, 1975). In this cumulative *pourquoi* tale, the mosquito sets off a series of events that culminates in the death of one of Mother Owl's owlets, and she refuses to wake the sun until the mosquito is punished. To this day, mosquitoes whine in people's ears to ask if everyone is still angry. Caldecott Award Book.

Cherokee Animal Tales, George F. Scheer, illustrated by Robert Frankenberg (New York: Holiday House, Inc., 1968). This collection of thirteen *pourquoi* tales from Cherokee storytellers explains the origin of fire and of the characteristics and features of animals and includes background information about the Cherokee people.

The Elephant's Child, Rudyard Kipling, illustrated by Lorinda Bryan Cauley (San Diego: Harcourt Brace Jovanovich, 1983). This illustrated single tale selected from Kipling's *Just So Stories* is the story of the result of the elephant's child's " 'satiable curiosity" about what the crocodile eats for dinner and explains why, as the result, elephants now have long trunks.

New Illustrated Just So Stories, Rudyard Kipling, illustrated by Nicolas (New York: The Trumpet Club, 1912, 1952). The book is a collection of twelve *pourquoi* stories that explain the origin of the features or traits of animals and the custom of people using written language to communicate.

MOTIVATION AND EXTENSION ACTIVITIES

Owls

1. At the beginning of the unit, students and the teacher brainstorm and record on one chart with the heading "True" (1) what they know (or think they know) to be true about owls (They are birds that are awake and hunt at night/nocturnal. They hunt and eat mice and other rodents. They have big eyes.), and (2) what they would like to learn about them (Are all owls big? What colors can owls be? Do male and female owls look different? Are owls really wise? Why are they called wise? Do owls live all over the world?). On a second chart with the heading "Not True or False," they record things that are not true about real owls that owl characters in books do (Talk. Wear clothes. Sit in chairs. Sleep in beds.).

The teacher uses this opportunity to introduce or review the terms *nonfiction*, which he or she adds under the heading "True" on the first chart, and *fiction,* which he or she adds under the heading "Not True or False" on the second chart. (For students who need a mnemonic device to remember the terms, the teacher points out that *false* and *fiction* begin with the same letter.)

Throughout the unit, students and the teacher verify or revise/correct and add information to the lists using the books suggested in this chapter and resource books and materials. They use, as one resource, the "Owls" issues of ***Zoobooks*** magazine (September 1987, vol. 4, no. 12, and June 1992, vol. 9, no. 9), published by Wildlife Education, Ltd., 930 Washington Street, San Diego, California 92103. Published monthly, ***Zoobooks*** magazines provide current information about groups of animals through brief text and colored photographs and diagrams with captions.

Animal Fact/Animal Fable, Seymour Simon, illustrated by Diane de Groat (New York: Crown Publishers, Inc., 1979) is another resource about animals. It provides factual information in an unusual and engaging format. The colorfully and accurately illustrated book presents scientific observations about the behavior of a variety of animals. For each animal, a true or false statement is presented on a right-hand page, and the reader guesses whether it is a fact or a fable (fiction) and turns the page to find out. Students and the teacher find answers to the questions "Are owls really wise?" and "Why are they called wise?" as they read "An Owl is a Wise Bird" in *Animal Fact/Animal Fable*.

2. Throughout the unit and during their research and reading, students and the teacher generate two lists of words (adjectives) and phrases that describe owls. On one chart, they list words and phrases that describe the attributes and features of real owls. On a second chart, they list words and phrases that describe fictional owl characters in the books they read in this unit. They compare and contrast them.

3. As they read *Good-Night Owl*, students and the teacher complete Activity 5 in Chapter 12, igh night.

4. Students use what they know and learn about the attributes and features of owls as they act out with costumes and/or masks, make and use puppets to dramatize, or create a dance/movements for the stories in this chapter. They choose background music that represents each character to be played at appropriate times during the play/ puppet show/dance/movements.

5. In "The Guest" in *Owl at Home*, Owl invites Winter inside to sit by the fire and warm itself. This is an example of personification, a type of figurative language in which animate, human, or personal qualities are given to inanimate things or abstract concepts or ideas. Students and the teacher discuss the use of personification in this story (and compare and contrast it to the use of personification in *Owl Moon* in Activity 10 of this chapter).

6. In "Strange Bumps" in *Owl at Home*, Owl is frightened by two bumps under the blanket that mysteriously move every time his legs move; and Owl, Otter, and Porcupine scare and comfort each other and themselves as they share the most frightening things they can imagine in bed during a sleep-over in "The Scariest Thing," in *Porcupine's Pajama Party*.

Students and the teacher tell and/or write and illustrate about fears of noises and sights of the night and/or of the dark they may have or have had. They tell how they cope(d) with or conquer(ed) them and whether there are/were any things or people that help(ed) them or give/gave them courage. They compare their experiences with those of characters in the books, including the two in this chapter. (See Activity 8 in Chapter 12, igh night, for a list of additional books.)

7. Owl thinks of things that are sad so that he can make "Tear-Water Tea" in *Owl at Home*. Students and the teacher generate and record (and illustrate) on a chart a list of things that are sad. To cheer themselves up, they make a second chart with a list of antonyms for words that mean "sad"—things that are happy.

8. Owl challenges himself to an impossible feat in "Upstairs and Downstairs" in *Owl at Home* when he tries to be in two places at once. Students and the teacher share (tell and/or write and illustrate about) how they have challenged themselves. They tell whether the task was possible and what was the result of the challenge.

9. Owl tries to make friends with the moon in "Owl and the Moon" in *Owl at Home*. Students and the teacher compare and contrast his approach and experience with Bear's in *Happy Birthday, Moon* (see Chapter 2, oo moon).

10. The visual imagery of the watercolor paintings and the verbal imagery created by the figurative language of the text combine to create a sense of mood and place in *Owl Moon*.

- Students and the teacher experiment with watercolor paints to create nighttime paintings of their own.
- They explore the way Yolen uses figurative language—metaphors, similes, and personification—to compare the unknown to the familiar as she describes an owling trip by moonlight. They identify and discuss the figurative language and visualize and/or draw/paint pictures of the images the descriptions evoke. Images include metaphors ("The moon made his face into a silver mask," "But I was a shadow as we walked home," and "The kind of hope that flies on silent wings under a shining Owl Moon"), similes ("The trees stood still as giant statues," "Somewhere behind us a train whistle blew, long and low, like a sad, sad song," "And when their voices faded away it was as quiet as a dream," "the snow below it was whiter than the milk in a cereal bowl," and "I could feel the cold as if someone's icy hand was palm-down on my back"), and personification ("Our feet crunched over the crisp snow and little gray footprints followed us," "my short, round shadow bumped after me," and "an echo came threading its way through the trees").
- They read and explore other books that feature figurative language. (See Activity 18 in Chapter 2, oo moon, Activity 12 in Chapter 4, y fly, Activity 13 in Chapter 13, oa goat, Activities 12 and 13 in Chapter 16, ar star, Activity 12 in Chapter 29, consonant-le fable, and Activity 8 in Chapter 32, c Frances Cinderella fancy.)

11. Students listen to (or read) **Owls in the Family** and discuss what they learn about owls—in the wild and in captivity—from this story based on the experiences of the author as a boy.

How and Why: *Pourquoi* Tales from around the World

12. The term *pourquoi tale*, which describes a type of folk tale, comes from the French word *pourquoi*, which means "why." These how and why tales have come from people's attempts to explain the (1) creation and workings of the elements of nature, (2) behavior and customs of people, and (3) features and traits of animals.

Students and the teacher approach their study of *pourquoi* tales in one of two ways:

- The teacher presents books by category, and they read and discuss them as a subunit. (Books are listed by progressive difficulty within subunits.)
- At the beginning of the unit, the teacher explains and displays, as headings on a chart, the three types of *pourquoi* tales. As they read or listen to a book, presented at random, students decide to which category it belongs, and they or the teacher write it under the appropriate heading. They explain their thinking behind their responses.

13. Students and the teacher create a bulletin board/wall display for the unit. They draw a picture that represents the main idea of each tale, or they photocopy the cover of the book. They either arrange pictures on the wall under headings by subunit categories or connect each picture to its place/culture or origin on a map by a string and pushpins or tacks. (See Activity 11 in Chapter 2, oo moon.)

14. Myths are typically more complex than *pourquoi* tales and are of three main types: nature, creation, and hero/ine. The first two types, nature and creation, are related in content to *pourquoi* tales, contain similar themes, and perform similar functions—they explain how or why. Students and the teacher read nature and creation myths—

Greek and Norse—and compare and contrast them to the *pourquoi* tales in this unit. (See Activity 15 in Chapter 18, er spider, in which "Pandora's Box" is compared to Anansi stories about buying Sky God's stories.)

15. In *Frederick*, by Leo Lionni (New York: The Trumpet Club, 1967), a mouse and his community discover and learn to celebrate his gift or talent. Students and the teacher read *Frederick* and compare and contrast it with *The Legend of the Indian Paintbrush*.

16. Inspired by the paintings of the sunsets in *The Legend of the Indian Paintbrush*, students and the teacher use watercolor paints to create their own sunset paintings.

17. *Before* they read *The Legend of the Bluebonnet: An Old Tale of Texas*, students and the teacher tell and/or write about their most valued possession. After they read the book, they tell how they might feel about sacrificing it for the good of their community and whether they would choose the same thing again if they knew they would have to give it up.

18. Students and the teacher read more legends of native American people from the "Native American Legend" series by Cohlene. (See Activity 13 in Chapter 24, oy boy.)

19. The sounds and rhythm of the first son's name in *Tikki Tikki Tembo*—Tikki tikki tembo-no sa rembo-chari bari ruchi-pip peri pembo—is a must to be read aloud. Students join in (individually or chorally) and say it with the reader as it recurs. They listen to a tape of the story (available from Scholastic) and join in when the name is read.

20. *The Rooster's Horns: A Chinese Puppet Play to Make and Perform* contains instructions for creating a shadow puppet theater and patterns for making paper and stick puppets. Students follow the directions in the book and perform the folktale as a shadow play.

21. Repetition is commonly used in traditional literature to lend strength to a statement or for emphasis. Students and the teacher discuss the use of repetition in *Why Mosquitoes Buzz in People's Ears: A West African Tale*, in other African folktales, and in other traditional literature. (See Activity 21 in Chapter 18, er spider.)

22. Like the first son's name in *Tikki Tikki Tembo*, the sounds and rhythm of the refrain from *The Elephant's Child* must be heard and repeated: "the great grey-green, greasy Limpopo River, all set about with fever-trees." Students, as they read or listen to the tale, repeat the phrase with expression as it recurs.

23. Storytellers and writers vividly represent the sounds that characters, objects, and actions make through the use of onomatopoeia, which are words that are similar to or contain the sound made—the buzz of a bee, for example.

- Students and the teacher identify and discuss the use of onomatopoeia in several African tales, including *Why Mosquitoes Buzz in People's Ears: A West African Tale*, *A Story a Story: An African Tale*, and *Who's in Rabbit's House: A Masai Tale* (Chapter 16, ar star, and Chapter 23, ou house). (See Activity 11 in Chapter 4, y fly, Activity 9 in Chapter 7, ay day, and Activity 1 in Chapter 25, oi noise, for books and activities that feature onomatopoeia.)

- They identify and discuss the use of onomatopoeia in books from other cultures, including *Good-Night Owl* (this chapter and Chapter 12, igh night); *Dakota Dugout* (Chapter 16, ar star); and *Over in the Meadow*, *Too Much Noise*, and *Blueberries for Sal* (Chapter 25, oi noise).

- They combine the techniques of repetition and onomatopoeia in response to descriptive phrases. The teacher (or students) writes descriptive phrases on slips of paper and places them in a basket or box. Individual students or in a group (round-robin style—each student and the teacher contributes a sound for each phrase) choose phrases and make up onomatopoeia for it, which they say three times. The teacher (or students) acts as scribe, approximates the sounds, and writes down the responses. One/several/all of the students illustrate it. For example, for "a frog landing on a lily pad," a group of five students generates the following and one student (or more) illustrates it:

bung bung bung
pu-ting pu-ting pu-ting
dingk dingk dingk
boing boing boing
bu-doing bu-doing bu-doing

Other descriptive phrases might include the following: a kitten lapping milk from a dish, a sudden clap of thunder, a rhinoceros chasing an enemy, snapping up a winter coat, walking in a mud puddle, a cat's purr while being patted, a plate smashing on the floor, air seeping out of a balloon, a door slamming shut, a dog growling at a burglar, a rabbit hopping through tall grass, a broom sweeping a dirty floor, a whale coming above the water to spout, a coyote singing to the moon, and a bat hitting a ball past second base.

24. Students and the teacher locate on a map and/or globe the places/cultures (depicted or of origin) in the books read in this chapter, including New England in the United States (***Owl Moon***); Saskatoon, Saskatchewan in Canada (***Owls in the Family***); Peru (***Moon Rope/Un lazo a la luna***); Southeastern Nigeria (***Why the Sun and the Moon Live in the Sky: An African Folktale by Elphinstone Dayrell***); Slovenia (***How the Sun Was Brought Back to the Sky***); Wyoming, Texas, and the high plains in the United States (***The Legend of the Indian Paintbrush***); Comanche culture and Texas in the United States (***The Legend of the Bluebonnet: An Old Tale of Texas***); rainforest and jungle areas (***Papagayo: The Mischief Maker***); eastern Africa, Kenya, and Tanzania (***The Orphan Boy: A Maasai Story***); China (***Tikki Tikki Tembo*** and ***The Rooster's Horns: A Chinese Puppet Play to Make and Perform***); Akan and Ashanti cultures and Ghana on the west coast of Africa (***Anansi the Spider: A Tale from the Ashanti***, ***A Story a Story: An African Tale***, ***Spider and the Sky God: An Akan Legend***, ***Oh, Kojo! How Could You!: An Ashanti Tale***, ***Why Mosquitoes Buzz in People's Ears: A West African Tale***); eastern Africa (***Who's in Rabbit's House: A Masai Tale***); India (***The Elephant's Child*** and ***New Illustrated Just So Stories***); Africa (***Lazy Lion***); North America and the southern Appalachian Mountains (***Kanahena: A Cherokee Story*** and ***Cherokee Animal Tales***); and Tsimshian culture in Canada (***The Loon's Necklace***).

TEACHER REFERENCE

Cloze Sentences

One-Syllable Words

Cloze Sentences 1

1. I <u>frown</u> or scowl when I am upset. I do not smile!
2. The actor took a <u>bow</u> at the end of the play.

3. A <u>cow</u> needs to be milked at least two times a day.

4. A <u>plow</u> is a useful tool for cleaning up after a snowstorm.

5. My kitchen is <u>down</u> the stairs from my bedroom.

6. The dog's <u>growl</u> let me know that it did not want me to pat it.

7. A person may <u>drown</u> if he or she does not know how to swim.

Cloze Sentences 2

1. A big <u>crowd</u> was cheering for the home team at the baseball game.

2. My father and mother showed me <u>how</u> to drive a car.

3. I heard an <u>owl</u> hooting from a tree last night.

4. A dog or a wolf may <u>howl</u> at the moon.

5. Deep, rich <u>brown</u> is the color of the dirt in my garden.

6. I need to finish my reading <u>now</u>. It cannot wait until later.

7. The <u>crown</u> that the king wore had belonged in his family for a long time.

Multisyllable Words

Cloze Sentences 3

1. I take a <u>shower</u> or a bath every morning before I get dressed.

2. I get <u>drowsy</u> when I do not get the sleep that I need.

3. <u>Sundown</u> is another name for sunset.

4. You may use a <u>towel</u> to dry yourself after a shower or a bath or after swimming.

5. The hunter used <u>gunpowder</u> to load his gun.

6. The <u>flower</u> I like to grow best in my garden is a rose.

7. A <u>prowler</u> is a person who goes around slowly and secretly looking for something to steal.

8. A <u>tower</u> is a tall part of a church or other building.

Dictations

1. <u>Down</u> at the <u>flower</u> garden a <u>brown</u> dog <u>growled</u> and <u>howled</u> at a <u>drowsy</u> old <u>owl</u> on the <u>prowl</u>.

2. The <u>clown</u> had on a <u>crown</u> and a <u>gown</u> as she rode a <u>sow</u> into <u>town</u>. The <u>crowd</u> cheered, and the <u>clown</u> took a <u>bow</u>.

3. At <u>sundown</u> after Mrs. <u>Brown</u> <u>plowed</u> her garden she took a <u>shower</u>, wiped herself on a <u>towel</u>, and sat <u>down</u> to rest. <u>How</u> good it felt to be <u>drowsy</u> <u>now</u> as the <u>owl</u> began to hoot and the dog started to <u>howl</u> at the moon.

4. On the <u>crown</u> of the hill that <u>overlooks</u> the <u>town</u> a <u>drowsy</u> <u>brown</u> <u>cow</u> stood munching grass and an old <u>sow</u> rolled in the mud. All of a sudden the "<u>pow</u>" of <u>gunpowder</u> made them run <u>down</u> to the barn for shelter.

ow   (ow)   owl

b	fr n	dr sy
br n	gr l	fl er
c	h	gunp der
cr d	h l	pr ler
cr n	n	sh er
d n	l	sund n
dr n	pl	t el
		t er

Name _____ Date _____

ow (ow) owl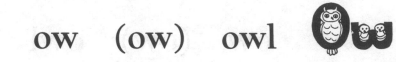

bow	frown	drowsy
brown	growl	flower
cow	how	gunpowder
crowd	howl	prowler
crown	now	shower
down	owl	sundown
drown	plow	towel
		tower

Name _____ Date _____

Word List 2

ow (ow) owl

Write a word from the Word List to complete each sentence.

1. I _____ or scowl when I am upset. I do not smile!

2. The actor took a _____ at the end of the play.

3. A _____ needs to be milked at least two times a day.

4. A _____ is a useful tool for cleaning up after a snowstorm.

5. My kitchen is _____ the stairs from my bedroom.

6. The dog's _____ let me know that it did not want me to pat it.

7. A person may _____ if he or she does not know how to swim.

Name _____ Date _____

Cloze Sentences 1

ow (ow) owl

Write a word from the Word List to complete each sentence.

1. A big _____ was cheering for the home team at the baseball game.

2. My father and mother showed me _____ to drive a car.

3. I heard an _____ hooting from a tree last night.

4. A dog or a wolf may _____ at the moon.

5. Deep, rich _____ is the color of the dirt in my garden.

6. I need to finish my reading _____. It cannot wait until later.

7. The _____ that the king wore had belonged in his family for a long time.

Name _____ Date _____

Cloze Sentences 2

ow (ow) owl

Write a word from the Word List to complete each sentence.

1. I take a _____ or a bath every morning before I get dressed.

2. I get _____ when I do not get the sleep that I need.

3. _____ is another name for sunset.

4. You may use a _____ to dry yourself after a shower or a bath or after swimming.

5. The hunter used _____ to load his gun.

6. The _____ I like to grow best in my garden is a rose.

7. A _____ is a person who goes around slowly and secretly looking for something to steal.

8. A _____ is a tall part of a church or other building.

Name _____ Date _____

Cloze Sentences 3

23   ou   house   OU

Houses

Anno's Counting House, Mitsumasa Anno (New York: Philomel Books, 1982). In this wordless cut-out picture book, readers use counters to discover mathematical concepts as they enact the story of ten children who move—one by one—from one house, at the beginning of the book, to another, at the end. Readers can reverse the process by reading the book backward.

A New House for Mole and Mouse, Harriet Ziefert, illustrated by David Prebenna (New York: Viking Penguin Inc., 1987). Easy-to-read repetitive and predictable text with supportive illustrations tells the story of Mole and Mouse as they try out everything in each room of their new house except the doorbell—until a surprise visitor rings it.

A Clean House for Mole and Mouse, Harriet Ziefert, illustrated by David Prebenna (New York: Viking Penguin Inc., 1988). Mole and Mouse (from ***A New House for Mole and Mouse*** by the same author) clean their house, and Mouse prevents Mole from using it right away so it will stay clean.

The Three Little Pigs: A British Folk Tale, (Glenview, Ill.: Scott, Foresman and Company, 1971, 1976). This easy-to-read version contains the basic plot and familiar refrains of the traditional tale of the ill-fated attempts by a wolf to blow down their houses of straw, sticks, and bricks and eat three pigs.

Goodbye House, Frank Asch (New York: The Trumpet Club, 1986). When the moving van is all packed, Baby Bear realizes he's forgotten something and he cannot leave until he returns to the empty house, visualizes his family's things where they had been, and says goodbye to each room.

The Napping House, Audrey Wood, illustrated by Don Wood (San Diego: Harcourt Brace Jovanovich, 1984). In this cumulative story, everyone except a flea is sleeping— "snoring granny, dreaming child, dozing dog, snoozing cat, slumbering mouse"—until the flea "bites the mouse, who scares the cat, who claws the dog . . ." and so on.

This Is the House That Jack Built, M. Twinn (Restrop Manor, England: Child's Play, 1977). This oversized version of the familiar cumulative nursery rhyme that follows Jack from single homeowner to groom has geometric shape cut-outs that reveal the next element to be added.

The House That Jack Built, Jenny Stow (New York: Dial Books for Young Readers, 1992). Colorful two-page illustrations of a Caribbean setting complement the traditional verses of the familiar cumulative Mother Goose rhyme.

The Magic Fish, Freya Littledale, illustrated by Winslow Pinney Pels (New York: Scholastic, 1966, 1985). When a poor fisherman puts back a fish he caught who is really a prince, his greedy wife demands more and more wishes for wealth and power until the fish sends her and the fisherman back to their original life in an old hut.

Lazy Lion, Mwenye Hadithi and Adrienne Kennaway (New York: The Trumpet Club, 1990). In this *pourquoi* tale, lazy Lion orders a variety of animals to make him a house, but he is dissatisfied with their efforts and even in heavy rain—when the animals take shelter in the homes they made—Lion does not find a house and wanders the African plain.

"Moving" and "Too Small," in ***Penrod Again***, Mary Blount Christian, illustrated by Jane Dyer (New York: Macmillan Publishing Company, 1987). In this sequel to ***Penrod's Pants*** by the same author, the friendship between Penrod Porcupine and Griswold the bear deepens as they share their daily lives, the possibility of Penrod moving away, cramped quarters, and holiday gifts. In "Moving," Griswold is upset when he learns that Penrod is moving and can't understand why his friend isn't sad until he finds that Penrod is moving to the house right behind his. In "Too Small," Griswold complains that his house is too small and Penrod that his house needs painting. They put all of Penrod's furniture (and Penrod) into Griswold's house while they paint Penrod's, and Griswold's house suddenly feels bigger to him after the job is finished and Penrod's things are removed.

Percy and the Five Houses, Else Homelund Minarik, illustrated by James Stevenson (New York: Viking, 1989). Percy, the beaver, had heard of a Book of the Month Club but not a House of the Month Club, until a fox sells him a membership. Percy finds that the houses he receives are not as good for him or his family as their lodge.

Mitchell Is Moving, Marjorie Weinman Sharmat, illustrated by José Aruego and Ariane Dewey (New York: Collier Books, 1978). When Mitchell the dinosaur announces that he is moving, Margo, his friend and neighbor of sixty years, does everything she can to prevent their separation and succeeds, in the end, when she moves, too—next door to him.

The Quilt Story, Tony Johnston, illustrated by Tomie dePaola (New York: G. P. Putnam's Sons, 1985). When her family travels west in a covered wagon, the quilt Abigail's mother made provides a warm and comforting familiarity. Many years later, one of Abigail's young relatives discovers the quilt in the attic, and it accompanies her, too, to a new home.

Three Little Pigs and the Big Bad Wolf, Glen Rounds (New York: The Trumpet Club, 1992). Bold text highlights key words in the well-known folk tale of a wolf's pursuit of three pigs in their houses of straw, sticks, and bricks and the triumph of the last pig, who outsmarts him.

The Three Little Pigs, Paul Galdone (New York: Clarion Books, 1970). In Galdone's version of the traditional story, only the third little pig, who built his house of bricks, survives—by his wits and courage—the threats of a wolf that eats his siblings, who make their houses of straw and sticks.

The Three Little Pigs, James Marshall (New York: Scholastic, 1989). Marshall's playful illustrations and colorful language combine to create a humorous retelling of the story of the pigs who build houses of straw, sticks, and brick and are pursued by a hungry wolf who eats all but the third pig, who outwits him.

Keep the Lights Burning, Abbie, Peter and Connie Roop, illustrated by Peter E. Hanson (Minneapolis, Minn.: Carolrhoda Books, 1985). In a story based on the experiences of Abbie Burgess, who kept the lighthouse lamps lit through a fierce winter storm in Maine in 1856, Abbie meets the challenge when her father is forced to leave her in charge of the lighthouse.

Why the Sun and the Moon Live in the Sky: An African Folktale by Elphinstone Dayrell, illustrated by Blair Lent (New York: Scholastic, 1968). Characters in this *pourquoi* tale wear costumes in this story of a visit from the water and his people that crowds the sun and his wife, the moon, out their house on earth and forces them to live in the sky.

The Little House, Virginia Lee Burton (Boston: Houghton Mifflin Company, 1942, 1969). Through the seasons and years, a little house, originally built in the country, watches the city grow closer and closer until she is surrounded by tall buildings, crowds of people, noise, and pollution. In the end, she is relocated to the country by the great-great-granddaughter of her first owner. Caldecott Award Book.

Dakota Dugout, Ann Turner, illustrated by Ronald Himler (New York: Macmillan Publishing Company, 1985). As she tells her granddaughter about the isolated and often difficult pioneer life through the seasons in a sod house on the prairies of Dakota, a woman reflects on the parts of the simple life that she misses.

Hansel and Gretel, Ruth Belov Gross, illustrated by Winslow Pinney Pels (New York: Scholastic, 1988). Deserted in the forest by their father and stepmother, Hansel and Gretel come upon the gingerbread house of a witch who eats children. Gretel saves her brother and herself by pushing the witch into the oven she is preparing for them.

Hansel and Gretel, James Marshall (New York: Scholastic, 1990). The traditional tale of two children banished to the woods by their father and stepmother, his domineering wife, and left to save themselves from the witch in the gingerbread house is interpreted with Marshall's contemporary language and comical illustrations.

The True Story of the 3 Little Pigs by A. Wolf, Jon Scieszka, illustrated by Lane Smith (New York: Scholastic, 1989). The wolf from the "Three Little Pigs" story tries to clear his name as he tells *his* side of the story, in which he claims he was framed and a cold caused him to sneeze and accidentally blow the pigs' houses down.

The Three Little Wolves and the Big Bad Pig, Eugene Trivizas, illustrated by Helen Oxenbury (New York: Margaret K. McElderry Books, 1993). In this humorous retelling of the familiar "Three Little Pigs" story with a contemporary setting, the animals' roles are reversed and the Big Bad Pig resorts to modern tools and technology to destroy the houses of the three "cuddly little wolves" made of bricks, cement, and metal; but all ends happily when the pig is transformed by the wolves' fourth house—made of fragrant flowers.

Who's in Rabbit's House?: A Masai Tale, Verna Aardema, illustrated by Leo and Diane Dillon (New York: The Dial Press, 1969, 1977). This retelling of a Masai folk tale is a play performed by villagers in masks and costumes. In the play, Rabbit refuses the aid of a series of her friends, who offer to help her get a frightening intruder out of her house, until frog, posing as a poisonous spitting snake, scares the creature—who turns out to be just a caterpillar.

The Man Who Kept House, Kathleen and Michael Hague, illustrated by Michael Hague (San Diego: Harcourt Brace Jovanovich, 1981). A man has a series of misadventures when he trades chores for a day with his wife, who he feels does not work as hard. When the wife returns from the fields, she finds the cow hanging from the roof and a humble husband with his head in the soup pot.

The Biggest House in the World, Leo Lionni (New York: Alfred A. Knopf, 1968). Father snail tells his son a fable about a snail who creates for himself a large, fancy shell only to discover that his house is too cumbersome to move and that he is left behind to starve when the other snails move on in search of food.

A House for Hermit Crab, Eric Carle (Saxonville, Mass.: Picture Book Studio, Ltd., 1987). Over several months, Hermit Crab settles into and decorates a new house with the help of his new friends. Just as he feels at home in the shell, he discovers he's outgrown it and must leave, but he does so confident to face the opportunities of the next challenge after his successes with the last.

Mister King, Raija Siekkinen, translated from the Finnish by Tim Steffa, illustrated by Hannu Taina (Minneapolis, Minn.: Carolrhoda Books, Inc., 1986). A lonely king who hasn't a single subject does not enjoy his beautiful house and kingdom until a huge cat arrives at his door. Biennale of Illustrations Bratislava (BIB) Grand Prix award for illustrations.

The Village of Round and Square Houses, Ann Grifalconi (Boston: Little, Brown and Company, 1986). A girl tells the story she heard from her grandmother, which explains why the women live in round houses and the men in square houses in their village beside a volcano, Mount Naka, in the Cameroons in Africa. Caldecott Honor Book.

The Magic Fish Rap, Bernice and Jon Chardiet, illustrated by Sam Viviano (New York: Scholastic, 1993). This is a contemporary rap version of the "Magic Fish" story, in which the fisherman's wife's greed for power and wealth demands more and more from the magic fish, whose life the fisherman saved, until the fish refuses to grant her wish and returns the fisherman and his wife to their original humble life and hut.

A House is a House for Me, Mary Ann Hoberman, illustrated by Betty Fraser (New York: Viking Penguin Inc., 1978). Rhyming text and detailed illustrations present the houses and shelters of people from different cultures, a variety of animals, familiar objects, children in a variety of houses, and the earth as a house for all.

A Very Special House, Ruth Krauss, illustrated by Maurice Sendak (New York: Harper & Row, 1953). This book's rollicking, repetitive text and whimsical illustrations create a child's dream—a house where a child can do all the things forbidden in a house that's not special: write on the walls, jump on the bed, swing on the doors, put his or her feet on the table, and bring home all the stray animals he or she wants.

The Maid and the Mouse and the Odd-shaped House: A Story in Rhyme, Paul O. Zelinsky (New York: Dodd, Mead & Co., 1981). A maid and a mouse's improvements to their comfortable house produce a result that they do not intend or expect. The odd shape of the house becomes the shape of a cat!

The Fisherman & His Wife, Jakob and Wilhelm Grimm, illustrated by John Howe (Mankato, Minn.: Creative Education Inc., 1983). The detail in the powerful illustrations that complement the text in this version of the "Magic Fish" story from the Grimm Brothers adds to the drama of this tale of greed and misuse of magic and wishes.

The Old Woman Who Lived in a Vinegar Bottle, Rumer Godden, illustrated by Mairi Hedderwick (London: Macmillan Children's Books, 1972). An old woman lives contentedly with her cat in their humble house (shaped like a vinegar bottle) until she spares the life of a magic fish. As the fish grants her wishes for increasing material possessions, she becomes more greedy and ungrateful, and he returns her to her old existence. When she realizes what she had become, she apologizes to the fish and, when offered return of all his gifts, asks for but one, which minimally changes her simple life.

"Pooh Goes Visiting," in ***Winnie-the-Pooh***, A. A. Milne, illustrated by Ernest H. Shepard (New York: Dell Publishing Co., Inc., 1926, 1954). This book introduces the adventures of a boy, Christopher Robin, and his toy bear, who's come to life as Winnie-the-Pooh, and their friends Piglet, Eeyore, Kanga and Roo, and Rabbit. In "Pooh Goes Visiting," Pooh visits Rabbit's house, eats a bit too much, and gets stuck in Rabbit's door when he tries to leave.

"Pooh Builds a House," in ***The House at Pooh Corner: Stories of Winnie-the-Pooh***, A. A. Milne, illustrated by Ernest H. Shepard (New York: E. P. Dutton, 1928, 1956). This book contains more stories of Christopher Robin and Pooh's friends in the Forest and introduces Tigger. In "Pooh Builds a House," on a snowy day Pooh and Piglet make a house for Eeyore at Pooh's Corner, but there's a problem. They use sticks from Eeyore's house at the other end of the Forest to contruct it!

Hansel and Gretel, The Brothers Grimm, illustrated by Lisbeth Zwerger (New York: Scholastic, 1988). The muted earth tones and carefully chosen details of the illustrations in Zwerger's interpretation of the traditional quest tale create a strong sense of its European origin.

Always Room for One More, Sorche Nic Leodhas, illustrated by Nonny Hogrogian (New York: Henry Holt Company, 1965). In this traditional Scottish folk song, generous Lachie MacLachlan welcomes everyone who passes by to join him, his wife, and their ten children in their "wee house" until it falls in. Grateful for his hospitality, his guests build him a new house—bigger than the first—where there would be "Always room for one more."

MOTIVATION AND EXTENSION ACTIVITIES

1. Throughout the unit, students and the teacher discuss the characteristics of the different houses in the books they read and how they are suited as shelters to their individual environments and cultures.

2. Ten children in *Anno's Counting House* move from one house at the beginning of the book to another house at the end. Readers then can reverse the process by reading the wordless book from the back and have the children move back to the first house.

Many of the books in this unit show characters leaving, moving from, or thinking about moving out of their houses to a new house: *Anno's Counting House*, *A New House for Mole and Mouse*, *Goodbye House*, "Moving" and "Too Small" in *Penrod Again*, *Percy and the Five Houses*, *Mitchell Is Moving*, *The Quilt Story*, *Why the Sun and the Moon Live in the Sky: An African Folktale by Elphinstone Dayrell*, *The Little House*, *Dakota Dugout*, *Hansel and Gretel* (Gross), *Hansel and Gretel* (Zwerger), *Who's in Rabbit's House,* and *A House for Hermit Crab*.

Students and the teacher share (tell and/or write and illustrate) about their experiences with moving (or having important people in their lives—friends or family—move) out of a house into a new house and/or school. They discuss their feelings and the challenges and victories that were part of the experience.

3. In a note to readers, Anno explains how to use counters to interact with *Anno's Counting House*. Students and the teacher follow his suggestions and create activities of their own for the book.

4. Students and the teacher select and complete Activities 9 and 10 in Chapter 1, ing king, related to *The Napping House*.

5. Verna Aardema's retelling of *Bringing the Rain to Kapita Plain: A Nandi Tale* uses a pattern and rhythm similar to the one in *This Is the House That Jack Built* and *The House That Jack Built*. Students and the teacher compare and contrast the books. (See Activity 14 in Chapter 15, ai rain.) They clap their hands, stamp their feet, and/or use rhythm instruments to punctuate the rhythmic patterns as the teacher or students read the books aloud.

6. "Too Small" in *Penrod Again* is similar in motif to several traditional tales from different cultures in which a house seems small and/or noisy until more things, people, or animals are added, which makes the house feel smaller and noisier. When the added elements are removed and the house returns to its original condition, it appears larger and less noisy to its inhabitants in comparison.

Students and the teacher compare and contrast "Too Small" in *Penrod Again* and the traditonal tales *Too Much Noise* by McGovern, *It Could Always Be Worse* by Zemach, and *Always Room for One More* by Nic Leodhas. (See Activity 2 in Chapter 25, oi noise.)

7. When they are reading *Percy and the Five Houses*, the teacher and/or students

brings in promotional mailings/advertisements (and books ordered, if they are available) from Book of the Month Clubs for students to look at. The teacher and/or students explain how the Clubs work, because this may be something with which many students are unfamiliar.

8. After they read and discuss **Keep the Lights Burning, Abbie**, students and the teacher learn more about lighthouses and Abbie Burgess by sharing the resource book **Beacons of Light: Lighthouses**, Gail Gibbons (New York: Morrow, 1990).

9. Students and the teacher select and complete activities related to **Why the Sun and the Moon Live in the Sky: An African Folktale by Elphinstone Dayrell** (Activity 15 in Chapter 2, oo moon, and Activity 23 in Chapter 22, ow owl).

10. The way in which Burton has drawn the Little House in her Caldecott Award–winning **The Little House**—with windows and curtains that look like eyes, a door that resembles a nose, and a door stoop that forms a mouth—personifies the building and makes her seem a much more convincing protagonist. Students and the teacher discuss the ways in which the illustrations and text complement each other in the book. They observe the changes in the countenance of the Little House—the way in which Burton shows her growing sadness as the book progresses and regaining her joy when she is moved and restored at the book's end. (See Activity 17 in Chapter 20, ur turtle, for an additional activity.)

11. As they read **Hansel and Gretel** (Gross), students and the teacher compare and contrast the stepmother as she is depicted in the text and illustrations with the fisherman's wife in **The Magic Fish** by Littledale in Chapter 31, g George magic stingy. Both books are illustrated by Winslow Pinney Pels, and there are striking similarities (and differences) between the two characters. Students read each character's part with expression, differentiating the voices. Students then listen to the tape of **The Magic Fish** (available from Scholastic) and compare their interpretation of the voices of the characters with the reader's on the tape.

12. Is there a more familiar (or sinister) house in all of traditional literature than the gingerbread house of the witch in the "Hansel and Gretel" story? Students and the teacher compare and contrast the text and illustrations of the three versions of the folk tale in this chapter: **Hansel and Gretel** (Gross, Zwerger, Marshall). They make gingerbread houses from gingerbread or graham crackers and candy ornaments.

13. For activities related to **Who's in Rabbit's House?: A Masai Tale**, students and the teacher see Activity 15 in Chapter 16, ar star, and Activity 23 in Chapter 22, ow owl.

14. The turn-about story pattern, as in **The Man Who Kept House**—in which characters exchange places for a time—is common in traditional literature. Students read other books from other cultures with the same plot and story pattern as **The Man Who Kept House** and compare and contrast their elements.

The Farmer in the Soup: Retold from the Norse Tale The Husband Who Was to Mind the House, Freya Littledale, illustrated by Molly Delaney (New York: Scholastic, 1987). (See Chapter 28, ou soup.)

Gone Is Gone: Or the Story of a Man Who Wanted to Do Housework, Wanda Gag (New York: Coward, McCann & Geoghegan, Inc., 1935). (See Chapter 28, ou soup.)

The three books provide an excellent opportunity to discuss gender stereotypes, in books and in real life, and students' responses to them.

15. *A House Is a House for Me* shows children in a variety of houses or shelters: in a treehouse, under a beach umbrella, inside a homemade tent made from a sheet draped over a table, building a snowfort, and beneath a blanket tent folded over a clothesline. Students and the teacher tell and/or write and illustrate a "A House Is a House for Me" book—as individuals or as contributors to a group book—patterned after Hoberman's book that includes the different houses or shelters they have had in their lives.

16. If possible, students and the teacher add to Hoberman's lengthy list of possible houses or shelters in *A House Is a House for Me*.

17. In an author's note, Zelinsky explains that the origin of the "tell and draw" story pattern of the anonymously written *The Maid and the Mouse and the Odd-shaped House: A Story in Rhyme* is found in American and British tradition and that this particular rhyme, which he adapted, was found in the notebook of a Connecticut schoolteacher in the late 1800s. In her class, students tooks turns adding a part of the picture as the story was read.

In a similar way, students draw the parts of the odd-shaped house as the teacher or a student reads it aloud. They make individual pictures or take turns and contribute to a group picture.

18. Characters in *The Magic Fish*, *The Magic Fish Rap*, *The Fisherman & His Wife*, and *The Old Woman Who Lived in a Vinegar Bottle* wish from the magic fish for bigger and more expensive houses. Students and the teacher compare and contrast the interpretations by the illustrators of the different houses—hut, house, cottage, and castle—in the four stories.

19. Students and the teacher draw a picture/diagram/sketch/blueprint of their own house (or room) and then construct and furnish a three-dimensional model from their plan using a variety of building materials, including craft/popsicle sticks, toothpicks, paper and cardboard, boxes, wood, and so on.

20. Students apply what they have learned about houses and shelters. They create a two-dimensional drawing/diagram/sketch/blueprint of a house or shelter from a culture different from their own and a three-dimensional model showing it in its appropriate setting. They invent an animal and provide information about its habitat, feeding and social habits, enemies, and means of protection and design a house or shelter appropriate to the animal's needs and environment—in two-dimensional and three-dimensional formats.

21. The walls in some houses in West Africa are decorated with patterns and designs using paints made from natural materials. Students and the teacher read about this custom in "Painted Walls (West Africa)" in *Kid Pix: A Multicultural Computer Activity Book*, Barbara Chan (Reading, Mass.: Addison-Wesley Publishing Company, 1993). The book contains essays that provide background information about twenty cultures around the world and detailed, step-by-step instructions that show children how to do drawing and painting activities using "Kid Pix" computer software. Presented cultures are marked on a world map in the front of the book. On the computer, students draw and decorate a mud house with a thatched roof and a painted house that they invent following the directions provided.

22. Students and the teacher locate on a map and/or globe the places/cultures (depicted or of origin) in the books read in this chapter, including the Caribbean (*The House That Jack Built*); Germany (*The Magic Fish*, *The Magic Fish Rap*, and *The Fisherman & His Wife*); Africa (*Lazy Lion*); England [*The Three Little Pigs: A British Folk Tale*, *Three Little Pigs and the Big Bad Wolf*, *The Three Little Pigs*

(Galdone, Marshall), *The True Story of the 3 Little Pigs by A. Wolf*, *The Three Little Wolves and the Big Bad Pig*, and *The Old Woman Who Lived in a Vinegar Bottle*]; the plains and prairie of the western United States (*The Quilt Story*); Maninicus Rock in Maine in the United States (*Keep the Lights Burning, Abbie*); southeastern Nigeria *Why the Sun and the Moon Live in the Sky: An African Folktale by Elphinstone Dayrell*); Dakota in the United States (*Dakota Dugout*); Germany [*Hansel and Gretel* (Gross, Zwerger, Marshall) and *Gone Is Gone: Or the Story of a Man Who Wanted to Do Housework*]; Masai culture and eastern Africa (*Who's in Rabbit's House?: A Masai Tale*); Norway (*The Man Who Kept House* and *The Farmer in the Soup: Retold from the Norse Tale The Husband Who Was to Mind the House*); hermit crab habitats in the world oceans (*A House for Hermit Crab*); Finland (*Mister King*); Tos and Naka Mountain in the Cameroons of Central Africa (*The Village of Round and Square Houses*); Bridgeport, Connecticut in the United States (*The Maid and the Mouse and the Odd-shaped House: A Story in Rhyme*); England (*Winnie-the-Pooh*; *The House at Pooh Corner: Stories of Winnie-the-Pooh*); and Scotland (*Always Room for One More*).

TEACHER REFERENCE

Cloze Sentences

One-Syllable Words

Cloze Sentences 1

1. An <u>out</u> in baseball may be three strikes.
2. <u>Sour</u> is the opposite of sweet.
3. The <u>couch</u> in our living room is so big that five of us can sit on it at one time.
4. A <u>mouse</u> took the cheese to its hole near the baseboard of the kitchen.
5. The <u>trout</u> that the fisherman hooked at the lake was 10 inches long.
6. A <u>loud</u> clap of thunder woke me up and let me know that the rainstorm had started.
7. The teacher was <u>proud</u> of the fine job his students did reading their books.
8. A black <u>cloud</u> in the sky showed that rain was on the way.

Cloze Sentences 2

1. I <u>found</u> the ring that I had lost a long time ago.
2. A <u>pound</u> of ground beef will feed my family for a whole meal.
3. Three cups of whole wheat <u>flour</u> is all that you need to make that cake.
4. In the <u>south</u> it is common to see palm trees.
5. Let me <u>count</u> the lunch tickets to see if they are all here.
6. A <u>hound</u> is a small dog with floppy ears that likes to go hunting.
7. The <u>sound</u> of rain on the roof is something I love to hear.
8. The <u>spout</u> of a whale can be seen from far away.

Cloze Sentences 3

1. The <u>house</u> across the street from ours is being painted and having its roof repaired.
2. Our dog likes to dig holes in the <u>ground</u> and hide his bones.
3. A <u>sprout</u> has begun to grow from the seeds I planted last week.
4. You do not need to <u>shout</u>! I can hear you when you just speak to me.
5. The weaver <u>wound</u> the yarn around a spool to save it.
6. A <u>round</u> shape has no corners or sides.

Multisyllable Words

Cloze Sentences 4

1. The <u>outfit</u> that I got at the clothing store included pants, a skirt, and a jacket.
2. We will go <u>outside</u> to have a picnic lunch.
3. If you speak <u>louder</u> I will hear you better than if you speak so softly.
4. She played so <u>loudly</u> on the trumpet that it hurt my ears.
5. I drove <u>around</u> the broken-down car that was stuck in the road.

Dictations

1. Lenny <u>found</u> a <u>mouse</u> in the <u>house</u> and let <u>out</u> a <u>loud</u> <u>shout</u>. <u>Without</u> a <u>sound</u> it <u>bounded</u> off the <u>counter</u> and <u>crouched</u> under the <u>couch</u>.

2. <u>Clouds</u> began to form in the sky and then, suddenly, came the <u>loud</u> <u>sound</u> of thunder. The fisherman grabbed his fishing <u>outfit</u> and the <u>trout</u> he'd just gotten and <u>shouted</u> to his <u>hound</u>. He <u>scouted</u> <u>around</u> and <u>found</u> a <u>round</u> hole in the <u>ground</u> for them to <u>crouch</u> in <u>out</u> of the storm.

3. The robber got <u>outside</u> the bank with the cash he had stolen in a <u>pouch</u> in his <u>trousers</u>. He drove <u>south</u> and <u>wound</u> his way <u>around</u> the cops that were <u>shouting</u> <u>loudly</u> for him to stop. When he <u>found</u> himself far away from the bank he got <u>out</u>, sat on the <u>ground</u>, and <u>without</u> a <u>sound</u> <u>proudly</u> <u>counted</u> his loot.

ou (ow) house OU

cl__d	p__nd	ar__nd
c__ch	pr__d	l__der
c__nt	r__nd	l__dly
fl__r	sh__t	__tfit
f__nd	s__nd	__tside
gr__nd	s__r	
h__nd	s__th	
h__se	sp__t	
l__d	spr__t	
m__se	tr__t	
__t	w__nd	

© 1995 by Cynthia Conway Waring

Name _____ Date _____

Word List 1

ou (ow) house

cloud	pound	around
couch	proud	louder
count	round	loudly
flour	shout	outfit
found	sound	outside
ground	sour	
hound	south	
house	spout	
loud	sprout	
mouse	trout	
out	wound	

Name _____ Date _____

Word List 2

ou (ow) house OU

Write a word from the Word List to complete each sentence.

1. An _____ in baseball may be three strikes.

2. _____ is the opposite of sweet.

3. The _____ in our living room is so big that five of us can sit on it at one time.

4. A _____ took the cheese to its hole near the baseboard of the kitchen.

5. The _____ that the fisherman hooked at the lake was 10 inches long.

6. A _____ clap of thunder woke me up and let me know that the rainstorm had started.

7. The teacher was _____ of the fine job his students did reading their books.

8. A black _____ in the sky showed that rain was on the way.

Name _____ Date _____

Cloze Sentences 1

ou (ow) house OU

Write a word from the Word List to complete each sentence.

1. I _____ the ring that I had lost a long time ago.

2. A _____ of ground beef will feed my family for a whole meal.

3. Three cups of whole wheat _____ is all that you need to make that cake.

4. In the _____ it is common to see palm trees.

5. Let me _____ the lunch tickets to see if they are all here.

6. A _____ is a small dog with floppy ears that likes to go hunting.

7. The _____ of rain on the roof is something I love to hear.

8. The _____ of a whale can be seen from far away.

Name _____ Date _____

Cloze Sentences 2

ou   (ow)   house   Oᴴ

Write a word from the Word List to complete each sentence.

1. The _____ across the street from ours is being painted and having its roof repaired.

2. Our dog likes to dig holes in the _____ and hide his bones.

3. A _____ has begun to grow from the seeds I planted last week.

4. You do not need to _____! I can hear you when you just speak to me.

5. The weaver _____ the yarn around a spool to save it.

6. A _____ shape has no corners or sides.

Name _____ Date _____

Cloze Sentences 3

ou (ow) house OU

Write a word from the Word List to complete each sentence.

1. The _____ that I got at the clothing store included pants, a skirt, and a jacket.

2. We will go _____ to have a picnic lunch.

3. If you speak _____ I will hear you better than if you speak so softly.

4. She played so _____ on the trumpet that it hurt my ears.

5. I drove _____ the broken-down car that was stuck in the road.

Name _____ Date _____

24   oy   boy

Boys and Challenge

Fortunately, Remy Charlip (New York: Four Winds Press, 1964). There is a good news–bad news pattern to the series of adventures a boy must brave between his home in New York City and a birthday party in Florida, and good events (fortunately) pictured with colored illustrations alternate with bad news (unfortunately) shown in black and white.

That's Good! That's Bad!, Margery Cuyler, illustrated by David Catrow (New York: Scholastic, 1991). A round-trip jungle adventure of a boy who leaves the zoo on the end of the string of a helium balloon is told with a good news (That's good!)–bad news (That's bad!) pattern.

The Hole in the Dike, Norma Green, illustrated by Eric Carle (New York: Scholastic, 1974). A young boy puts his finger in a hole in a dike until it can be repaired and saves his town in Holland from being flooded.

A Crocodile's Tale: A Philippine Folk Story, José and Ariane Aruego (New York: Scholastic, 1972). Threatened by a crocodile that he's just saved and disappointed by the advice of a basket and a hat, a boy perseveres and is saved by a monkey.

Arrow to the Sun: A Pueblo Indian Tale, Gerald McDermott (New York: The Viking Press, 1974). In this combination quest and *pourquoi* tale from a Pueblo myth, the Boy, the son of the Sun, is ridiculed on earth by his peers because he has no father, and he leaves to search for him. Made into an arrow, he travels to the Sun, proves himself by enduring four trials, is transformed and filled with the Sun's power, and returns to earth, where he is respected. Tells how the spirit of the Sun was brought to the earth. Caldecott Award Book.

Crow Boy, Taro Yashima (New York: Penguin Books, 1955). Once taunted, shunned, and called Chibi or "tiny boy" at school, a boy earns everyone's respect and the new name of Crow Boy when he shows his knowledge of nature and talent for imitating crows' calls. Caldecott Honor Book.

The Old, Old Man and the Very Little Boy, Kristine L. Franklin, illustrated by Terea D. Shaffer (New York: Atheneum, 1992). Not until he is old himself does the boy understand what the wise old man in his village had told him about the universality of growing old when he was a small boy sitting at the old man's feet—that inside his old body there lived a little boy.

The Wreck of the Zephyr, Chris Van Allsburg (Boston: Houghton Mifflin Company, 1983). An old man tells the tale of a boy whose consuming pursuit of proving himself the best sailor takes him to a strange shore, where he learns to sail above the water, and whose pride causes him to crash his sailboat far from the sea, surrounding the event with mystery.

Star Boy, Paul Goble (New York: Macmillan Publishing Company, 1983). Star Boy—born in the Sky World and scarred on his face and banished to earth because of his mother's disobedience—returns to the Sky World and asks his grandfather, the Sun, to bless his marriage and remove his scar. This *pourquoi* tale explains the origin of the Morning and Evening Stars. Contains information about the Blackfoot culture and tipis.

Clamshell Boy: A Makah Legend, Terri Cohlene, illustrated by Charles Reasoner (Mahwah, N.J.: Watermill Press, 1990). The legend of the Makah people from the Pacific Northwest tells how Clamshell Boy, who comes to life from the tears of a distraught mother, saves a group of children taken captive by Basket Woman, a giant who eats children.

Dancing Drum: A Cherokee Legend, Terri Cohlene, illustrated by Charles Reasoner (Mahwah, N.J.: Watermill Press, 1990). In this legend of the Cherokee people, Dancing Drum first ends periods of drought and flood and then plays his drum, which pleases Grandmother Sun, who shines down on his People and their land.

Ka-ha-si and the Loon: An Eskimo Legend, Terri Cohlene, illustrated by Charles Reasoner (Mahwah, N.J.: Watermill Press, 1990). Given powers from his grandfather through a loon messenger, Ka-ha-si helps his People when he finds food, defeats a giant, and protects the land from attacking mountains in this legend of the Eskimo people.

Quillworker: A Cheyenne Legend, Terri Cohlene, illustrated by Charles Reasoner (Mahwah, N.J.: Watermill Press, 1990). In the Cheyenne legend, Wihio uses his Power of Sky-Reaching to prevent Quillworker from being taken by the giant buffalo, and together they are taken to live in the heavens as stars, with Wihio as the brightest, the North Star.

Turquoise Boy: A Navajo Legend, Terri Cohlene, illustrated by Charles Reasoner (Mahwah, N.J.: Watermill Press, 1990). According to the Navajo legend, Turquoise Boy sees that his People work hard and wants to give them something to make their lives easier. After he proves himself worthy, he is given horses to give to his People.

Rain Player, David Wisniewski (New York: Clarion Books, 1991). With the help of Jaguar, Quetzal, and the sacred water, Pik brings rain to his parched land and earns the name Rain Player when he challenges and defeats the rain god in *pok-a-tok*, a game of ball. The author's note includes information about the Maya culture.

The Orphan Boy: A Maasai Story, Tolowa M. Mollel, illustrated by Paul Morin (New York: Clarion Books, 1990). In this *pourquoi* story, a star disappears from the sky and an orphan boy mysteriously appears to live with a childless old man, who learns the price of curiosity. His insatiable interest in the boy's secret powers betrays the boy's trust and sends him back to the sky as the planet Venus. Notes about the author contain information about the Maasai and the author's life in Kenya and Tanzania.

The Boy Who Held Back the Sea, Thomas Locker (New York: Dial Books for Young Readers, 1987). Rich oil paintings combine with detailed text to tell the story of the Dutch boy who saves his town from flooding by holding his finger over a hole in the dike until help comes.

Evan's Corner, Elizabeth Starr Hill, illustrated by Nancy Grossman (New York: Holt, Rinehart and Winston, 1967). When Evan has what he wanted most—a place of his own in the corner of the two-room apartment he shares with seven other members of his family—he finds that he's not happy until he helps his younger brother, who admires him, to fix a corner of his own.

Island Boy, Barbara Cooney (New York: The Trumpet Club, 1988). Matthais, the youngest of twelve, ignores the disregard of his older siblings and leaves the island where they were raised to distinguish himself sailing aboard a schooner, and he later returns to raise a family and live the rest of his full life on the island.

MOTIVATION AND EXTENSION ACTIVITIES

1. The boys in each of the books in this unit encounter challenge—some physical, some psychological—and distinguish themselves by their responses. Often, they are rewarded with respect—self-respect or the respect of others—and sometimes they remain misunderstood. Throughout the unit, as they read and discuss the suggested books, students and the teacher consider the theme of challenge, response, and respect.

2. Individuals or groups of students (round-robin, with each person adding the next event) tell and/or write and illustrate their own "Good News! Bad News!" adventure story following the pattern of ***Fortunately*** and ***That's Good! That's Bad!***. Illustrators decide whether there will be a pattern to the drawings as well as the text.

3. The two versions of the story of the boy who saves his town in Holland from flood by plugging a hole in a dike with his finger are strikingly different. ***The Hole in the Dike*** is told with simple text and plot and colorful, bold collage and paint illustrations, whereas ***The Boy Who Held Back the Sea*** is written with challenging text and more complicated plot and sophisticated oil paintings. Students and the teacher compare and contrast the two interpretations of the traditional Dutch tale.

4. Originally, ***Arrow to the Sun: A Pueblo Indian Tale*** was a film. Its vibrant illustrations, which incorporate Pueblo designs, are central to the presentation of the tale. Students and the teacher read the books and view the film versions (available from Weston Woods) of ***Arrow to the Sun: A Pueblo Indian Tale, Anansi the Spider: A Tale from the Ashanti*** (Chapter 2, oo moon, Chapter 18, er spider, and Chapter 22, ow owl), ***The Stonecutter: A Japanese Folk Tale***, and ***The Magic Tree: A Tale from the Congo*** (Chapter 31, g George magic stingy) written by McDermott. They compare and contrast the book and film versions and discuss the difference in the illustrations

chosen by the same illustrator for the tales from four different cultures. They note how the music chosen in the film version contributes to the interpretation of each tale.

5. In *Arrow to the Sun: A Pueblo Indian Tale*, the Boy seeks help in his quest from Corn Planter and Pot Maker, but receives none. It is the wise Arrow Maker who makes him into an arrow. When given the four trials to endure by his father, "not afraid" the Boy relies on his own courage. Finally, after the last trial, the Kiva of Lightning, the Boy is changed and full of the Sun's power.

Students and the teacher discuss the sources of power and strength available to the hero/ines in quest tales—the characters in the four McDermott books (in Activity 4 in this chapter), for example—and in other books. Do they act from their own strength and efforts, are they given help from others (earthly or natural), are they aided by supernatural powers or magic, or are they enabled by a combination of sources?

6. In the traditional hero/ine quest, *Arrow to the Sun: A Pueblo Indian Tale*, the Boy is challenged by four trials to prove himself to his father, the Sun: the four chambers of ceremony—the Kiva of Lions, the Kiva of Serpents, the Kiva of Bees, and the Kiva of Lightning. In the book, there are illustrations for each trial but no text. Students create stories/text (tell and/or write) for each of the trials. They compare the effectiveness of their stories and the illustrations together with the illustrations alone. They consider why McDermott may have chosen not to use text in this part of the tale.

7. Students apply what they have learned about quest tales to write their own quest tales. They are given cards with the following: (1) description of a hero/ine, (2) a goal or wish, and (3) a source of power—their own strength, courage, and effort; help from earthly or natural sources; aid from supernatural powers or magic; or combination of sources. They are also given several unrelated objects in a box. They tell and/or write and illustrate a quest tale that uses all of the elements.

8. Like the Boy in *Arrow to the Sun: A Pueblo Indian Tale*, Chibi in *Crow Boy* was isolated and shunned by his peers—until a sensitive teacher recognized and helped others see that Chibi, like everyone, has his own special talents and gifts.

Students and the teacher share (tell and/or write and illustrate) about times when they (or someone else) may have felt isolated or ridiculed. They tell what or who (if anything or anyone) helped them through that difficult time. They discuss the ways in which people discover their talents or gifts and/or earn special names of respect, including the characters in books suggested for this unit: the Boy (the arrow) in *Arrow to the Sun: A Pueblo Indian Tale*, Chibi (Crow Boy) in *Crow Boy*, Quillworker (Seeker-or-Seven-Brothers) in *Quillworker: A Cheyenne Legend*, and Pik (Rain Player) in *Rain Player*. They also consider the characters in books in other units: Little Gopher (He-Who-Brought-the-Sunset-to-the-Earth) in *The Legend of the Indian Paintbrush* by dePaola, Frederick the mouse (the poet) in *Frederick* by Lionni, She-Who-Is-Alone (One-Who-Dearly-Loved-Her-People) in *The Legend of the Bluebonnet: An Old Tale of Texas* (Chapter 22, ow owl), and Little Burnt One (Little Firefly) in *Little Firefly: An Algonquin Legend* (Chapter 32, c Frances Cinderella fancy). (See Activity 5 in Chapter 18, er spider, and Activities 15 and 16 in Chapter 22, ow owl, for additional activities related to gifts or talents.)

9. Who is the old man who tells the tale in *The Wreck of the Zephyr*, and what caused his limp? Students and the teacher discuss the identity of the old man and how the suggestion that he was the boy who sailed the Zephyr affects their response to the tale.

10. After the legend in each of the books in the "Native American Legends" series by Cohlene, there is a section that contains information, photographs, maps, time lines, and drawings about the culture of origin and depicted. Students and the teacher discuss this background information as they read the books in the series suggested for this unit: *Clamshell Boy: A Makah Legend, Dancing Drum: A Cherokee Legend, Ka-ha-si and the Loon: An Eskimo Legend, Quillworker: A Cheyenne Legend,* and *Turquoise Boy: A Navajo Legend.*

11. After reading *Ka-ha-si and the Loon: An Eskimo Legend,* students and the teacher learn more about the Eskimo or Inuit people. They read *Mama, Do You Love Me?* by Joosse (see Chapter 3, open syllable go). They learn about Eskimo or Inuit boats, umiaks, by reading "Picture Story (The Arctic)" in *Kid Pix around the World: A Multicultural Computer Activity Book* and follow directions in the chapter to make a picture story on an umiak paddle using the computer. They record the suggested adventure, Ka-ha-si's adventures, and adventures of their own. *Kid Pix around the World: A Multicultural Computer Activity Book,* Barbara Chan (Reading, Mass.: Addison-Wesley Publishing Company, 1993), contains essays that provide background information about twenty cultures around the world and detailed, step-by-step instructions that show children how to do drawing and painting activities using "Kid Pix" computer software. Presented cultures are marked on a world map in the front of the book.

12. In *Quillworker: A Cheyenne Legend,* the sequence of buffalo messengers that precede the buffalo bull—Buffalo Calf and Buffalo Cow, who increase in size and foretell one who is larger that is to come—follows the same pattern as in *The Three Billy Goats Gruff* (Chapter 13, oa goat). Students and the teacher compare and contrast the pattern or motif in the two stories.

13. The story of *The Orphan Boy: A Maasai Story* comes from the Maasai/Masai people of Kenya and Tanzania in eastern Africa. Students and the teacher read two additional picture books about or from the Maasai/Masai culture: *Masai and I,* by Kroll, and *Who's in Rabbit's House?: A Masai Tale,* by Aardema. (See Activity 15 in Chapter 16, ar star.)

14. After reading *Evan's Corner* and *Island Boy,* students and the teacher share (tell and/or write and illustrate) about a place of their own, like Evan's corner, or a special place, like Matthais's island, that means or has meant a lot to them.

15. Students and the teacher locate on a map and/or globe the places/cultures (depicted or of origin) in the books read in this chapter, including New York City and Florida in the United States (*Fortunately*); jungle areas of the world (*That's Good! That's Bad!*); Holland (*The Hole in the Dike* and *The Boy Who Held Back the Sea*); the Philippines (*A Crocodile's Tale: A Philippine Folk Story*); Acoma Pueblo culture in New Mexico in the United States (*Arrow to the Sun: A Pueblo Indian Tale*); Wyoming, Texas, and the high plains in the United States (*The Legend of the Indian Paintbrush*); Comanche culture and Texas in the United States (*The Legend of the Bluebonnet: An Old Tale of Texas*); Japan (*Crow Boy* and *The Stonecutter: A Japanese Folk Tale*); Africa (*The Old, Old Man and the Very Little Boy*); oceans of the world (*The Wreck of the Zephyr*); Blackfoot culture, the northern Great Plains, and Montana in the United States and Alberta, Canada (*Star Boy*); Makah culture, the coast of the Pacific Northwest, and Cape Flattery in Washington state in the United States (*Clamshell Boy: A Makah Legend*); Cherokee culture in Georgia, Tennessee, and North Carolina in the United States (*Dancing Drum: A Cherokee Legend*); the coast of

Greenland, northern Asia and North America, and the Bering Sea (***Ka-ha-si and the Loon: An Eskimo Legend***); Cheyenne culture, Lake Superior and the Great Plains in the United States (***Quillworker: A Cheyenne Legend***); Navajo culture in Arizona and New Mexico and the southwestern United States (***Turquoise Boy: A Navajo Legend***); Maya culture in Mexico, Belize, Honduras, Guatemala, and El Salvador (***Rain Player***); Maasai/Masai culture in eastern Africa, Kenya, and Tanzania (***The Orphan Boy: A Maasai Story***); and the seacoast of Maine in the United States (***Island Boy***).

TEACHER REFERENCE

Cloze Sentences

One-Syllable Words

Cloze Sentences 1

1. A <u>toy</u> is something fun that is used for playing.
2. On a hot day it is a <u>joy</u> for me to go swimming.
3. The <u>boy</u> sitting with me is my brother.

Multisyllable Words

4. When I <u>enjoy</u> something I like doing it.
5. The baby was <u>annoying</u> his sister when he pulled her hair.
6. An <u>oyster</u> is a shellfish that lives in shallow water near seacoasts and is used as food.
7. Something that is <u>royal</u>, like a throne, belongs to a king or a queen.

Cloze Sentences 2

1. A <u>soybean</u> is a small bean used for food that is grown in China, Japan, and the United States.
2. <u>Corduroy</u> is a thick cotton cloth that has close bumps and feels like velvet.
3. A <u>decoy</u> helped the hunter lead birds into a trap.
4. Many trees can be <u>destroyed</u> by a forest fire.
5. The boy had a <u>joyless</u> look as he sadly looked for his missing dog.
6. The hotel <u>employs</u> more than one cook now that it has gotten so big.

Dictations

1. The <u>boy</u> and I were <u>employed</u> to <u>destroy</u> weeds around the <u>soybean</u> plants. He <u>enjoyed</u> it, but the <u>joyless</u> chore <u>annoyed</u> me.

2. The hunter told the <u>boy</u> of his plan to <u>employ</u> <u>decoys</u> to attract ducks. It <u>annoyed</u> the <u>boy</u> to think of the hunter's <u>joy</u> while all of those ducks were being <u>destroyed</u>.

3. A cook was <u>employed</u> to prepare a <u>royal</u> dinner of <u>oysters</u> with <u>soybean</u> stuffing. The <u>royalty</u> <u>enjoyed</u> the dinner and, as a result, the cook will <u>enjoy</u> full-time <u>employment</u>.

oy (oy) boy

b	ann	ing
j	cordur	
t	dec	
	destr	ed
	empl	s
	enj	
	j	less
	ster	
	r	al
	s	bean

Name _____ Date _____

Word List 1

oy (oy) boy

boy	**annoying**
joy	**corduroy**
toy	**decoy**
	destroyed
	employs
	enjoy
	joyless
	oyster
	royal
	soybean

Name _____ Date _____

Word List 2

oy (oy) boy

Write a word from the Word List to complete each sentence.

1. A _____ is something fun that is used for playing.

2. On a hot day it is a _____ for me to go swimming.

3. The _____ sitting with me is my brother.

4. When I _____ something I like doing it.

5. The baby was _____ his sister when he pulled her hair.

6. An _____ is a shellfish that lives in shallow water near seacoasts and is used as food.

7. Something that is _____, like a throne, belongs to a king or a queen.

Name _____ Date _____

oy (oy) boy Oy

Write a word from the Word List to complete each sentence.

1. A _____ is a small bean used for food that is grown in China, Japan, and the United States.

2. _____ is a thick cotton cloth that has close bumps and feels like velvet.

3. A _____ helped the hunter lead birds into a trap.

4. Many trees can be _____ by a forest fire.

5. The boy had a _____ look as he sadly looked for his missing dog.

6. The hotel _____ more than one cook now that it has gotten so big.

Name _____ Date _____

© 1995 by Cynthia Conway Waring

Cloze Sentences 2

25   oi   noise

BOOK LIST ═══

Noise

I Hear a Noise, Diane Goode (New York: E. P. Dutton, 1988). One night a child and his mother are whisked out his bedroom window by a monster, who takes them home. The adventure is short lived: The monster's mother scolds the monster and makes it take them back!

Noisy Nora, Rosemary Wells (New York: Dial Books for Young Readers, 1973). In a humorous rhyming story, Nora the mouse represents the plight of all middle siblings. She has to wait while Mother and Father are busy with baby Jack and big sister Kate—that is, until she gets their attention with some *Noise*!

Too Much Noise, Ann McGovern, illustrated by Simms Taback (New York: Scholastic, 1967). When Peter can't stand the noise in his house, the wise man of the village advises him to put in his house a cow, donkey, sheep, hen, and dog and then to let them go. By comparison, the original noises of his home seem quiet.

Good-Night Owl, Pat Hutchins (New York: The Trumpet Club, 1972). One by one, the daytime animals in this cumulative story make noise that keeps Owl awake during the day, but in the end he achieves his goal of revenge when he screeches at night and awakens them.

"Too Small," in ***Penrod Again***, Mary Blount Christian, illustrated by Jane Dyer (New York: Macmillan Publishing Company, 1987). In this sequel to ***Penrod's Pants*** by the same author, the friendship between Penrod Porcupine and Griswold the Bear deepens as they share their daily lives, the possibility of Penrod moving away, cramped quarters, and holiday gifts. In "Too Small," Griswold complains that his house is too small and Penrod that his needs painting. They put all of Penrod's furniture (and Penrod) into Griswold's house while they paint Penrod's, and Griswold's house suddenly feels bigger to him after the job is finished and Penrod's things are removed.

Night Noises, Mem Fox, illustrated by Terry Denton (New York: The Trumpet Club, 1989). One evening, as Lily dozes by the fire, only her dog is aware of the noises that announce the arrival of her large extended family and forty-seven friends, who surprise her with a ninetieth birthday party.

Dakota Dugout, Ann Turner, illustrated by Ronald Himler (New York: Macmillan Publishing Company, 1985). As she tells her granddaughter about the isolated and often difficult pioneer life through the seasons in a sod house on the prairies of Dakota, a woman reflects on the parts of the simple life that she misses.

Over in the Meadow, Ezra Jack Keats (New York: Four Winds Press, 1971). Keats's collage and paint illustrations for this traditional counting rhyme show animal mothers and their young in their habitats making characteristic noises and engaged in typical activities.

Blueberries for Sal, Robert McCloskey (New York: The Viking Press, 1948). Two mothers—one human and one bear—take their children blueberry picking and get mixed up with each other on Blueberry Hill. In the end, everyone listens for familiar noises of family, gets sorted out, and goes down the side of the hill toward home.

The Cat Who Wore a Pot on Her Head, Jan Slepian and Ann Seidler, illustrated by Richard E. Martin (New York: Scholastic, 1980). With a pot on her head to escape the noise of her busy family, Bendemolena the cat can't tell if her mother said to put the "fish on to bake," "bish in the lake," or "soap in the cake."

It Could Always Be Worse: A Yiddish Folk Tale, Margot Zemach (New York: Farrar, Straus and Giroux, 1976). Crowded into a small hut with his family, a man goes for advice to the Rabbi, who tells him to put more and more animals into the hut with them. When the man can take the noise no longer, the Rabbi suggests he put the animals out, and suddenly the man finds his hut peaceful, spacious—and quiet. Caldecott Honor Book.

Papagayo: The Mischief Maker, Gerald McDermott (San Diego: Harcourt Brace Jovanovich, 1980, 1992). This *pourquoi* tale explains moon phases. Papagayo, the parrot, annoys the nocturnal animals during the day, but he becomes their hero one night when his noisy plan saves their beloved thinning moon from the teeth of the hungry moon-dog.

Always Room for One More, Sorch Nic Leodhas, illustrated by Nonny Hogrogian (New York: Henry Holt and Company, 1965). In this traditional Scottish folk song, generous Lachie MacLachlan welcomes everyone who passes by to join him, his wife, and their ten children in their "wee house" until it falls in. Grateful for his hospitality, his guests build him a new house—bigger than the first—where there would be "Always room for one more."

MOTIVATION AND EXTENSION ACTIVITIES

1. The storytellers and writers of several of the stories in this unit use onomatopoeia to represent the sounds and noises that characters (human and animal), objects, and actions make. Onomatopoeia are words that are similar to or contain the sound made— the buzz of a bee, for example. Students and the teacher identify and discuss the use of onomatopoeia in books from this unit: *Too Much Noise, Good-Night Owl, Night Noises; Dakota Dugout, Over in the Meadow, Blueberries for Sal, It Could Always Be Worse*, and *Papagayo: The Mischief Maker*.

African storytellers frequently use onomatopoeia to represent sounds in their tales.

Students and the teacher extend their consideration of the use of onomatopoeia as they identify and discuss its use in African storytelling. (See Activity 23 in Chapter 22, ow owl, for a list of African tales.) They use onomatopoeia in response to descriptive phrases. (See Activity 23 in Chapter 22, ow owl, for a description of this activity.) They explore the use of onomatopoeia in other books. (See Activity 11 in Chapter 4, y fly, and Activity 9 in Chapter 7, ay day, for books and activities that feature onomatopoeia.)

2. Several of the books in this unit contain a motif or pattern that is common in traditional literature. In these stories, a house seems too noisy and/or too small to its inhabitants. Then more things, people, or animals are added, which makes the house feel noisier and smaller. When the added elements are removed and the house returns to its original condition, it appears less noisy and larger to its inhabitants in comparison.

Students and the teacher identify and discuss this motif in the following stories in this unit: *Too Much Noise*, "Too Small" in *Penrod Again*, and *It Could Always Be Worse*. They compare and contrast the tales. For example, Peter in *Too Much Noise* and "the poor unfortunate man" in *It Could Always Be Worse* follow the advice of a wise man and the Rabbi, respectively. Penrod Porcupine and Griswold Bear in "Too Small" in *Penrod Again* achieve the same result by chance when they put all of Penrod's furniture in Griswold's house while they paint the walls of Penrod's house. A fourth book in the unit, *Always Room for One More*, does not follow the same pattern, but it might if students write an extended ending or sequel in which Lachie, his wife, and their ten children move into their new, quiet house without guests.

3. *Always Room for One More* is a well-known Scottish song passed down orally for generations. A section following the story in the book contains definitions of the Scottish words and the music for the song. Some students may have difficulty reading the Scottish dialect, though modified. The teacher reads the book aloud so that students can focus on the rhythm and richness of the language, the Caldecott Award–winning illustrations, and the plot. As they listen to (or read) *Always Room for One More*, students make predictions about the meanings of the Scottish words with which they may be unfamiliar. They confirm or correct their hypotheses by reading on in the story and by consulting the list of Scottish words in the back of the book.

Students and the teacher try the tale as a song after they have read it through at least once. The author, Nic Loedhas, offers a gentle suggestion—that one needs to be "flexible" in using the tune. If the tune is too difficult, students and the teacher tap the beat with their feet, clap it with their hands, or mark it with rhythm instruments.

4. Many of the stories in this unit invite dramatization. With a few simple props (and costumes and/or masks and scenery, if they wish) and a lot of noise, students as actors or puppeteers dramatize their choice of stories. (See Activity 17 in Chapter 2, oo moon, for an activity related to *Papagayo: The Mischief Maker*.)

5. Students and the teacher locate on a map and/or globe the places/cultures (depicted or of origin) in the books read in this chapter, including Australia (*Night Noises*); the prairie of the western United States (*Dakota Dugout*); Maine (*Blueberries for Sal*); Jewish culture in eastern Europe (*It Could Always Be Worse*); rainforest and jungle areas (*Papagayo: The Mischief Maker*); and Scotland (*Always Room for One More*).

Cloze Sentences

One-Syllable Words

Cloze Sentences 1

1. <u>Point</u> to the word you are reading, and then we will know where you are in the story.
2. I <u>boil</u> eggs for at least three minutes if I want them cooked until they are hard.
3. At the <u>joint</u> my arms, legs, and fingers can bend.
4. An <u>oink</u> from the pigpen let us know that at least one pig was inside.
5. The <u>coin</u> in my pocket may be a penny, a nickel, a dime, a quarter, or a half dollar.
6. The ground was <u>moist</u> after the rain last night.

Cloze Sentences 2

1. After you <u>join</u> the math team, we will have ten members.
2. I put potting <u>soil</u> in the pots when I grow plants inside the house.
3. Food may <u>spoil</u> if you do not keep it cool on a hot day.
4. Farmers are used to <u>toil</u>, which is very hard work.
5. The loud <u>noise</u> from the fire truck's siren woke me up.
6. I took the <u>foil</u> wrapper off the gum before I put it in my mouth.
7. <u>Oil</u> is used to light some lanterns.

Multisyllable Words

Cloze Sentences 3

1. The room was so <u>noisy</u> that I didn't hear what the teacher was saying.
2. To <u>avoid</u> hitting the car that was broken down in the road, we passed on the right.
3. Because the <u>toilet</u> was broken, we did not use the bathroom near our classroom.
4. The rags were <u>oily</u> after I wiped off the motor and checked the oil in the car.
5. The candy bar was wrapped in <u>tinfoil</u>—a very thin sheet of silver paper.
6. My mother showed me how to <u>embroider</u> a flower on my shirt using different stitches.

Dictations

1. If you <u>soil</u> the cloth that I am <u>embroidering</u>, it will be <u>spoiled</u>.
2. I didn't see the <u>point</u> in <u>oiling</u> the <u>joints</u> of my car until they got rusty and <u>noisy</u>. It will take a lot of <u>toil</u> to <u>moisten</u> the <u>joints</u> and <u>oil</u> them. Now I know that I can <u>avoid</u> the problem by <u>oiling</u> them before they get <u>noisy</u>!
3. It was a <u>noisy</u> time in the lunchroom, the air was <u>moist</u> and hot from cooking, and I didn't like the <u>oily</u> <u>boiled</u> fish that was being sold. So I <u>avoided</u> the things that were <u>spoiling</u> my lunch and used my <u>coins</u> to get a peanut butter and jelly sandwich wrapped in <u>tinfoil</u>. Then I <u>joined</u> students in a spot with less <u>noise</u>.

oi (oy) noise

b l   l   av d

c n   nk   embr der

f l   p nt   n sy

j n   s l   ly

j nt   sp l   tinf l

m st   t l   t let

n se

Name _____ Date _____

Word List 1

oi   (oy)   noise

boil	oil	avoid
coin	oink	embroider
foil	point	noisy
join	soil	oily
joint	spoil	tinfoil
moist	toil	toilet
noise		

Name _____ Date _____

oi (oy) noise

Write a word from the Word List to complete each sentence.

1. _____ to the word you are reading, and then we will know where you are in the story.

2. I _____ eggs for at least three minutes if I want them cooked until they are hard.

3. At the _____ my arms, legs, and fingers can bend.

4. An _____ from the pigpen let us know that at least one pig was inside.

5. The _____ in my pocket may be a penny, a nickel, a dime, a quarter, or a half dollar.

6. The ground was _____ after the rain last night.

Name _____ Date _____

Cloze Sentences 1

oi (oy) noise

Write a word from the Word List to complete each sentence.

1. After you _____ the math team, we will have ten members.

2. I put potting _____ in the pots when I grow plants inside the house.

3. Food may _____ if you do not keep it cool on a hot day.

4. Farmers are used to _____, which is very hard work.

5. The loud _____ from the fire truck's siren woke me up.

6. I took the _____ wrapper off the gum before I put it in my mouth.

7. _____ is used to light some lanterns.

Name _____ Date _____

Cloze Sentences 2

oi (oy) noise

Write a word from the Word List to complete each sentence.

1. The room was so _____ that I didn't hear what the teacher was saying.

2. To _____ hitting the car that was broken down in the road, we passed on the right.

3. Because the _____ was broken, we did not use the bath-room near our classroom.

4. The rags were _____ after I wiped off the motor and checked the oil in the car.

5. The candy bar was wrapped in _____ —a very thin sheet of silver paper.

6. My mother showed me how to _____ a flower on my shirt using different stitches.

Name _____ Date _____

26 aw straw

BOOK LIST

Straw, Straw, and More Straw

The Three Little Pigs: A British Folk Tale, (Glenview, Ill.: Scott, Foresman and Company, 1971, 1976). This easy-to-read version contains the basic plot and familiar refrains of the traditional tale of the ill-fated attempts by a wolf to blow down their houses of straw, sticks, and bricks and eat three pigs.

There's a Hole in the Bucket, Nadine Bernard Westcott (New York: Harper & Row, 1990). Henry and Liza trade a series of problems and solutions after Henry discovers a hole in the bucket as he gets water from the well. The circle of responses and the song are completed when Henry needs water for the sharpening stone and discovers that the hole in the bucket is perfect for giving the napping Liza a surprise shower.

"Cinderumpelstiltskin: Or the Girl Who Really Blew It," in ***The Stinky Cheese Man and Other Fairly Stupid Tales***, Jon Scieszka, illustrated by Lane Smith (New York: Viking, 1992). This book contains eleven humorous modern retellings of well-known traditional tales. In "Cinderumpelstiltskin: Or the Girl Who Really Blew It," the narrator interweaves elements of the "Cinderella" and "Rumpelstiltskin" stories into one silly tale in which her stepsisters rename Cinderella "Cinderumpelstiltskin."

Rumpelstiltskin: A Tale Told Long Ago by the Grimm Brothers, Edith H. Tarcov, illustrated by Edward Gorey (New York: Scholastic, 1973). Simple line drawings with occasional gold illustrate this easy-to-read version of the traditional fairy tale, in which a strange little man appears to the miller's daughter and offers to spin straw into gold for the king (which her father had boasted she could do) if she gives him her first child should she become queen. After the baby is born, he agrees to release her from her agreement if, in three days, she can discover his name.

Three Little Pigs and the Big Bad Wolf, Glen Rounds (New York: The Trumpet Club, 1992). Bold text highlights key words in this well-known folk tale of a wolf's pursuit of three pigs in their houses of straw, sticks, and bricks and the triumph of the last pig, who outsmarts him.

The Three Little Pigs, Paul Galdone (New York: Clarion Books, 1970). In Galdone's version of the traditional story, only the third pig, who built his house of bricks, survives— by his wits and courage—the threats of a wolf that eats his siblings, who make their houses of straw and sticks.

The Three Little Pigs, James Marshall (New York: Scholastic, 1989). Marshall's playful illustrations and colorful language combine to create a humorous retelling of the story of the pigs who build houses of straw, sticks, and brick and are pursued by a hungry wolf who eats all but the third pig, who outwits him.

The True Story of the 3 Little Pigs by A. Wolf, Jon Scieszka, illustrated by Lane Smith (New York: Scholastic, 1989). The wolf from the "Three Little Pigs" story tries to clear his name as he tells *his* side of the story, in which he claims he was framed and a cold caused him to sneeze and accidentally blow the pigs' houses down.

The Three Little Wolves and the Big Bad Pig, Eugene Trivizas, illustrated by Helen Oxenbury (New York: Margaret K. McElderry Books, 1993). In this humorous retelling of the familiar "Three Little Pigs" story with a contemporary setting, the animals' roles are reversed and the Big Bad Pig resorts to modern tools and technology to destroy the houses of the three "cuddly little wolves" made of bricks, cement, and metal; but all ends happily when the pig is transformed by the wolves' fourth house—made of fragrant flowers.

Rumpelstiltskin, Paul Galdone (New York: Clarion Books, 1985). The colorful illustrations that fill the pages with detail and emotion in this retelling communicate the enormity of the task of spinning all of the straw into gold.

Rumpelstiltskin: Retold from the Brothers Grimm, Donna Diamond (New York: Holiday House, 1983). Diamond's double-full-page, black and white, pencil-drawn illustrations use light and shadow to create a dramatic, almost theatrical, mood in this version of the Grimm Brothers' traditional fairy tale of straw spun to gold.

Rumpelstiltskin: From the German of the Brothers Grimm, Paul O. Zelinsky (New York: E. P. Dutton, 1986). The rich, textured oil painting illustrations of interior and exterior scenes complement the text, which Zelinsky adapted from one of the earliest of several of the Grimm Brothers' own versions of the tale. A note from the author includes information about the Grimm Brothers, the history of the tale, and Zelinsky's process of developing the text for the book.

MOTIVATION AND EXTENSION ACTIVITIES

1. To introduce the unit, the teacher brings in two kinds of straw: (1) hollow, threshed grain, and (2) drinking straws—paper, plastic, and glass (including a scientist's pipette). Students and the teacher explore the physical properties of the straws and describe, compare, and contrast the two kinds of straws. They compile a list of ways in which the two kinds of straw are the same and different and record them on a chart with illustrations/diagrams. The lists might include the following:

Two Kinds of Straw: Grain and Drinking

Same	*Different*
long and thin	
hollow	Grain straw was grown, drinking straw was not.

Same	*Different*
light (not heavy)	People use drinking straw for drinking liquids.
can blow or suck through	
can look through them	Grain straw is used in farming.
	The miller's daughter in ***Rumpelstiltskin*** was commanded to spin grain straw, not drinking straw.

and so on

2. What were the first drinking straws made of? When was the first patent for paper drinking straws established? Who patented the first paper drinking straw? What was the first drinking straw made out of? How was it made? When was the first machine for making drinking straws invented?

In the beginning of the unit, students and the teacher learn some of the history of drinking straws and their relationship to the hollow stalk of threshed grain (the answer to the first question). They make a drinking straw by hand, explore how a drinking straw works, construct a straw medicine dropper and a straw atomizer, and make and play a straw oboe and a water trombone using a straw. They learn how to bend a straw without touching it, spear a raw potato with a straw (really!), make straw wheels to move a book across a surface, find the center of balance, and construct a straw balance scale. They engage in all of these activities as they explore and complete the science experiments in the "Clutching at Straws" chapter of *Simple Science Experiments with Everyday Materials,* Muriel Mandell, illustrated by Frances Zweifel (New York: Sterling Publishing Co., Inc., 1990), a collection of ninety-nine science experiments that use household objects and common materials and that includes, for each experiment, materials needed, directions for the experiment, a description of what to expect to happen or to observe, and an explanation of why the result occurred—the scientific principle that was demonstrated. Chapters are organized by the main material used in the experiment—straws, paper, lemons, dairy products, string, and soap.

3. After they explore the physical properties of straw, students experiment, in the role of the wolf, with attempting to blow down small, three-dimensional models of the pigs' houses—made of straw, sticks, and bricks (or Lego® blocks). They huff, and they puff, and they describe the results (orally or in writing) of their experiment and compare and contrast them to the experiences of the wolf in several versions of the "Three Little Pigs" story: ***The Three Little Pigs: A British Folk Tale, Three Little Pigs and the Big Bad Wolf, The Three Little Pigs*** (Galdone, Marshall), and ***The True Story of the 3 Little Pigs by A. Wolf***. (See the "Three Tales of Three" unit in Chapter 8, ee seeds, for additional activities related to the "Three Little Pigs" story.)

4. The music for the song ***There's a Hole in the Bucket*** is included in the book, so students and the teacher can read *and* sing about the familiar straw that needed an axe because it was too long to fix the bucket—while they clap their hands, stamp their feet, and/or use rhythm instruments to mark the beat.

5. The traditional fairy tale "Rumpelstiltskin" contains perhaps the most famous straw in all of literature—the straw spun to gold by the strange little man who appears to the miller's daughter. Students and the teacher read and discuss the five versions of the story: "Cinderumpelstiltskin: Or the Girl Who Really Blew It" in ***The Stinky Cheese***

Man and Other Fairly Stupid Tales, *Rumpelstiltskin: A Tale Told Long Ago by the Grimm Brothers*, *Rumpelstiltskin*, *Rumpelstiltskin: Retold from the Brothers Grimm*, and *Rumpelstiltskin: From the German of the Brothers Grimm*. They compare and contrast the versions. They compare and contrast the different ways in which Rumpelstiltskin disappears in his rage at the end. In the Tarcov and Galdone versions, he stamps his feet and vanishes into the ground; in the Diamond version, he tears himself in two; and in the Zelinsky version, he flies away on the same cooking spoon he had ridden around the fire in the forest the night before. They share which ending they like best, which ending they feel communicates his rage most effectively, and which was the most frightening or eerie.

They select a favorite from among the versions. They share the criteria on which they based their choice. They include in their discussion, for example, an evaluation of (1) the text (language, difficulty of words, amount of text, type font), (2) the illustrations (use of space, color, and light; creation of a sense of place, or setting, and time; the way in which the characters and their emotions are depicted; and personal response), and (3) how well the text and illustrations work together to convey the story's meaning.

6. Zelinsky's *Rumpelstiltskin: From the German of the Brothers Grimm* contains an author's note in which he provides information about the Brothers Grimm—Jacob and Wilhelm—who collected folk tales in Germany in the early 1800s, about the history of the several versions of the tale, and about how Zelinsky selected and developed the text for his book. Before they begin reading the different retellings of "Rumpelstiltskin," students and the teacher discuss this background information.

7. Faerie Tale Theatre (CBS/Fox Video, Industrial Park Drive, Farmington Hills, Michigan 48024) offers a film version of "Rumpelstiltskin." Students and the teacher view the film and compare and contrast the story in two media: book and film.

8. Rumpelstiltskin's rage at the end of the tale demands a dramatic response. Students present an exuberant reading or dramatization—a play or puppet show—with costumes and/or masks, scenery, and props.

9. "Rumpelstiltskin" is one of the best known of the traditional fairy tales, and the miller's daughter is one of the most famous fairy tale daughters. Students and the teacher consider "Rumpelstiltskin"—in its traditional and modern versions—as part of their exploration of "Modern Fairy Tale Daughters and Princesses" in the following chapter (Chapter 27, au daughter).

10. "This is the last straw!" Ellie, in the "For Better or For Worse" comic strip cartoon shown here, uses the word *straw* as part of an idiomatic expression when she's telling her children, who have been fighting, that "This is it, the end, all I can take!" The children—partly because of the context (they are fighting over who will get the last drinking straw in a box) and partly because they are young (and young children tend to interpret language at a less abstract level)—interpret her statement literally.

Students and the teacher discuss the humor of the cartoon and how misinterpretation of words and phrases as literal that are intended figuratively or idiomatically can often result in funny situations, at best, and confusion or miscommunication (as experienced by the characters in the comic strip). Successful readers are able to interpret words and expressions beyond their literal definitions. Many students need support and practice to develop these skills.

- Students and the teacher discuss other idiomatic expressions that use the word *straw*, including "the straw that broke the camel's back," "straw man," "to pick the short straw," "straw dog," "straw boss," and "clutching at straws."
- They extend their exploration of idiomatic expressions and word play by reading and discussing other books that feature them.

    They read three books by Fred Gwynne, in which a girl imagines literally the statements she hears adults make, which include idiomatic expressions: *The King Who Rained* (New York: Prentice-Hall Books for Young Readers, 1970), *A Chocolate Moose for Dinner* (New York: The Trumpet Club, 1976), and *A Little Pigeon Toad* (New York: The Trumpet Club, 1988).

    Students listen to or read books from the "Amelia Bedelia" series by Peggy Parish, in which Amelia Bedelia, the maid, interprets words literally and misses the nuances of language.

    They challenge each other to homophone riddles in *Eight Ate: A Feast of Homonym Riddles*, Marvin Terban, illustrated by Giulio Maestro (New York: Clarion Books, 1982).

    They explore idioms in *In a Pickle and Other Funny Idioms*, Marvin Terban, illustrated by Giulio Maestro (New York: Clarion Books, 1983).

- Together, students and the teacher tell and/or write and illustrate other idiomatic expressions. On a piece of paper held lengthwise and divided in half from top to bottom, they draw, first on the left, a picture of the literal meaning (as the girl in the Gwynne books might do) and second, on the right, a picture of the idiomatic/figurative meaning. They bind a set of phrases contributed by a group of students into a group book. (See Activities 15 and 16 in Chapter 5, closed syllable cats and kittens, Activity 16 in Chapter 17, or corn, and Activity 11 in Chapter 28, ou soup, for additional books and activities related to idioms.)

    11. Students and the teacher locate on a map and/or globe the places/cultures (depicted or of origin) in the books read in this chapter, including England [*The Three Little Pigs: A British Folk Tale*, *Three Little Pigs and the Big Bad Wolf*, *The Three Little Pigs* (Galdone, Marshall), *The True Story of the 3 Little Pigs by A. Wolf*, and *The Three Little Wolves and the Big Bad Pig*] and Germany ("Cinderumpelstiltskin: Or the Girl Who Really Blew It" in *The Stinky Cheese Man and Other Fairly Stupid Tales*, *Rumpelstiltskin: A Tale Told Long Ago by the Grimm Brothers*, *Rumpelstiltskin*, *Rumpelstiltskin: Retold from the Brothers Grimm*, and *Rumpelstiltskin: From the German of the Brothers Grimm*.

TEACHER REFERENCE

Cloze Sentences

One-Syllable Words

Cloze Sentences 1

1. I like to <u>draw</u> with markers and crayons.
2. I hurt my <u>jaw</u> and my teeth when I hit my mouth on the dashboard of the car.

3. I heard the baby <u>bawl</u> after he fell out of his crib.

4. The <u>fawn</u> hid from the deer hunter after the doe and buck were shot.

5. The <u>paws</u> of a cat left footprints on the ground after it rained.

6. I use a <u>straw</u> to sip milk or soda.

7. The <u>lawn</u> needs to be mowed each week or the grass gets too long.

8. I get up at <u>dawn</u> each morning so I see the sun rise every day.

Cloze Sentences 2

1. I hope that the snow on the roads will <u>thaw</u> when the sun shines later today.

2. The <u>claws</u> of the cat scratched my arm when she jumped off my lap.

3. I saw a <u>hawk</u> swoop down from the sky and catch a mouse.

4. I need a <u>saw</u> to cut this thick board.

5. When he was a baby, my son liked to <u>crawl</u> on his hands and knees before he walked.

6. I <u>yawn</u> with my mouth wide open when I start to get sleepy.

7. The old woman wore a <u>shawl</u> around her shoulders when she felt cold.

8. It is against the <u>law</u> to speed while driving.

Multisyllable Words

Cloze Sentences 3

1. I had an <u>awful</u> day on Friday after I had a super day on Thursday.

2. The <u>outlaw</u> hid the stolen cash after she robbed the bank.

3. An <u>awkward</u> person is clumsy.

4. My family enjoys doing <u>jigsaw</u> puzzles together.

5. A <u>seesaw</u> at the park needs a pair of children to take turns going up and down.

Dictations

1. I stayed up until <u>dawn</u> doing a <u>jigsaw</u> puzzle. I felt <u>awful</u> as I <u>yawned</u> and <u>crawled</u> to the couch, put a <u>shawl</u> over myself, and fell asleep.

2. The <u>outlaw</u> spent an <u>awful</u> night trying to escape the <u>law</u>. At <u>dawn</u> he gave up and <u>crawled</u> inside a barn to <u>thaw</u> his frozen hands and feet. With a <u>yawn</u>, he fell asleep in the <u>straw</u> he <u>saw</u> inside.

3. The mouse <u>crawled</u> on its tiny <u>paws</u> across the <u>lawn</u>, but it was not yet <u>dawn</u> and a <u>hawk</u> swooped down and grabbed it with its <u>claws</u>. The mouse let out an <u>awful</u> <u>bawl</u> as the <u>hawk</u> crushed it in its <u>jaws</u>.

aw (aw) straw

b	l		l	ful
cl	s		l	n	kward
cr	l		p	s	jigs
d	n			s	outl
dr			sh	l	sees
f	n		str	
h	k		th	
j			y	n	

Name _____ Date _____

Word List 1

aw (aw) straw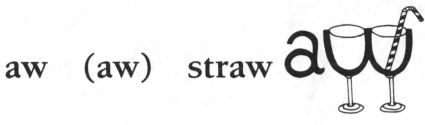

bawl	law	awful
claws	lawn	awkward
crawl	paws	jigsaw
dawn	saw	outlaw
draw	shawl	seesaw
fawn	straw	
hawk	thaw	
jaw	yawn	

Name _____ Date _____

Word List 2

aw (aw) straw

Write a word from the Word List to complete each sentence.

1. I like to _____ with markers and crayons.

2. I hurt my _____ and my teeth when I hit my mouth on the dashboard of the car.

3. I heard the baby _____ after he fell out of his crib.

4. The _____ hid from the deer hunter after the doe and buck were shot.

5. The _____ of a cat left footprints on the ground after it rained.

6. I use a _____ to sip milk or soda.

7. The _____ needs to be mowed each week or the grass gets too long.

8. I get up at _____ each morning so I see the sun rise every day.

Name _____ Date _____

Cloze Sentences 1

aw (aw) straw

Write a word from the Word List to complete each sentence.

1. I hope that the snow on the roads will _____ when the sun shines later today.

2. The _____ of the cat scratched my arm when she jumped off my lap.

3. I saw a _____ swoop down from the sky and catch a mouse.

4. I need a _____ to cut this thick board.

5. When he was a baby, my son liked to _____ on his hands and knees before he walked.

6. I _____ with my mouth wide open when I start to get sleepy.

7. The old woman wore a _____ around her shoulders when she felt cold.

8. It is against the _____ to speed while driving.

Name _____ Date _____

Cloze Sentences 2

aw (aw) straw

Write a word from the Word List to complete each sentence.

1. I had an _____ day on Friday after I had a super day on Thursday.

2. The _____ hid the stolen cash after she robbed the bank.

3. An _____ person is clumsy.

4. My family enjoys doing _____ puzzles together.

5. A _____ at the park needs a pair of children to take turns going up and down.

Name _____ Date _____

Cloze Sentences 3

27 au daughter

BOOK LIST ══

Modern Fairy Tale Daughters and Princesses

Princess Smartypants, Babette Cole (New York: G. P. Putnam's Sons, 1986). To protect the single life with her pets that she prefers, Princess Smartypants gives each prince who comes to call a challenging task. One comes who can accomplish them all, but her singlehood is preserved when he turns into a frog the first time she kisses him.

The Paper Bag Princess, Robert N. Munsch, illustrated by Michael Martchenko (Toronto, Canada: Annick Press Ltd., 1980). When a fire-breathing dragon destroys her castle, incinerates her clothes, and captures her intended, Prince Ronald, Princess Elizabeth sets off, wearing a paper bag, to rescue him. After she outwits the dragon, the ungrateful Ronald criticizes Elizabeth for not looking like a princess in her disheveled state, and she decides not to marry him.

"The Princess and the Bowling Ball" and "Little Red Running Shorts," in ***The Stinky Cheese Man and Other Fairly Stupid Tales***, Jon Scieszka, illustrated by Lane Smith (New York: Viking, 1992). This book contains eleven humorous modern retellings of well-known traditional tales. In "The Princess and the Bowling Ball," the prince puts his bowling ball under his mattresses to be certain to marry the princess he prefers, and they live dishonestly ever after. In "Little Red Running Shorts," the narrator rewrites and shortens the story of the wolf and Red (who wears running shorts in his version), and they get angry, refuse to do a retake, and leave the narrator (and readers) with a blank page.

Red Riding Hood, James Marshall (New York: Dial Books for Young Readers, 1987). Marshall's contemporary language and details and comic-like illustrations distinguish this humorous version of the tale, in which Granny is most upset at having her reading disturbed, not at having a wolf appear at her bedside or swallow her whole.

Flossie & the Fox, Patricia C. McKissack, illustrations by Rachel Isadora (New York: Scholastic, 1986). On her way to take a basket of eggs to a neighbor for her grandmother, Flossie meets and outsmarts a fox by taking advantage of his vanity. Conversational dialect and glowing illustrations create the rural southern United States setting for the drama featuring one of literature's most independent heroines.

Sleeping Ugly, Jane Yolen, illustrated by Diane Stanley (New York: Scholastic, 1981). Justice triumphs in this hilarious modern fairy tale parody of the "Sleeping Beauty" story with Princess Miserella, who is beautiful outside but mean inside (and spoiled), and Plain Jane, her opposite.

The Mapmaker's Daughter, M. C. Helldorfer, illustrated by Jonathan Hunt (New York: Macmillan Publishing Company, 1991). Longing for an adventure of her own, Suchen, the mapmaker's daughter, sets out to save the prince from the witch's spell. Aided by three magic objects from her father, she succeeds, is celebrated, and sets out on another adventure.

The Girl Who Loved the Wind, Jane Yolen, illustrated by Ed Young (New York: Harper & Row, 1972). To keep his only daughter, Danina, safe from any sadness, a merchant shuts her away in his house, where she is content until the wind sings his mysterious song. When she learns from him of the world—not always happy but filled with possibility and change—the house becomes a prison and Danina leaves, carried on her own cape by the wind.

Many Moons, James Thurber, illustrated by Louis Slobodkin (San Diego: Harcourt Brace Jovanovich, 1943, 1970). In this modern fable, when none of the wise members of the king's court can think of a way to get the moon for the ill Princess Lenore, it is the jester and Princess Lenore herself who show real wisdom. Caldecott Award Book.

The Practical Princess, Jay Williams, illustrated by Friso Henstra (New York: Parents' Magazine Press, 1969). Given the gift of common sense by a fairy, the ever-practical Princess Bedelia destroys a dragon, disposes of an unwanted suitor, rescues herself and a long-captive prince from a tower by using his long beard as a ladder, and marries the prince (but only after she makes him shave and get a haircut).

MOTIVATION AND EXTENSION ACTIVITIES

1. A number of modern fairy tales have been written recently. Although not folk tales in the purest sense of having been passed down through oral tradition, these stories, like those written by Hans Christian Andersen many years ago and long considered fairy tales, share many of the elements of traditional fairy tales. Readers discover, however, that the young women in the modern tales—daughters and princesses—are quite different from their traditional counterparts.

Students and the teacher make a chart on which they list the characteristics of traditional and modern fairy tale daughters and princesses. At the beginning of the unit, they brainstorm as many words (adjectives) and phrases as they can think of that describe daughters and princesses in traditional fairy tales in one column on a chart. Throughout the unit, as they read and discuss books, they verify or revise/correct and add information to the list. As they read and discuss the modern fairy tales suggested for this unit, they write words and phrases in the second column of the chart that describe daughters and princesses in modern fairy tales. The chart might include the following:

Fairy Tale Daughters and Princesses

Traditional	*Modern*
pretty	brave, courageous
weak	capable
waiting for Prince Charming	practical, use common sense
beautiful	adventuresome
dependent	not beautiful, but kind
beautiful on the outside, ugly or mean inside	beautiful outside and inside
not intelligent or clever	independent
timid	intelligent
impractical	strong

and so on

They make a second chart on which they list endings to fairy tales: traditional and modern. At the beginning of the unit, they brainstorm and summarize what they know (or think they know) about traditional fairy tale endings, which they record in one column on the chart. Throughout the unit, they verify or revise/correct and add information as they read and discuss books. As they read and discuss the modern fairy tales, they summarize and list endings from modern fairy tales in the second column of the chart. The second chart might include the following:

Endings to Fairy Tales

Traditional	*Modern*
prince kisses daughter/ princess and wakes her	daughter/princess saves herself/the prince or solves a problem no one else can
daughter/princess lives happily ever after	daughter/princess celebrated and respected for her deeds
the woodcutter comes and saves daughter/princess	daughter/princess goes on another adventure
daughter/princess marries prince	daughter/princess refuses to marry prince
daughter/princess becomes queen, rich	daughter/princess returns after adventure to previously satisfying life
	daughter/princess overcomes enemy, or evil or wicked person

and so on

They make a third chart on which they compile a list of elements, motifs, patterns, and conventions common to both traditional and modern fairy tales. At the beginning of the unit, they brainstorm what they know (or think they know) about fairy tales. Through-out the unit, they verify or revise/correct and add information as they read and discuss books. The third chart might include the following:

Elements, Motifs, Patterns, and Conventions
Common to Both Traditional and Modern Fairy Tales

problems, challenges, adventures, quests	repetition
hero or heroine	chants
good fairies, fairy godmothers	wishes
enemy or wicked person (witch, unwanted suitor, evil fairies/elves)	rescues
	magic
spells, curses	numbers (three)
inner and outer beauty compared	magic objects
castles, towers, dungeons	kings, queens
fire-breathing dragons, monsters	trickery
evil, haunted places	dead parent(s)
invisible or changing forms/ transformations	
long sleep/enchantment	

and so on

2. Some students may not have had much experience with traditional literature and may not know many traditional fairy tales. They may need to listen to and/or read traditional tales before they are able to benefit from the activities described in this unit.

The following list (in alphabetical order by title) suggests traditional fairy tales that are not included in the Book List or Activities for this unit. Fairy tales about the following traditional fairy tale characters are listed in other units: The Frog Prince (Chapter 14, old gold), Rumpelstiltskin (Chapter 26, aw straw), and Cinderella (Chapter 32, c Frances Cinderella fancy).

Beauty and the Beast, Jan Brett (New York: The Trumpet Club, 1989).

Beauty and the Beast, Marianna Mayer, illustrated by Mercer Mayer (New York: Four Winds Press, 1978).

Lazy Jack, Tony Ross (New York: The Trumpet Club, 1986).

Rapunzel, Bernice Chardiet, illustrated by Julie Downing (New York: Scholastic, 1982, 1990).

Snow White, Brothers Grimm, translated from the German by Paul Heins, illustrated by Trina Schart Hyman (Boston: Little, Brown and Company, 1974).

Snow-White and the Seven Dwarfs, Brothers Grimm, translated by Randall Jarrell, illustrated by Nancy Ekholm Burkert (New York: Farrar, Straus and Giroux, 1972).

Snow White and the Seven Dwarfs, Freya Littledale, illustrated by Susan Jeffers (New York: Scholastic, 1980).

Snow-White and Rose-Red, Barbara Cooney (New York: Delacorte Press, 1965).

The Twelve Dancing Princesses, Freya Littledale, illustrated by Isadore Seltzer (New York: Scholastic, 1988).

  3. In *Princess Smartypants*, the name of the prince who attempts each challenging task fits some element of the task. Princess Smartypants asks Prince Compost, for example, to protect her garden from slugs and Prince Bashthumb to chop down some trees. Students and the teacher think of some other difficult tasks Princess Smartypants could have given princes to do and corresponding names for the princes.
  4. After they read *The Paper Bag Princess*, students and the teacher tell and/or write and illustrate a short or long ending that shows what Elizabeth does after she decides not to marry Prince Ronald.
  5. Before or after they read *Flossie & the Fox*, students listen to the book read aloud so that they can focus on the verbal richness, the illustrations, and the plot as they listen to it.
  6. The modern and often humorous versions of fairy tales often provide older students with motivation to read and study traditional tales. Students and the teacher compare and contrast elements and themes in Scieszka's "The Princess and the Bowling Ball" in *The Stinky Cheese Man and Other Fairly Stupid Tales* and in a more traditional retelling of the "Princess and the Pea" story: *The Princess and the Pea*, Janet Stevens (New York: Scholastic, 1982). Lavishly dressed animals are the characters in Stevens's adaptation of the traditional tale, in which the prince and his mother (who considers herself the best judge of real princesses) travel the world over but find only noisy, clumsy, greedy, and graceless prospects until a soggy princess arrives in a rainstorm, feels the pea beneath twenty mattresses, and claims the prince.
  Students and the teacher compare and contrast elements and themes in the modern versions of the "Little Red Riding Hood" story—Scieszka's "Little Red Running Shorts" in *The Stinky Cheese Man and Other Fairly Stupid Tales*, Marshall's *Red Riding Hood*, and McKissack's *Flossie & the Fox*, with its modern, liberated Red Riding Hood character, Flossie—and in traditional retellings of the tale:

  ♦ *Little Red Riding Hood*, illustrated by Karen Schmidt (New York: Scholastic, 1986). In the end of this easy-to-read traditional retelling, the wolf dies when he tries to run after Little Red Riding Hood's grandmother sews rocks into his stomach.

  ♦ *Little Red Riding Hood*, illustrated by Trina Schart Hyman (New York: Holiday House, 1983). This traditional retelling of the Grimm fairy tale is illustrated with detailed drawings and border designs that provide a rich setting for the story and complement the equally complex text.

  Students and the teacher compare and contrast elements and themes in Yolen's modern parody of the "Sleeping Beauty" story, *Sleeping Ugly*, and in traditional retellings:

  ♦ *The Sleeping Beauty*, Freya Littledale, illustrated by Brenda Dabaghian (New York: Scholastic, 1984). In this easy-to-read traditional retelling, a slighted fairy puts a curse on Briar Rose. In spite of the king's precautions to protect his daughter, true to prophecy, at age fifteen she pricks her finger on a spindle, and she (and the castle inhabitants) sleeps for a hundred years until the prince awakens her with a kiss.

- **The Sleeping Beauty**, Trina Schart Hyman (Boston: Little, Brown and Company, 1977). Against dark and often shadowy backgrounds, the close-up studies of the faces of characters—the humble as well as the royal—of the illustrations give the reader glimpses into the emotional dimensions of the drama of the tale.
- **The Sleeping Beauty**, Jane Yolen, illustrated by Ruth Sanderson (New York: Alfred A. Knopf, 1986). The dramatic use of light and detail in the oil painting illustrations contributes to the richness of the traditional retelling of the classic romantic fairy tale of the long-awaited and well-loved daughter awakened after a hundred-year enchantment by the prince's kiss.

7. **Lon Po Po: A Red-Riding Hood Story from China** is a version of the "Red Riding Hood" story from another culture. Students and the teacher read **Lon Po Po: A Red-Riding Hood Story from China**, a Caldecott Award Book by Ed Young (New York: Scholastic, 1989). They compare and contrast it with the three versions of the traditional tale they have read: two traditional retellings of the original Grimm Brothers' tale from Germany—**Little Red Riding Hood** by Littledale and **Little Red Riding Hood** by Hyman—and McKissack's **Flossie & the Fox** from the rural south of the United States.

8. At the end of the unit, students and the teacher discuss and summarize the characters, plots, themes, elements, motifs, patterns, and conventions common to both traditional and modern fairy tales and the differences they have discovered.

9. Students and the teacher discuss roles of men and women in different cultures and times in history and gender stereotypes in books and real-life experiences.

10. Students apply what they have learned about daughters and princesses in traditional and modern fairy tales.

- Students generate or are given a problem that might be encountered in a fairy tale (A dragon is threatening the kingdom. A witch has cast a spell. A prince has been captured by evil elves. The king has been imprisoned in a tower. A spell of darkness has been cast over the land.). They tell and/or write two fairy tales using traditional fairy tale components (see Activity 8 in this chapter)—one a traditional tale with a traditional daughter/princess and the other a modern tale with a modern daughter/princess.

- Individual students tell and/or write and illustrate their own modern versions of familiar traditional fairy tales like "The Princess and the Bowling Ball" and "Little Red Running Shorts" in **The Stinky Cheese Man and Other Fairly Stupid Tales**, Marshall's **Red Riding Hood, Flossie and the Fox**, and **Sleeping Ugly**.

- Students in a group tell (and a scribe records) a modern version of a familiar traditional fairy tale (as in the preceding activity), round-robin with each person adding a part that logically follows the previous part, and illustrate it.

- Students (individually or in a group) retell/rewrite and illustrate a familiar traditional fairy tale and change the hero or heroine from a traditional character to a modern daughter or princess. They then revise any part of the tale that, consequently, must change for the tale to continue to make sense (for example, the reactions of other characters, as in the repeated reaction of the characters that Suchen meets in **The Mapmaker's Daughter**: "Run out of explorers? All out of brave knights? Sending princes and ladies these days?").

- Students (individually or in a group) retell/rewrite and illustrate only the ending of a familiar traditional fairy tale to change it into a more modern tale.

- Students (individually or in a group) tell and/or write and illustrate what happened to the character(s) in a familiar traditional fairy tale after the given ending. A short extended ending would be part of the tale. A longer extension might be a sequel similar to **The Frog Prince Continued** by Scieszka. (See Chapter 14, old gold.)
- Students (individually or in a group) retell/rewrite and illustrate a familiar traditional fairy tale from the point of view of a character different from the original or from the principal(s), as Scieszka does in **The True Story of the 3 Little Pigs** by A. Wolf. (See the "Three Tales of Three" unit in Chapter 8, ee seeds.)
- Students (individually or in a group) switch principal characters in their illustrated retelling/rewritten version of a familiar traditional fairy tale, as Turkle does in **Deep in the Forest** (a wordless picture book version of the "Goldilocks and the Three Bears" story in which a young bear visits the house of three people) and as Trivizas does in **The Three Little Wolves and the Big Bad Pig** (in which roles of the principal characters are reversed). (See the "Three Tales of Three" unit in Chapter 8, ee seeds.)

11. Students and the teacher view popular film/video versions of traditional fairy tales such as "Snow White," "Cinderella," and "Beauty and the Beast" and film versions produced by film companies such as Faerie Tale Theatre (CBS/Fox Video, Industrial Park Drive, Farmington Hills, Michigan 48024) and Rabbit Ears Productions, Inc. (Westport, Connecticut). They compare and contrast the different film versions of a single tale and a film and book version of a tale.

12. Not all of the girls and young women in traditional fairy tales are the same, as Janet, the heroine of **Wild Robin**, and Signy, the heroine of **Half a Kingdom: An Icelandic Folktale**, demonstrate. Although Jeffers's retelling is based on an old tale, the female character of **Wild Robin** is brave and strong, and she saves her brother in the end. In **Wild Robin**, by Susan Jeffers (New York: E. P. Dutton, 1976), Janet saves her wild and lazy brother Robin, whom she loves dearly, by overcoming a shadowy creature in Fairyland, where the Queen of fairies is holding him captive. Similarly, even though **Half a Kingdom: An Icelandic Folktale** is based on a tale from the folk tradition in Iceland, its heroine Signy, a resourceful peasant girl, uses her knowledge of her environment and excellent problem-solving skills to do what none of the wisest and strongest men in the kingdom can do—find and return the king's lost son and collect the reward of half the kingdom (**Half a Kingdom: An Icelandic Folktale**, Ann McGovern, illustrated by Nola Langner, New York: Scholastic Book Services, 1977).

After they have read several traditional and modern fairy tales and without the teacher giving any background to the story, students and the teacher read **Wild Robin**. They discuss whether this appears to be a modern or traditional fairy tale based on the criteria they have developed during their study in this unit (and referring to the charts in Activity 1 in this chapter). They may be surprised to discover that it is traditional. Later, after some time has elapsed and students would not be expecting the same result, they follow the same procedure with **Half a Kingdom: An Icelandic Folktale**.

The teacher shows students how to check copyright dates in the front or back of a book to see when it was written/published and where to look for information and author's notes that indicate whether a tale is original and modern or an adaptation or retelling of a traditional tale.

13. Students and the teacher locate on a map and/or globe the places/cultures (depicted or of origin) in the books read in this chapter, including the rural south of the

United States (*Flossie & the Fox*); Germany (*Little Red Riding Hood* by Schmidt and Hyman); China (*Lon Po Po: A Red-Riding Hood Story from China*); and Iceland (*Half a Kingdom: An Icelandic Folktale*).

TEACHER REFERENCE

Cloze Sentences

One-Syllable Words

Cloze Sentences 1

1. Some folks think that a ghost can <u>haunt</u> an old house at Halloween.
2. A <u>vault</u> is a safe or a compartment at a bank where things of value are kept.
3. It is not a person's <u>fault</u> if something happens that he or she did not cause.
4. A <u>jaunt</u> is a short trip made for fun.
5. When something is the <u>cause</u> of an event, it makes it happen.
6. When we <u>haul</u> a lot of wood, we need to use a truck.

Multisyllable Words

Cloze Sentences 2

1. The <u>author</u> of the book was signing <u>autographs</u> at the bookstore.
2. <u>Auto</u> means "car" and is a short form of the word <u>automobile</u>.
3. <u>Because</u> he did a good job on it, the teacher gave the student a good mark on his test.
4. We <u>applaud</u> or clap for a performer, actor, or actress when a play is over.
5. We will not find a <u>dinosaur</u> like the Brontosaurus alive today because it is extinct.
6. <u>August</u> is the last summer month, and it comes after July and before September.
7. The <u>exhaust</u> from a truck or a car can leave a bad smell in the air and can add to the smog.
8. A person may take <u>laundry</u> to a <u>laundromat</u> if he or she has dirty clothes to <u>launder</u> and no washer or dryer at home.
9. My <u>daughter</u> is my female child.

Dictations

1. I have the <u>autograph</u> of an <u>author</u> of books about <u>dinosaurs</u> and <u>haunted</u> houses. He keeps his manuscripts locked in a <u>vault</u> at the bank <u>because</u> he wants them to be safe.

2. On a hot <u>August</u> day <u>Paul</u> had to <u>haul</u> our <u>laundry</u> to the <u>laundromat</u> in his <u>automobile</u>. It was not his <u>fault</u> that he had to <u>launder</u> it there. The <u>exhaust</u> pipe broke that vents our dryer at home. I <u>applaud</u> him <u>because</u> he did the job for all of us. It was just a short <u>jaunt</u> to the <u>laundromat</u> from our house, so he was not <u>exhausted</u> from the trip.

3. Last <u>August</u> my <u>daughter</u> had an <u>automobile</u> crash during a short <u>jaunt</u> to the <u>laundromat</u>. A man who had rented a <u>U-Haul</u>® truck admitted that it was his <u>fault</u>. He said he was distracted <u>because</u> the <u>exhaust</u> pipe on the truck was dragging on the ground. I <u>applaud</u> his willingness to say that he <u>caused</u> the crash, and I hope his mistake will not <u>haunt</u> him.

au (aw) daughter

c___se   appl___   d___d___ghter

f___lt   ___gust   dinos___r

h___l   ___thor   exh___st

h___nt   ___to   l___nder

j___nt   ___tographs   l___ndromat

v___lt   ___tomobile   l___ndry

bec___se

Name _____ Date _____

au (aw) daughter

cause	applaud	daughter
fault	August	dinosaur
haul	author	exhaust
haunt	auto	launder
jaunt	autographs	laundromat
vault	automobile	laundry
	because	

Name _____ Date _____

Word List 2

au (aw) daughter

Write one or more words from the Word List to complete each sentence.

1. Some folks think that a ghost can _____ an old house at Halloween.

2. A _____ is a safe or a compartment at a bank where things of value are kept.

3. It is not a person's _____ if something happens that he or she did not cause.

4. A _____ is a short trip made for fun.

5. When something is the _____ of an event, it makes it happen.

6. When we _____ a lot of wood, we need to use a truck.

Name _____ Date _____

Cloze Sentences 1

au (aw) daughter

Write one or more words from the Word List to complete each sentence.

1. The _____ of the book was signing _____ at the bookstore.

2. _____ means "car" and is a short form of the word _____ .

3. _____ he did a good job on it, the teacher gave the student a good mark on his test.

4. We _____ or clap for a performer, actor, or actress when a play is over.

5. We will not find a _____ like the Brontosaurus alive today because it is extinct.

6. _____ is the last summer month, and it comes after July and before September.

7. The _____ from a truck or a car can leave a bad smell in the air and can add to the smog.

8. A person may take _____ to a _____ if he or she has dirty clothes to _____ and no washer or dryer at home.

9. My _____ is my female child.

Name _____ Date _____

Cloze Sentences 2

28 ou soup

BOOK LIST

Soup, Stew, and Broth

Growing Vegetable Soup, Lois Ehlert (San Diego: Harcourt Brace & Company, 1987). Giant text and word labels for all items pictured combine with Ehlert's brilliant illustrations to show the stages of growth and tools used as a child and father grow vegetables and make soup. Includes recipe for vegetable soup.

"Birthday Soup," in ***Little Bear***, Else Holmelund Minarik, illustrated by Maurice Sendak (New York: Harper & Row, 1957). This book is a collection of four stories about Little Bear and his sensitive Mother Bear, who is always nearby to support and enjoy him. In "Birthday Soup," when he thinks that Mother Bear has forgotten his birthday, Little Bear makes birthday soup to share with his friends, and Mother Bear arrives with the cake just in time to join the party.

"Split Pea Soup," in ***George and Martha: Five Stories about Two Great Friends***, James Marshall (New York: Scholastic, 1972). This first book in the series introduces the friendship of two hippopotamuses, George and Martha, as they discover each other's likes, dislikes, and habits and cheer each other on through some misadventures. In "Split Pea Soup," Martha makes split pea soup again and again until she and George confess that they don't like it and would rather eat chocolate chip cookies.

Mouse Soup, Arnold Lobel (New York: Scholastic, 1977). A mouse insists that the soup a weasel wants to make of him needs stories, so the mouse tells four—about bees and mud, large stones, crickets, and a thorn bush—and, while the weasel goes on a difficult search for those items, the mouse escapes.

The Wolf's Chicken Stew, Keiko Kasza (New York: The Trumpet Club, 1987). Rather than make chicken stew from the hen as she is, a wolf decides to fatten her up by putting pancakes, doughnuts, and cake on her porch, but he finds he can't eat her when her thankful chicks smother him with kisses and call him "Uncle Wolf."

Chicken Soup with Rice: A Book of Months, Maurice Sendak (New York: Scholastic, 1962). In a rhyme with a repeated refrain, a little boy—as himself or transformed into other things—celebrates and eats chicken soup with rice every month of the year in a variety of contexts and places around the world.

Stone Soup, Ann McGovern, illustrated by Winslow Pinney Pels (New York: Scholastic, 1968, 1986). A hungry traveler tricks a woman into making and serving him soup by asking for a stone and a series of food items to make it cook faster, smell and taste better, be fit for a king, and thicken.

The Farmer in the Soup: Retold from the Norse Tale The Husband Who Was to Mind the House, Freya Littledale, illustrated by Molly Delaney (New York: Scholastic, 1987). Tired of her husband's complaining about everything she does, a farmer's wife changes places with him for a day, which ends with the cow swinging from the roof by a rope and a husband who never complains again sitting in the soup pot.

Vegetable Soup, Jeanne Modesitt, illustrated by Robin Spowart (New York: Macmillan Publishing Company, 1988). New to the neighborhood, two rabbits try to borrow carrots from their neighbors but are offered a variety of vegetables they have never eaten before instead, so they make vegetable soup and invite everyone to share it. Includes recipe for simple vegetable soup.

Mean Soup, Betsy Everitt (San Diego: Harcourt Brace Jovanovich, 1992). Horace's mother shows him how to stir away a bad day with her recipe for mean soup: boiling water, salt, screams, growls, bared teeth, stuck-out tongues, bangs with a spoon, and Horace's "best dragon breath."

The Man Who Kept House, Kathleen and Michael Hague, illustrated by Michael Hague (San Diego: Harcourt Brace Jovanovich, 1981). A man has a series of misadventures when he trades chores for a day with his wife, who he feels does not work as hard. When the wife returns from the fields, she finds the cow hanging from the roof and a humble husband with his head in the soup pot.

Stone Soup: An Old Tale, Marcia Brown (New York: Charles Scribner's Sons, 1947). When the townspeople hear that three soldiers are coming, they hide their food, but the hungry and clever soldiers teach them how to make stone soup with just three round stones *and* their hidden food.

Stone Soup, John Warren Stewig, illustrated by Margot Tomes (New York: The Trumpet Club, 1991). Grethel leaves home to seek her fortune, arrives hungry in a village of stingy people who hide their food, and uses her magic stone—and a few additions from their food stores—to make enough soup for them all.

The Boy and the Ghost, Robert D. San Souci, illustrated by J. Brian Pinkney (New York: The Trumpet Club, 1989). A boy leaves home to earn money to help his poor family, stops at a haunted house that has a treasure free to anyone who can stay in the house from sunset to sunrise, and—kept busy making his meal of soup—meets the challenge and takes home the money.

The Talking Eggs: A Folktale from the American South, Robert D. San Souci, illustrated by Jerry Pinkney (New York: Scholastic, 1989). Accustomed to being made to do all of the work by her mean older sister and mother, Blanche is rewarded for an act of kindness to an old woman, who takes her home, shows her strange and wondrous things, and gives her a gift of talking eggs that produce riches. Caldecott Honor Book.

Princess Furball, Charlotte Huck, illustrated by Anita Lobel (New York: Scholastic, 1989). A motherless princess escapes marriage to an Ogre planned by her father and uses the dresses that were in her dowry, soup herbs from the cook who raised her, and her mother's golden treasures to win the heart of the young king, who marries her.

Gone Is Gone: Or the Story of a Man Who Wanted to Do Housework, Wanda Gag (New York: Coward, McCann & Geoghegan Inc., 1935). Gag's version of the day a husband and wife trade chores, which ends with the cow hanging from the roof and the husband in the soup, uses the language and conversational style of the German storyteller who told her the tale when she was a child.

"Too Many Cooks . . ." and Other Proverbs, illustrated by Maggie Kneen (New York: Simon & Schuster, 1992). Colorful drawings of the activities of a variety of animals illustrate over twenty proverbs. A glossary describes proverbs and explains each saying.

MOTIVATION AND EXTENSION ACTIVITIES

1. Before or after they read "Split Pea Soup" in ***George and Martha: Five Stories about Two Great Friends***, the teacher brings in split pea soup for students to try. They make a graph that shows how many people like and don't like split pea soup. Then everyone (who likes them) eats chocolate chip cookies, and they make a graph of how many people like and don't like chocolate chip cookies. They compare and contrast the graphs and propose reasons for the differences they observe.

2. In addition to ***Mouse Soup***, Arnold Lobel has written another collection of mouse stories—***Mouse Tales*** (New York: Harper & Row, 1972). Students and the teacher read the mouse stories from ***Mouse Tales***: "The Wishing Well," "Clouds," "Very Tall Mouse and Very Short Mouse," "The Mouse and the Winds," "The Journey," "The Old Mouse," and "The Bath."

3. Three versions of the familiar "Stone Soup" story are suggested for this unit: ***Stone Soup*** (McGovern), ***Stone Soup: An Old Tale*** (Brown), and ***Stone Soup*** (Stewig).

- Students and the teacher compare and contrast the elements in the three versions. Allusions to "stone soup" are often made in conversation and in books. Students and the teacher share whether they have heard references made to "stone soup." They discuss what this saying means beyond the literal level.

- They choose their favorite version and make stone soup following its recipe in the text.

- They make three pots of stone soup by following the recipes in the text in each of the three books. Each person chooses a favorite and indicates the criteria on which he or she based the selection.

- They write recipe cards (3″ × 5″ index cards) for stone soup as it is presented in each book: "McGovern's Famous Stone Soup," "Brown's French Style Stone Soup," and "Stewig's Stone Soup, Not Stew."

4. Three versions of the "Farmer in the Soup" story are suggested for this unit: *The Farmer in the Soup: Retold from the Norse Tale The Husband Who Was to Mind the House* (Littledale), *The Man Who Kept House* (Hague), and *Gone Is Gone: Or the Story of a Man Who Wanted to Do Housework* (Gag). The turn-about story pattern of these books, in which characters exchange places for a time, is common in traditional literature. Students and the teacher compare and contrast the elements of the three books, including characters, plot, setting, theme, text, and illustrations.

5. The three "Farmer in the Soup" stories, *The Farmer in the Soup: Retold from the Norse Tale The Husband Who Was to Mind the House* (Littledale), *The Man Who Kept House* (Hague), and *Gone Is Gone: Or the Story of a Man Who Wanted to Do Housework* (Gag), raise questions about gender stereotypes and roles. Students and the teacher discuss gender stereotypes and roles in books and in real life and students' responses to them.

6. *Vegetable Soup* contains the recipe that the rabbits in the book follow to make soup from the vegetables their neighbors give them. Students and the teacher follow the recipe to make vegetable soup, and they invite the neighbors to share it.

7. In *Mean Soup*, Horace learns how to get over a bad day when his mother teaches him how to make mean soup by tossing his frustrations and a few loud noises into the pot. Students and the teacher share (tell and/or write and illustrate) about bad days they have had and what they did to get through them. They compare and contrast Horace's story with the story of another boy who has a bad day—in fact, a "terrible, horrible, no good, very bad day"—Alexander in *Alexander and the Terrible, Horrible, No Good, Very Bad Day* by Viorst (Chapter 7, ay day). They compare and contrast Horace's and Alexander's mothers' reactions to their sons' bad days in the two books. They make a pot of "mean soup."

8. *The Boy and the Ghost* and *The Talking Eggs: A Folktale from the American South* are written and illustrated by the same people—Robert D. San Souci and J. (Jerry) Brian Pinkney. Students and the teacher discuss the similarities and differences in the two books.

9. *The Talking Eggs: A Folktale from the American South* and *Princess Furball* are two variants of the "Cinderella" story in which soup or stew is an important element. For activities related to the two books, see Chapter 32, c Frances Cinderella fancy.

10. Because Gag uses the language and conversational style of the German storyteller who told her the tale when she was a child, the language in *Gone Is Gone: Or the Story of a Man Who Wanted to Do Housework* may be difficult for some students to read. The teacher (or students) reads the book aloud for some students so that they can focus on the plot, illustrations, and descriptions.

11. Successful readers are able to interpret words and expressions beyond their literal meanings or definitions. Many students need support and practice to develop abilities to recognize and use the relationships between/among words (synonyms, antonyms, homophones, homographs, homonyms, and analogies) and understandings of literary allusions and idiomatic and proverbial expressions as they read. *"Too Many Cooks..." and Other Proverbs*, with its humorous and colorful illustrations of familiar proverbs and section that defines proverbs and provides explanations of each saying in the book, introduces students to proverbs. Most students benefit from many experiences and activities involving proverbial and idiomatic expressions that are best provided in the context of units of study.

- Students and the teacher read and discuss *"Too Many Cooks ..." and Other Proverbs* and the explanatory section at the end of the book.

- They read and discuss other books that feature word play, including idiomatic and proverbial expression. (See Activities 15 and 16 in Chapter 5, closed syllable cats and kittens, Activity 16 in Chapter 17, or corn, and Activity 10 in Chapter 26, aw straw, for lists of books and additional activities.)

- They visualize and/or draw the literal meanings of statements related to the "Soup, Stew, and Broth" unit. On a piece of paper held lengthwise and divided in half from top to bottom, they draw first—on the left—a picture of the literal meaning and second—on the right—a picture of the idiomatic/figurative meaning. They bind a set of phrases contributed by a group of students into a group book. The statements might include the following:

> The fog was as thick as pea soup.
>
> She always stews before she takes a test.
>
> You lost your car keys? Now you're in a real stew.
>
> It sure is soupy out tonight. I can hardly see where I am going.
>
> When he souped up his engine, I could hear his car three blocks away!
>
> We're having stone soup tonight. Tomorrow is pay day.

12. Students and the teacher locate on a map and/or globe the places/cultures (depicted or of origin) in the books read in this chapter, including Spain, Bombay in India, and the Nile River in Egypt (***Chicken Soup with Rice: A Book of Months***); Norway (***The Farmer in the Soup: Retold from the Norse Tale The Husband Who Was to Mind the House*** and ***The Man Who Kept House***); France (***Stone Soup: An Old Tale***); Virginia and Alabama in the United States (***The Boy and the Ghost***); Creole culture and Louisiana in the southern United States (***The Talking Eggs: A Folktale from the American South***); and Germany (***Gone Is Gone: Or the Story of a Man Who Wanted to Do Housework***).

TEACHER REFERENCE

Cloze Sentences

One-Syllable Words

Cloze Sentences 1

1. The <u>wound</u> that the deer got during hunting season has healed and it is fine now.

2. In her <u>youth</u> the woman was a fine athlete, but as she has grown older she runs more slowly.

3. We were given a <u>tour</u> of the school we visited by the students who attend it.

4. A <u>group</u> of children crowded around the teacher's desk.

5. The <u>soup</u> that I made for lunch with the tomatoes from my garden was a bit too hot at first, but it cooled down after I spooned some into my bowl.

6. <u>You</u> are the person that I am speaking to right now.

7. I took a different <u>route</u> on my way home today and I got lost.

Cloze Sentences 2

1. A <u>troupe</u> of several actors and actresses came to join our acting company to put on a play.

2. <u>Mousse</u> made from frozen whipped cream and chocolate can be a wonderful dessert.

Multisyllable Words

3. The <u>youthful</u> attitude of the elderly man made him seem less old than he was.

4. We got a <u>souvenir</u> at the store to help us remember our trip.

5. When I follow my daily <u>routine</u>, I do things the same way each day.

6. We took a <u>detour</u> when the road we take home was torn up for repairs.

7. The oatmeal was <u>soupy</u> when I put in too much milk.

Cloze Sentences 3

1. He will <u>recoup</u> his money when you repay the loan he gave you.

2. <u>Caribou</u> is the name of a number of different reindeer that live in North America.

3. Traffic was <u>rerouted</u> when the road was being repaired.

4. A <u>tourist</u> likes to travel around to visit different places.

5. A <u>cougar</u> is a large brown wild animal that is also known as a panther, mountain lion, or puma.

Dictations

1. We invite <u>you</u> to join us and a <u>group</u> of <u>youthful</u> <u>tourists</u> for lunch. We will have <u>soup</u> and sandwiches with <u>mousse</u> for dessert. It will be a day that differs from the <u>routine</u> as the <u>tourists</u> share the <u>souvenirs</u> they have collected on their <u>tour</u>.

2. The <u>youthful</u> acting <u>troupe</u> that joined us to put on the play had a <u>tour</u> of the town. The <u>youths</u> were <u>rerouted</u> by a <u>detour</u> because the road was muddy after a rainstorm, but they were a happy <u>group</u> of <u>tourists</u>. I tell <u>you</u>, they took photographs of the <u>soupy</u> road as a <u>souvenir</u>!

3. We took a bunch of <u>youths</u> on a <u>tour</u> of the hills. These <u>tourists</u> did not have the <u>routine</u> <u>tour</u> because we saw a <u>wounded</u> <u>cougar</u> and a <u>group</u> of <u>youthful</u> <u>caribou</u> as we followed the <u>route</u> <u>through</u> the hills.

ou ($\overline{oo}$) soup

gr p   carib
m sse   c gar
r te   det r
s p   rec p
t r   rer ted
tr pe   r tine
w nd   s py
y   s venir
y th   t rist
                 y thful

Name _____ Date _____

Word List 1

ou (o͞o) soup

group · caribou

mousse · cougar

route · detour

soup · recoup

tour · rerouted

troupe · routine

wound · soupy

you · souvenir

youth · tourist

· youthful

Name _____ Date _____

Word List 2

ou ($\overline{oo}$) soup

Write a word from the Word List to complete each sentence.

1. The _____ that the deer got during hunting season has healed and it is fine now.

2. In her _____ the woman was a fine athlete, but as she has grown older she runs more slowly.

3. We were given a _____ of the school we visited by the students who attend it.

4. A _____ of children crowded around the teacher's desk.

5. The _____ that I made for lunch with the tomatoes from my garden was a bit too hot at first, but it cooled down after I spooned some into my bowl.

6. _____ are the person that I am speaking to right now.

7. I took a different _____ on my way home today and I got lost.

Name _____ Date _____

Cloze Sentences 1

ou (o͞o) soup

Write a word from the Word List to complete each sentence.

1. A _____ of several actors and actresses came to join our acting company to put on a play.

2. _____ made from frozen whipped cream and chocolate can be a wonderful dessert.

3. The _____ attitude of the elderly man made him seem less old than he was.

4. We got a _____ at the store to help us remember our trip.

5. When I follow my daily _____ , I do things the same way each day.

6. We took a _____ when the road we take home was torn up for repairs.

7. The oatmeal was _____ when I put in too much milk.

Name _____ Date _____

Cloze Sentences 2

ou (o͞o) soup

Write a word from the Word List to complete each sentence.

1. He will _____ his money when you repay the loan he gave you.

2. _____ is the name of a number of different reindeer that live in North America.

3. Traffic was _____ when the road was being repaired.

4. A _____ likes to travel around to visit different places.

5. A _____ is a large brown wild animal that is also known as a panther, mountain lion, or puma.

Name _____ Date _____

Cloze Sentences 3

29   consonant-le   fable

Modern Fables

"The Tortoise and the Hair" and "The Really Ugly Duckling," in *The Stinky Cheese Man and Other Fairly Stupid Tales*, Jon Scieszka, illustrated by Lane Smith (New York: Viking, 1992). This book is a collection of eleven humorous modern retellings of well-known traditional tales. In "The Tortoise and the Hair," the Hare challenges the Tortoise to run faster than the Hare can grow his hair. In "The Really Ugly Duckling," the ugly duckling fails to fulfill his traditional destiny of becoming the beautiful and revered swan; he grows up to be just a plain and ugly duck.

The Tortoise and the Hare: An Aesop Fable, Janet Stevens (New York: Scholastic, 1984). In Stevens's humorous retelling of the familiar Aesop fable with a contemporary setting, Tortoise's friends help him train for the race and Hare wears jogging shorts and Tortoise wears running shoes.

The Principal's New Clothes, Stephanie Calmenson, illustrated by Denise Brunkus (New York: Scholastic, 1989). In this modern version of Hans Christian Andersen's "The Emperor's New Clothes" story and fable, Mr. Bundy, the principal, is the emperor and a kindergarten student is the child who speaks up with the truth that the principal is wearing only his underwear.

A House for Hermit Crab, Eric Carle (Saxonville, Mass.: Picture Book Studio, Ltd., 1987). Over several months, Hermit Crab settles into and decorates a new house with the help of his new friends. Just as he feels at home in the shell, he discovers he's outgrown it and must leave, but he does so confident to face the opportunities of the next challenge after his successes with the last.

Mister King, Raija Siekkinen, translated from the Finnish by Tim Steffa, illustrated by Hannu Taina (Minneapolis, Minn.: Carolrhoda Books, Inc., 1986). In this modern fable, a lonely king who hasn't a single subject does not enjoy his beautiful house and kingdom until a huge cat arrives at his door. Biennale of Illustrations Bratislava (BIB) Grand Prix award for illustrations.

Fables, Arnold Lobel (New York: Scholastic, 1980). A variety of animals are the characters in the short tales in this collection of twenty humorous and contemporary modern fables, with morals written and illustrated by Arnold Lobel. Caldecott Award Book.

Frederick's Fables: A Leo Lionni Treasury of Favorite Stories, Leo Lionni (New York: Random House, 1985). Full text of and selected illustrations from thirteen animal fables illuminate human themes through the experiences and adventures of small animals: mice, caterpillars, chameleons, rabbits, fish, crocodiles, birds, snails, and frogs.

Many Moons, James Thurber, illustrated by Louis Slobodkin (San Diego: Harcourt Brace Jovanovich, 1943, 1970). In this modern fable, when none of the wise members of the King's court can think of a way to get the moon for the ill Princess Lenore, it is the jester and Princess Lenore herself who show real wisdom. Caldecott Award Book.

The Foolish Tortoise, Richard Buckley, illustrated by Eric Carle (New York: Scholastic, 1985). Tired of being encumbered and slow, Tortoise takes off his shell in this rhyming story and fable and finds that he's far too vulnerable without its protection.

Everyone Knows What a Dragon Looks Like, Jay Williams, illustrated by Mercer Mayer (New York: Four Winds Press, 1976). In this modern fable, when the wise councilors call on the Great Cloud Dragon to protect the city of Wu from attack, only a humble boy, the city's gate sweeper, is able to look beyond appearances and treat with respect the old man who arrives to save them.

Amos & Boris, William Steig (New York: Penguin Books, 1971). This tender story and modern fable celebrates the reciprocity of friendship as a mouse is able to save a friend— a whale who rescued him from drowning in the sea years before.

MOTIVATION AND EXTENSION ACTIVITIES

1. At the beginning of the unit, the teacher reads aloud a fable with an explicit (stated) moral and asks students "What kind of story is this?" If students recognize it as a fable, the teacher asks "What is a fable?" Students make observations about the story/ fable, which the teacher records.

The teacher (or students) read several more traditional fables (possibly from the list of suggested books that follows in Activity 2 in this chapter). Together, students and the teacher generate a list of elements common to and necessary for a story to be considered a fable (a definition). They discuss the purpose of fables and how this relates to the length of traditional fables. They discuss the moral (or lesson)—explicit (or stated) or implicit—and the use of animals who speak as people and who represent the characteristics of humans. Throughout the unit, as each new fable is read and discussed, students refer to the list of fable elements (definition) and revise or correct and add information.

2. The teacher's (or students') reading of a few fables may be sufficient to enable some students to remember others that they have heard or to begin to understand the form. Other children may not have had much experience with traditional literature and may not know many (or any) fables. They may need to listen to and/or read additional fables before they are able to benefit from the activities described in this unit. Allusions to fables or to characters or morals in fables are often made in conversation and in books. It is important for fables to be part of students' experiences with literature.

The following list suggests sources of additional traditional fables to supplement the traditional fables included in the Activities in this unit.

Fables from Aesop (Greece, 600 B.C.)

City Mouse-Country Mouse and Two More Mouse Tales from Aesop, illustrated by John Wallner (New York: Scholastic, 1970).

City Mouse-Country Mouse and Two More Mouse Tales from Aesop, illustrated by Marian Parry (New York: Scholastic, 1970).

The Boy Who Cried Wolf, Freya Littledale, illustrated by James Marshall (New York: Scholastic, 1975).

Tales from Aesop, J. P. Miller (New York: Random House, 1976).

Three Aesop Fox Fables, Paul Galdone (New York: Clarion Books, 1971).

Aesop's Fables, Michael Hague (New York: Holt, Rinehart and Winston, 1985).

The Aesop for Children, illustrated by Milo Winter (Chicago: Rand McNally & Co., 1919, 1947).

Aesop's Fables Retold in Verse, Tom Paxton, illustrated by Robert Rayevsky (New York: William Morrow & Company, Inc., 1988).

Fables from India

Seven Blind Mice, Ed Young (New York: Philomel Books, 1992).

The Blind Men and the Elephant, Karen Backstein, illustrated by Annie Mitra (New York: Scholastic, 1992).

Once a Mouse . . . : A Fable Cut in Wood, Marcia Brown (New York: Atheneum, 1961). Caldecott Award Book.

The Jatakas: Tales of India, Ellen C. Babbitt (New York: The Century Co., 1912).

Fables from Africa

Anansi Goes Fishing, Eric A. Kimmel, illustrated by Janet Stevens (New York: Holiday House, 1992).

Anansi Finds a Fool, Verna Aardema, illustrated by Bryna Waldman (New York: Dial Books for Young Readers, 1992).

Oh, Kojo! How Could You!, Verna Aardema, illustrated by Marc Brown (New York: The Trumpet Club, 1984).

Traveling to Tondo: A Tale of the Nkundo of Zaire, Verna Aardema, illustrated by Will Hillenbrand (New York: Scholastic, 1991).

Fables from Leonardo da Vinci (Italy, 1452–1519)

Fables of Leonardo da Vinci, interpreted and transcribed by Bruno Nardini, illustrated by Adriana Saviozzi Mazza (Northbrook, Ill.: Hubbard Press, 1972).

A Fable from Chaucer's Canterbury Tales (England, 1386–1387)

Chanticleer and the Fox, Barbara Cooney (New York: Thomas Y. Crowell Company, 1958).

Fables from Different Cultures around the World

Feathers and Tails: Animal Fables Retold, David Kherdian, illustrated by Nonny Hogrogian (New York: Philomel Books, 1992).

3. As students read or listen to traditional and modern fables, they make a list of animals and the characteristics of people they represent. They discuss similarities and differences of the human characteristics represented by animals in fables from different cultures.

4. Are the themes in modern fables the same as or different from the themes in traditional tales? Are the morals (lessons) similar? Do they have the same animal characters? Students and the teacher compare and contrast the themes, morals, and characters they discover in the modern and traditional fables they listen to or read.

5. The modern, humorous versions of fables such as "The Tortoise and the Hair" and "The Really Ugly Duckling" in *The Stinky Cheese Man and Other Fairly Stupid Tales* and *The Tortoise and the Hare: An Aesop Fable* often provide older readers with motivation to read and study traditional literature. Students and the teacher compare and contrast the modern and traditional versions of the two fables.

- They compare and contrast "The Tortoise and the Hair" in *The Stinky Cheese Man and Other Fairly Stupid Tales* by Scieszka and *The Tortoise and the Hare: An Aesop Fable* by Stevens with *The Hare and the Tortoise* by Wildsmith (Chapter 20, ur turtle) and "The Hare and the Tortoise" in *The Aesop for Children* by Winter and "The Tortoise and the Hare" in *Aesop's Fables Retold in Verse* by Paxton (Activity 2 in this chapter). (See Activities 10, 11, 12, 13, 15, and 16 in Chapter 20, ur turtle, for additional activities related to tortoises in fables.)

- They compare and contrast "The Really Ugly Duckling" in *The Stinky Cheese Man and Other Fairly Stupid Tales* by Scieszka with *The Ugly Duckling*, Lilian Moore, illustrated by Daniel San Souci (New York: Scholastic, 1987), a recent retelling of the familiar fable written by Hans Christian Andersen.

- They tell and/or write and illustrate their own modern versions of the "The Tortoise and the Hare" fable.

6. *The Principal's New Clothes* is a modern retelling with contemporary characters and setting of Hans Christian Andersen's "The Emperor's New Clothes" story and fable. Students and the teacher compare and contrast *The Principal's New Clothes* and two versions of the "The Emperor's New Clothes" fable: *The Emperor's New*

Clothes, Hans Christian Andersen, retold and illustrated by Nadine Bernard Westcott (Boston: Little, Brown and Company, 1984) and *The Emperor's New Clothes*, Hans Christian Andersen, retold by Ruth Belov Gross, illustrated by Jack Kent (New York: Scholastic, 1977). They tell and/or write a moral (lesson) for the fables—modern and traditional—and discuss whether their moral is the same or different for the fables from two different times in history.

The Westcott book contains a paper doll of the emperor and changes of clothes for him to wear. Students follow the suggestions in the book to trace, cut out, and decorate the clothes and to design additional outfits for him to wear.

7. *A House for Hermit Crab* is a modern fable about adjusting to change and challenge and seeing them as opportunities for new growth and success. Students and the teacher discuss *A House for Hermit Crab* with other books about change, especially moving to a new home. (See Activity 2 in Chapter 23, ou house.) They tell and/or write a moral (lesson) for this fable with an implied moral.

8. In *Mister King*, the king learns an important lesson about ruling, serving, and caring from a cat. Students and the teacher discuss this theme and tell and/or write a moral (lesson) for this fable with an implied moral.

9. The thirteen fables about animals compiled as a collection with full text and selected illustrations in *Frederick's Fables: A Leo Lionni Treasury of Favorite Stories* are each available as a single title. They are *Frederick, Fish Is Fish, Alexander and the Wind-Up Mouse, The Biggest House in the World, Geraldine, the Music Mouse, Tico and the Golden Wings, Cornelius, Swimmy, In the Rabbitgarden, Theodore and the Talking Mushroom, A Color of His Own, The Greentail Mouse*, and *The Alphabet Tree*. Students and the teacher compare the single copies of the fables with their complete illustrations with those edited for the collection. They tell and/or write morals (lessons) for the fables with implied morals. They discuss the common theme(s) of the Lionni animal fables when considered together.

10. The wisdom of the young—Princess Lenore—and the "foolish"—the jester—in *Many Moons* contrasts with the "wisdom" of the members of the King's court. Students and the teacher discuss the theme of the meaning of wisdom in *Many Moons*, tell and/or write a moral (lesson) for this fable with an implied moral, and complete additional activities related to the book (Activity 18 in Chapter 2, oo moon, and selected Activities in Chapter 27, au daughter).

11. The theme of looking beyond the external to the inner qualities of a person is common in fables and in other traditional literature forms. The characters in fairy tales, for example, are often plain on the outside but kind, strong, and loving within. (See Chapter 27, au daughter.) Students and the teacher discuss this theme in *Everyone Knows What a Dragon Looks Like*. They compare the character of the boy Han, the humble gate sweeper of the city, and those of the "wise" councilors. They consider the characters in *Many Moons* who serve the same function—the wise Princess Lenore and the jester—compared to the members of the King's court.

12. Williams uses figurative language (similes and a metaphor) in *Everyone Knows What a Dragon Looks Like* to compare the unknown to the more familiar in his description of the old man as he transforms into the dragon. The dragon is "taller than the tallest tree, taller than the tallest tower," "the color of sunset shining through rain," and "His claws and teeth glittered like diamonds. His eyes were noble like those of a proud horse." Students and the teacher identify and discuss the use of figurative language in this passage. (See Activity 18 in Chapter 2, oo moon, Activity 12 in Chapter 4, y fly,

Activity 13 in Chapter 13, oa goat, Activities 12 and 13 in Chapter 16, ar star, Activity 10 in Chapter 22, ow owl, and Activity 8 in Chapter 32, c Frances Cinderella fancy, for more activities that feature figurative language.) They invent and draw a dragon and describe it for a partner to draw using figurative language without showing the original. (See Activity 18 in Chapter 2, oo moon, for more specific directions for the activity.)

13. In Lionni's heart-warming modern fable about friendship, "Fish Is Fish" in *Frederick's Fables: A Leo Lionni Treasury of Favorite Stories*, a friend—a frog— saves another—a fish who is stranded out of the water on land. Students and the teacher compare and contrast and "Fish Is Fish" in *Frederick's Fables: A Leo Lionni Treasury of Favorite Stories* and *Amos & Boris*, in which the plot is similar: A mouse, Amos, saves his friend, Boris the whale, who is stranded out of water on land, as well.

14. The theme of a tiny animal saving a much larger one is common in fables. The motivation is not always friendship, however. Sometimes it is a debt of gratitude. Students and the teacher compare and contrast *Amos & Boris* with three retellings of the familiar "Lion and Mouse" fable from Aesop: "The Lion and the Mouse" in *Aesop's Fables*, Michael Hague (New York: Holt Rinehart and Winston, 1985); *City Mouse-Country Mouse* and *Two More Mouse Tales from Aesop*, John Wallner (New York: Scholastic, 1970); and *The Aesop for Children*, Milo Winter (Chicago: Rand McNally & Co., 1919, 1947).

15. Throughout the unit and at its end, students apply what they learn about fables.

- They read *Animal Fact/Animal Fable*, Seymour Simon, illustrated by Diane de Groat (New York: Crown Publishers, Inc., 1979). The colorfully and accurately illustrated book presents scientific observations about the behavior of a variety of animals. For each animal, a true or false statement is presented on a right-hand page, and the reader guesses whether it is a fact or a fable (fiction) and turns the page to find out. They decide whether the title is accurate. (These are animal facts and fictions, not fables.) If they decide it is not, they provide a better title.
- They write explicit morals (lessons) for fables that have implicit morals.
- Different retellings of a single fable frequently have different morals. Students choose their preference and give reasons for their choice.
- They identify and compare and contrast a traditional fable that has elements similar to those in a modern fable or another traditional fable—similar theme, plot (incident), moral, character(s), setting, and so on.
- They tell and/or write and illustrate a modern version of a traditional tale with modern characters and setting as in *The Principal's New Clothes, The Tortoise and the Hare* by Stevens, and *Fables* by Lobel.
- They tell and/or write and illustrate their own fables—with explicit or implicit morals—using the characters they have read about or their own.
- They dramatize fables—modern, traditional, or their own—and create costumes, masks, movements, voices, and/or music that clearly shows the characteristics their character(s) represent.
- They consider the differences and similarities of themes among fables from different cultures and times in history.

16. Students and the teacher locate on a map and/or globe the places/cultures (depicted or of origin) in the books read in this chapter, including Greece (*City Mouse-*

Country Mouse and Two More Mouse Tales from Aesop (illustrated by Wallner and Parry), *The Boy Who Cried Wolf, Tales from Aesop, Three Aesop Fox Fables, Aesop's Fables, The Aesop for Children, Aesop's Fables Told in Verse, The Tortoise and the Hare: An Aesop Fable*, and *The Hare and the Tortoise* (Wildsmith); India (*Seven Blind Mice, The Blind Men and the Elephant, Once a Mouse . . .: A Fable Cut in Wood*, and *The Jatakas: Tales of India*); Africa (*Anansi Goes Fishing, Anansi Finds a Fool, Oh, Kojo! How Could You!*, and *Traveling to Tondo: A Tale of the Nkundo of Zaire*); Italy (*Fables of Leonardo da Vinci*); England (*Chanticleer and the Fox*); India, Russia, West Africa, Czechoslovakia, Armenia, Greece, Yurok Indian culture, Italy, Eskimo cultures, Germany, France, China, Muskogee Indian culture, and Kutchin Indian culture (*Feathers and Tails: Animal Fables Retold*); Denmark *The Ugly Duckling* and *The Emperor's New Clothes* (Westcott and Gross); Finland (*Mister King*); and China (*Everyone Knows What a Dragon Looks Like*).

TEACHER REFERENCE ═══

Cloze Sentences

MultiSyllable Words

Cloze Sentences 1

1. We like to <u>paddle</u> our boat across the lake at sunset.
2. His <u>cradle</u> is the bed that the baby likes best because it rocks.
3. If you <u>mumble</u> and do not speak clearly, I cannot understand what you are saying.
4. The <u>bugle</u> that she plays in the band is a small brass instrument like a trumpet.
5. The <u>bottle</u> of milk broke when I dropped it, and glass shattered all over the counter.
6. I <u>stumble</u> over rocks if I hike when I am tired.
7. A <u>fable</u> is a story that teaches a lesson and has animals that act like people.

Cloze Sentences 2

1. I collected a tiny smooth green <u>pebble</u> and five larger stones when I was at the beach.
2. We sat at a picnic <u>table</u> when we ate lunch at the park.
3. She grabbed the <u>handle</u> of the hammer and started to nail down the boards.
4. A <u>single</u> bed is made for comfortable sleeping for one person.
5. We put buckets on the <u>maple</u> trees in the spring to catch the sap, which we boil to make syrup.
6. A <u>puddle</u> is fun to splash in after a rainstorm.
7. The <u>stable</u> where the horses and cattle are kept is behind the barn.

Cloze Sentences 3

1. We lit a <u>candle</u> when the lights went out during the storm.
2. The <u>poodle</u> that we saw at the dog show had long curly hair.

3. The book that we need is in the <u>middle</u> of the shelf. Five books are on each side of it.

4. I had a <u>sample</u> of the cheese at the store to see if I like it before I got some.

5. We made <u>apple</u> pie when we got back from picking at the orchard.

6. A <u>simple</u> math problem is not hard to do.

Dictations

1. It was a <u>battle</u> for the toddler to be <u>able</u> to take a <u>couple</u> of <u>simple</u> steps. It was hard for us to <u>muffle</u> our <u>giggles</u> as we saw him <u>wobble</u>, <u>wiggle</u>, and <u>stumble</u> and then <u>topple</u> over. When he got tired, we did not see him cry or even <u>sniffle</u>! We saw him just <u>guzzle</u> milk from his <u>bottle</u> with the rubber <u>nipple</u>, <u>cuddle</u> up with his <u>rattle</u>, and fall asleep under the <u>table</u>.

2. It is not a <u>simple</u> matter for us to feed the <u>cattle</u> and horses after they <u>stumble</u> into the <u>stable</u> at the end of the day. A tired and hungry cow or horse can <u>trample</u> a person, so it is important to be <u>nimble</u> to be <u>able</u> to <u>handle</u> them. A <u>simple</u> <u>bridle</u> may be <u>ample</u> to <u>handle</u> a <u>single</u> horse without a <u>struggle</u>, but we do not get in the <u>middle</u> of a <u>tangle</u> of horses. It is too much of a <u>gamble</u>!

3. It is fun to <u>amble</u> over to the zoo to see the <u>nimble</u> monkeys from the <u>jungle</u> as they <u>dangle</u> from the branches and <u>tumble</u> together as they play. They are never <u>idle</u>. It is <u>impossible</u> to <u>stifle</u> our <u>giggles</u> as they jump <u>hurdles</u>, <u>babble</u> back and forth, and <u>gobble</u> their food.

consonant-le   fable

cand	app	bug
hand	bott	crad
mumb	midd	fab
samp	padd	map
simp	pebb	pood
sing	pudd	stab
stumb		tab

Name _____   Date _____

Word List 1

consonant-le   fable

candle	apple	bugle
handle	bottle	cradle
mumble	middle	fable
sample	paddle	maple
simple	pebble	poodle
single	puddle	stable
stumble		table

Name _____   Date _____

consonant-le   fable

Write a word from the Word List to complete each sentence.

1. We like to _____ our boat across the lake at sunset.

2. His _____ is the bed that the baby likes best because it rocks.

3. If you _____ and do not speak clearly, I cannot understand what you are saying.

4. The _____ that she plays in the band is a small brass instrument like a trumpet.

5. The _____ of milk broke when I dropped it, and glass shattered all over the counter.

6. I _____ over rocks if I hike when I am tired.

7. A _____ is a story that teaches a lesson and has animals that act like people.

Name _____ Date _____

Cloze Sentences 1

consonant-le   fable

Write a word from the Word List to complete each sentence.

1. I collected a tiny smooth green _____ and five larger stones when I was at the beach.

2. We sat at a picnic _____ when we ate lunch at the park.

3. She grabbed the _____ of the hammer and started to nail down the boards.

4. A _____ bed is made for comfortable sleeping for one person.

5. We put buckets on the _____ trees in the spring to catch the sap, which we boil to make syrup.

6. A _____ is fun to splash in after a rainstorm.

7. The _____ where the horses and cattle are kept is behind the barn.

Name _____ Date _____

Cloze Sentences 2

consonant-le   fable

Write a word from the Word List to complete each sentence.

1. We lit a _____ when the lights went out during the storm.

2. The _____ that we saw at the dog show had long curly hair.

3. The book that we need is in the _____ of the shelf. Five books are on each side of it.

4. I had a _____ of the cheese at the store to see if I like it before I got some.

5. We made _____ pie when we got back from picking at the orchard.

6. A _____ math problem is not hard to do.

Name _____ Date _____

30 tion immigration

BOOK LIST

Stories of Immigration

Watch the Stars Come Out, Riki Levinson, illustrated by Diane Goode (New York: E. P. Dutton, 1985). A little girl learns that she shares her great grandmother's traits—red hair, the love of a good story, and pleasure in watching the stars come out—as her grandmother tells the story her mother told of her immigration to the United States from Europe.

How Many Days to America?: A Thanksgiving Story, Eve Bunting, illustrated by Beth Peck (New York: Clarion Books, 1988). A family with two young children flees their village filled with soldiers in the Caribbean aboard a small fishing boat and arrives in time to celebrate Thanksgiving in the United States.

I Hate English!, Ellen Levine, illustrated by Steve Bjorkman (New York: Scholastic, 1989). Mei Mei's family moves from Hong Kong to New York City's Chinatown, and although she understands English, Mei Mei resists speaking it until her sensitive teacher discovers a way to help her want to speak the new language.

Molly's Pilgrim, Barbara Cohen, illustrated by Michael J. Deraney (New York: Bantam Doubleday Dell Publishing Group, Inc., 1983). Molly, who has recently immigrated with her family to the United States from Russia, is ridiculed at school because of her language, accent, and clothes until she learns about pilgrims and Thanksgiving in the United States, and she and her mother teach her classmates and teacher a new meaning for the word *pilgrim* when her mother makes a pilgrim doll—one that looks just like she did as a girl in Russia.

The Long Way to a New Land, Joan Sandin (New York: Harper & Row, 1981). Invited to join his uncle's family in America when drought causes famine in Sweden, Carl Erik's family immigrates by boat to the United States in 1868. A map at the beginning of the book shows their journey.

The Long Way Westward, Joan Sandin (New York: Harper & Row, 1989). This book continues the story of Carl Erik's family (from ***The Long Way to a New Land*** by the same author), emigrants from Sweden to the United States, as they leave New York City and travel west in "emigrant train cars" to Minnesota to join Carl Erik's uncle and his family. A map at the beginning of the book records their journey.

Pettranella, Betty Waterton, illustrated by Ann Blades (Toronto, Ontario: Douglas & McIntyre Ltd., 1980). When her family immigrates to Canada, Pettranella promises her grandmother, who stays behind, that she will plant the seeds her grandmother gives her when they get to their new home.

Penny and the Four Questions, Nancy E. Krulik, illustrated by Marina Young (New York: Scholastic, 1993). Penny learns about friendship when she shares the reading of the four questions at their Passover Seder and the *afikomen* and gift with a girl who has recently immigrated to the United States from Russia.

The Keeping Quilt, Patricia Polacco (New York: Simon & Schuster, 1988). The author tells and illustrates the story of a quilt made from clothing of family members who immigrated with her great grandmother to New York City from Russia and that has been a central part of her family's daily life and celebrations and passed from mother to daughter for four generations.

An Ellis Island Christmas, Maxinne Rhea Leighton, illustrated by Dennis Nolan (New York: Viking, 1992). With their mother, Krysia and her two brothers leave Poland and travel by steamship to join their father (who had gone ahead to find and prepare a home) in the United States and arrive at Ellis Island on Christmas Eve.

My Grandmother's Journey, John Cech, illustrated by Sharon McGinley-Nally (New York: Bradbury Press, 1991). Korie's grandmother tells her stories about meeting gypsies and surviving the revolution and civil war in her village in Germany, giving birth to Korie's mother while hiding during World War II, and immigrating to the United States.

Immigrant Girl: Becky of Eldridge Street, Brett Harvey, illustrated by Deborah Kogan Ray (New York: Holiday House, 1987). Ten-year-old Becky tells about the busy life and traditions of her family on the East Side of New York City in 1910, who have recently immigrated from Russia to escape the organized massacres of the Jewish people. A glossary contains pronunciations and definitions of Yiddish words used in the text.

MOTIVATION AND EXTENSION ACTIVITIES

NOTE: When studying and discussing immigration, one needs to be sensitive to individual differences, needs, and life experience. For personal reasons, it may be difficult for some students and teachers to discuss family or to obtain the information that would enable them to participate in many of the following activities. The teacher needs to be sensitive to and aware of these factors when planning the unit, before suggesting activities, and as they read and share books.

1. The words *immigrant* and *emigrant* are easily confused. An immigrant is a person who comes into a new country, culture, or region to live or settle there. An emigrant is a person who leaves or exits from one country, culture, or region to live or settle in another. The "Introduction" and "New Beginnings" sections of "Behind the Scenes" in the Reading Rainbow special edition of *Watch the Stars Come Out* (see Activity 2 in this chapter) and the author's note at the end of *The Long Way Westward* provide clear explanations of the terms.

Students and the teacher discuss the words and the concepts they represent at the beginning of the unit. (For students who need a mnemonic device to remember the terms, the teacher points out that *immigrant* and *into* and *emigrant* and *exit*, in the explanation in the preceding paragraph, begin with the same letters.)

2. Reading Rainbow Library has produced a special edition of **Watch the Stars Come Out** written by Marsha Cohen, MaryAnn Gray, and Barbara A. McCall and illustrated by Kris Nielsen (New York: Reading Rainbow Gazette, Inc., 1987). It contains the full text and illustrations of the book, "Behind the Scenes" background information, and suggested activities to accompany the book.

Students and the teacher explore and discuss the background information and complete selected activities from the special edition after they share **Watch the Stars Come Out**. They use critical thinking and evaluative skills to evaluate the accuracy or current validity of some of the information presented in the special edition.

* On page 38, the culture of the United States (which is called America—a term that represents North, Central, and South America, not solely the United States) is described with the "melting pot" metaphor, which emphasizes the blending of cultural and ethnic identity in a more uniform culture. A metaphor that many people prefer is a "salad bowl" metaphor, which emphasizes preservation of the integrity and separateness of cultural and ethnic identity within a diverse culture.

* Students and the teacher consider the statement made on page 39—"After all, we are all immigrants—the only difference is *when* our families first landed on American shores"—in light of the experiences of many people in the United States—the Native Americans.

* They discuss the cultural bias and ethnocentrism implicit in the presentation of Thanksgiving in the "Pilgrims Were Immigrants" section (pages 35 and 36) from the European settlers' point of view only, especially the statement "Today, we share the Pilgrims' early feelings of gratitude by setting aside a day to remember these settlers." Not only does this statement omit recognition of Native Americans' experiences of the first Thanksgiving in the United States referred to in this section and mentioned briefly earlier in the passage, but it also makes a statement about a "we" that disregards the experiences and feelings of Native Americans and other people who do not feel that same sentiment about Thanksgiving.

* They read the rest of the special edition section carefully and look for other examples to evaluate critically.

3. A unit on immigration lends itself to map and time-line activities. Students and the teacher create a large map and time line wall/bulletin board display (or add to one they have been developing for other units of study) and locate in time and space each book they read and share. They draw a picture that represents the main idea or an important or exciting event in each book or photocopy the cover and connect it to the date and places (of origin/departure and destination/arrival) with strings and tacks or push-pins.

4. Students may have immigrated to their current country/culture, and some, recently. Others may have friends or family who have done so. They share their experiences as they read and discuss the books in the unit. They compare and contrast their experiences and feelings (or those of people they know) with those of characters in the books.

5. During the unit, students and the teacher collect and bring in to share informa-

tion and artifacts or special objects that relate to their own family history (or that of friends). They do the following:

- Make a family tree that shows as many generations of family on maternal and paternal sides as possible.
- Make a map that shows routes of immigration of members of their family and indicates places of origin/departure and destination/arrival or shows where generations of family have always lived if they are native to a location.
- Construct a time line that shows important dates in their own life and in their family's history.
- Compile the information they have collected for the preceding three activities of this Activity on a group map and time line (See Activity 3 in this chapter.)
- Trace the history of last and first names of family members to discover whether any were changed if/when family members immigrated to their current country/ culture.
- Bring in or make models/drawings of artifacts or special items from their countries/ cultures of origin: photographs, clothing/costumes, coins, stamps, flags (or pictures of flags), postcards, and so on.
- Interview family members or friends about their memories of past events and family/ community history (including experiences they may have had or heard about) and record their stories on audio and/or videotape (and transcribe or take notes).
- Take the role of a person from the past (family or community member or friend) and have a partner interview them in front of an audio and/or videorecorder.
- Prepare and share food(s) from their countries/cultures of origin.
- Teach games from their countries/cultures of origin.
- Share about traditions, celebrations, holidays, or interesting facts about their countries/cultures of origin.
- Teach some words from the language of their countries/cultures of origin.
- Tell and/or write and illustrate a story from the point of view of a family or community member or friend from the past: in her/his country/culture or origin, while immigrating, when arriving in the new country/culture, when settling in the new country/culture.
- Dramatize (as actor or puppeteer) the story in the preceding activity.
- Play and/or teach a song or music from their countries/cultures of origin.
- Do and/or teach a dance/movements from their countries/cultures of origin.
- Draw and/or paint or construct pictures or three-dimensional habitats of their countries/cultures of origin that include native vegetation and animals.
- Tell and/or dramatize (as actor or puppeteer) a traditional folk tale, joke, riddle, or proverb from their countries/cultures of origin.

6. Students and teachers may have had to learn a language different from the language of their countries/cultures of origin. They share (tell and/or write and illustrate) their experiences learning a new language and compare and contrast their experiences and Mei Mei's in *I Hate English!*. They discuss whether someone (or something) like

the teacher, Nancy, in the book made the process easier. They share how it felt at the beginning and how it is now to adjust to a new and unfamiliar language, environment, and culture.

7. *Before* they read (or listen to) **Molly's Pilgrim**, students make a pilgrim doll out of clothespins, as Molly's mother and the students in her class do in the book. They discuss the word *pilgrim* before they read or talk about the book and record a list of definitions/phrases that describe a pilgrim. After they read **Molly's Pilgrim**, they discuss the word *pilgrim* again, make changes in and/or add to their definitions, and discuss the process they have just shared. They discuss any experiences they (or people they know who are immigrants to a new country) have had that are similar to Molly's and/or her mother's. They discuss Thanksgiving as traditionally celebrated in the United States from the point of view of the European settlers and consider the event from the points of view of Native Americans or people from other cultures. Students and the teacher read and discuss other books that present diverse experiences with Thanksgiving in the United States including **How Many Days to America?: A Thanksgiving Story**.

8. As they read (or listen to) **Molly's Pilgrim** and/or **Immigrant Girl: Becky of Eldridge Street**, students and teachers who do not understand or speak Yiddish (the language of Jewish people in Eastern Europe) make predictions about the meaning of the Yiddish words with which they may be unfamiliar. They confirm or correct their hypotheses by reading on in the story and by consulting students, teachers, or friends/family who do understand and speak Yiddish (or the glossary in the back of **Immigrant Girl: Becky of Eldridge Street**, which contains pronunciations and definitions of the Yiddish words in that book).

9. There is a film version of **Molly's Pilgrim**. Students and the teacher view the film and compare and contrast the story presented in two media.

10. While Carl Erik's family was living in Sweden, they received a letter from his Uncle Axel and cousin Anna Stina that described their new life and America (the United States) and encouraged them to join their family (**The Long Way to a New Land**). Students and the teacher write a letter (or letters) to Uncle Axel or Anna Stina from the point of view of Carl Erik that tells about their journey from Sweden to Anoka, Minnesota, where they are finally reunited with them (which is described in **The Long Way to a New Land** and in its sequel, **The Long Way Westward**).

11. Students and/or teachers who have immigrated from another country or culture (or know someone who has) share (tell and/or write and illustrate) about something they were given from their previous home to take to their new one, like the seeds that Pettranella's grandmother gave her to take to Canada in **Pettranella**.

12. Penny's new friend, Natasha, in **Penny and the Four Questions** brought a nesting doll from Russia when she immigrated with her family to the United States, and Krysia and her mother in **An Ellis Island Christmas** brought her two dolls with them from Poland. The teacher or students show nesting dolls or toys like Natasha's, and those who have immigrated (or know people who have) share dolls, toys, games, or other special items that they were able to bring from their previous home country or culture.

13. It was often difficult to leave family and friends behind when people left their countries of origin to immigrate to a new country/culture. Characters in many of the books in this unit express the difficulty of this reality. In addition, people could not always take with them all of the special and important things from their homes to their new homes when they emigrated. The childrens' mother in **How Many Days to America?: A Thanksgiving Story**, for example, finds it difficult but necessary to leave

behind her chair and bedcover. Krysia, in **An Ellis Island Christmas**, believes that she is leaving behind the larger of her two treasured dolls.

Students and the teacher discuss the feelings expressed by friends and family/community members, shown by the characters in books, and that they have felt themselves (if they have been in a similar situation) when forced to leave loved ones or treasured items behind when leaving one country/culture for another.

14. Penny and her family, in **Penny and the Four Questions**, share Passover Seder with Natasha's family, and Becky and her family, in **Immigrant Girl: Becky of Eldridge Street**, share their first Passover Seder on the East Side of New York with family and friends. Students and teachers who share Passover Seder with their family and/or friends share (tell and/or write and illustrate) about their experiences. Those who share other celebrations, traditions, and/or holidays from their countries/cultures of origin tell and/or write about and illustrate or create a three-dimensional model of them.

15. Like countless other immigrants, Krysia, in **An Ellis Island Christmas**, first sees the Statue of Liberty on the New York City skyline as she approaches the United States for the first time and enters the new country through Ellis Island. Students or teachers who have visited the Statue of Liberty and/or Ellis Island share (tell and/or write and illustrate) about their experiences and bring in photographs, postcards, and other related items of interest. They share stories they may have heard from family/community members or friends about the Statue of Liberty or Ellis Island, especially those related to immigration.

16. Students and the teacher locate on a map and/or globe the places/cultures (depicted or of origin) in the books read in this chapter, including New York City in the United States and Europe (**Watch the Stars Come Out**); Caribbean islands (**How Many Days to America?: A Thanksgiving Story**; Hong Kong in China and Chinatown in New York City in the United States (**I Hate English!**); Russia (**Molly's Pilgrim**); Gothenbury in Sweden, Hull and Liverpool in England, and New York City in the United States (**The Long Way to a New Land**); New York City in New York, Philadelphia and Pittsburgh in Pennsylvania, Crestline in Ohio, Fort Wayne in Indiana, Chicago in Illinois, LaCrosse in Wisconsin, and St. Paul and Anoka in Minnesota in the United States (**The Long Way Westward**); Manitoba in Canada (**Pettranella**); Russia (**Penny and the Four Questions** and **The Keeping Quilt**); Poland and Ellis Island in New York City in the United States (**An Ellis Island Christmas**); Germany (**My Grandmother's Journey**); and Grodno in Russia and the East Side of New York City in the United States (**Immigrant Girl: Becky of Eldridge Street**).

TEACHER REFERENCE ═══

Cloze Sentences

Multisyllable Words

Cloze Sentences 1

1. The <u>motion</u> of the ship made us seasick.

2. The winner of the <u>election</u> won by more than a thousand votes.

3. At the <u>auction</u> I offered the most money and had the highest bid for the table, so it was sold to me.

4. You may locate the <u>information</u> you need in a dictionary because it lists a number of facts.
5. After our <u>conversation</u> I understood you better, so I am glad that we talked.
6. My cat shows <u>affection</u> when she purrs and rubs against my leg.
7. There was <u>construction</u> on the road, so I had to take a detour on my way home to avoid the spots that were torn up.

Cloze Sentences 2

1. The <u>introduction</u> to the book gave me the background information I needed as I began to read it.
2. I have a <u>collection</u> of stamps and coins from all over the world.
3. The <u>direction</u> of the wind shown by the weather vane today is west.
4. Workers are nearing <u>completion</u> of the school addition, and when it is completely done we can move back into the building.
5. It is hard to make a <u>selection</u> at a restaurant when there are a lot of meals to choose from on the menu.
6. I put <u>lotion</u> on my sunburn and it helped heal my skin while it lessened the pain.

Cloze Sentences 3

1. We waited at the railroad <u>station</u> for the train to arrive.
2. The <u>invitation</u> included the time and location of the party.
3. <u>Emotion</u> can be a strong feeling like fear, happiness, or sadness.
4. During our <u>vacation</u> every year, we travel and visit members of our family.
5. <u>Immigration</u> involves leaving one location to live in another.
6. <u>Protection</u> from crime is provided by policemen and women.

Dictations

1. After the <u>completion</u> of the <u>election</u>, there was a lot of <u>emotion</u>. A <u>collection</u> of supporters was on hand at the <u>station</u> to meet the winner, show her their <u>affection</u>, and give their <u>congratulations</u>. During a <u>conversation</u> at the <u>station</u>, she made an <u>invitation</u> to them to attend her victory party. The <u>invitation</u> included <u>information</u> about the party's <u>location</u> with <u>directions</u>.

2. <u>Cooperation</u> among fire fighters and police provided temporary <u>protection</u> at their <u>stations</u> for those who escaped the fire, which caused the <u>destruction</u> of a number of apartments. It was a time of much <u>emotion</u> and <u>exhaustion</u> as, in the midst of the <u>commotion</u>, <u>information</u> and <u>directions</u> were given to the people left without homes. <u>Collection</u> and <u>distribution</u> of food and clothing may be the <u>solution</u> to a <u>fraction</u> of the needs, but after <u>consumption</u> of the <u>rations</u> more <u>action</u> will be needed in <u>connection</u> with the fire victims. Some may respond to <u>invitations</u> from <u>relations</u> in other <u>sections</u> of town to stay with them, but there will still remain the need for <u>location</u> of homes for the others.

tion (shun) immigration

affec	informa
auc	introduc
collec	invita
comple	lo
construc	mo
conversa	protec
direc	selec
elec	sta
emo	vaca
immigra	

Name _____ Date _____

Word List 1

tion   (shun)   immigration

affection	information
auction	introduction
collection	invitation
completion	lotion
construction	motion
conversation	protection
direction	selection
election	station
emotion	vacation
immigration	

Name _____ Date _____

tion (shun) immigration

Write a word from the Word List to complete each sentence.

1. The _____ of the ship made us seasick.

2. The winner of the _____ won by more than a thousand votes.

3. At the _____ I offered the most money and had the highest bid for the table, so it was sold to me.

4. You may locate the _____ you need in a dictionary because it lists a number of facts.

5. After our _____ I understood you better, so I am glad that we talked.

6. My cat shows _____ when she purrs and rubs against my leg.

7. There was _____ on the road, so I had to take a detour on my way home to avoid the spots that were torn up.

Name _____ Date _____

Cloze Sentences 1

tion   (shun)   immigration

Write a word from the Word List to complete each sentence.

1. The _____ to the book gave me the background information
   I needed as I began to read it.

2. I have a _____ of stamps and coins from all over the world.

3. The _____ of the wind shown by the weather vane today
   is west.

4. Workers are nearing _____ of the school addition, and
   when it is completely done we can move back into the building.

5. It is hard to make a _____ at a restaurant when there are
   a lot of meals to choose from on the menu.

6. I put _____ on my sunburn and it helped heal my skin
   while it lessened the pain.

Name _____ Date _____

© 1995 by Cynthia Conway Waring

Cloze Sentences 2

tion (shun) immigration

Write a word from the Word List to complete each sentence.

1. We waited at the railroad _____ for the train to arrive.

2. The _____ included the time and location of the party.

3. _____ can be a strong feeling like fear, happiness, or sadness.

4. During our _____ every year, we travel and visit members of our family.

5. _____ involves leaving one location to live in another.

6. _____ from crime is provided by policemen and women.

Name _____ Date _____

Cloze Sentences 3

31 g George magic stingy

BOOK LIST ═══

George and Martha

George and Martha: Five Stories about Two Great Friends, James Marshall (New York: Scholastic, 1972). This first book in the series introduces the friendship of two hippopotamuses, George and Martha, as they discover each other's likes, dislikes, and habits and they cheer each other on through some misadventures.

George and Martha Encore: More Stories about Two Great Chums, James Marshall (Boston: Houghton Mifflin Company, 1973). The two hippo friends expand their horizons and enrich their friendship as they dance, study French, wear disguises, disagree about sunburns, and share consolation over a disappointing garden.

George and Martha Rise and Shine: About Two Fine Friends, James Marshall (New York: The Trumpet Club, 1976). Hippos George and Martha learn more about each other in this collection of five stories as they show their fears, hobbies, and stubborn sides and as George celebrates all of Martha as president of the "Martha Fan Club."

George and Martha One Fine Day: Five Stories about Two Best Friends, James Marshall (Boston: Houghton Mifflin Company, 1978). George and Martha, hippo friends, cheer each other on and irritate each other in five short stories about their friendship.

George and Martha Tons of Fun: Five Stories about the Best of Friends, James Marshall (Boston: Houghton Mifflin Company, 1980). In this collection of five stories, hippos George and Martha get angry, get sick, get a funny picture taken, get hypnotized, get caught stealing cookies from the cookie jar, and get a birthday gift.

George and Martha Back in Town: Five Stories about Two Dear Friends, James Marshall (New York: The Trumpet Club, 1984). George and Martha know each other well enough to tease each other, help each other save face, trick each other, get angry at each other, and forgive each other.

George and Martha Round and Round: Five Stories about the Best of Friends, James Marshall (Boston: Houghton Mifflin Company, 1988). The familiar hippos share a range of activities, mishaps, and emotions; but, as always, they forgive each other in time to celebrate their friendship at the book's end.

The Magic Fish, Freya Littledale, illustrated by Winslow Pinney Pels (New York: Scholastic, 1966, 1985). When a poor fisherman puts back a fish he caught who is really a prince, his wife greedily demands more and more wishes for wealth and power until the fish sends her and the fisherman back to their original life in an old hut.

Peter and the North Wind: Retold from the Norse Tale The Lad Who Went to the North Wind, Freya Littledale, illustrated by Tory Howell (New York: Scholastic, 1971, 1988). After it blows their flour away, Peter goes to the North Wind to get it back and receives a magic cloth that gives food, a magic goat that makes gold, and a magic stick that hits at command and protects him from an innkeeper who tries to steal Peter's magic objects.

The Elves and the Shoemaker, Freya Littledale, illustrated by Brinton Turkle (New York: Scholastic, 1975). A poor shoemaker and his wife receive good fortune when, by magic, two elves make shoes to be sold in their shop, and they repay the gift by making clothes and shoes for the elves.

Anansi and the Moss-Covered Rock, Eric A. Kimmel, illustrated by Janet Stevens (New York: Scholastic, 1988). In this trickster tale, with the help of a magic moss-covered rock, lazy but cunning Anansi the Spider tricks all of the animals in the forest out of their food until Little Bush Deer, who's been watching all the time, turns the tables and teaches Anansi a lesson.

The Magic Tree: A Tale from the Congo, Gerald McDermott (New York: Penguin Books, 1973). A rejected twin brother leaves his unloving mother and finds a magic tree that fulfills all of his emotional and material wishes as long as he keeps their source a secret. He is happy until he is drawn back home, brags of his good fortune, reveals his secret, and loses all.

The Stone-Cutter: A Japanese Folk Tale, Gerald McDermott (New York: Penguin Books, 1975). A humble stonecutter's contentment as he cuts rock from a mountain pleases a magic spirit, who grants him wish after wish for increasing power. He becomes prince, sun, cloud, and mountain—a mountain being cut by a humble stonecutter—and there he remains, no longer watched over by the spirit.

Oh, Kojo! How Could You!: An Ashanti Tale, Verna Aardema, illustrated by Marc Brown (New York: The Trumpet Club, 1984). Lazy Anansi, the old man, tricks lazy Kojo, the young man, into trading gold for a dog, cat, and dove, who appear useless; but they prove their value when they enable Kojo to receive, and later regain, a magic ring as a reward for an act of kindness. This *pourquoi* and trickster tale tells why the Ashanti people treat their cats better than their dogs.

The Whale's Song, Dyan Sheldon, illustrated by Gary Blythe (New York: Scholastic, 1990). Lilly learns about the magic of the whales in her grandmother's lap, and she dreams, offers her gift into the sea, and waits. One night, by moonlight, the whales return a gift: They call her name.

Strega Nona: An Old Tale, Tomie dePaola (Englewood Cliffs, N.J.: Prentice-Hall Inc., 1975). After Strega Nona leaves and tells Big Anthony not to touch her pasta pot, he uses her magic chant to make it start making pasta but can't remember exactly how to make it stop. Pasta overflows the pot and house and fills the town until Strega Nona returns, stops the pot, and comes up with a perfect solution. She gives Big Anthony a fork! Caldecott Honor Book.

Strega Nona's Magic Lessons, Tomie dePaola (New York: Scholastic, 1982). Big Anthony disguises himself as Antonia so that Strega Nona will teach him her magic, but she teaches him a lesson instead.

Sylvester and the Magic Pebble, William Steig (New York: Scholastic, 1969). One summer day, Sylvester the donkey discovers a magic wish-granting pebble and, in his haste to escape a lion, foolishly wishes he were a rock. He remains a rock until the next spring, when his parents picnic by the rock, find the pebble, and wish he were there with them. Caldecott Award Book.

Magical Hands, Marjorie Barker, illustrated by Yoshi (Saxonville, Mass.: Picture Book Studio, 1989). Before he goes to work making barrels, William, the cooper, gives his three friends their wishes—to have their chores done for them by "magic" on their birthdays— and William's "magical hands" do not go unrewarded on his own birthday.

Dragon Kite of the Autumn Moon, Valerie Reddix, illustrated by Jean and Mou-sien Tseng (New York: Lothrop, Lee & Shepard Books, 1991). By Chinese tradition, each year Grandfather and Tad-Tin make and fly a kite and cut its string to release their troubles on Kite Day, but this year, with Grandfather seriously ill and unable to help him make a kite, Tad-Tin chooses to fly and release his special dragon kite, made by Grandfather to celebrate Tad-Tin's birth, and its magic touches and heals Grandfather.

Kenji and the Magic Geese, Ryerson Johnson, illustrated by Jean and Mou-sien Tseng (New York: Simon & Schuster Books for Young Readers, 1992). After rice crops are flooded in their town in Japan, Kenji brings magic and good fortune to his family when he flies their prized painting of geese on his kite.

The Magic Fish Rap, Bernice and Jon Chardiet, illustrated by Sam Viviano (New York: Scholastic, 1993). This is a contemporary rap version of the "Magic Fish" story, in which the fisherman's wife's greed for power and wealth demands more and more from the magic fish (whose life the fisherman saved), until the fish refuses to grant her wish and returns the fisherman and his wife to their original humble life and hut.

The Fisherman & His Wife, Jakob and Wilhelm Grimm, illustrated by John Howe (Mankato, Minn.: Creative Education Inc., 1983). The detail in the powerful illustrations that complement the text in this version of the "Magic Fish" story from the Grimm Brothers adds to the drama of this tale of greed and misuse of magic and wishes.

The Old Woman Who Lived in a Vinegar Bottle, Rumer Godden, illustrated by Mairi Hedderwick (London: Macmillan Children's Books, 1972). An old woman lives contentedly with her cat in their humble house (shaped like a vinegar bottle) until she spares the life of a magic fish. As the fish grants her wishes for increasing material possessions, she becomes more greedy and ungrateful, and he returns her to her old existence. When she realizes what she had become, she apologizes to the fish and, when offered return of all his gifts, asks for but one, which minimally changes her simple life.

Stingy

Stone Soup, Ann McGovern, illustrated by Winslow Pinney Pels (New York: Scholastic, 1968, 1986). A hungry traveler tricks a woman into making and serving him soup by asking for a stone and a series of food items to make it cook faster, smell and taste better, be fit for a king, and thicken.

Stone Soup: An Old Tale, Marcia Brown (New York: Charles Scribner's Sons, 1947). When the townspeople hear that three soldiers are coming, they hide their food, but the hungry and clever soldiers teach them how to make stone soup with just three round stones *and* their hidden food.

Stone Soup, John Warren Stewig, illustrated by Margot Tomes (New York: The Trumpet Club, 1991). Grethel leaves home to seek her fortune, arrives hungry in a village of stingy people who hide their food, and uses her magic stone—and a few additions from their food stores—to make enough soup for them all.

The Stingy Baker, Janet Greeson, illustrated by David LaRochelle (Minneapolis: Carolrhoda Books, Inc., 1990). In this *pourquoi* tale from the United States that explains one of the origins of the baker's dozen, a stingy baker learns generosity from a dissatisfied witch customer, who casts a spell on his shop and cookies, and from an angel, who breaks the spell.

MOTIVATION AND EXTENSION ACTIVITIES

George and Martha

1. Throughout the "George and Martha" unit, students and the teacher share (tell and/or write and illustrate) stories from their own experiences that are similar to those of the two hippo friends in the books. They share about special friendship(s) they have or have had.

2. As they read the "George and Martha" books, students and the teacher compile a list of words (adjectives) and phrases that describe George and another list that describes Martha. They discuss the ways in which they are alike and different and how dealing with differences and similarities works in friendships between/among friends. They share (tell and/or write and illustrate) about time(s) when they have celebrated their similarities or have had to deal with differences in their friends.

3. Before or after they read "Split Pea Soup" in ***George and Martha: Five Stories about Two Great Friends***, the teacher brings in split pea soup for students to try. Students and the teacher make a graph that shows how many people like and don't like split pea soup. Then everyone (who likes them) eats chocolate chip cookies, and they make a graph of how many people like and don't like chocolate chip cookies. They compare and contrast the graphs and propose reasons for the differences they observe.

4. In each of the stories in the "Magic" unit, characters are aided by a source outside themselves—by magic (supernatural spirits or powers or magic objects). This is a common motif or pattern in traditional literature. The drama of each story is the result of the character's response to the magical gift, and their destiny (and the ending of the story) is shaped by their choice. In some stories, a character is unselfish, thankful, wise, and humble, and all ends well; but in many stories characters are greedy, ungrateful, foolish, and boastful, and they lose all that they have gained.

Throughout the unit, students and the teacher discuss the motif of magic and individual character's response. They record books, as they read (or listen to) them, on two charts that have, as headings, character descriptions/response to magic (on the first chart: "Unselfish, Thankful, Wise, and Humble," and on the second chart "Greedy, Ungrateful, Foolish, and Boastful").

5. ***The Magic Tree: A Tale from the Congo*** was originally a film before McDermott made it into a book. Students and the teacher discuss the illustrations in the book and consider how its origin as a film influenced the artwork.

6. If weather, time, and resources permit, students and the teacher make and fly kites inspired by ***Dragon Kite of the Autumn Moon*** and ***Kenji and the Magic Geese***.

7. Audiotapes are available (from Scholastic) of two of the versions of the "Magic Fish" story suggested for this unit: ***The Magic Fish*** and ***The Magic Fish Rap***. After they read the books, students and the teacher listen to the tapes and compare and contrast the taped interpretations of the stories and their own interpretations, including the voices they assigned to the characters in the books. They move, clap, and/or stamp their feet to the rhythm as they join the tape in a second reading of ***The Magic Fish Rap***.

8. Winslow Pinney Pels illustrated ***The Magic Fish*** (in this chapter) and Gross's retelling of ***Hansel and Gretel*** (Activity 11 in Chapter 23, ou house). There are striking similarities (and differences) between the fisherman's wife and the stepmother, respectively. Students and the teacher compare and contrast the two characters as they are depicted in the text and illustrations. They generate a list of words (adjectives) and phrases that describe each character and note which characteristics/traits are similar and which are different.

9. Many of the stories in this chapter lend themselves to dramatization. Students—as actors or puppeteers—dramatize stories. They use what they know about the characters to differentiate voices and to read (or deliver) their parts with expression. (See Activities 7 and 8 in this chapter for activities related to ***The Magic Fish***.)

10. There is a remarkable difference in the illustrations and text in three of the versions of the "Magic Fish" story suggested for this unit: ***The Magic Fish, The Magic Fish Rap***, and ***The Fisherman & His Wife***. Students and the teacher compare and contrast the illustrations and text in the three books, choose their favorite, and give the criteria on which they based their selection.

11. There is a film version of the book ***The Fisherman & His Wife***. Students and the teacher view the film and compare and contrast the story presented in the two media.

12. As they read ***The Old Woman Who Lived in a Vinegar Bottle***, students and the teacher make predictions about what the old woman will wish for next and identify the clues they used to make their guesses. At the end of the third to last page, they stop at "except" and finish the story, telling which gift they think the old woman would want to keep and why. They read on (or listen to the rest of the book) to test their hypotheses.

13. In ***The Old Woman Who Lived in a Vinegar Bottle***, the once kind, generous, and polite old woman desires more and more and her appreciation, gratitude, and satisfaction decrease until the magic fish finally sends a greedy, ungrateful old woman back to her old existence. In the end, she realizes the errors of her ways and apologizes to the fish, who offers to give her back the material possessions, but she refuses all but a weekly hot meal to share with her cat and is happy once again with what she has.

Students and the teacher compare and contrast this story—particularly the ending—with the three other "Magic Fish" stories they have read: ***The Magic Fish, The Magic Fish Rap***, and ***The Fisherman & His Wife***. They compile three lists of words (adjectives) and phrases that describe the old woman (1) in the beginning of the story (kind, humble, unselfish, polite, generous, content, happy, and so on), (2) in the middle of the story (greedy, materialistic, boastful, bossy, "grabby", rude, pushy, "hoity toity", and so on), and (3) at the end of the story (apologetic, sorry, thankful, happy, content, humble). They note how the old woman's facial expressions in the illustrations change to reflect her attitude in the three sections of the book.

14. Several of the books in this unit center around a theme of greed and desire for power and material possessions. Rather than be content with themselves and their circumstances, characters seek identity, satisfaction, and/or recognition from external sources. Students tell and/or write a moral (lesson) for the books that incorporates the theme.

15. Five of the stories in this unit follow a similar story pattern: the four "Magic Fish" stories—***The Magic Fish, The Magic Fish Rap, The Fisherman & His Wife***, and ***The Old Woman Who Lived in a Vinegar Bottle***—and ***The Stone-Cutter: A Japanese Folk Tale***. In these stories, a series of events (resulting from the magical granting of wishes) elevate characters to positions of material wealth and power above their original circumstances; and, in the end, because of their greed the magical source retreats after leaving the character back where he or she began, with his or her original circumstances (or, in the case of Tasaku in ***The Stone-Cutter: A Japanese Folk Tale***, in a worse situation). Students and the teacher make a diagram of the story shape of these books.

Stingy

16. After they read the books suggested for this unit that feature stingy characters—***Stone Soup*** (McGovern, Brown, Stewig) and ***The Stingy Baker***—students and the teacher compile a list of words that mean the same or nearly the same as (synonyms) *stingy*, including *selfish, hoarding, cheap, penny-pinching, miserly, chintzy, greedy, grudging*, and *tight-fisted*. They generate a list of words that mean the opposite or nearly the opposite of (antonyms) *stingy*, including *generous, giving, charitable, helpful, considerate, hospitable, kind, thoughtful*, and *unselfish*. The teacher introduces or reviews the dictionary and the thesaurus as resource books.

16. Students and the teacher locate on a map and/or globe the places/cultures (depicted or of origin) in the books in this chapter, including Germany [***The Magic Fish, The Elves and the Shoemaker, The Magic Fish Rap, The Fisherman & His Wife***, and ***Hansel and Gretel*** (Gross)]; Norway (***Peter and the North Wind***); Africa (***Anansi and the Moss-Covered Rock***); the Congo (***The Magic Tree: A Tale from the Congo***); Japan (***The Stone-Cutter: A Japanese Folk Tale*** and ***Kenji and the Magic Geese***); Ashanti culture and Ghana on the west coast of Africa (***Oh, Kojo! How Could You!:***

An Ashanti Tale); world oceans (*The Whale's Song*); Italy (*Strega Nona: An Old Tale* and *Strega Nona's Magic Lessons*); Taiwan and China (*Dragon Kite of the Autumn Moon*); England (*The Old Woman Who Lived in a Vinegar Bottle*); and France (*Stone Soup: An Old Tale*).

TEACHER REFERENCE

Cloze Sentences

One-Syllable Words

Cloze Sentences 1

1. The <u>change</u> the clerk at the store gave me was two dimes.
2. We used the <u>gym</u> during the winter to practice basketball and to have our games.
3. The <u>stage</u> was filled with actors and actresses as they took bows after they performed the play.
4. The <u>gem</u> that I like best to wear in jewelry is the ruby.
5. A <u>huge</u> problem is so large that it is hard to solve.
6. A cotton <u>gin</u> is a tool used to take the seeds out of cotton.
7. <u>George</u> can be the first name of a boy or man, the nickname for Georgiana, or a last name for a man or a woman.
8. A person's <u>age</u> is how old he or she is.

Multisyllable Words

9. We were <u>gentle</u> with the tiny kitten—patting it softly and using only kind and low voices when we were near it.

Cloze Sentences 2

1. A <u>stingy</u> person spends the smallest amount of money possible and does not share with others.
2. Mothers and fathers protect their children from <u>danger</u> that might harm them.
3. <u>Magic</u> is used by witches and fairies to make things happen and to cast spells.
4. The <u>tragic</u> car crash caused us to feel very sad.
5. <u>Giants</u> in fairy tales are huge and powerful men and women.
6. After he took <u>gymnastics</u> for many years, the gymnast became a skilled acrobat.
7. We need to <u>digest</u> the food that we eat so that our body can use it.
8. <u>Hydrogen</u> is a colorless gas that combines with oxygen in water (H_2O).
9. The teacher asked us to leave a one-inch <u>margin</u> on both sides of our paper when we wrote our reports.

Dictations

1. After the <u>danger</u> of frost is past, I plant <u>cabbages</u> that I sell in late summer. They are simple to <u>digest</u> and very good in coleslaw. I delight in the <u>magic</u> of the <u>changes</u>

in the garden over the summer, and I <u>lounge</u> after the weeding is done. I don't make a <u>gigantic</u> <u>wage</u>, but gardening is a <u>gem</u> of a hobby that I like to <u>indulge</u> in!

2. <u>George</u> the <u>gymnast</u> was a <u>large</u>, <u>gentle</u> man with a wide <u>range</u> of skills. He had studied <u>gymnastics</u> in the <u>gym</u> starting at the <u>age</u> of five and had performed his <u>magic</u> on <u>stage</u> by the time he was nine. He had a <u>giant</u> following until a <u>tragic</u> fall during a <u>gymnastics</u> show put an end to his days on <u>stage</u>.

3. <u>Scrooge</u> was a miser who found out at an old <u>age</u> about the <u>tragic</u> results of being <u>stingy</u>. As he <u>aged</u>, the <u>gentle</u> man became hardened and more of a penny pincher, giving the smallest <u>wages</u> possible to the men he hired. Near the end of his life, visits by <u>magical</u> beings <u>changed</u> the <u>stingy</u> <u>Scrooge</u> into a <u>gem</u> of a man filled with <u>generosity</u>.

g (j) George magic stingy

e

a   dan r

chan   di st

   m   ntle

   orge   hydro n

hu

sta

                 i

n   ant

                     ma c

                     mar n

                     tra c

             y

m   mnastics

                     stin

Name _____ Date _____

Word List 1

g (j) George magic stingy

e

age   danger
change   digest
gem   gentle
George   hydrogen
huge
stage

i

gin   giant
                            magic
                            margin
                            tragic

y

gym   gymnastics
                            stingy

Name _____ Date _____

Word List 2

g   (j)   George   magic   stingy

Write a word from the Word List to complete each sentence.

1. The _____ the clerk at the store gave me was two dimes.

2. We used the _____ during the winter to practice basketball and to have our games.

3. The _____ was filled with actors and actresses as they took bows after they performed the play.

4. The _____ that I like best to wear in jewelry is the ruby.

5. A _____ problem is so large that it is hard to solve.

6. A cotton _____ is a tool used to take the seeds out of cotton.

7. _____ can be the first name of a boy or man, the nickname for Georgiana, or a last name for a man or a woman.

8. A person's _____ is how old he or she is.

9. We were _____ with the tiny kitten—patting it softly and using only kind and low voices when we were near it.

Name _____ Date _____

Cloze Sentences 1

g (j)   George   magic   stingy

Write a word from the Word List to complete each sentence.

1. A _____ person spends the smallest amount of money possible and does not share with others.

2. Mothers and fathers protect their children from _____ that might harm them.

3. _____ is used by witches and fairies to make things happen and to cast spells.

4. The _____ car crash caused us to feel very sad.

5. _____ in fairy tales are huge and powerful men and women.

6. After he took _____ for many years, the gymnast became a skilled acrobat.

7. We need to _____ the food that we eat so that our body can use it.

8. _____ is a colorless gas that combines with oxygen in water (H_2O).

9. The teacher asked us to leave a one-inch _____ on both sides of our paper when we wrote our reports.

Name _____ Date _____

© 1995 by Cynthia Conway Waring

Cloze Sentences 2

32   c   Frances

Cinderella   fancy

BOOK LIST

Frances the Badger Stories

A Bargain for Frances, Russell Hoban, illustrated by Lillian Hoban (New York: Harper & Row, 1970). Frances, the badger, and her friend Thelma learn about trust in friendship and about trading and making bargains through a difficult incident with a tea set that they both want.

Bedtime for Frances, Russell Hoban, illustrated by Garth Williams (New York: Harper & Row, 1960). In a series of episodes, little Frances the badger and her wise parents successfully deal with a common childhood fear—night noises and sights.

A Birthday for Frances, Russell Hoban, illustrated by Lillian Hoban (New York: Harper & Row, 1969). Birthdays are wonderful—unless they're your little sister Gloria's! Frances, the badger, struggles with jealousy and learns about giving.

Best Friends for Frances, Russell Hoban, illustrated by Lillian Hoban (New York: Harper & Row, 1969). After rejecting her little sister Gloria's invitation to play, Frances herself is shunned by her friend Albert. Frances learns that a sister can be a friend, too, and Albert learns to include girls in his circle of friends.

Bread and Jam for Frances, Russell Hoban, illustrated by Lillian Hoban (New York: Harper & Row, 1964). Frances decides that she wants to eat only bread and jam, and her wise parents allow her to do just that and give her an opportunity to discover for herself the value of variety.

A Baby Sister for Frances, Russell Hoban, illustrated by Lillian Hoban (New York: Harper & Row, 1964). When everything changes with the birth of her little sister Gloria, Frances, with the patient support of her parents, is able to work through her feelings of rejection and displacement. She returns from running away to the dining room having resolved her feelings and secure in her new role as big girl in the family.

Cinderella Stories

"Cinderumpelstiltskin: Or the Girl Who Really Blew It," in ***The Stinky Cheese Man and Other Fairly Stupid Tales***, Jon Scieszka, illustrated by Lane Smith (New York:

Viking, 1992). This book contains eleven humorous modern retellings of well-known traditional tales. In "Cinderumpelstiltskin: Or the Girl Who Really Blew It," the narrator interweaves elements of the "Cinderella" and "Rumpelstiltskin" stories into one silly tale, in which her stepsisters rename Cinderella "Cinderumpelstiltskin."

Walt Disney's Cinderella, Walt Disney Productions (New York: Random House, 1974). This book, from the movie, adds an industrious and creative mouse community who help Cinderella get ready for the ball, the fairy godmother's chant "Bibbidi Bobbidi Boo!", and the characters of the King and the Grand Duke to the familiar fairy tale.

Cinderella, Barbara Karlin, illustrated by James Marshall (New York: The Trumpet Club, 1989). Contemporary expressions, conversational language, and comical Marshall illustrations combine in this humorous retelling of the "Cinderella" story, in which her fairy godmother joins Cinderella, the prince, and her family to live in the palace.

Little Firefly: An Algonquian Legend, Terri Cohlene, illustrated by Charles Reasoner (Mahwah, N.J.: Watermill Press, 1990). Little Firefly—ridiculed, called "Little Burnt One," and made to do most of the work by her sisters—is led by her dead mother's voice in a dream to see and marry the great hunter, The Invisible One. Contains information about the Algonquian culture and maps, time line, photographs, drawings, and paintings.

The Rough-Face Girl, Rafe Martin, illustrated by David Shannon (New York: G. P. Putnam's Sons, 1992). Shannon's rich paintings complement Martin's retelling of the Algonquian "Cinderella" legend, in which the hard-working and scarred Rough-Face Girl, not her cruel older sisters, confidently succeeds in seeing and marrying the Invisible Being, who was hidden from all others.

Yeh-Shen: A Cinderella Story from China, Ai-Ling Louie, illustrated by Ed Young. Recorded more than 1000 years before the oldest Western variant, this version of the "Cinderella" story tells of an orphan girl, made to do the work by her stepmother and sister, who is visited by a kind old uncle and enabled to attend the Festival in beautiful clothes and golden shoes by the magic powers of the spirit of her pet fish, whom her stepmother kills. After the Festival, she reclaims one of her tiny shoes, lost in flight, and marries the king.

Mufaro's Beautiful Daughters: An African Tale, John Steptoe (New York: Scholastic, 1987). Two sisters, kind Nyasha and jealous, greedy, and bad-tempered Manyara, journey to be judged by the King as he chooses a wife. Nyasha acts kindly to those she meets on her way and discovers that they (and the garden snake she'd befriended at home) had been the King in disguise, who rewards her by marrying her and making her sister their servant. Caldecott Honor Book.

The Talking Eggs: A Folktale from the American South, Robert D. San Souci, illustrated by Jerry Pinkney (New York: Scholastic, 1989). Accustomed to being made to do all of the work by her mean older sister and mother, Blanche is rewarded for an act of kindness to an old woman, who takes her home, shows her strange and wondrous things, and gives her a gift of talking eggs that produce riches. Caldecott Honor Book.

Princess Furball, Charlotte Huck, illustrated by Anita Lobel (New York: Scholastic, 1989). A motherless princess escapes marriage to an Ogre planned by her father and uses the dresses that were in her dowry, soup herbs from the cook who raised her, and her mother's golden treasures to win the heart of the young king, who marries her.

Cinderella, Charles Perrault, retold by Amy Ehrlich, illustrated by Susan Jeffers (New York: Dial Books for Young Readers, 1985). Jeffers's paintings, occasionally presented as full two-page illustrations, capture the actions and emotions of the characters—principals and supporting—in Ehrlich's retelling of the classic tale of rags to riches.

Cinderella, Charles Perrault, translated and illustrated by Diane Goode (New York: Alfred A. Knopf, 1988). The soft colors and details of Goode's illustrations set this version of Perrault's "Cinderella" story in the place and time of its recording, in seventeenth-century France during the reign of King Louis XIV.

Cinderella: Or the Little Glass Slipper, translated from the French of Charles Perrault and illustrated by Marcia Brown (New York: Charles Scribner's Sons, 1954). Brown's Caldecott Award–winning illustrations accompany the more challenging vocabulary and text of her translation of Perrault's tale of justice and forgiveness. Caldecott Award Book.

Moss Gown, William H. Hooks, illustrated by Donald Carrick (New York: Clarion Books, 1987). Banished from the plantation home of her beloved father by her two cruel sisters, kind-hearted Candace is able to win the heart of a Young Master at the ball and later to be reunited with her father by the moss gown—magic only by starlight—given her by the mysterious witch woman. This tale is from the oral tradition of southern United States and contains elements of the "King Lear" and "Cinderella" stories.

Fancy Stories

Just Plain Fancy, Patricia Polacco (New York: Bantam Doubleday Dell Publishing Group, 1990). Naomi's wish for something fancy in their plain life in an Amish community is answered when she finds an unusual egg, and her fears about the reception her chick named "Fancy" will receive from the elders are unfounded because they are full of appreciation for "God's handiwork" when they see the peacock she's raised.

Hannah's Fancy Notions: A Story of Industrial New England, Pat Ross, illustrated by Bert Dodson (New York: The Penguin Group, 1988). At first, Hannah's father calls her idea of making a bandbox (hatbox), in which her sister can carry her clothes on the stagecoach on her way to her job at a mill, "fancy notions"—but making the boxes provides a steady enough income for their family that Hannah's sister can leave her factory job and live at home full time.

MOTIVATION AND EXTENSION ACTIVITIES

Frances the Badger Stories

1. Books in the "Frances" story series portray the challenges faced by children as they explore their relationships with family and friends and the world. Students and the

teacher share (tell and/or write and illustrate) stories from their own experiences that are similar to those of the characters in the "Frances" stories.

2. Frances's parents are depicted as exceptionally wise, sensitive, and supportive. Students and the teacher compare and contrast Frances's parents and parents in other books (some of whom are more sensitive and supportive than others), including *Little Fox Goes to the End of the World* by Tompert, *Mama, Do You Love Me?* by Joosse, and *The Runaway Bunny* by Brown (Chapter 3, open syllable go), *Alexander and the Terrible, Horrible, No Good, Very Bad Day* by Viorst (Chapter 7, ay day), *Peter's Chair* by Keats (Chapter 9, ow grow), *Little Bear* by Minarik (Chapter 19, ir birthday, and Chapter 28, ou soup), *Noisy Nora* by Wells (Chapter 25, oi noise), and *Mean Soup* by Everitt (Chapter 28, ou soup).

3. Frances often creates and sings songs that are an important part of the "Frances" stories. Students and the teacher make up their own tunes for Frances's songs as they read the books aloud.

4. Audiotapes are available (from Scholastic) of the "Frances" stories. After they read (or listen to) the books, students and the teacher listen to the tapes and compare and contrast the taped interpretations of the stories and their own interpretations. They consider the voices assigned to characters on the tapes and in their own readings and the tunes given the songs that Frances sings. (See Activity 3 in this chapter.)

5. Students and the teacher eat bread and jam before or after they read *Bread and Jam for Frances*.

Cinderella Stories

6. The books suggested for the "Cinderella" stories unit are but a few of hundreds of variants of the tale from different times in history and from cultures all around the world. Included are several authors' and illustrators' retellings and interpretations of perhaps the best-known variant, recorded by Charles Perrault in 1697 in France.

There are theories about why variants of tales exist. Some propose that a tale originates in a single culture and is carried by its storytellers to other places and cultures. Others believe that a story, like the "Cinderella" story, develops in different cultures independently as a reflection of universal themes of human experience and of common human needs (emotional, physical, psychological, and spiritual), desires, beliefs and values, relationships, strengths and weaknesses, and challenges and victories.

Throughout the unit, students and the teacher compare and contrast the variants of the "Cinderella" story represented by the suggested books.

- They discuss themes common to wonder or "fairy" tales: justice as good rewarded, the virtue of looking beyond external appearances to a person's inner qualities, and other themes they identify.

- They consider the typical characters in wonder or fairy tales: the fairies (and fairy godmothers) and other magical or supernatural characters for whom the stories were originally named, and the one-dimensional characters that represent the good in people and their opposites, which represent their evil or wicked qualities.

- They discuss the power of names or naming in traditional literature, including the negative connotations of Cinderella, Little Burnt One (*Little Firefly: An Algonquian Legend*), The Rough-Face Girl, Princess Furball, and Cinderbritches [*Cinderella* (Goode)]. They compare the negative names given to Cinderella with the names of respect that reflect their talents or gifts given to characters in stories in other units. (See Activity 8 in Chapter 24, oy boy.)

◆ They identify and discuss familiar sayings that reflect themes common to traditional wonder tales, such as "Goodness triumphs" or "Beauty is only skin deep," and they tell and/or write morals/sayings that reflect the themes. (Goode's version of Perrault's *Cinderella* has its own explicit moral after the story.)

◆ They consider similarities and differences in themes, motifs, plot (including endings), setting, characters, and other elements in these stories from different cultures and times in history.

◆ They identify elements in the tales that reflect the specific culture or place (depicted or of origin)—setting (including animals and vegetation), customs and values or beliefs, food, shelters, and so on.

◆ They note differences in writing styles and illustrations in the books.

◆ They collect, read, and share additional variants of the "Cinderella" story.

7. After they read *Walt Disney's Cinderella*, students and the teacher view the Disney film version and the film version of "Cinderella" from Faerie Tale Theatre (CBS/ Fox Video, Industrial Park Drive, Farmington Hills, Michigan 48024). They discuss the similarities and differences between the more popularized contemporary Disney interpretation and the traditional versions they have read, seen, and/or listened to.

8. San Souci frequently uses figurative language in his descriptions in *The Talking Eggs: A Folktale from the American South*. Students and the teacher identify and discuss the figurative language in the book and books in other units. (See Activity 18 in Chapter 2, oo moon, Activity 12 in Chapter 4, y fly, Activity 13 in Chapter 13, oa goat, Activities 12 and 13 in Chapter 16, ar star, Activity 10 in Chapter 22, ow owl, and Activity 12 in Chapter 29, consonant-le fable, for books and activities that feature figurative language.)

9. Obedient to the old woman's directions, Blanche in *The Talking Eggs: A Folktale from the American South* takes only the plain-looking eggs and passes by the beautiful gold and silver eggs decorated with jewels that she would have preferred, and she is rewarded with wealth and riches. Students and the teacher relate this part of the story to the theme of the importance of looking beyond a person's external appearance to their inner qualities common in traditional wonder or fairy tales, including those suggested for this unit.

10. An audiocassette tape recording of *Cinderella* (Goode) narrated by Jessica Lange is available to accompany the book. After they read (or listen to) the book, students and the teacher listen to the tape and compare and contrast the taped interpretation of the story and their own interpretation, including the voices with which they read the characters' parts.

Fancy Stories

11. At the beginning of the "Fancy" stories unit, students and the teacher offer and record what the word *fancy* means to them. Then they consult resource books, including a dictionary and a thesaurus, and they add definitions. As they read *Just Plain Fancy* and *Hannah's Fancy Notions: A Story of Industrial New England*, they discuss what *fancy* meant to different characters in the books.

12. Students may not be familiar with the time in history that encompasses the

industrial period of nineteenth-century New England depicted in **Hannah's Fancy Notions: A Story of Industrial New England**.

- They learn more about this period of time in the history of New England and the United States through resource books and materials.

- They add **Hannah's Fancy Notions: A Story of Industrial New England** to a time line they have developed as part of their study of literature.

- After they read the book, they read and discuss the information in an "About This Book" section at the end of the book about the origin of the story, hatboxes (or bandboxes), and young women working in factories and mills during this time.

13. Students and the teacher locate on a map and/or globe the places/cultures (depicted or of origin) in the books read in this chapter, including France [retellings of Perrault's "Cinderella" story: "Cinderumpelstiltskin" in **The Stinky Cheese Man and Other Fairly Stupid Tales**, **Walt Disney's Cinderella**, **Cinderella** (Karlin and Marshall), **Cinderella** (Ehrlich and Jeffers), **Cinderella** (Goode), and **Cinderella: Or the Little Glass Slipper** (Brown)]; Algonquian culture from the Great Lakes to the Atlantic Ocean in Canada and the United States (**Little Firefly: An Algonquian Legend** and **The Rough-Face Girl**); China (**Yeh-Shen: A Cinderella Story from China**); Zimbabwe and southern Africa (**Mufaro's Beautiful Daughters**); Creole culture and Louisiana in the southern United States (**The Talking Eggs**); eastern North Carolina and the southern United States (**Moss Gown**); Amish culture in Pennsylvania in the United States (**Just Plain Fancy**); and Lowell and Boston, Massachusetts in the United States (**Hannah's Fancy Notions: A Story of Industrial New England**).

TEACHER REFERENCE

Cloze Sentences

One-Syllable Words

Cloze Sentences 1

1. After I <u>slice</u> the bread, we can make ourselves a sandwich.
2. Outer <u>space</u> can be reached by rockets and other spacecraft.
3. A wooden <u>fence</u> around the garden keeps animals from getting into it.
4. A <u>cent</u> is another name for a penny.
5. <u>Mice</u> are small animals that my cat likes to chase and eat.
6. I can tell by the smile on your <u>face</u> that you are happy.
7. An <u>ice</u> cube in a glass keeps a drink cold.

Multisyllable Words

Cloze Sentences 2

1. <u>Icy</u> roads after the snowstorm made it difficult to drive.
2. I like to use a <u>pencil</u> when I write so that I can erase when I want to change something.
3. The <u>entrance</u> to the store was blocked, so we went in the back door.

4. <u>Cinderella</u> had to claim her lost glass slipper in order to marry the prince.
5. If you ask my <u>advice</u>, I will tell you what I think is best.
6. <u>Frances</u> the badger in books by Russell Hoban has a sister named Gloria.
7. If it is hard for you to <u>decide</u>, just take your time until you make your choice.

Cloze Sentences 3

1. The <u>cigar</u> that my grandfather is smoking was made from tobacco leaves grown near our home.
2. We drank cold <u>cider</u> that was made from the apples at the orchard.
3. We left the <u>city</u> and went to a small town that was much less crowded.
4. Eating the <u>spicy</u> food made our eyes water.
5. They wore their <u>fancy</u> clothes to the formal dance.
6. Flowered patterns in the <u>lacy</u> white curtains allowed sunlight to shine into the room.

Dictations

1. <u>Twice</u> <u>since</u> I spoke with you some <u>mice</u> have gotten under the <u>space</u> in the <u>cedar</u> <u>fence</u> near the <u>entrance</u> to my yard and have filled their <u>faces</u> with the <u>slices</u> of bread I put out for the birds. I need your <u>advice</u> about filling up the <u>space</u> in the <u>fence</u>. I cannot <u>decide</u> on a <u>decent</u> way to mend the <u>fence</u> that will <u>conceal</u> the patch. I do not want to <u>deface</u> the <u>fence</u> as I <u>displace</u> the <u>mice</u>!

2. We need your <u>advice</u> about <u>exciting</u> things to do in the <u>city</u>. <u>Since</u> it is the <u>chance</u> of a lifetime, we want to be near the <u>center</u> of activity. If it is <u>icy</u>, we will want a parking <u>space</u> by the <u>entrance</u> to the hotel, but we have to <u>face</u> it that it will cost more than a few <u>cents</u> for a good <u>space</u>. We cannot <u>decide</u> between a <u>fancy</u> restaurant and one that has <u>excellent</u> <u>spicy</u> food. I will take my <u>fancy</u> <u>lace</u> dress, and my husband will get himself a <u>decent</u> <u>cigar</u> to <u>celebrate</u>.

3. <u>Frances</u> <u>decided</u> to <u>celebrate</u> her graduation, so she invited her family to come to the <u>city</u> to <u>rejoice</u> with her. She had <u>celery</u> and other vegetables with dip, a <u>fancy</u> cake with <u>lacy</u> <u>icing</u>, and a <u>choice</u> of <u>cider</u> or a <u>spicy</u> punch with <u>ice</u>. At the end of the party, everyone stood in a <u>circle</u> at the <u>entrance</u> to her apartment and <u>embraced</u> <u>Frances</u> and lifted their <u>voices</u> to <u>celebrate</u> the <u>excellent</u> job she had done and the fine <u>choices</u> she had yet to make.

c   (s)   Frances

Cinderella   fancy

e

nt   advi
fa   entran
fen   Fran   s
i
mi
sli
spa

i

der
gar
nderella
ty
de   de
pen   l

y

fan
i
la
spi

Name _____ Date _____

c   (s)   Frances

Cinderella   fancy

e

cent   advice
face   entrance
fence   Frances
ice
mice
slice
space

i

cider
cigar
Cinderella
city
decide
pencil

y

fancy
icy
lacy
spicy

Name _____ Date _____

c   (s)   Frances

Cinderella   fancy

Write a word from the Word List to complete each sentence.

1. After I _____ the bread, we can make ourselves a sandwich.

2. Outer _____ can be reached by rockets and other space-craft.

3. A wooden _____ around the garden keeps animals from getting into it.

4. A _____ is another name for a penny.

5. _____ are small animals that my cat likes to chase and eat.

6. I can tell by the smile on your _____ that you are happy.

7. An _____ cube in a glass keeps a drink cold.

Name _____ Date _____

Cloze Sentences 1

c (s) Frances

Cinderella fancy

Write a word from the Word List to complete each sentence.

1. _____ roads after the snowstorm made it difficult to drive.

2. I like to use a _____ when I write so that I can erase when I want to change something.

3. The _____ to the store was blocked, so we went in the back door.

4. _____ had to claim her lost glass slipper in order to marry the prince.

5. If you ask my _____, I will tell you what I think is best.

6. _____ the badger in books by Russell Hoban has a sister named Gloria.

7. If it is hard for you to _____, just take your time until you make your choice.

Name _____ Date _____

c (s) Frances

Cinderella fancy

Write a word from the Word List to complete each sentence.

1. The _____ that my grandfather is smoking was made from tobacco leaves grown near our home.

2. We drank cold _____ that was made from the apples at the orchard.

3. We left the _____ and went to a small town that was much less crowded.

4. Eating the _____ food made our eyes water.

5. They wore their _____ clothes to the formal dance.

6. Flowered patterns in the _____ white curtains allowed sunlight to shine into the room.

Name _____ Date _____

Cloze Sentences 3

33   qu   quilt

Quilt Stories

The Josefina Story Quilt, Eleanor Coerr, illustrated by Bruce Degen (New York: Harper & Row, 1986). Pa is reluctant to let Faith take her old pet hen, Josefina, in their covered wagon as they travel west in 1850, and her misadventures nearly cause Josefina's demise, but she proves her worth along the way. Faith records their journey in a patchwork quilt.

The Quilt Story, Tony Johnston, illustrated by Tomie dePaola (New York: G. P. Putnam's Sons, 1985). When her family travels west in a covered wagon, the quilt Abigail's mother made provides a warm and comforting familiarity. Many years later, one of Abigail's young relatives discovers the quilt in the attic, and it accompanies her, too, to a new home.

Patchwork Tales, Susan L. Roth and Ruth Phang (New York: Atheneum, 1984). In this book, illustrated with colorful wood block prints, a little girl's grandmother tells her the stories represented by each block in her mother's patchwork sampler quilt, and she asks her grandmother to sew her stories into a quilt for her. Includes directions for a simple, doll-size cloth patchwork quilt.

Tar Beach, Faith Ringgold (New York: Scholastic, 1991). Ringgold's "Tar Beach" story quilt was adapted and combined with text and paintings in this book about Cassie's fantasy flight of the spirit amid the stars above New York City from the rooftop of her apartment building (Tar Beach).

Aunt Harriet's Underground Railroad in the Sky, Faith Ringgold (New York: Crown Publishers, Inc., 1992). Cassie and her brother Be Be (from *Tar Beach* by the same author) learn about slavery—and freedom—while flying aboard a fantasy train on the Underground Railroad, whose conductor is Harriet Tubman. Contains background information about Harriet Tubman and the Underground Railroad, including a short bibliography of further readings and a map of routes.

The Rag Coat, Lauren Mills (Boston: Little, Brown and Company, 1991). Children in a small Appalachian coal mining town learn the meaning of community when the Quilting Mothers make Minna a coat from their cloth rags so that she can attend school.

The Patchwork Quilt, Valerie Flournoy, illustrated by Jerry Pinkney (New York: Dial Books for Young Readers, 1985). Every day Tanya's beloved Grandma sits in her favorite chair sewing pieces of fabric and the stories of the lives of her family into a patchwork quilt, until she becomes ill. Then Tanya works on it until Grandma recovers and can finish it.

The Keeping Quilt, Patricia Polacco (New York: Simon & Schuster, 1988). The author tells and illustrates the story of a quilt made from clothing of family members who immigrated with her great grandmother to New York City from Russia and that has been a central part of her family's daily life and celebrations and passed from mother to daughter for four generations.

Sweet Clara and the Freedom Quilt, Deborah Hopkinson, illustrated by James Ransome (New York: Alfred A. Knopf, 1993). Aided by the quilt onto which she sews a map pattern of the Underground Railroad, Clara is reunited with her mother and sister and, with them and a friend, escapes to freedom.

MOTIVATION AND EXTENSION ACTIVITIES

1. People from cultures around the world create quilts and other pieces of fabric art that are beautiful to look at as well as functional and that preserve, for generations, family and community stories and folklore. Students and the teacher explore this art form.

- Bring in and share quilts that students/teacher, family/community members, or friends own and/or have made and tell about the history, stories, and lives they represent.
- Attend quilt exhibits at museums, historical societies, continuing education courses, and quilt supply stores.
- Learn more about quilts and quilting through visits by guest speakers/presenters and resource books and materials.

2. Students and the teacher extend their exploration of quilts by making their own quilts out of fabric and/or paper.

Fabric Quilts

- Make a quilt top from one large piece of fabric, on which students and the teacher draw pictures/designs with fabric crayons, pens, or markers.
- Piece fabric quilt tops (patchwork designs or crazy quilts) using scraps of cloth sewn together. (It is often helpful to plan the designs with geometric shapes on graph paper first.)
- Applique fabric designs onto a large piece of fabric.

Paper Quilts

- Cut out geometric shapes or designs from colored paper or from light-colored paper, which students and the teacher color with crayons, colored pencils, markers, or paints. They assemble the shapes or designs into an applique design, a patchwork pattern, or a crazy quilt and fasten (glue, paste) them onto a paper background.

- Cut out geometric shapes or designs from fabric and assemble them into an applique design, a patchwork pattern, or a crazy quilt and fasten (glue, paste) them onto a paper background.
- Use "Kid Pix" or other computer drawing and painting programs to create quilts and other fabric art designs from paper.

Students and the teacher read and follow directions for making fabric art designs on the computer in three chapters in *Kid Pix around the World: A Multicultural Computer Activity Book*, Barbara Chan (Reading, Mass.: Addison-Wesley Publishing Company, 1993), that describe traditional fabric arts from three different cultures. They read "Patchwork Quilts (United States)," which describes a paper patchwork crazy quilt, "Kinglist Cloth (Benin)," which describes paper applique cloths that tell stories with pictures and symbols, and "Good-Bye Cloth (Ghana)," which describes a pieced wall hanging made from several separate paper Good-Bye or Adinkra cloths made on the computer (traditionally made by applying dye on fabric using stamps made from calabash squashes). The book contains essays that provide background information about twenty cultures around the world and detailed, step-by-step instructions that show children how to do drawing and painting activities using "Kid Pix" computer software. Presented cultures are marked on a world map in the front of the book.

3. In *The Josefina Story Quilt*, Faith makes a patchwork quilt that records events from her family's journey west in the United States in a covered wagon in the mid-1800s. An author's note that follows the story provides additional information about travel by covered wagon and about quilts. Students and the teacher read and discuss the information from the author's note. They make a two-sided six-patch patchwork quilt design on paper that summarizes each of the six chapters of *The Josefina Story Quilt*—one patch for each chapter. They use a format similar to the following: In the six blocks on the left, they record the main idea of an exciting or important event from each chapter by drawing a picture. In the six blocks on the right (with the chapter titles written in them), they record the same information in a few words.

4. In *The Quilt Story*, Abigail is often comforted by the quilt her mother made for her, especially during their journey in a covered wagon to build a new house and life in the western United States. Years later, another little girl, a young relative of Abigail's, finds the quilt in an attic and, mended by her mother, it comforts her, too, during a move to a new house.

Students and the teacher share (tell and/or write and illustrate) their own experiences with moving to a new house. They tell whether something (or someone), like the familiar quilt in *The Quilt Story*, helped make the transition process easier. They read and discuss other books about characters leaving, moving from, or thinking about moving out of their homes. (See Activity 2 in Chapter 23, ou house, for a list of suggested books and activities.)

5. *The Josefina Story Quilt* and *The Quilt Story* are both about families with young children who journey west in the United States in a covered wagon. Students and the teacher compare and contrast the two books.

6. The stories of her first patchwork quilt square and her wedding and of her daughter's childhood that the grandmother tells her granddaughter in *Patchwork Tales* are represented by patchwork quilt squares in a sampler quilt. In some of the patches, the actual fabric from an event depicted is sewn into the patch. Students plan and/or create a quilt from paper or cloth that records important events or stories in their lives

or the lives of family members or friends. (See Activity 2 in this chapter for ideas for making simple quilts out of paper or cloth.)

7. The granddaughter in **Patchwork Tales** asks her grandmother to make her a sampler patchwork quilt that tells her stories. That would be quite an undertaking for a little girl. The book includes directions for a simple, doll-size cloth patchwork quilt that is a more realistic first quilting project. Students and the teacher follow the directions in the book to make the small cloth quilt.

8. Ringgold's **Tar Beach** book is based on a fabric story quilt with the same title that she finished in 1988 and is on display at the Guggenheim Museum in New York City. In the quilt, the words of the story (adapted for the book) are written on strips of fabric, which are part of the borders at the top and bottom of the quilt. Ringgold's illustrations for the book are acrylic paintings with borders that are photographs of blocks from the actual cloth quilt. After the story, the book contains a full-page color photograph of the quilt and information about Ringgold's life and art and about the quilt and book titled **Tar Beach**.

Students and the teacher read and discuss the background information about **Tar Beach** and its creator, discuss the themes and images it presents, and explore the artwork in the book and the cloth quilt and the ways in which they are related. (See Activity 2 in Chapter 4, y fly, for activities related to the theme of wishes and flying.)

9. The author and illustrator of **Aunt Harriet's Underground Railroad in the Sky**, Faith Ringgold, chose to end the book with a quilt—a quilt commemorating the hundredth anniversary of Harriet Tubman's first trip on the Underground Railroad. Students and the teacher discuss her choice of final illustration and consider what they have learned about Ringgold's life, the quiltmaking in her family, and her art.

10. In **The Rag Coat**, Minna's story quilt contains pieces of fabric that are part of the lives and important events of many of the people in her community, and, through sharing those stories, she connects with several children at school in a deeper way. But Minna's story quilt is not a bed covering. It is a coat, made for her by the Quilting Mothers after her father dies from the coal miner's cough so she can attend school during the cold months.

Students and the teacher think of and record as many different quilted products and uses for quilts as they can. They bring in and share examples of as many items on their list as possible. The list might include bed covers, coats, jackets, vests, pants, pocketbooks, change purses, eye glass cases, bookmarks, jewelry, hats, aprons, wall hangings, pillow tops, pot holders and mitts, hot pads, tea cozies, ornaments, baby bibs and clothing, and so on.

11. Each of the patches that Grandma in **The Patchwork Quilt** sews into a patch for the quilt comes from something worn or used by a member of her family. While she is sick, Tanya realizes that Grandma is missing from the quilt, and she cuts a piece of cloth from the old quilt on the bed where Grandma is sleeping and adds it to the quilt. The quilt in **The Keeping Quilt** is made from clothing of family members a century earlier and is part of making and keeping memories of the daily events and special celebrations of members of the author's family for four generations.

Students and the teacher make a class community quilt with at least one patch for every member. They make a quilt from paper or cloth (using the suggestions from Activity 2 of this chapter). If possible, each person brings in a scrap of cloth that represents an important story or event in their lives while part of the class community, or they draw a picture illustrating a memorable event of their time together. The teacher gives each student a photograph of himself or herself with the completed quilt at the end of their time together.

12. Students and the teacher locate on a map and/or globe the places/cultures (depicted or of origin) in the books read in this chapter, including Benin and Ghana in Africa ["Kinglist Cloth (Benin)" and "Good-Bye Cloth (Ghana)" in *Kid Pix around the World: A Multicultural Computer Activity Book*]; California and the plains and prairies of the western United States (*The Josefina Story Quilt* and *The Quilt Story*); New York City in the United States (*Tar Beach*); routes of the Underground Railroad (*Aunt Harriet's Underground Railroad in the Sky* and *Sweet Clara and the Freedom Quilt*); the Appalachian Mountain region in the United States (*The Rag Coat*); and Russia (*The Keeping Quilt*).

TEACHER REFERENCE

Cloze Sentences

One-Syllable Words

Cloze Sentences 1

1. We felt the <u>quake</u> of the ground beneath us as the volcano erupted.
2. Sometimes a person has to <u>quit</u> a job to start another one.
3. My dog got <u>quills</u> from a porcupine in his mouth, so we took him to the vet to have them removed.
4. It is important to be <u>quiet</u> in the library so that everyone can read and study.
5. A <u>quiz</u> is a short test.
6. If I <u>quote</u> a person, I repeat the words that he or she said.

Cloze Sentences 2

1. We made a <u>quilt</u> to cover my bed using scraps of cloth that we stitched together.
2. I <u>squint</u> my eyes when the sun is shining brightly.
3. A <u>queen</u> is a female ruler or the wife of a king.
4. <u>Quick</u> action by fire fighters is needed to save lives because fires travel fast.

Multisyllable Words

5. The party went by so <u>quickly</u> that I was surprised that it was time to go home.
6. The hospital will <u>equip</u> the operating room with all of the instruments needed for the operation.

Cloze Sentences 3

1. During the <u>conquest</u> the village was overtaken by force.
2. Checking for all of the <u>equipment</u> needed at the games—including balls, bats, and gloves—is one of the jobs of the baseball coach.
3. We attended a <u>banquet</u> last night that was quite a feast!

4. Writers use <u>quotation</u> marks to show when they repeat the words spoken by another person.

5. When I call the hotel to <u>inquire</u> about a room for us, I will ask about the number of beds.

6. The <u>quicksand</u> was so wet and deep that a cow was not able to get out and was swallowed up.

7. The speaker spoke so <u>quietly</u> that we were not able to hear him.

Dictations

1. I will call to <u>inquire</u> about the <u>quake</u> that destroyed hundreds of homes and farm <u>equipment</u> in England. Witnesses were <u>quoted</u> as saying that the <u>quake</u> came <u>quietly</u> and <u>quickly</u> in the night and that aftershocks did not <u>quit</u> for days. The <u>queen</u> was <u>quick</u> to declare a state of emergency.

2. Our <u>quiz</u> in English class was <u>quite</u> a challenge! I found myself <u>squinting</u> in the dim light as I continued my <u>quest</u> for <u>quotation</u> marks that indicated the direct <u>quotes</u> that were part of the test. I looked over the <u>quiz</u> <u>quickly</u> one last time before I <u>quit</u> and handed it in.

3. In the <u>quiet</u> of the night my dog <u>Queen</u> went into the woods and got <u>quite</u> a number of <u>quills</u> in her mouth in a fight with a porcupine. I called the vet to <u>inquire</u> about what to do, and she told me to come <u>quickly</u> to her office, where she had the <u>equipment</u> <u>required</u> to remove the <u>quills</u>.

qu (kw) quilt

ake   ban et

een   con est

ick   e ip

iet   e ipment

ills   in ire

ilt   ickly

it   icksand

iz   ietly

ote   otation

s int

Name _____ Date _____

Word List 1

qu (kw) quilt

quake	banquet
queen	conquest
quick	equip
quiet	equipment
quills	inquire
quilt	quickly
quit	quicksand
quiz	quietly
quote	quotation
squint	

Name _____ Date _____

qu (kw) quilt

Write a word from the Word List to complete each sentence.

1. We felt the _____ of the ground beneath us as the volcano erupted.

2. Sometimes a person has to _____ a job to start another one.

3. My dog got _____ from a porcupine in his mouth, so we took him to the vet to have them removed.

4. It is important to be _____ in the library so that everyone can read and study.

5. A _____ is a short test.

6. If I _____ a person, I repeat the words that he or she said.

Name _____ Date _____

qu (kw) quilt

Write a word from the Word List to complete each sentence.

1. We made a _____ to cover my bed using scraps of cloth that we stitched together.

2. I _____ my eyes when the sun is shining brightly.

3. A _____ is a female ruler or the wife of a king.

4. _____ action by fire fighters is needed to save lives because fires travel fast.

5. The party went by so _____ that I was surprised that it was time to go home.

6. The hospital will _____ the operating room with all of the instruments needed for the operation.

Name _____ Date _____

Cloze Sentences 2

qu (kw) quilt

Write a word from the Word List to complete each sentence.

1. During the _____ the village was overtaken by force.

2. Checking for all of the _____ needed at the games—including balls, bats, and gloves—is one of the jobs of the baseball coach.

3. We attended a _____ last night that was quite a feast!

4. Writers use _____ marks to show when they repeat the words spoken by another person.

5. When I call the hotel to _____ about a room for us, I will ask about the number of beds.

6. The _____ was so wet and deep that a cow was not able to get out and was swallowed up.

7. The speaker spoke so _____ that we were not able to hear him.

Name _____ Date _____

Cloze Sentences 3

34   x   fox

BOOK LIST ═══════════════════════════════════════

Fox Tales

Rosie's Walk, Pat Hutchins (New York: The Macmillan Company, 1968). In this book with few words, the action is in the illustrations. While Rosie, the hen, walks nonchalantly through the barnyard completely unaffected by the fox that wants to eat her for dinner, the fox is thwarted at every turn by one mishap after another.

Henny Penny, H. Werner Zimmermann (New York: Scholastic, 1989). Amusing water-color illustrations and easy-to-read large print combine to tell the familiar cumulative story of a hen who, after she is hit on the head by an acorn, passes on her panic about the sky falling to an increasing collection of friends and leads them, on the way to tell the king, to an untimely end in the fox's cave.

Hattie and the Fox, Mem Fox, illustrated by Patricia Mullins (New York: The Trumpet Club, 1966). The suspense builds in this story with a repetitive refrain when Hattie, the hen, is the only animal in the barnyard who notices in the bushes first a nose, then two eyes, then two ears, . . . and, finally, *all* of a—fox!

The Hungry Fox and the Foxy Duck, Kathleen Leverich, illustrated by Paul Galdone (New York: Parents Magazine Press, 1978). A wise duck outsmarts a hungry fox by insisting that the shared meal he proposes be eaten properly. The meal is postponed as the fox gets a table, plates and cups, and a tablecloth—a large, *red* tablecloth that excites a bull, who shares the field with the duck and conveniently chases the fox away.

Percy and the Five Houses, Else Homelund Minarik, illustrated by James Marshall (New York: Viking, 1989). Percy, the beaver, had heard of a Book of the Month Club but not a House of the Month Club, until a fox sells him a membership. Percy finds that the houses he receives are not as good for him or his family as their lodge.

The Fox Went out on a Chilly Night: An Old Song, Peter Spier (New York: The Trumpet Club, 1961). Spier's illustrations for the well-known traditional song show in detail a fox's successful hunting exploits one night in a farmer's poultry yard and the feast he happily shares afterward with his family. Caldecott Honor Book.

One Fine Day, Nonny Hogrogian (New York: Macmillan Publishing Company, 1971). In this cumulative tale, a fox drinks a woman's milk, and she cuts off his tail. To get the milk she requests in trade for sewing on his tail, the fox must satisfy the requests of a series of characters. Caldecott Award Book.

Moon Rope/Un lazo a la luna: A Peruvian Folktale, Lois Ehlert, translated into Spanish by Amy Prince (San Diego: Harcourt Brace Jovanovich, 1992). Written in English and Spanish, this adaptation of a Peruvian *pourquoi* legend tells the adventures of mole and fox as they climb to the moon on a grass rope ladder and why moles live underground and a fox's face is in the moon.

Three Aesop Fox Fables, Paul Galdone (New York: Clarion Books, 1971). The fox is tricked in the first two fables, but wins in the third, in this collection of three fox fables from Aesop: "The Fox and the Grapes," "The Fox and the Stork," and "The Fox and the Crow."

Fox's Dream, Tejima (New York: Philomel Books, 1985, 1987). The poetic prose and *New York Times* Best Illustrated Children's Book Award–winning illustrations capture a lonely fox's winter dream-wish for family and its fulfillment when he meets a vixen.

Flossie & the Fox, Patricia C. McKissack, illustrations by Rachel Isadora (New York: Scholastic, 1986). On her way to take a basket of eggs to a neighbor for her grandmother, Flossie meets and outsmarts a fox by taking advantage of his vanity. Conversational dialect and glowing illustrations create the rural southern United States setting for the drama featuring one of literature's most independent heroines.

Chicken Little, Steven Kellogg (New York: The Trumpet Club, 1985). Kellogg's story is a modern, humorous retelling of the traditional tale with a contemporary setting and police rather than a king. In the end, the plotting and poultry-loving fox villain is sentenced to prison and a vegetarian diet, and the hen tells her grandchildren the story under an oak tree she plants (from the acorn, of course).

Mother Goose and the Sly Fox, Chris Conover (New York: Farrar, Straus and Giroux, 1989). Rich, two-page illustrations alternate with illustrated text in Conover's story set in Holland, in which Mother Goose tricks Fox, who tricked her seven goslings.

Doctor De Soto, William Steig (New York: Scholastic, 1982). Tiny Doctor De Soto, mouse and dentist, and his wife outsmart the large and hungry fox, who comes to their office to have a tooth pulled, with good thinking and a secret formula that glues the gullible and easily flattered fox's teeth together. Newbery Honor Book.

Tales for a Winter's Eve, Wendy Watson (New York: Farrar, Straus and Giroux, 1988). The evening after little Freddie, the fox, hurts his paw while skiing, his grandmother, Bert Blue Jay, and Nellie Mouse each tell the fox family a humorous story about other animals that live on Vinegar Lane.

Father Fox's Pennyrhymes, Clyde Watson, illustrated by Wendy Watson (New York: Scholastic Book Services, 1971). In Watson's detailed illustrations, a variety of foxes dressed in rural Vermont farm clothes dramatize the action and add comments that provide the context for a collection of short rhymes.

Chanticleer and the Fox, Geoffrey Chaucer, adapted and illustrated by Barbara Cooney (New York: Thomas Y. Crowell Company, 1958). In this traditional fable, the fox's flattery tricks proud Chanticleer, the rooster, into crowing with his eyes closed so he can capture Chanticleer, but Chanticleer outsmarts the fox and escapes his mouth when he tricks the fox into speaking.

MOTIVATION AND EXTENSION ACTIVITIES

1. At the beginning of the unit, students and the teacher brainstorm and record on one chart with the heading "True" (1) what they know (or think they know) to be true about foxes (They are often red. They look like dogs. They eat poultry.), and (2) what they would like to learn about them (What do they use their long noses and big ears for? Do they live alone? Do they live in caves or dens?). On a second chart with the heading "Not True or False," they record things that are not true about real foxes that fox characters in books do (Talk. Wear clothes. Sell things. Go to the dentist. Ski.).

The teacher uses this opportunity to introduce or review the terms *nonfiction*, which he or she adds under the heading "True" on the first chart, and *fiction*, which he or she adds under the heading "Not True or False" on the second chart. (For students who need a mnemonic device to remember the terms, the teacher points out that *false* and *fiction* begin with the same letter.)

Throughout the unit, students and the teacher verify or revise/correct and add information to the lists using the books suggested in this chapter and resource books and materials. They use, as one resource, the "Wild Dogs" (1985 and April 1988, vol. 5, no.7) and the "City Animals" (June 1987, vol. 3, no. 9, and May 1991, vol. 8, no. 8) issues of ***Zoobooks*** magazine, published by Wildlife Education, Ltd., 930 Washington Street, San Diego, California 92103. Published monthly, ***Zoobooks*** magazines provide current information about groups of animals through brief text and colored photographs and diagrams with captions.

Animal Fact/Animal Fable, Seymour Simon, illustrated by Diane de Groat (New York: Crown Publishers, Inc., 1979) is another resource about animals. It provides factual information in an unusual and engaging format. The colorfully and accurately illustrated book presents scientific observations about the behavior of a variety of animals. For each animal, a true or false statement is presented on a right-hand page, and the reader guesses whether it is a fact or a fable (fiction) and turns the page to find out. Students discover information about wolves (another wild dog and close relative of the fox) and find an answer to the question "Do they live alone?" as they read "A Wolf Lives Alone" in ***Animal Fact/Animal Fable***.

2. Throughout the unit and during their research and reading, students and the teacher generate lists of words (adjectives) and phrases that describe foxes. On one chart, they list words and phrases that describe the attributes and traits of fictional fox characters in the books they read in this unit. The list might include sly, clever, sneaky, calculating, aggressive, dangerous, meat-eating (especially poultry), wicked, crafty, villain, fast-talking, always hungry, tricky, scary, almost always male, howling, easily flattered, pointed nose, big ears, bushy tail, red, shrewd, swallow people whole, plotting, untrustworthy, and so on. (If they look up the word *fox* in a dictionary, they find that foxes are considered sly and crafty and that the word *fox* has come to mean a sly or crafty person.)

On a second chart, they list words and phrases that describe the attributes and traits of real foxes. They discover and record the following about real foxes: shy, watchful, loyal, excellent and devoted parents, cautious, intelligent, nocturnal, patient, excellent hunters, wild dogs, bushy tailed, long noses (and excellent sense of smell), big, long ears (for sensing danger), chase their prey, fast runners, omnivores (eat plants, fruits, berries, and insects when meat is scarce), strong, muscular, strong sense of family, do not have powerful jaws (so cannot kill large animals alone), long-distance runners, travel in packs (extended family units), leap to catch prey, do not kill many domestic animals, hunt animals harmful to farm crops (mice, rats), no proven case of a wild dog attacking or killing a human, and so on.

As they do their research, students and the teacher compare and contrast the words (adjectives) and phrases used to describe fox characters in fiction and those used to describe real foxes. They consider how fox characters in books have come to be associated with the traits they have. They propose some reasons: Perhaps nocturnal animals cannot be observed closely or accurately by most people; possibly shy, cautious, intelligent, watchful animals could be viewed as sly, sneaky, or calculating especially if they have been observed to threaten the livelihood of poultry farmers; and so on. They discuss whether fairy tales and children's books portray foxes realistically and/or fairly and whether they think that fictional representations of foxes (and wolves) predispose people to make unrealistic and unfair judgments about other wild dogs.

Students and the teacher read and consider **The True Story of the 3 Little Pigs by A. Wolf** by Scieszka (Chapter 8, ee seeds), in which the wolf shares his point of view and thoughts; **The Three Little Wolves and the Big Bad Pig** by Trivizas (Chapter 8, ee seeds), a retelling of the traditional "Three Little Pigs" story sympathetic to the wolves, whose roles are reversed with a pig; and **The Wolf's Chicken Stew**, in which the wolf changes from an antagonist at the book's beginning to a more sympathetic character at the book's end (Chapter 6, vowel-consonant-e syllable cake). (See Activity 25 in Chapter 8, ee seeds, for an activity related to points of view.)

Students use what they know and learn about the attributes and features of foxes (and wolves) as they act out with costumes and/or masks, make and use puppets to dramatize, create a dance/movements for the stories in this chapter. They choose background music that represents each character to be played at appropriate times during the play/puppet show/dance/movements.

3. The text of **Rosie's Walk** describes the simple actions of a hen as she walks from one side of the barnyard to the other. She is totally unaffected by the drama that occurs behind her as the fox has one misadventure after another.

Students and the teacher read and discuss **Rosie's Walk**. They decide for themselves, for example, whether Rosie knows that the fox is behind her.

After they discuss the book, students retell or rewrite the book and dramatize the different versions.

+ They describe the actions and (mis)adventures of the fox.
+ They tell the story from the point of view of the fox. The fox tells the story in the first-person and shares her/his thoughts, feelings, motivations, and reactions.
+ They dramatize--act out or perform a puppet show--the original or the retellings of the book.

4. Students and the teacher discuss the characterization and comical, contemporary illustrations of Ferd, the shrewd business fox, who sells Percy, the beaver, a membership to the House of the Month Club in *Percy and the Five Houses*.

5. Spier's *The Fox Went Out On A Chilly Night: An Old Song* contains the music for the song on a left-hand page and all of the verses, written out fully, on the facing right-hand page.

Students and the teacher sing the song after they have read and discussed the book (if they were able to resist singing during the first reading!). They clap their hands, stamp their feet, and/or use rhythm instruments to mark the beat and accompany their singing.

6. *One Fine Day* is an example of a specific type of cumulative tale. It is a dynamic cumulative tale variation with a chain reaction or dominoes pattern. This is a story pattern in which a series of characters are added who respond negatively to the desired outcome of the central character. Then an event stops the negative cycle and reverses it toward a positive outcome and begins a chain reaction, like falling dominoes, that achieves the desired outcome of the protagonist.

In this story, the fox asks the cow for milk, and she refuses unless he gets her some grass. He asks the field for grass, who refuses unless he gets some water. The fox continues, and all of the characters he asks in a series respond negatively with the condition that he satisfy their request, until a kind miller satisfies the fox's request made of him. This stops and reverses the negative cycle and starts a positive chain reaction that satisfies all of the characters and, finally, the old woman who helps the fox achieve his desired outcome when she sews on his tail. Students and the teacher observe and discuss this story pattern in *One Fine Day* and in other cumulative tales. (See Activity 5 in Chapter 12, igh night.)

7. Students and/or family/community members or teachers who speak and read Spanish read aloud *Moon Rope/Un lazo a la luna: A Peruvian Folktale*.

8. *Moon Rope/Un lazo a la luna: A Peruvian Folktale* is a *pourquoi* tale that tells why moles live underground and why a fox's face is seen in the moon. Students and the teacher read and discuss other *pourquoi* stories. (See Chapter 22, ow owl.) They dramatize *Moon Rope*, as actors wearing masks and/or costumes or as puppeteers.

9. Introductory material for *Moon Rope/Un lazo a la luna: A Peruvian Folktale* provides background information about folk literature and the Peruvian culture, from which this tale comes. Ehlert based her collage illustrations on "ancient Peruvian textiles, jewelry, ceramic vessels, sculpture, and architectural detail" and uses the food, animals, and colors important to that culture in her pictures and designs. After they listen to or read the book and the teacher shares this background information, students and the teacher experiment with collage pictures and designs using colored and metallic paper.

10. For his *Three Aesop Fox Fables*, Galdone has chosen three of the numerous traditional and modern fables that feature the fox as a character. Students and the teacher read and discuss other traditional and modern fables with fox characters. They discuss the characteristics of humans that foxes typically represent in fables. (See Chapter 29, consonant-le fable, for lists of additional traditional and modern fables.)

11. The habits and ways of the fox are more realistically represented in *Fox's Dream* than in most fiction. Students and the teacher compare and contrast the features, traits, and habits of the fox depicted in the fiction book *Fox's Dream* and in the nonfiction resource books and materials they have researched with the features, traits, and habits of foxes portrayed in the other fiction books in this unit.

12. After they read *Flossie & the Fox*, the teacher (or students) reads the book

aloud so that students can focus on the verbal richness, the illustrations, and the plot as they listen to it. (See Activity 6 in Chapter 27, au daughter, for an additional activity that considers Flossie and other daughters/heroines in modern stories.)

13. The ending of Kellogg's *Chicken Little*, in which the fox is punished by being put on a vegetarian diet while in prison, perpetuates the misconception that foxes are carnivores exclusively. Students and the teacher evaluate the validity of the ending of Kellogg's *Chicken Little* based on their research, in which they discover that foxes are omnivores who eat fruits, berries, and plants when meat is not available. They reread *Three Aesop Fox Fables* by Galdone and discuss the dietary habits of foxes as they are depicted in the three fables.

14. In *Mother Goose and the Sly Fox*, Conover uses a variety of words in addition to *said* to describe how the characters speak. When six of Mother Goose's seven goslings come for breakfast and make their complaints, the ways in which they make their comments are described with a series of words beginning with *w*: "whispered," "whined," "whimpered," "worried," "warbled," and "weaseled," and later they "gabbled" and "grouched." The fox cubs "yowled," "howled," and "yipped" and Fox "howled."

Students and the teacher extend this list of words that mean the same or nearly the same as (synonyms) *said* and compile as long a list as possible. The teacher introduces or reviews the dictionary and the thesaurus as resource books. Students take turns saying the word *said* with inflection and emphasis, which provide clues for others to guess which synonym for *said* they dramatize.

15. After they read *Mother Goose and the Sly Fox*, students and the teacher read and share another variation of the Grimm folktale—*Nanny Goat and the Seven Little Kids* retold by Eric A. Kimmel and illustrated by Janet Stevens (New York: Holiday House, 1990). In the humorous version with a contemporary setting, the characters are changed—a wolf tricks seven goat kids—but his tricks and fate are the same. Students and the teacher compare and contrast the two versions of the folktale.

16. There is an audiotape of *Doctor De Soto* (available from Scholastic). After they read (or listen to) the book, students and the teacher listen to the tape and compare and contrast the taped interpretation of the story and their own interpretations. They consider the voices assigned to the characters on the tape and in their own readings.

17. Before or after students read *Tales for a Winter's Eve* (or while the teacher reads the book aloud), they eat their teacher's "famous lighter-than-air muffins" like the ones the woodchuck children and Mr. Raccoon, the governor, eat in "Grammer's Tale" in the book (especially if it happens to be snowing outside).

18. The traditional fable *Chanticleer and the Fox* is an adaptation of one of Chaucer's *Canterbury Tales*, the "Nun's Priest's Tale." The teacher provides students with historical context and background information about Chaucer and *Canterbury Tales*. Because the language in *Chanticleer and the Fox* may be difficult for some students to read, the teacher (or students) reads the book aloud for some students so that they can focus on the plot, illustrations, and descriptions.

19. Students and the teacher locate on a map and/or globe the places/cultures (depicted or of origin) in the books read in this chapter, including Peru (*Moon Rope/Un lazo a la luna: A Peruvian Folktale*); Greece (*Three Aesop Fox Fables*); the rural south of the United States (*Flossie & the Fox*); Germany and Holland (*Mother Goose and the Sly Fox*); Germany (*Nanny Goat and the Seven Little Kids*); rural Vermont in the United States (*Tales for a Winter's Eve* and *Father Fox's Pennyrhymes*); and England (*Chanticleer and the Fox*).

Cloze Sentences

One-Syllable Words

Cloze Sentences 1

1. The <u>wax</u> used in making a candle melts easily as it burns.
2. The large <u>ox</u> was trained to pull a cart and a plow on the farm.
3. When I first saw the <u>fox</u> it looked like a dog, but when it got closer I noticed its red fur and large bushy tail.
4. We <u>mix</u> together flour, butter, and milk to make batter for pancakes.
5. We used an <u>ax</u> to chop down a small tree.
6. <u>Six</u> eggs is the same as half a dozen.

Cloze Sentences 2

1. I hope that we will be able to <u>fix</u> the broken parts on our car and will not have to get a new one.
2. I packed the gifts in a cardboard <u>box</u>, and then I mailed it at the post office.
3. I pay my property <u>tax</u> to the town where I live, and the money is used for roads, police protection, and schools.
4. If I sit <u>next</u> to the board, I can see the lesson better than if I sit far away.

Multisyllable Words

5. I look in the <u>index</u> at the back of a book to see what it contains and to find the pages where things can be found.
6. If we <u>exhale</u> air from our lungs under water when we are swimming, we form bubbles.

Cloze Sentences 3

1. I like to <u>explore</u> carefully a place that I have never been before to see what I can discover.
2. When you <u>express</u> yourself clearly, I know what you think and feel.
3. A balloon will <u>expand</u> to a larger size if you blow air into it.
4. An <u>extremely</u> cold day is much colder than most days.
5. When firecrackers <u>explode</u>, there is a loud noise and a colorful display in the sky.
6. We <u>expect</u> it to snow in the winter but not in the summer where we live.
7. An <u>extinct</u> animal like the dinosaur does not exist any more.

Dictations

1. I went to the hospital last week to <u>explore</u> the pain I had been having, and <u>unexpectedly</u> I had my <u>appendix</u> removed. I did not <u>expect</u> it to be so painful, but it was an <u>extremely</u> <u>complex</u> operation. I was glad that you called to <u>express</u> good wishes. I will

explore with my doctor when I can return to my job. I expect that may be in six days if I am not lax in doing my exercises and if it does not tax me too much.

2. We did an experiment to explore the extent to which a person can exhale into balloons of different sizes before they explode. It was an excellent context in which to extract information about this complex area of study. We will express to the people at the laboratory how extremely grateful we are that they extended the invitation to us to complete the experiment and did not exclude us.

3. The petting zoo considered extremely carefully the need to exclude some animals from its collection. I expect that six oxen and a red fox will be removed, but that may not be the full extent of it. They may need to explore the need to exclude more animals if the tax on the zoo complex becomes extremely large during the next year. If the tax is less, they may be able to expand and there will be an influx of new animals.

x (ks) fox

a		e	hale
bo		e	pand
fi		e	pect
fo		e	plode
mi		e	plore
ne	t	e	press
o		e	tinct
si		e	tremely
ta		inde	
wa			

Name _____ Date _____

Word List 1

x (ks) fox

ax	exhale
box	expand
fix	expect
fox	explode
mix	explore
next	express
ox	extinct
six	extremely
tax	index
wax	

Name _____ Date _____

x   (ks)   fox

Write a word from the Word List to complete each sentence.

1. The _____ used in making a candle melts easily as it burns.

2. The large _____ was trained to pull a cart and a plow on the farm.

3. When I first saw the _____ it looked like a dog, but when it got closer I noticed its red fur and large bushy tail.

4. We _____ together flour, butter, and milk to make batter for pancakes.

5. We used an _____ to chop down a small tree.

6. _____ eggs is the same as half a dozen.

Name _____   Date _____

Cloze Sentences 1

x (ks) fox

Write a word from the Word List to complete each sentence.

1. I hope that we will be able to _____ the broken parts on our car and will not have to get a new one.

2. I packed the gifts in a cardboard _____ , and then I mailed it at the post office.

3. I pay my property _____ to the town where I live, and the money is used for roads, police protection, and schools.

4. If I sit _____ to the board, I can see the lesson better than if I sit far away.

5. I look in the _____ at the back of a book to see what it contains and to find the pages where things can be found.

6. If we _____ air from our lungs under water when we are swimming, we form bubbles.

Name _____ Date _____

Cloze Sentences 2

x (ks) fox

Write a word from the Word List to complete each sentence.

1. I like to _____ carefully a place that I have never been before to see what I can discover.

2. When you _____ yourself clearly, I know what you think and feel.

3. A balloon will _____ to a larger size if you blow air into it.

4. An _____ cold day is much colder than most days.

5. When firecrackers _____ , there is a loud noise and a colorful display in the sky.

6. We _____ it to snow in the winter but not in the summer where we live.

7. An _____ animal like the dinosaur does not exist any more.

Name _____ Date _____

Cloze Sentences 3

Appendix A

Teaching Strategies

LEVELS OF READING SUPPORT

Four basic stages of reading are presented. They are described in order by the kind of support provided for students: listening (teacher read-aloud), oral cloze reading, supported reading, and independent reading. In real-life reading and in *Developing Independent Readers*, reading occurs along a continuum that encompasses the four stages. Often lines blur as progress involves transition from one stage to the next. Individual readers also often need different kinds and levels of support at different times and with different texts.

Listening (Teacher Read-Aloud)

It has been widely recognized that none of us outgrows the benefits and pleasures of listening to fine books read aloud. Sharing books in this way enables students and teachers to enjoy books together. It provides students with vicarious experiences and background information. Learners have important experiences with book language and formats.

Reading aloud provides opportunities for modeling and making explicit important aspects of the reading process. The teacher begins by modeling the previewing of a book. During the reading, students and teacher discuss and respond to storyline, themes, concepts, and vocabulary. Together, they ask and discuss questions at and beyond the literal level. They relate their own experiences and compare their feelings to those of characters. They identify the author's and characters' points of view. The teacher demonstrates how to make and confirm or correct predictions about plot. They explore new or specialized vocabulary. The teacher highlights figurative and descriptive language and idiomatic expressions. The teacher's oral reading provides a model for reading fluency and expression.

Occasionally, but not so often that it interrupts the flow or experience of the book, the teacher deletes words for students to fill in orally. (Students listen to the story and look at the illustrations and do not necessarily look at the text.) Generally, the teacher deletes words at or near the ends of sentences so that information the student can use to predict a word is available preceding it. At the beginning, the teacher omits words that are highly predictable. These are words with which the teacher is confident students will have success—often rhyming or repeated words or phrases. Later, the teacher deletes words that carry the most meaning (often nouns and verbs). At times the teacher gives the student an initial sound to aid in predicting. Together they determine whether the predicted word fits by cross-checking using semantic, syntactic, and grapho-phonic cues in combination. They also confirm or correct predictions about plot and vocabulary as they read.

Oral Cloze Reading

During oral close reading, skills modeled and practiced during listening are reinforced and built on. Now students look at the text as well as the illustrations as the teacher reads aloud. After they preview the book together, the teacher points to words while he or she reads aloud. Students follow along and fill in by reading words aloud when the teacher hesitates.

First, the teacher pauses and omits sight words (usually starting with one or two— often "a, I, the, to, is"). The teacher increases the number of words deleted as students are able. Then, in addition to sight words, the teacher begins to omit words in a sequence similar to that followed in listening: rhyming or repeated words and words that carry the most meaning—nouns and verbs (especially names of characters and "mother, father, boy, girl, dog, cat"). The emphasis, at this point, is to have students predict a word that makes sense (semantic) and sounds right (syntactic). Students use first letter clues (grapho-phonic) to confirm or correct their predictions. At times the teacher rereads a sentence or passage to help students regain the sense of meaning and language flow. This models a rereading strategy and helps students use cross-checking and self-correcting strategies.

In the beginning, the teacher deletes words at or near the ends of sentences. Most of the information precedes the omitted word, which makes predicting easier. Later, the teacher omits words at or near the beginning of sentences. This is a more difficult task. Readers need to read on (beyond the word) to gather information following the deleted word. Often, readers also need to reread the sentence or passage from the beginning to regain meaning and language flow in order to cross-check to confirm or correct a response.

As soon as possible, in addition to sight words, the teacher omits words containing the grapho-phonic elements as they are introduced in the sequence described in *Developing Independent Readers*.

As experience with oral cloze reading progresses, students naturally begin to take over more text. They begin to use strategies to read more words as the teacher reads them aloud, not only the ones for which the teacher hesitates. The teacher allows his or her voice to fade and regain strength in response to the amount of support the student needs at any given moment. The teacher reads less and less of the text and, in essence, students and teacher exchange places. Students begin to point and read; the teacher fills in.

Supported Reading

At this point, the nature of the reading has changed sufficiently to signal a new stage. Students have taken over pointing to words as they read. They now use productive strategies independently much of the time. They have the beginning of a sufficient critical mass of words (element and sight words) to engage in the reading process with increasing independence.

The teacher rarely fills for students. As a general rule, the teacher does not give or supply a word at this stage of reading. The goal is to have the students use, as independently as possible, the productive strategies that have been established. The teacher reminds students to use strategies—explicitly or by carefully chosen responses or questions. The teacher gives students ample time to think and work out challenges independently. If students have made good attempts to use the time to think and use strategies yet they continue to be unable to determine a word that is important to text meaning, the teacher gives clues. If the word is not important to text meaning, the teacher may advise students to abandon it.

The teacher often gives nonverbal clues so that fluency is not interrupted. For example, the teacher simply points to the part of the illustration that represents the word or points toward an object in the room which may provide a clue. The teacher pantomimes words and makes hand gestures. The teacher moves his or her hand in a circle for the word *around*, for example, or points to the ceiling for *up*. The teacher points from the end set of quotation marks to the word *said* which immediately follows (and says, if necessary, "I see talking marks. Someone *said* something."). This technique helps many students adopt this strategy independently. *Said* is a high-frequency word with which many learners with special needs experience great difficulty.

The teacher gives verbal clues as well. Meaning/semantic clues include contextual ("It says the _____ barked at the cat. What animal barks?") and pragmatic ("Remember, this is a fairy tale. How do fairy tales usually begin?"). Meaning clues that use relationships between words include synonyms ("It's the same as _____." or "It means _____."), antonyms ("It's the opposite of _____." or "It means not _____."), and analogies ("Cats meow. Dogs _____." or "Lemons are sour. Sugar is _____."). To provide structural/syntactic clues, the teacher rereads the sentence/passage with expression or intonation. This provides further information and reestablishes language structure and flow for students. Grapho-phonic clues include "It begins with _____." or "It rhymes with _____."

The teacher gives less and less of this support as students are able to take over clue giving for themselves. As students gain more skill and confidence, the teacher gives them more and more time to work out text without support. The need for time to think—uninterrupted, silent, comfortable time—cannot be overemphasized. In individual work and in group situations (where teachers often need to help students give each other this most important gift), the supportive atmosphere that is so critical at this stage is very often *silent*!

Paired or small group reading gives students opportunities to practice and model strategies for their peers. In group reading there are three essential understandings: (1) We give each other the gift of comfortable, silent time in which to think; (2) we do not give help to the reader unless and until the reader asks for help; and (3) we do not give the word, we give clues—meaning and structure first and grapho-phonic last. Pairs or groups of students who have developed and become comfortable with this kind of supportive atmosphere work together. They give each other quiet time to work out challenges, and they wait in supportive silence to be asked to help. They remind each other to use strategies, and they act out and give verbal clues.

Independent Reading

At this stage of reading, students are able independently to use productive strategies for reading. They use structural analysis and syllable division strategies in combination with other strategies for reading multisyllabic words. Reading continues to improve as students read progressively difficult books. This is because readers have mastered a process and are actively seeking meaning.

At the beginning of this stage, readers often look to the teacher for support when they encounter a challenging word or confusion in their reading. When the teacher asks students, at the end of a passage, why the teacher smiled or nodded for them to return to the text, students often answer "You wouldn't help me (or give me the word) because I can do it myself." Having gained this confidence in their own abilities, students are much more able, willing, and enthusiastic about choosing to read independently in their classrooms and out of school.

At this point, some students have developed sufficient strategy and process awareness. They can generalize strategies for learning new elements from the elements presented. These students do not need to continue the *Developing Independent Readers* program. They are no longer beginning readers!

Other learners are not as easily able to generalize and need to continue further with the *Developing Independent Readers* lessons. They need continued supported opportunities to practice and apply additional elements, language skills, and modeled strategies.

Timing for each learner is individual.

STRATEGIES BEFORE AND FOLLOWING READING

Previewing Books—A First Response

Sharing a new book with students is always exciting! If teachers present books about which they genuinely feel enthusiastic, it is not difficult to communicate that feeling. The first and primary response to a book is one of sharing and enjoying it together.

When possible, the teacher includes students in the choice-making process. The teacher places several theme books of similar difficulty on the table in front of students, who choose the book to read next.

Together, students and teacher discuss the title, and they progress, page by page, throughout the book. They look at and discuss the illustrations, identify possible traits in characters, talk about special or unusual words and important concepts, and discuss background information. They also pose questions and make predictions about outcomes of the plot, which they verify or correct during reading. If the book is a mystery or has a trick ending, students and teacher stop previewing before key details or events are given away.

From the beginning of the program, the teacher guides this process. Students soon take it over independently. Then the teacher serves as a support and is a person with whom to share the excitement and anticipation of a new book. The teacher continues to bring attention to key vocabulary and concepts that may not be evident from the illustrations.

Previewing books is a strategy that helps students choose books from libraries and classroom collections. It is an important life-long habit to establish.

Retelling

When they resume reading a book from a previous session, the teacher asks students to retell the story up to the point where they stopped reading. Occasionally, the teacher asks students to retell an entire story. Some learners benefit more from this activity than others. Some students need support with the process.

The teacher encourages students to include the basic elements of narrative in the summarized account. These elements include main ideas, points of view, characters, settings, plot, emotions, and ending or conclusion. When necessary, students use the illustrations as a guide. Later, they retell without reference to the illustrations. The teacher directs the process more at the beginning of the program and withdraws support as students become more independent.

Review Reading

After students complete a brief retelling of the passage that was read previously, they (or the teacher) reread just enough text, often the last page, to reestablish flow of the storyline. This procedure provides an important transition to the text, reestablishes fluency, and reinforces rereading as a strategy during the reading process.

STRATEGIES DURING READING

During shared reading, the teacher focuses discussion on characters and setting, plot, concepts, and vocabulary. In addition, the teacher responds to students' hesitations, apparent confusions, and miscues. The teacher models or explicitly restates productive strategies when encountering an unknown word or a difficult part in text. The goal is to help students broaden and balance the repertoire of active responses they can give, questions they can ask themselves, and strategies they can use while reading.

The teacher often asks questions of or responds to students who are reading fluently and successfully. This affirms and brings productive strategies to conscious awareness and builds learners' confidence. The teacher describes and commends positive behaviors by saying, for example, "What I noticed about your reading today is that you said 'blank' and read on to find out words, and they popped into your head." Or "You reread and figured out that word. Good reading (or thinking or detective work)." Or "You figured that out yourself. You didn't need me to help you!"

Whether readers are just learning to search for and use cues or have previously become overreliant on a cueing system or strategy, the teacher asks a balance of questions. The teacher's responses use a variety of strategies and cueing systems to encourage a balance of responses by students. If readers tend to rely too heavily on grapho-phonic cues, the teacher draws attention to semantic and syntactic cues. Successful readers frequently reread to work out challenging words. Modeling this powerful strategy is especially effective to help students focus on semantic and syntactic cues. Conversely, if students overrely on semantic and syntactic information, the teacher makes responses and asks questions that point out and highlight grapho-phonic information.

The teacher also models questions that encourage readers to confirm their responses by cross-checking using other cueing systems. The teacher encourages students to self-correct if their responses are not confirmed by cross-checking, when meaning is interrupted, or when what they have read does not make sense.

Productive strategies that successful readers use during reading include the following.

Anticipating Meaning

The use of this strategy begins with the understanding that reading is a meaning-seeking process and that text communicates meaning. Able readers expect that a story will make sense and that language in books will sound right. As they read, they sample or sound grapho-phonic information while anticipating a word (or words) consistent with meaning and language structure and order.

Reading On

When skilled readers encounter an unknown or challenging word, they often omit the word and say "blank." Some readers pause rather than say "blank," and this indicates that they have omitted a word. Then they read the text following the word to gather more information on which to base a response that fits in the blank.

Rather than say "blank" or pause to signal the omission of the unknown words, readers may predict words. They base their predictions on grapho-phonic information and the preceding and anticipated meaning and language structure and order. They then read on to confirm or correct the prediction.

Rereading

When successful readers encounter a challenging word or difficult part in text, they often reread the sentence or passage from the beginning to regain meaning and language flow. If necessary, they also sample or sound again grapho-phonic information. This strategy helps readers make and confirm responses.

This is analogous to high-jumpers who are interrupted as they run to the bar and have to stop before completing the jump. They do not jump from a standing position in front of the bar. They go back to the starting line and run again. They get a running start to regain momentum.

Cross-Checking

Skilled readers often confirm or correct predictions by cross-checking. They take information from one cueing system and check it against information from other cueing systems. Cross-checking is represented by the central question:

> How did I know it was that word and what else could I use to make sure it is the right word?

For example, to read the word *puppy*, the reader cross-checks the following information. The story reads: "The girl saw an animal in her yard. It was a little _____ that was barking and jumping at the end of its leash." The reader knows from text meaning (semantics) that the word describes a small animal that barks and jumps and is on a leash. The reader predicts the word *dog*. The reader confirms the prediction with further semantic information. The illustration shows a small dog. The reader continues to confirm the response by using information from language structure and order (syntax). The word follows an article *a* and an adjective *little*, so it must be a noun. The word *dog* is a noun and continues to be confirmed. Finally, the reader cross-checks the previous information with information from letter-sound correspondences (grapho-phonic). The word begins with a *p*. The reader corrects the prediction. The word must be puppy. The reader rereads the passage to further confirm the response. The word *puppy* makes sense in the story, sounds right with the rest of the words in the sentence, and contains the expected letters.

Self-Correcting

Successful readers self-correct when their predictions are not confirmed by cross-checking. They independently correct responses when meaning is interrupted—when what they have read does not make sense, sound right, or look right.

RESPONSES AND QUESTIONS THAT SUPPORT THE DEVELOPMENT AND USE OF STRATEGIES DURING READING

Sample responses and questions that teachers can use to highlight strategies that use information from each cueing system are discussed in this section. Responses and questions that encourage cross-checking and self-correcting strategies follow. Examples are organized by category. They are presented in random order within categories. Order of presentation does not imply priority for use. These examples are suggestive and illustrative. Teachers develop and use their own styles of response and questioning.

Use of Information from Multiple Cueing Systems

The teacher provides responses and asks questions that encourage students to use information simultaneously from multiple cueing systems: (1) meaning (semantic), (2) language structure and order or grammar (syntax), and (3) letter-sound correspondences (grapho-phonic). The three central questions that students need constantly to ask themselves about a predicted response are as follows:

1. Does the word make sense? (semantic)
2. Does the word sound right there? (syntactic)
3. Are these the letters that represent the sounds in the word I predicted? (grapho-phonic)

Semantic (Meaning)

1. I noticed that you were thinking about the story as you were reading. Good thinking!
2. I noticed that you were looking at the pictures to help you read that word. Good detective work!
3. Does that (the word) make sense?
4. Hmmm . . . Could that happen?
5. Is there such a word as _____? It sounded a little funny to me.
6. You read "_____." Is that right?
7. Think about the story. What would make sense? or What might happen next? or What do you think could happen?
8. Take a look at the picture. or What is he doing in the picture? or What is that a picture of? (Or the teacher points to the illustration.)
9. How do fairy tales usually begin? (Once upon a time . . .) How do fairy tales usually end? (Happily ever after . . .)
10. He's writing a letter. What word usually begins letters? (Dear . . .)

Syntactic (Language Structure and Order or Grammar)

1. I noticed that you were listening to yourself read to decide if it sounded right. Great!
2. Does that (the word) sound right?
3. Would that word fit there?
4. Do we say that (talk) that way?
5. Does that sound like talking? Does that sound like talking in books?
6. Reread from the beginning to check.
7. Sample the sounds and keep reading.
8. Try reading ahead for more clues.
9. Let's read it again (or reread it) together.
10. Hmmm . . . Do people talk like that?

Grapho-Phonic (Letter-Sound Correspondences)

1. You are looking carefully at the words while you are pointing to make sure your voice matches. Great reading!
2. Do you think the word looks like _____ ?
3. What letters do you think you would see in _____ ? (beginning, middle, end)
4. You read _____ . How does _____ begin (end)? How does the word in the book begin (end)?
5. Are these the letters you thought you would see? Are these the sounds in the word you predicted?
6. It ends with ay as in "day" (or rhymes with "day").
7. Let's sound that one together.
8. I see a silent *e* at the end, so the *a* is (_____).
9. It could be _____ , but look at the letters.
10. What does it begin with? Could it be _____ ?

Cross-Checking and Self-Correcting Strategies

1. How did you know it was that word? How else?
2. Are you right? Check to see.
3. You stopped for a moment (or looked like you were thinking about that part) just before you fixed that. What were you thinking? What did you notice? What did you use?
4. What did you use to figure that out? What were you thinking that helped you?
5. Is there any other way you could know?
6. Were you thinking about the story while you looked at that word?
7. Can you find two ways to check that word?
8. Tell me two ways that you knew it was that word. Any other way?
9. I noticed that you looked at the picture and used the first sound to read that word. Did you use anything else?

10. What else could you use/ask to find out if it's the right word?

11. Is that right? How do you know? Is there another way that helps you know?

12. Try sampling or sounding and read on to see if a word pops into your head.

13. Listen to yourself reading as you look at the word. What sounds right and looks right?

14. What helped you know that? Anything else?

15. Were you right? How did you know that you were? Any other way?

16. That makes sense and sounds right. Now check the letter. or How does that begin or end?

17. Try that again. How did you know that word was _____ ? What did you use? Anything else?

18. Could you use something else to check/to make sure?

19. It could be _____ , but also try _____ .

20. What could you do here? What else?

21. What are some of your choices now? Which one, do you think, would work best here?

22. What could you try? What else?

23. What do you think it could be? How could you tell?

24. What do you know that might help? What else?

25. Check to find out if what you read makes sense, sounds right, and looks right to you.

26. There was something not quite okay on that page. Can you find it? What can you use to fix it?

27. When that didn't sound right, you went back to fix it.

28. Why did you stop (or hesitate) there? What did you do to fix that part?

29. I noticed that you fixed that part all by yourself.

30. Did I need to help you with that? No, *you* did all the work!

31. I noticed that you sampled sounds and read on to figure that out yourself.

32. You decided to reread that part to get a running start to check that word. Did it work?

33. I noticed that you were looking at the illustrations/pictures to help you change the word that didn't make sense there.

34. I noticed that you stopped for a moment. Were you thinking about the story when you fixed that part?

SYLLABLE DIVISION AND STRUCTURAL ANALYSIS STRATEGIES FOR READING AND WRITING

From the beginning of *Developing Independent Readers*, during shared reading the teacher models syllable division and structural analysis strategies. The teacher shows students how to use the thumb to "make the word shorter." The teacher covers endings

(-s, -ing, -ed, -less) and other structural elements in multisyllabic words. The teacher also covers the second word in compound words and syllables after the first in multisyllabic words and moves his or her thumb to expose consecutive syllables. The teacher continues to model this strategy until students use it independently as they read.

Words chosen for the Word List for each unit are single syllable through Chapter 6, which introduces compound words. Subsequent chapters include compound and multisyllabic words for syllable division and structural analysis practice. During activities that use the Word Lists, the teacher models dividing words with pencil loops under single syllables (as shown next).

Syllable Division Strategies

The teacher models the following syllable division strategies to read or check the spelling of words that have more than one syllable.

Compound words: Divide between the two words in a compound word—**pancake**.

Multisyllabic words: Underline the vowel sounds, circle the consonant sounds (qu and consonant digraphs—ch, sh, th, ph, wh—represent one consonant sound), and follow the strategies for dividing.

Syllable Division

Strategy 1: One Consonant Sound

rāven

Divide *before* one consonant sound.
The first syllable is an open syllable.
The vowel in the first syllable is long.

or   If the word does not make sense there or you do not recognize the word:

rŏbin

Divide *after* one consonant sound.
The first syllable is a closed syllable.
The vowel in the first syllable is short.

• **With one consonant sound: Try it long, then try it short.**

Syllable Division

Strategy 2: Two Consonant Sounds

răbbit

Divide *between* two consonant sounds.
The first syllable is a closed syllable.
The vowel in the first syllable is short.

or   If the word does not make sense there or you do not recognize the word:

Āpril

Divide *before* the two consonant sounds. (They may be a consonant blend.)
The first syllable is an open syllable.
The vowel in the first syllable is long.

Syllable Division

Strategy 3: Three Consonant Sounds

cŏnstant

Divide after the *first* consonant sound.
The first syllable is a closed syllable.
The vowel in the first syllable is short.

or   If the word does not make sense there or you do not recognize the word:

ĕndless

Divide after the *second* consonant sound.
The first syllable is a closed syllable.
The vowel in the first syllable is short.

```
┌─────────────────────────────────────────────────────────────┐
│                                                             │
│        Mnemonic for Syllable Division Strategies 1, 2, and 3: │
│                                                             │
│                                                             │
│        1    You may see a **raven** or a **robin**          │
│                                                             │
│                                                             │
│        2    or a **rabbit** in **April**,                   │
│                                                             │
│                                                             │
│        3    which is **constant** and **endless**.          │
│                                                             │
│                                                             │
└─────────────────────────────────────────────────────────────┘
```

Open, Closed, and Vowel-Consonant-e Syllables

The teacher presents the relationship among open syllable, closed syllable, and vowel-consonant-e syllables: A single vowel in an open syllable is at the end of the syllable and out in the open with no letter(s) following it to close it in, so it can represent its name. In a closed syllable, a consonant letter (or letters) follows the vowel and acts like a gate, and the vowel represents a short sound. In a vowel-consonant-e syllable, the silent *e* cancels or neutralizes the effect of the one consonant that follows the vowel, and the vowel is in a second open context and represents the long sound. Both open contexts for single vowels are represented on the Letter-Sound Key Word/Picture Cards as a (ā)-(in the open), e (ē)-(in the open), i (ī)-(in the open), o (ō)-(in the open), and u (ū)-(in the open).

The teacher offers an analogy to aid students' understanding and recall of the symbols that represent the long (or open) sound " ¯ " (macron) and short (or closed) sound " ˘ " (breve) of vowels: When a garden hose is held long and straight like the " ¯ ", it is open and water flows through easily; when a hose is bent like the " ˘ ", the water is closed off and cannot flow as well.

Students often benefit from the following explanation. Vowels and consonants are on two separate teams. Vowels *love* to represent (or say) their own names (or long sounds)—(ā), (ē), (ī), (ō), (ū)—which they can do when they are at the end of a syllable or word and out in the open in an open syllable. In a closed syllable, at least one consonant closes in the vowels like a gate so that it can only say its short sound—(ă), (ĕ), (ĭ), (ŏ), (ŭ). In a vowel-consonant-e syllable, a special vowel team member—silent super *e* (complete with a cape and key that fits the keyhole in the gate)—opens the gate. The vowel, in the open once again, represents its long sound (says its name).

Students contrast the following sets of words, which the teacher prepares with vowels in red and consonants in black.

Open	Closed	Open
-	˘	-
a	at	ate
me	met	mete
hi	hid	hide
ho	hop	hope
tu	tub	tube

(<u>tu</u>na, <u>tu</u>ba)

Appendix B

Reproducible Master

for

Lesson Plan Student Record

THE LESSON PLAN STUDENT RECORD ══════════════════

The Lesson Plan Student Record suggests a format and sequence for teachers to use to present lessons for each element in *Developing Independent Readers*. Teachers use it to record the specific activities completed by students. A reproducible master for photocopying is included. Teachers fill in student name(s) and element for each unit.

The Lesson Plan Student Record lists the following in a column format: activity presented, materials needed, dates completed, and notes about performance. Activities are listed in a suggested sequence. Starred double lines (*****) indicate suggested beginning and ending points for single sessions of approximately fifteen minutes each. Several activities can be combined for sessions of more than fifteen minutes.

Space is provided in the "Sustained Reading in Context and Motivation and Extension Activities" sections. Teachers list books read and can include pages completed. They can record observations of students during the reading process and include notes about the strategies students use. Teachers can record the specific Motivation and Extension Activities completed and notes about individual student responses. Teachers can add activities, materials, and books to reflect individual learning and teaching styles and needs.

Lesson Plan Student Record   Name: _____

Activity   Element: **Materials**   **Dates and Notes**
Sustained Reading in Context and Motivation and Extension Activities

* *

Auditory Pattern Discovery   Word List 1
(color coded)

Visual Pattern Discovery   Word List 1
(color coded)

Word List Reading   Word List 1
with Oral Sentences   (color coded)

Theme and Key Word Clue Game   Word List 1
(color coded)

Introduction of New Card(s)   Letter-Sound Key Word/Picture Card(s)

* *

Sustained Reading in Context and Motivation and Extension Activities

* *

Word List Clue Game   Word List 2

* *

Sustained Reading in Context and Motivation and Extension Activities

* *

Letter-Sound Key Word Practice   Letter-Sound Key Word/Picture Cards
(new and review)

3 frames exposed _____   1 frame exposed _____

Sound-Letter Practice   (Teacher refers to Letter-Sound
Key Word/Picture Cards)

oral _____   oral and sorting _____   oral and written _____

* *

Sustained Reading in Context and Motivation and Extension Activities

* *

Spelling and Reading List Words   Word List 2
for Cloze Sentences

Cloze Sentences   Cloze Sentence Sheets

* *

Sustained Reading in Context and Motivation and Extension Activities

* *

Dictation and Editing

* *

Sustained Reading in Context and Motivation and Extension Activities

Appendix C

Reproducible Masters

for

Letter-Sound Key Word/Picture

Cards

and

Mask

Letter-Sound Key Word/Picture Cards are approximately 3″ × 5″ in size. They are made by photocopying the reproducible masters which follow onto white card stock. Each card is divided vertically by lines into three segments or frames, with the following information represented:

1. On the left is the letter or letters that represent a phoneme/sound.
2. In the middle is the sound represented by the letter(s) which is enclosed within parentheses.
3. On the right is a key word and picture. For most sounds, the letters are embedded in the picture.

Teachers may choose to color some of the Key Pictures, including old gold (a waterbased pigment ink gold marker is available from ZIG POSTERMAN), p   pumpkin, v   valentine, w   water, and y   yarn. Procedures for using Letter-Sound Key Word/Picture Cards begin on page xv. A card is used as a mask to cover the last two frames (middle

and right) of each card during the One Frame Exposed activity of Letter-Sound Key
Word Practice (page xv). A template for making a mask from colored card stock or oaktag
follows.

Template
for
Mask

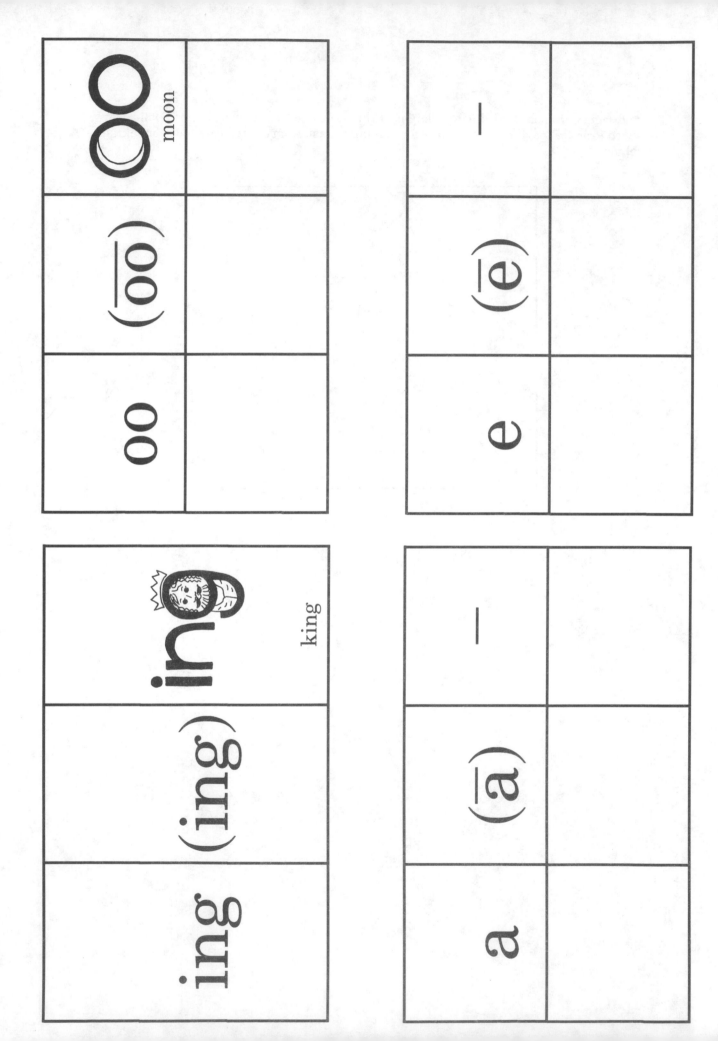

fly

—	(ō)	o

	(ī)	y

—	(ī)	i

—	(ū)	u

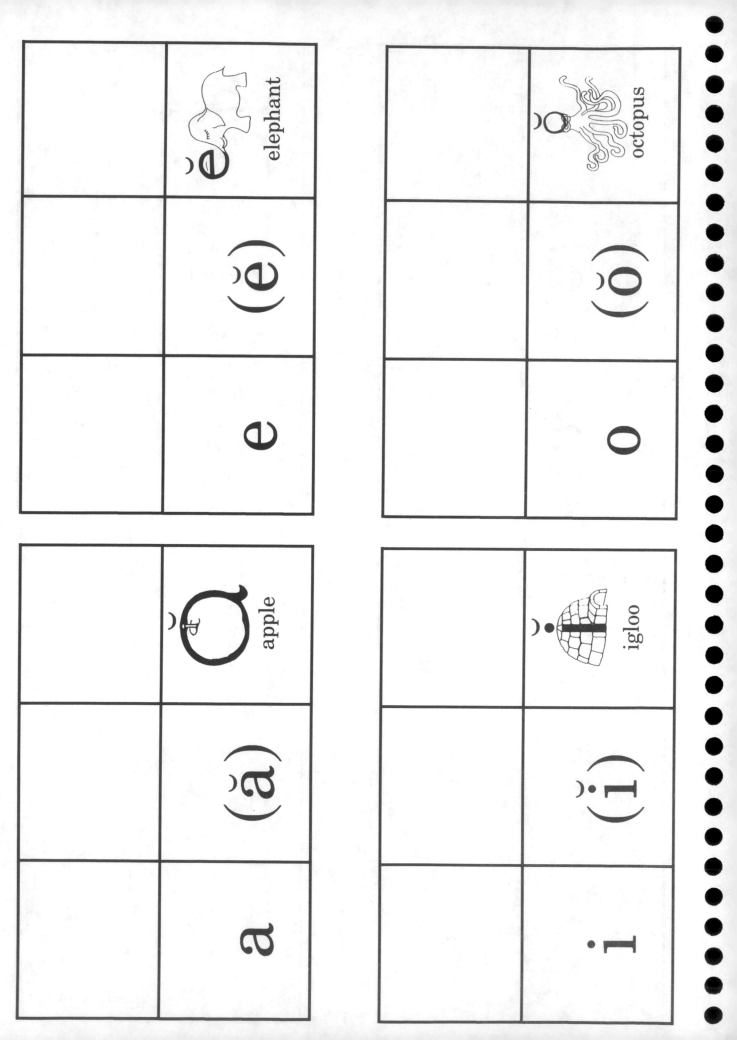

elephant (ĕ) e

octopus (ŏ) o

apple (ă) a

igloo (ĭ) i

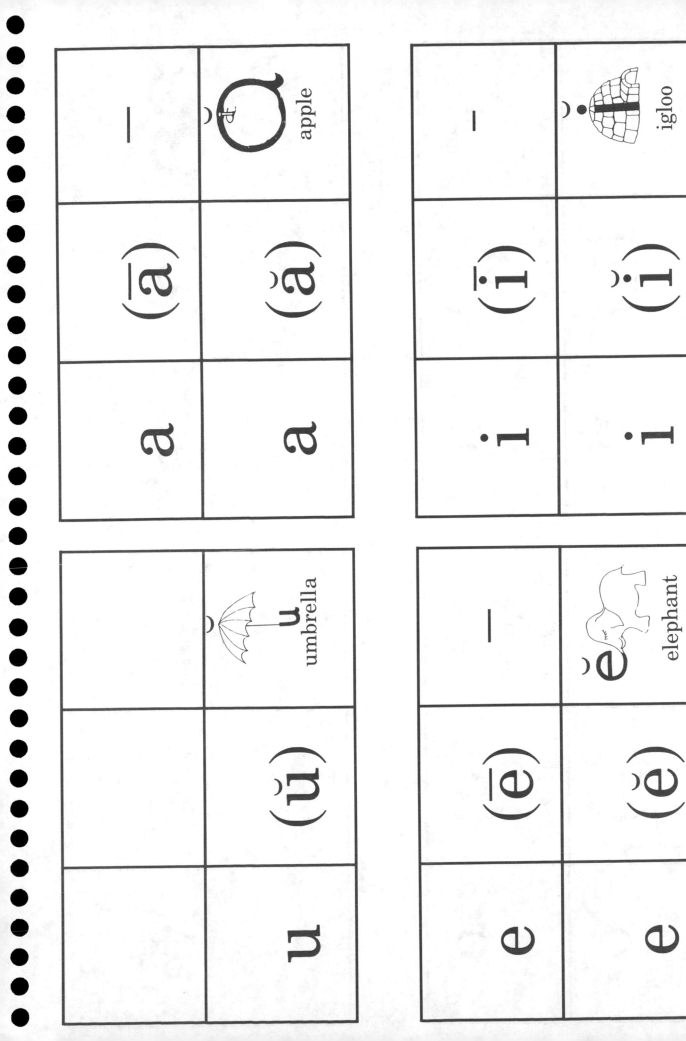

	(ā)	a
apple	(ă)	a

	(ī)	i
igloo	(ĭ)	i

	(ŭ)	u
umbrella		

	(ē)	e
elephant	(ĕ)	e

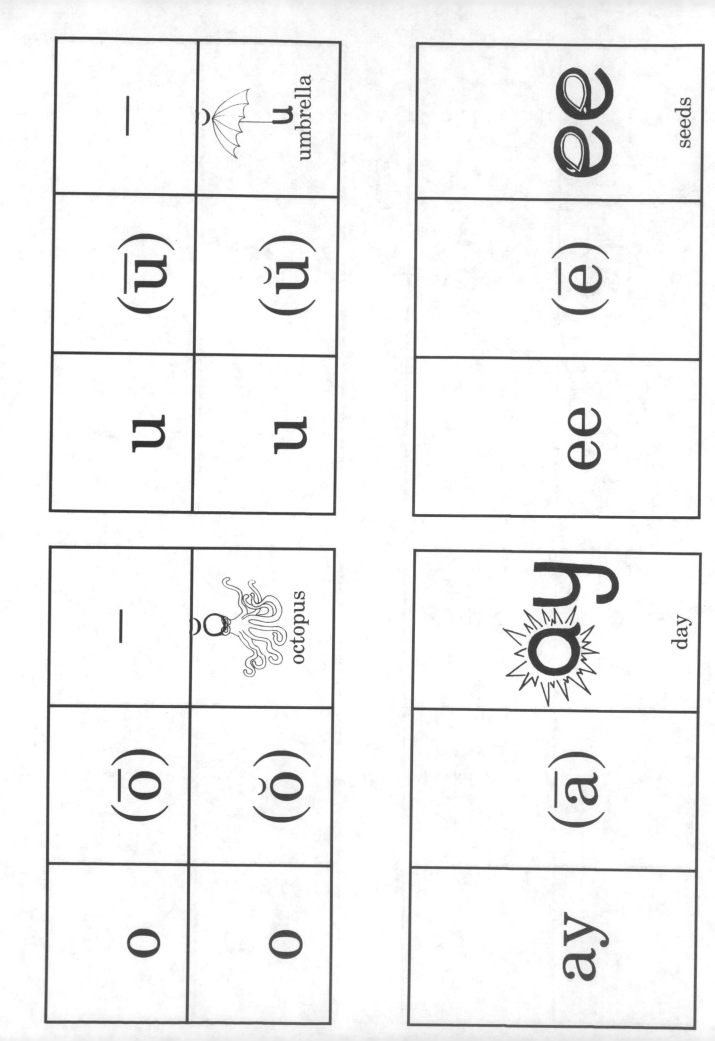

u

umbrella

(ū) u

(ŭ) u

—

octopus

(ō) o

(ŏ) o

—

ee

seeds

(ē)

ee

ay

day

(ā)

ay

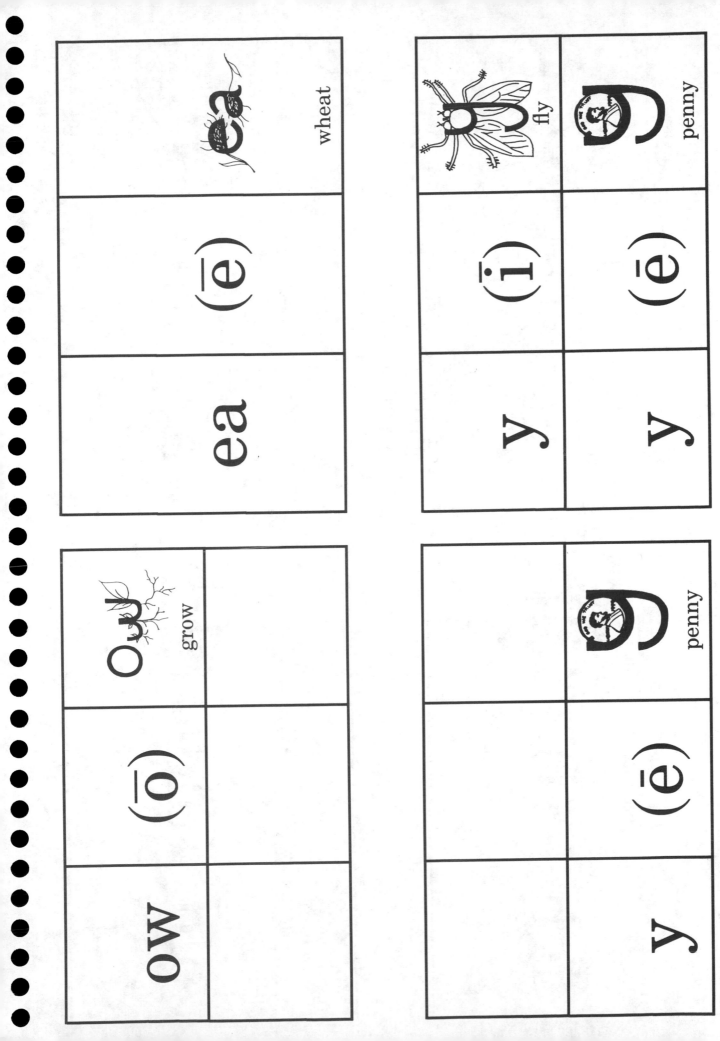

ea (ē) wheat

ow (ō) grow

y (ī) fly

y (ē) penny

y (ē) penny

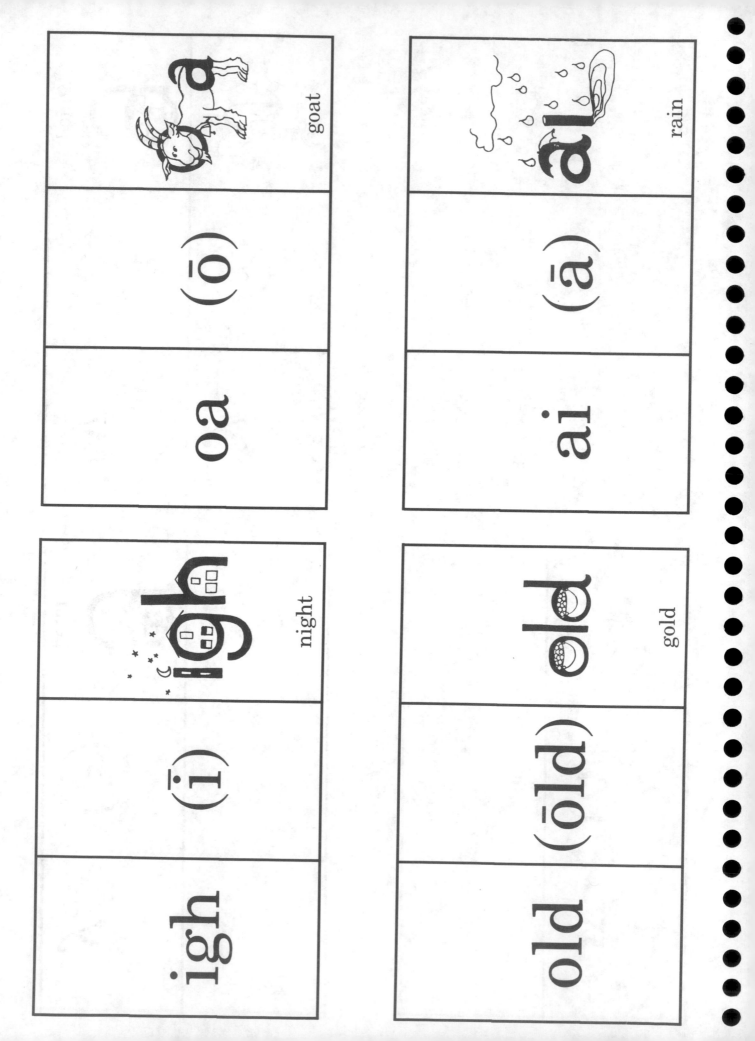

oa   (ō)   goat

ai   (ā)   rain

igh   (ī)   night

old   (ōld)   gold

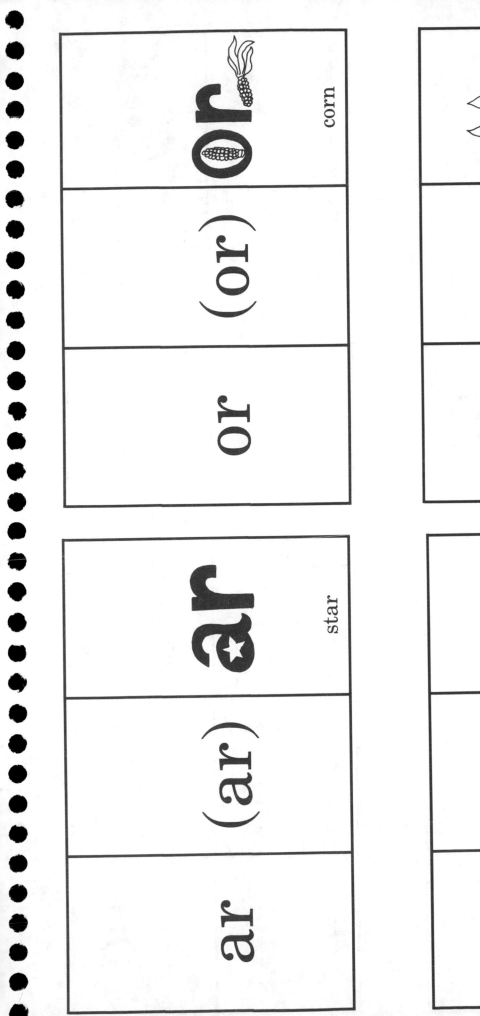

| **or** | (or) | or |
| corn | | |

| **ar** | (ar) | ar |
| star | | |

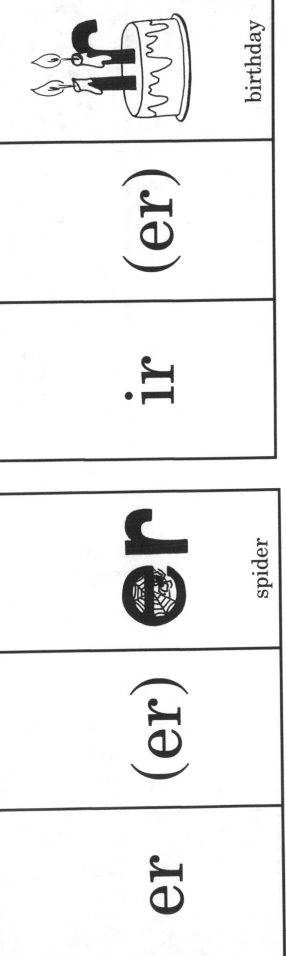

| **ir** | (er) | ir |
| birthday | | |

| **er** | (er) | er |
| spider | | |

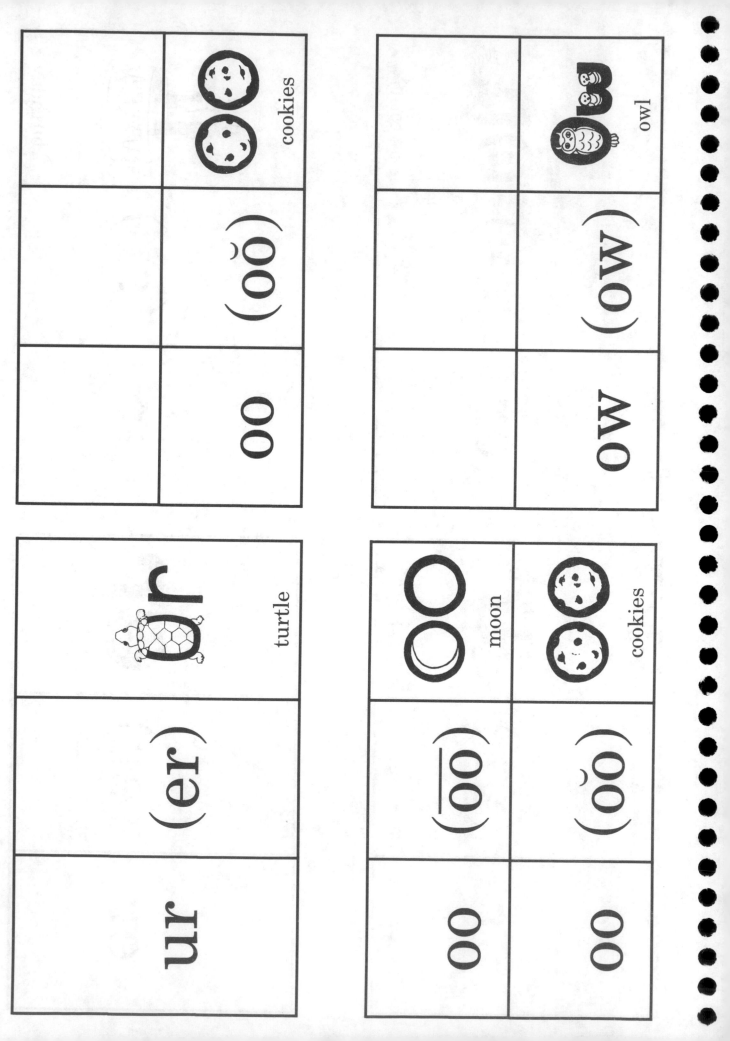

| | (o͝o) | oo |
| cookies | | |

| | (ow) | ow |
| owl | | |

| turtle | (er) | ur |

| moon | (o͞o) | oo |
| cookies | (o͝o) | oo |

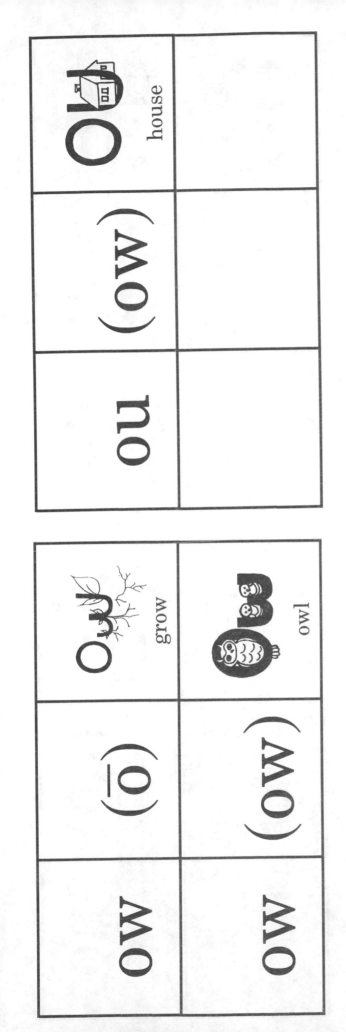

house

grow

owl

(ow)

ou

(ō)

(ow)

ow

ow

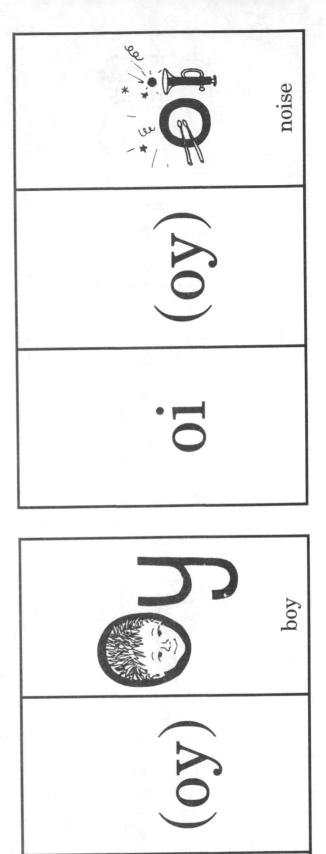

noise

boy

(oy)

oi

(oy)

oy

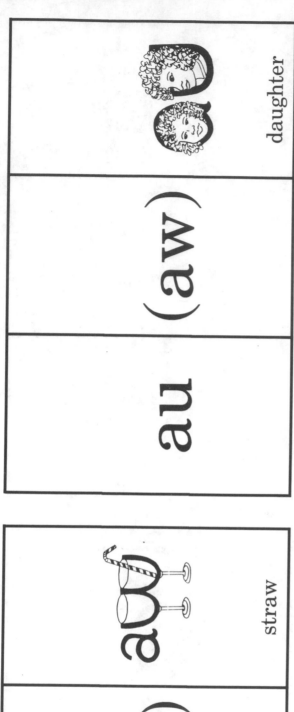

daughter

(aw)

au

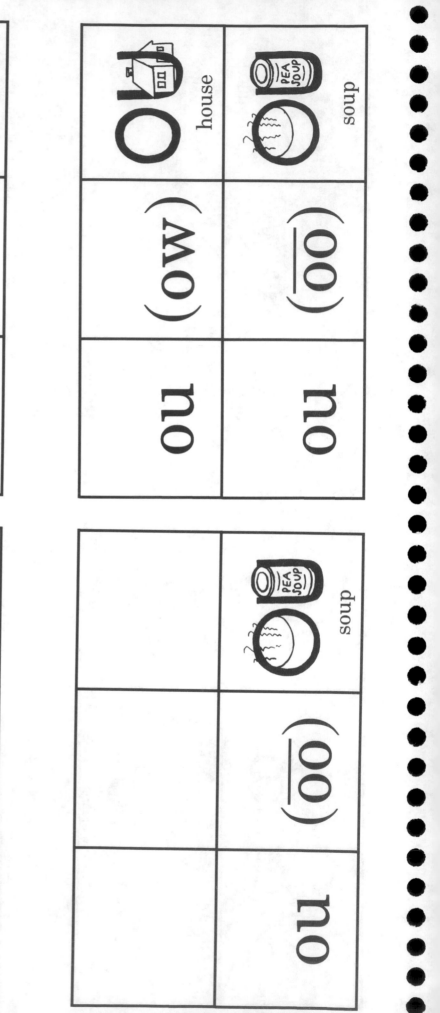

house

(ow)

ou

soup

$\overline{oo}$

ou

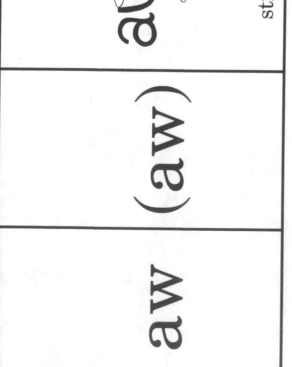

straw

(aw)

aw

soup

$\overline{oo}$

ou

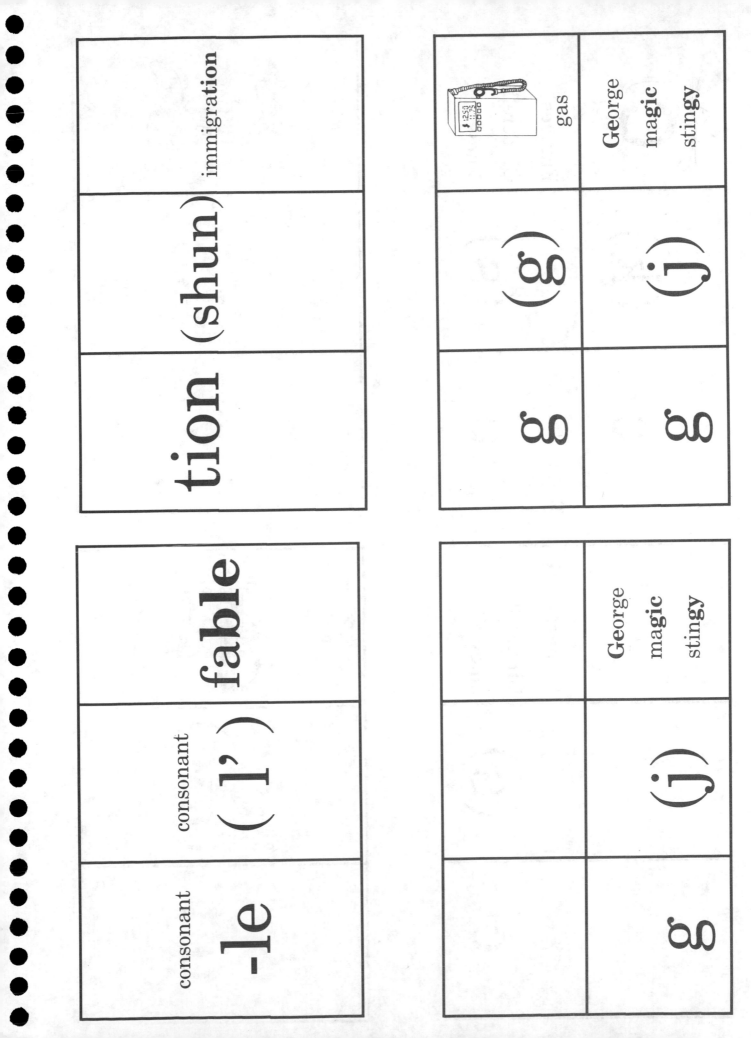

tion | (shun) | immigration

-le | (l') | fable
consonant | consonant

gas | (g) | g
George
magic
stingy | (j) | g

George
magic
stingy | (j) | g

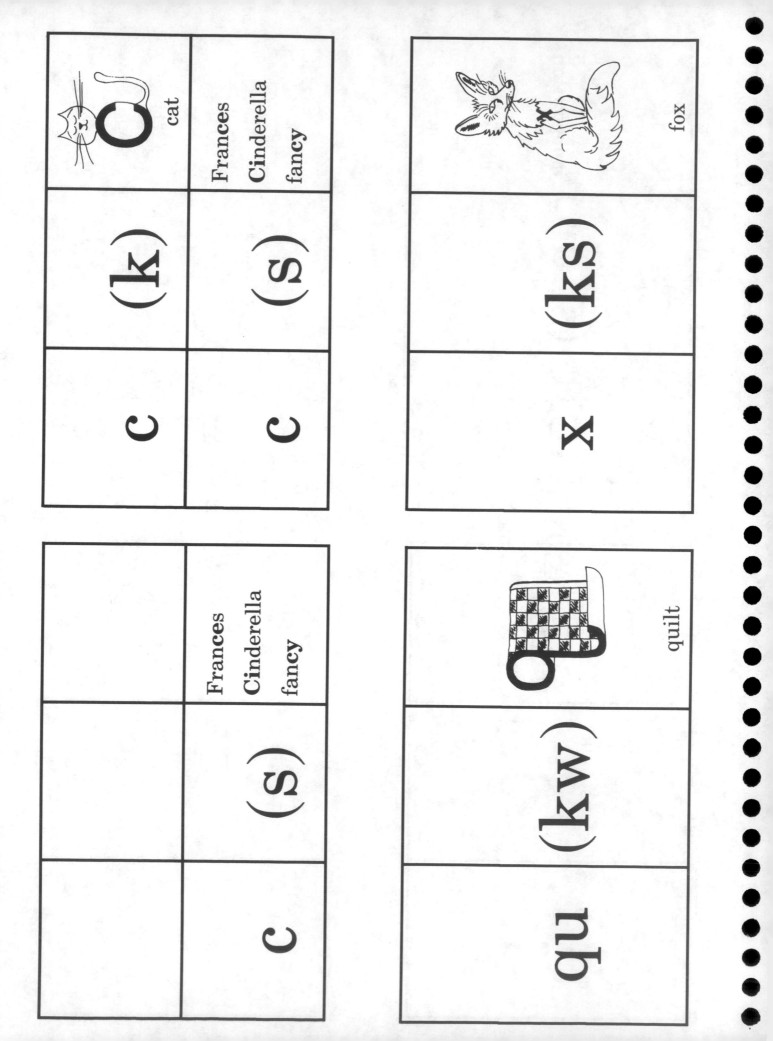

cat
c (k)

Frances / Cinderella / fancy
c (s)

fox
x (ks)

Frances / Cinderella / fancy
c (s)

quilt
qu (kw)

Consonant Sounds

b	(b)	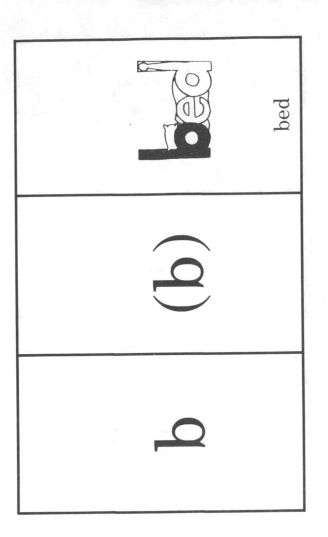
		bed

d	(d)	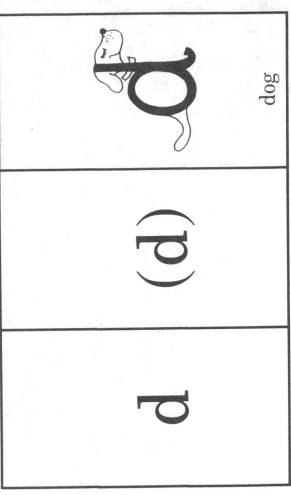
		dog

c	(k)	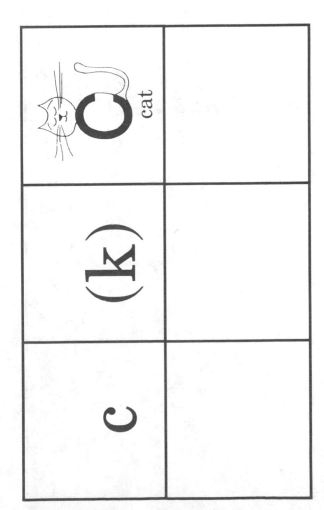
		cat

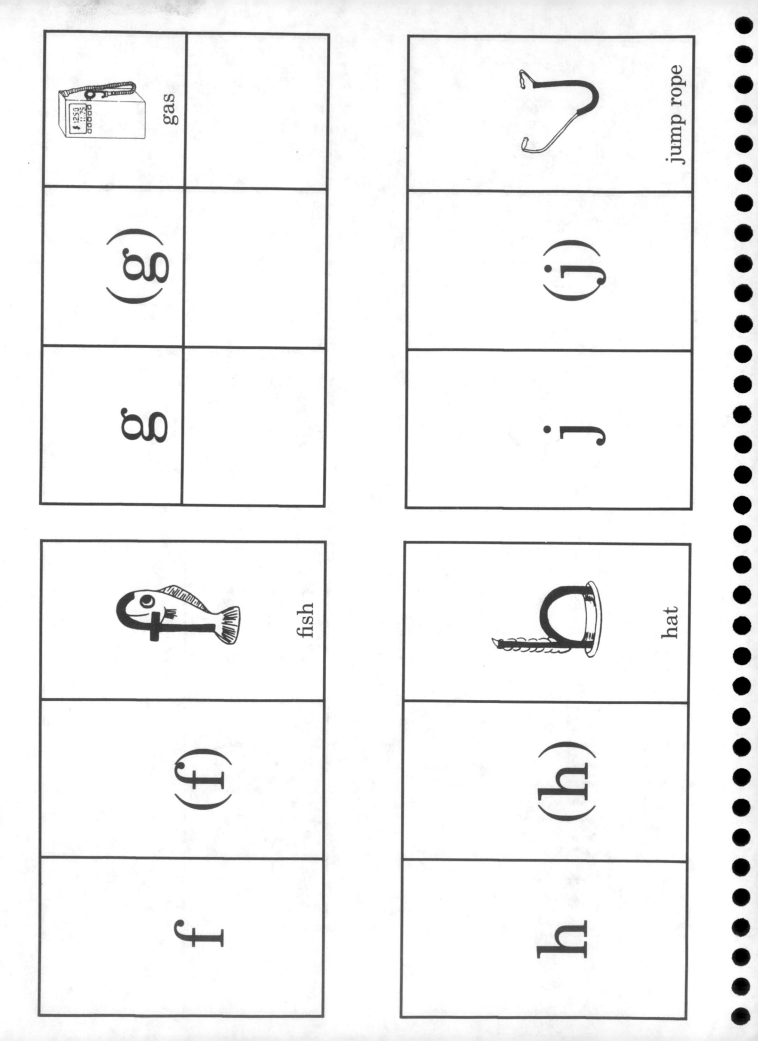

gas

g g

jump rope

(j) j

fish

(f) f

hat

(h) h

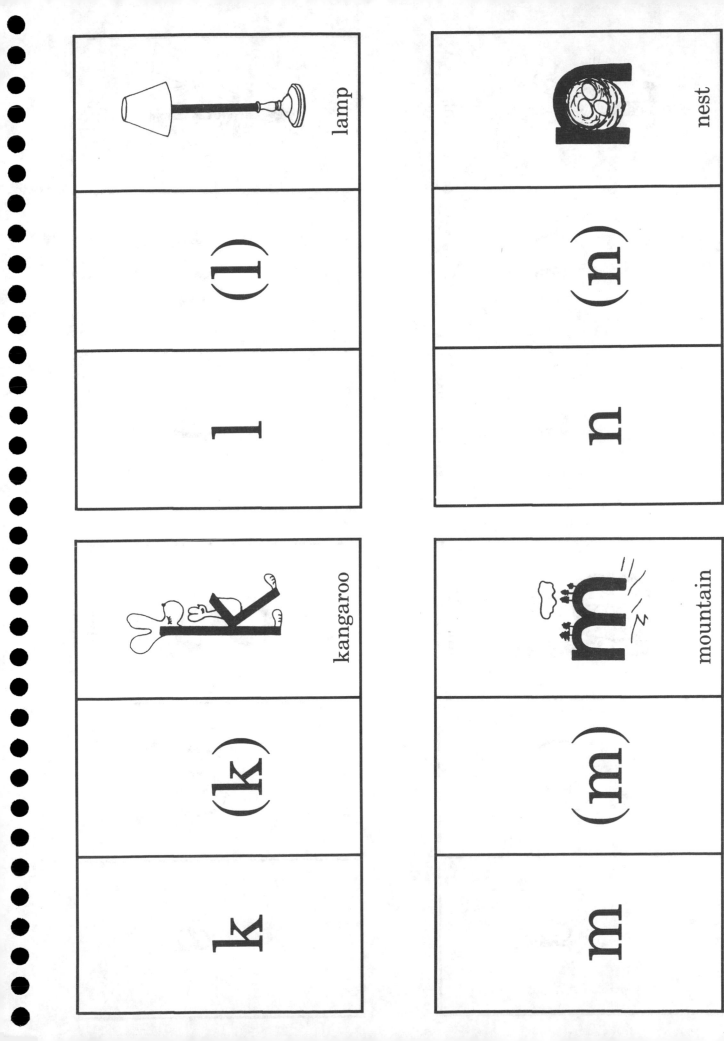

lamp

(l)

l

nest

(n)

n

kangaroo

(k)

k

mountain

(m)

m

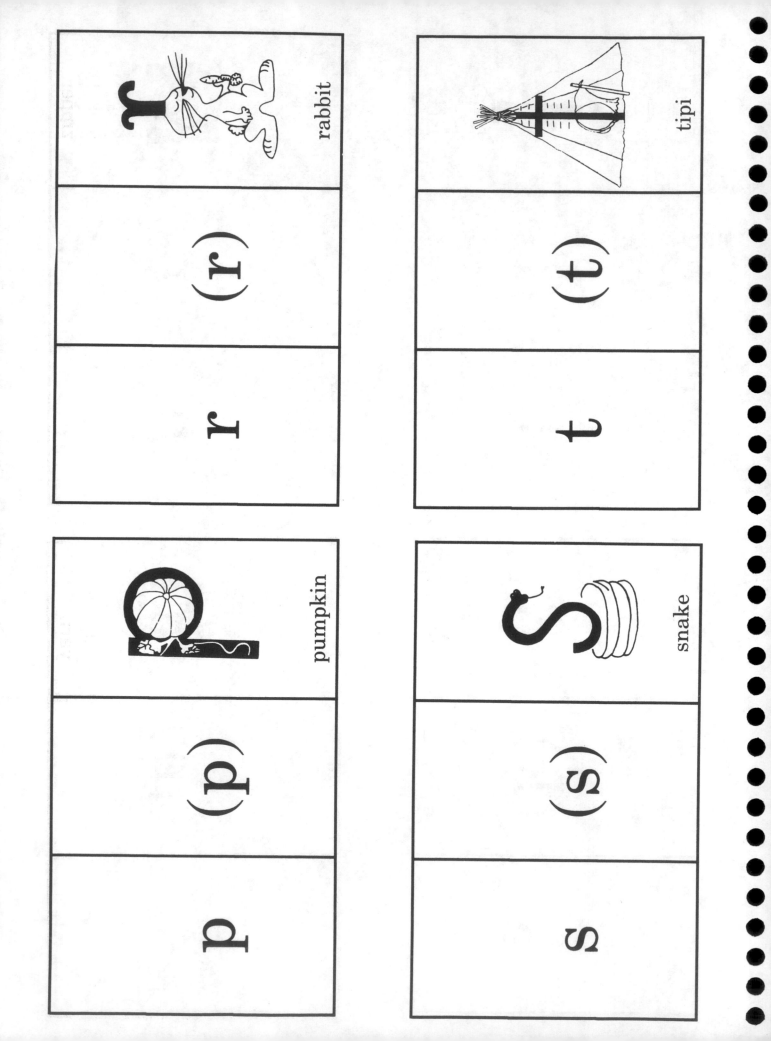

rabbit

(r)

r

tipi

(t)

t

pumpkin

(p)

p

snake

(s)

s

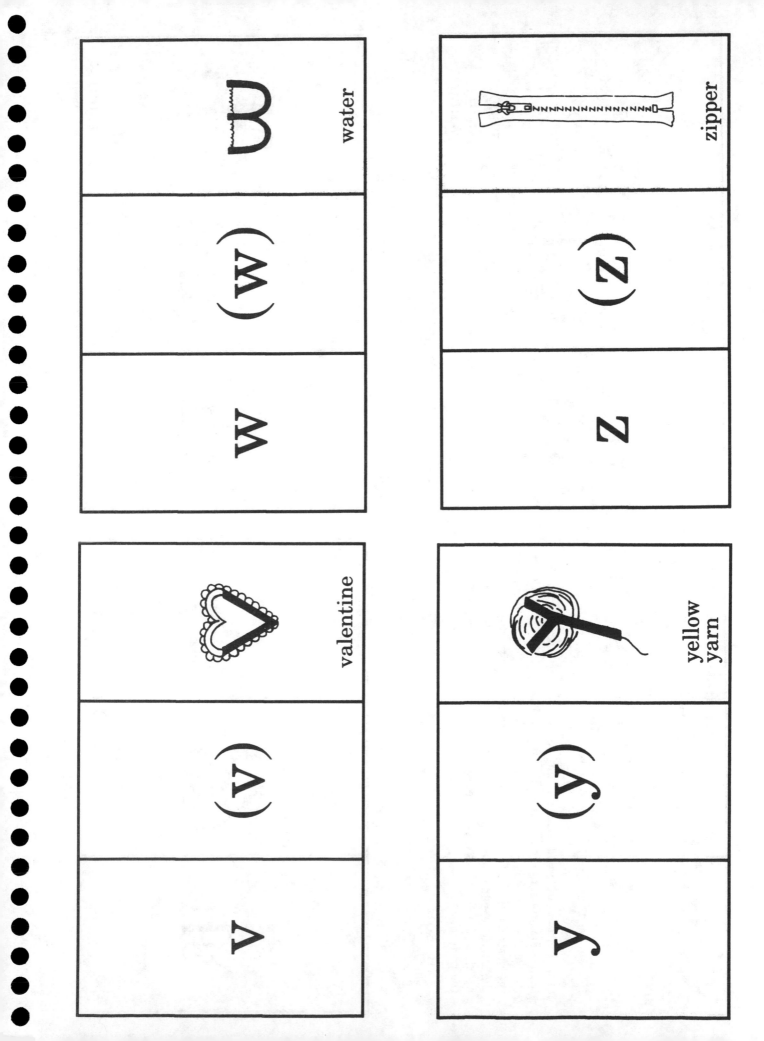

W   (w)   w

water

Z   (z)   z

zipper

V   (v)   v

valentine

Y   (y)   y

yellow
yarn

Consonant Digraphs

Teachers may add hand motions corresponding to the pictures to help some students remember and retrieve consonant digraphs. For *ch* the teacher pretends to sneeze, with the index finger forming a *c* under the nose; for *sh* the teacher forms an *s* in the air as if tracing the fin of the shark to signal the *s* of the *sh* combination; for *th* the teacher puts up his or her thumb as it is represented in the *t* of the *th* combination in the picture.

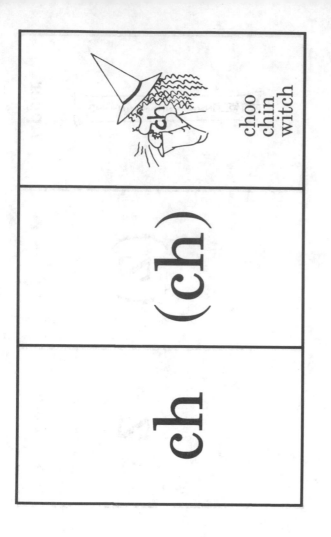

choo
chin
witch

(ch)

ch

the
thumb

(th)

th

sh!
shark

(sh)

sh

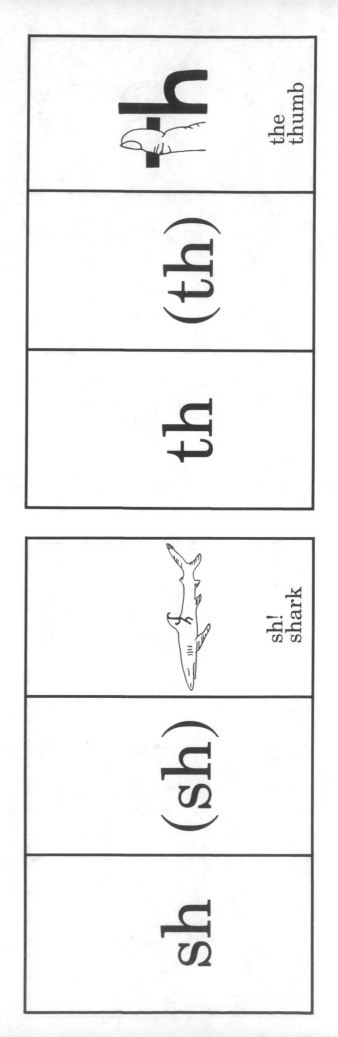

Appendix D
Alphabet Knowledge

Alphabet Knowledge Record

Student: Date: Recorder:

1. Alphabet Sequence
says/sings

A B C D E F G H I J K L M N O P Q R S T U V W X Y Z

2. Letter-Sound Correspondences for Reading

	N	S		N	S
P			p		
S			s		
F			f		
A*			a*		
M			m		
B			b		
T			t		
H			h		
K			k		
E*			e*		
W			w		
O*			o*		
Z			z		
J			j		
			a		
R			r		
U*			u		
C*			c*		
N			n		
Q			q		
Y*			y*		
G*			g*		
D			d		
V			v		
X			x		
			g*		
I*			i*		
L			l		
CH			ch		
SH			sh		
TH			th		

3. Upper- and Lowercase Letters Written to Dictation

	UC	LC
1. Tt		
2. Vv		
3. Rr		
4. Gg		
5. Ee		
6. Ii		
7. Xx		
8. Ss		
9. Nn		
10. Dd		
11. Mm		
12. Qq		
13. Ll		
14. Yy		
15. Cc		
16. Uu		
17. Jj		
18. Oo		
19. Hh		
20. Bb		
21. Zz		
22. Ww		
23. Pp		
24. Kk		
25. Ff		
26. Aa		

4. Letter-Sound Correspondences

	S	L
1. (m)		
2. (t)		
3. (ō)		
4. (z)		
5. (b)		
6. (ŭ)		
7. (g)		
8. (ĭ)*		
9. (r)		
10. (w)		
11. (ă)		
12. (k)*		
13. (ē)*		
14. (y)		
15. (j)*		
16. (ŏ)		
17. (n)		
18. (ā)		
19. (l)		
20. (ĕ)		
21. (f)		
22. (ū)		
23. (s)*		
24. (d)		
25. (h)		
26. (ĭ)*		
27. (v)		
28. (p)		
29. (kw)		
30. (ks)		
31. (sh)		
32. (th)		
33. (ch)		

DIRECTIONS FOR ADMINISTRATION

Note: An asterisk (*) next to items on the Alphabet Knowledge Record indicates that there is more than one way to spell a sound.

1. Alphabet Sequence

Materials: • Alphabet Knowledge Record

Say: "Please say or sing the alphabet."

Record: Circle each letter the student says/sings in order, leaving omitted letters unmarked. Indicate whether the student says or sings the response.

2. Letter-Sound Correspondences for Reading

Materials: • Alphabet Knowledge Record

• Uppercase letters written on separate cards for the twenty-six letters of the alphabet and consonant digraphs *ch*, *sh*, and *th* arranged in order of presentation indicated on the Alphabet Knowledge Record.

• Lowercase letters written on separate cards for the twenty-six letters of the alphabet (including *a* and a, *g* and g) and consonant digraphs *ch*, *sh*, and *th* arranged in order of presentation indicated on the Alphabet Knowledge Record.

Say: (1) "What is the *name* of this letter?"
(2) "What *sound* does it spell?"

Prompt: "Do you know another way to spell that sound?"

Record: After exposing each card, write the student's responses in the appropriate column for Name (N) and Sound (S) for upper- and lowercase letters on the Alphabet Knowledge Record.

3. Upper- and Lowercase Letters Written to Dictation

Materials: • Alphabet Knowledge Record

• Student Response Sheet for Upper- and Lowercase Letters Written to Dictation (folded in half from top to bottom)

• Pencil for student

Say: "After I say the name of a letter, please write it here." (Point to each number as needed.) "Write the uppercase/capital and the lowercase/small letter for each one."

Prompt: "Do you know another way to write that letter?" or "That is the upper (or lower) case. Do you know how to write the lower (or upper) case letter?"

Record: Write the student's responses on the Alphabet Knowledge Record.

4. Sound-Letter Correspondences for Writing

Materials: • Alphabet Knowledge Record

• Student Response Sheet for Sound-Letter Correspondences for Writing (folded in half from top to bottom)

• Pencil for student

Say: "After I say a sound, please write the letter that spells that sound. If more than one letter spells the sound, write those letters. You may use uppercase/capital letters *or* lowercase/small letters. You do not need to write both."

Note: An asterisk (*) on the Alphabet Knowledge Record indicates more than one way to spell a sound.

Prompt: "Do you know another way to spell that sound?"

Record: Write the student's responses on the Alphabet Knowledge Record. A Key for Sound-Letter Correspondences follows.

KEY FOR SOUND-LETTER CORRESPONDENCES

1. (m)	m		18. (ā)	a
2. (t)	t		19. (l)	l
3. (ō)	o		20. (ĕ)	e
4. (z)	z		21. (f)	f
5. (b)	b		22. (ū)	u
6. (ŭ)	u		23. (s)	s, c
7. (g)	g		24. (d)	d
8. (ī)	i, y		25. (h)	h
9. (r)	r		26. (ĭ)	i, y
10. (w)	w		27. (v)	v
11. (ă)	a		28. (p)	p
12. (k)	c, k		29. (kw)	q
13. (ē)	e, y		30. (ks)	x
14. (y)	y		31. (sh)	sh
15. (j)	j, g		32. (th)	th
16. (ŏ)	o		33. (ch)	ch
17. (n)	n			

Student Response
Upper- and Lowercase Letters Written to Dictation

Student: _____ Date: _____ Recorder: _____

1. _____

2. _____

3. _____

4. _____

5. _____

6. _____

7. _____

8. _____

9. _____

10. _____

11. _____

12. _____

13. _____

14. _____

15. _____

16. _____

17. _____

18. _____

19. _____

20. _____

21. _____

22. _____

23. _____

24. _____

25. _____

26. _____

Student Response
Sound-Letter Correspondences for Writing

Student: _____ Date: _____ Recorder: _____

1. _____

2. _____

3. _____

4. _____

5. _____

6. _____

7. _____

8. _____

9. _____

10. _____

11. _____

12. _____

13. _____

14. _____

15. _____

16. _____

17. _____

18. _____

19. _____

20. _____

21. _____

22. _____

23. _____

24. _____

25. _____

26. _____

27. _____

28. _____

29. _____

30. _____

31. _____

32. _____

33. _____

NOTES

NOTES